W9-CIQ-859

THE BRITISH ACADEMICS

THE BRITISH ACADEMICS

A. H. Halsey *and* M. A. Trow

with the assistance of Oliver Fulton

'Only about the peculiar behaviour of our own profession do we choose to remain naive. . . . A deeper study would, of course, entail investigation of our personal history and our present inclinations as these are influenced by our relation to the class structure and our cultural and social milieu.'

(Gunnar Myrdal, *Asian Drama*, The Twentieth Century Fund, 1968, Vol. 1, p. 6)

Harvard University Press
Cambridge, Massachusetts
1971

Library of Congress Catalog Card Number 76–151285
SBN 674–08210–9

Printed in Great Britain

ACKNOWLEDGEMENTS

In the course of this long study which began in 1963 we have acquired many debts. The greatest of these is to the very large number of British university teachers, of every rank and subject, who gave up the time necessary to answer our questions either during intensive and lengthy interviews or by mailed questionnaires.

Transatlantic collaboration has been made possible by support from many institutions. First among these, perhaps, is the Committee on Higher Education and we are particularly grateful to its chairman, Lord Robbins, and its chief social statistician, Professor Claus Moser, who made the original survey data available from their study in 1962 and gave us permission to return to those members of their representative national sample of British university teachers who were willing to answer a further questionnaire from us. We might mention here that Professor Moser's unit for the study of higher education at the London School of Economics is now engaged in a further research project which includes repeating many of the items included in our own 1964 survey.

At various stages of our work support and assistance were provided by Nuffield College and the Department of Social and Administrative Studies at Oxford; the Elmhurst Foundation; Sussex University; the Atlas Computer at Harwell; the data processing facilities at the Oxford Regional Hospital Board; the Center for Advanced Study in the Behavioral Sciences at Palo Alto, California; the Department of Sociology of the University of California, Berkeley; the Survey Research Center and the Institute of International Studies, both also at Berkeley; and the U.S. Office of Education.

We have had help at various times with interviewing, the administration of the questionnaire survey, typing and criticism of manuscript from Peter Collison, Mrs. Catherine Chandler, Miss Katherine Lloyd, Mrs. Margaret Ralph, Mrs. Cleo Stokes, Mrs. J. R. Parker, Miss E. Webster and Miss Stephanie Wood.

Oliver Fulton's important and valuable contribution to the study, and especially his assistance in the analysis of our 1964 and 1965 surveys, is acknowledged on the title page. His essay on the Colleges of Advanced Technology is printed as Appendix A.

Finally, we would like to offer tribute to Professor Edward Shils of the Universities of Cambridge and Chicago, whose advice and guidance, particularly in the early stages of our work, was invaluable to us.

A.H.H.
M.A.T.

CONTENTS

APPENDICES

TABLES AND GRAPHS

INTRODUCTION

When we began to think about this book in 1963 we were seeking an answer to an intriguing question. How would academic men in Britain adapt themselves and their institutions to a period of expansion and redefinition of higher education? There were other questions we could have asked. The sociology of higher education has a considerable literature which is, in turn, but a small part of a more voluminous writing on universities.[1] We could have tackled the problem of the changing role of the intellectual in modern society or we could have asked how the academic professions fitted in to the general expansion of the professions in the twentieth century. We were, however, quickly convinced that our first question also raised, if it did not presuppose, answers to the second and third and we decided to make it central to our study. There was in any case an immediate and practical reason for doing so. The Robbins Committee[2] reported in that year and in its Appendix III Professor Claus Moser offered a valuable, and the first, sociographic description of the British university teaching professions. Our question required an essay in the sociological analysis of the academic role. Appendix III was never intended to be that. It was written, as is so much social research in Britain, for an official enquiry. In this particular case a landmark was set up in the use of modern methods of information gathering by a public investigation. The sample survey is a powerful and economical technique and Professor Moser, the author of the

[1] See A. H. Halsey, 'The Study of the University Teacher', *Universities Quarterly*, March 1963, and the Select Bibliography below, pp. 548–50.

[2] Committee on Higher Education Report, Cmnd. 2154, H.M.S.O. 1963. This report, with its five appendices, was the work of a committee appointed by the Prime Minister in 1961 under the Chairmanship of Lord Robbins. It is a monumental description of British higher education in the period 1961–3. Appendix III contains a statistical description of the university teaching professions. We shall refer to Appendix III and to the Report generally throughout this book.

Appendix, is a virtuoso of it. The derivation and meaning of his findings are always crystal clear and his tables are, so to say, highly readable. However, given the reticence one would expect of an official body of public researchers, the enquiry was confined to the class of facts (age, sex, qualifications, previous posts, hours of work, etc.) which could be left to 'speak for themselves' with the minimum of interpretation either by the researchers or by the respondents. In consequence Appendix III was an astringent essay on the social arithmetic of the university teacher. It recorded the vital statistics of these professions at a critical moment in their history.

Our task, as we saw it, was to take the enquiry further in order to provide a sociological portrait of the academic professions, describing and analysing their collective self-conceptions in relation to the programme of institutional expansion in which the Robbins Report would involve them. This suggested a further survey of the Robbins respondents designed to collect their relevant opinions and attitudes[1] and to this end we conducted prolonged interviews with 100 serving university teachers representing a rough cross-section of the British academics. These interviews guided us in deciding on the content of the new survey.

Most discussion of university expansion has been about students–their numbers, quality, origins, outlook and, to a lesser extent, their destinations. The same questions, we felt, had to be asked about university teachers who are, so to say, the academic succession. The government is of course the final arbiter of student numbers and university resources but the university teachers themselves are the managers of expansion. Their assumptions and preoccupations were therefore of vital interest in any attempt to discern the outcome of the Robbins proposals for expansion to take 17 per cent of the relevant age group into some form of higher education by 1980. How far would academic opinion support the Robbins proposals? Would academic support take the form of desire for a modest expansion of the highly selective system which already existed? Or would it envisage the transformation of that system in the direction of mass higher education?

These questions, we anticipated, would evoke attitudes which in part were rooted in political predispositions but also in the concep-

[1] We are indebted to the Robbins Committee for their permission to return to the same sample of respondents. For details of the research procedures see below, pp. 508–10.

tions held by academics of both the quality of university life and the role they saw themselves as playing within it.

Again the main emphasis in expansion plans was put upon the need to teach more students, but the role of the university teacher is one which also carries with it the obligation to extend the frontiers of intellectual culture as well as to transmit it. We were aware too that teaching and research to some extent divide the loyalties of academics. We knew that the experience of expansion in American higher education had led to increasing recognition of the research role of the academic in the double sense of both visibility and reward for those with high reputations in research and a consequential erosion of the quality of undergraduate teaching. How far were these pressures already at work in the British universities? Were British academics, as we suspected, relatively strongly oriented to teaching compared with their American counterparts? And what consequences for the balance between teaching and research were envisaged by the university teachers?

Nevertheless our question could not be answered solely on the basis of a follow-up of the survey reported in Appendix III, albeit grounded in preliminary interviews. The outlook of university teachers was clearly conditioned by the traditions of the universities in which they served. The history of the universities, their changing functions in society, the evolution and manner of their control, administration and organisation had to be thoroughly explored if we were to understand the assumptions and preconceptions to which contemporary academics were habituated. We had therefore also to undertake a study of the rise of the university professions at least from the Victorian beginnings of the provincial universities. We began this as a necessary precondition, along with our interviews, for deciding on the exact form and content of the new survey.

In one sense the universities *are* the university teachers in their composite role as teachers, researchers and administrators. The university, in this same sense, is the organisational framework which is designed or evolved to facilitate the academic role, to protect certain forms of intellectual activity and at the same time to mediate between them and external social demands. It was therefore necessary to include, and convenient to begin with, an account of the organisational framework, tracing the changing relations between university and society.

Part I of the book accordingly begins with an analysis of the changing functions of universities in industrial societies and a more detailed exploration of the British universities in the light of the development of industrialism in that country. Out of this history, we suggest, a distinctive conception of university organisation and functions became entrenched in university thinking and in Part II we have attempted to compare these traditional ideas with the realities of university development during the expansion of the 1960's. The university, in Britain especially, is a peculiar organisation. It could be described as an organisation for community where the community is that of scholars. We therefore look closely at the external influences on university autonomy and academic self-government as they are modified by the expansion of universities and the multiplication of their student numbers.

Within this institutional setting we then turn in Part III of the book to analyse the academic career, its hierarchy of ranks, its relation to the prestige of different institutions, its material conditions and its style of life. This discussion in turn leads us to Part IV where we look directly at the self-conceptions of university teachers in different institutions, different subjects and at different ranks and analyse attitudes to the various facets of university life against the background of an expanding system. Here we use our survey material to try to explain variations in opinion and finally to derive a typology of orientations which we try to relate to institutional developments in our concluding chapter.

PART I

UNIVERSITY AND SOCIETY

Chapter 1

THE CHANGING FUNCTIONS OF UNIVERSITIES

Some kind of intellectual life goes on in all societies. There are always processes of cultural transmission to each new generation. There is, in other words, always teaching and hence the possibility of 'men of knowledge'. Where there are specialised guardians of highly prized elements in the culture we have the prototype of the academic man. Societies also change and where intellectual discovery is the agent of change there is the possibility of 'men of new knowledge'. In the modern world the discovery of new knowledge has been institutionalised as research and thereby, over a wide range of scientific enquiry, has acquired a cumulative character. The implications for economic growth and social change of this recent development are vast and probably as yet largely unrealised. Academic men were not especially prominent in the beginning of this revolution in the creation of knowledge, but have become so since the middle of the nineteenth century. Thus higher education has become one of the means of creating a new form of society, economically rich, organised in larger economic and political units, connected by increasingly elaborate networks of communications and above all containing large investments of skill and resources in further economic and social change through the extending applications of science to human activity.

The Unbound Prometheus is David Landes' apt title for a description of the inter-related set of changes which began with the Industrial Revolution in eighteenth-century England, i.e. 'the first historical instance of the breakthrough from an agrarian handicraft economy to one dominated by industry and machine manufacture'.[1]

The historical primacy of Britain in the early revolution of

[1] David S. Landes, *The Unbound Prometheus: technological change and industrial development in Western Europe from 1750 to the present*, Cambridge University Press, 1969.

industrial technique has had special consequences for the subsequent development of organised science and education in general and universities in particular. It meant, among other things, that an industrial middle class developed before the system of modern or reformed universities, and thus outside the university system. On one side this middle class developed attitudes that were by no means favourable to the universities either for their sons or for their managerial and technical employees. On the other side there was little interest in this new middle class within the ancient foundations of Oxford and Cambridge, which functioned mainly to serve the needs of the upper classes and those intending to enter the Anglican ministry.

More generally, this historical background suggests part of the explanation for the distinctive position of academic men in contemporary Britain. But as well as national peculiarities the academic role has common elements which derive basically from the intrinsic social and cultural imperialism of the new form of society. Landes' summary of the character of the relevant societies is as follows.

> Industrialisation in turn is at the heart of a larger, more complex process often designated as *modernisation*. This is that combination of changes–in the mode of production and government, in the social and institutional order, in the corpus of knowledge and in attitudes and values–that make it possible for a society to hold its own in the twentieth century; that is, to compete on even terms in the generation of material and cultural wealth, to sustain its independence, and to promote and accommodate to further change. Modernisation comprises such developments as urbanisation (a concentration of the population in cities that serve as nodes of industrial production, administration, and intellectual and artistic activity); a sharp reduction in both death-rates and birth-rates from traditional levels (the so-called demographic transition); the establishment of an effective, fairly centralised bureaucratic government; the creation of an educational system capable of training and socialising the children of a society to a level compatible with their capacities and best contemporary knowledge; and of course, the acquisition of the ability and means to use an up-to-date technology.[1]

Advanced industrial societies everywhere have developed institutions of higher education which, through technological innovation by research and through educating and training recruits for the professions, form an essential part of the economy. Universities, in

[1] *Ibid.*, p. 6.

which teaching and research are combined, form a more or less important part of these structures of higher education–more important in the U.S.A.[1] and Great Britain, less in France and the U.S.S.R. where specialised training institutions have a large place. In general, however, academic men have come to occupy a position at the apex of teaching and research mainly through the development of universities. The university is only one of the possible forms of organisation for transmitting and creating knowledge: it is the combination of teaching and research which, while permitting wide variation between its elements and emphases, defines the distinctive character of the university as a social institution. The place of this institution in the British version of an emerging system of higher education is our main concern in Chapter 2.[2]

The characteristics of the British as of all modern systems of education are products of adaptation to a changing society. Changes in social structure create changes in the structure and functions of universities which in turn promote or impede further changes in society. This kind of interaction dates at least from medieval Europe. Thus explanation of the character of universities and the role of academic men within them requires in principle an examination of the history of every aspect of social structure. Society sets changing supply and demand conditions for universities and thereby closely constrains the choice of functions open to them. For example, there have been changes in the employment opportunities for graduates over the course of industrialisation and in the demand for the intellectual output of university teachers and research workers. The internal life of universities has accordingly changed, and the explanation of these changes lies in changes in the religious, economic and political structure of society.

The main trends in the development of the general relation between

[1] Cf. T. Parsons and G. M. Platt, 'Considerations on the American Academic System', *Minerva*, Vol. 6, No. 4, Summer 1968.

[2] By the word 'system' we refer to the web of social relationships and the institutional division of labour which are involved in advanced teaching and research and which in turn form part of the wider process of formal education in schools, colleges and institutes. Such a system is a sociological abstraction. It may be more or less consciously organised, controlled and standardised in the forms and procedures of its constituent units. There was no popular conception of a British system of higher education before the Robbins Report. Far less was there an administrative entity. Indeed, a centralised direction for higher education remains a contentious issue of policy with all its attendant problems of defining the legitimate degree of autonomy of academic institutions and the division of powers between central and local government, governing bodies and the numerous professional, business, academic and civic interests.

the universities and society are clear enough. In the nineteenth and twentieth centuries there has been a transformation in the functions of universities for the economy, an increase in state control, and a widening of social class connection both in the recruitment of students and in the training of professional people.

The European universities were, in the middle ages, an organic part of religious rather than economic life and the subsequent growth of economic functions for them with the rise of industrialism is part of a broader process of secularisation of learning which can be traced at least as far back as the fourteenth century. In the fifteenth century the European universities–some seventy in all–'constituted an intellectual commonwealth embodying the same ideal'[1] and they were based on a common religion, language and culture. The schismatic effects of the Reformation and the rise of nationalisms undermined the foundations of university life in the following centuries, but when the universities began to respond to the scientific revolution and its effects in industry and government during the nineteenth century, a new period of expansion and prestige opened for them which led to the diversified modern secular systems of higher education. Thus, in the nineteenth and twentieth centuries, pressure from economic development evoked response from the universities or the setting up of other institutions of higher education which gradually linked the universities to the economy through the market for professional manpower, through research activities in the applied sciences and through a slowly widening consumption of 'high culture'. A new commonwealth of educated men has emerged in the form of international coteries of experts involved in science and scholarship, the management of economic enterprise and economic growth and intellectual and cultural activities of every kind.

This fundamental change in their functions has brought the universities increasingly into the political arena, financed and managed more and more by national governments. In responding to the manpower and research needs of modernisation universities have outstripped the capacity or willingness of the private purse. In any case, in recent decades, a conscious attempt to plan and manage economic growth and military efficiency has become more or less universal among the governments of industrial and industrialising countries and has led to the development of a new sphere of science

[1] Eric Ashby, *Universities: British, Indian, African*, Weidenfeld and Nicolson, 1966, p. 4.

policy which relates the polity to the scientific community. Consequently, universities everywhere attract increasing governmental interest and control, no matter what the political constitution of the country in which they are placed.

The political significance of the modern university, moreover, does not stem solely from new relations to the productive system. It is also a result of class and status struggles over the distribution of opportunity afforded by a university education. The trend is towards more democratic entry into an expanded and diversified system of higher education which offers chances for mobility through professional qualifications and a generally superior life style for those in possession of the culture of the educated.[1] Over a period of emerging industrialism in Europe and America the universities have served as an avenue of recruiting and educating political, industrial and social élites which have become larger and more diversified during the course of industrialisation and which have had to absorb some men from the lower social strata to secure their development and maintenance.

Thus, the secularisation of higher learning, and especially the incorporation of science into research and teaching, has increased the potential of the universities as sources of technological, and therefore of social, change until now they form part of the economic foundations of a new type of society. In this new technological society educational institutions have expanded, not only to exercise research functions, but also to play a central role in the economy and system of stratification as agencies for the selection, training and placement of individuals in an ever-widening range of professional and quasi-professional occupations and in a corresponding hierarchy of life styles.

Movement towards these conditions has been uneven among the Western industrial countries and university systems have accordingly diversified.[2] But the direction of movement is common despite political and social differences. Democratisation and expansion have been more or less successful and accompanied by a greater or lesser degree of differentiation within higher education systems. At one end of the spectrum, large numbers and a wide range of vocational

[1] The extension of university opportunities to women is a subsidiary element in political movements aimed to 'universalise' access to higher education. See Annie Rogers, *Degree by Degrees*, Oxford University Press, 1938, and Vera Brittain, *The Women of Oxford*, George G. Harrap, 1960.

[2] See Ashby, *op. cit.*, for a more extended discussion and an analysis of the transplantation of the Western university to India and Africa.

studies are gathered under the university umbrella in the United States and, at the other end, a system of specialised institutions in which the university as such constitutes a relatively minor part has developed in Russia. The American and Russian systems of higher education represent the two dominating and contrasting forms at the present time just as university development in the middle of the nineteenth century was dominated by the German idea of the university.

British conceptions of the university still exercise considerable sway over the ex-colonial territories in Africa and the Caribbean and British intellectual traditions retain extraordinary dominance over the educated Indian,[1] but the U.S.A. and the Soviet Union now receive rather than send the would-be planner of new universities. A Royal Commission on Oxford and Cambridge in 1922 could say that 'the two senior Universities of the Empire have also now the chance of becoming to a much greater extent than formerly centres of research, and of graduate study for the whole Empire and for American and foreign guests'.[2] A generation later David Riesman, surveying the American universities, asserted that 'we can no longer look abroad for our models of cultural and educational advance, Europeans and Japanese, West Africans and Burmese now come here to look for models or invite American professors to visit and bring with them the "American Way" in higher education'.[3] Western Europe was becoming a cultural province of North America.

The American system was dominated by the German idea of a university in the early nineteenth century. But in the second half of the century, after the Civil War, it expanded more rapidly than any other as a heterogeneous, large-scale and internally differentiated set of competitive educational enterprises serving the needs of a rapidly growing economy and unhampered by a restrictive class hierarchy or undue dominance from a metropolitan élite centre. The expansion of the Russian system dates from the Revolution of 1917 and owes a great deal to central political control which has directed the supply of graduates to the needs of planned economic growth and has

[1] Cf. Edward Shils, 'The Intellectual Between Tradition and Modernity: The Indian Situation', *Comparative Studies in Society and History*, Supplement I, 1961, pp. 81–7. 'India was, and remains, an intellectual province of London, Oxford and Cambridge.'

[2] Report of the Royal Commission on Oxford and Cambridge, 1922, Cmd. 1588, para. 33.

[3] David Riesman in A. H. Halsey *et al.* (eds.), *Education, Economy and Society*, The Free Press, 1961, p. 481.

regulated the number of places accordingly, giving special emphasis to the supply of professional engineers.

In his comparative analysis of the changing functions of modern universities over the course of the last hundred years, Joseph Ben-David has shown that the willingness and capacity of universities 'to recognise and develop innovations into new disciplines depended on the existence of a decentralised competitive market for academic achievements ... and on their direct, or government-mediated relationship to the different classes of society'.[1] A highly differentiated organisation is needed to carry out the greatly increased and increasingly varied functions of higher education and research. 'Such complex academic organisation has arisen in the United States and the Soviet Union. In spite of the vast difference in the formal organisation of their higher education and research, both countries have developed clearly differentiated functions of pure as well as applied research and purely scientific and scholarly education along-side highly practical professional training. And both countries managed to create a much greater variety of academic roles than the European countries.'[2]

Our main concern in this book is with Britain, which was the first country to be influenced by the development of the German universities in the nineteenth century. Influence, however, did not mean repetition. As Ben-David has put it 'what emerged was something rather baffling to observers accustomed to use the German "idea of the university" as a yardstick of measuring academic accomplishment. ... They admired English universities for the quality of their graduates; criticised them for their mediocre performance in many fields and their seeming indifference towards the active promotion of research; and were mystified by the nevertheless brilliant work of some English scientists.'[3] We turn to an exploration of the particular form of British university development in the next chapter.

[1] Joseph Ben-David and Awraham Zloczower, 'Universities and Academic Systems in Modern Societies', *European Journal of Sociology*, Vol. 1, 1962.
[2] *Ibid.*, p. 82. [3] *Ibid.*, p. 62.

Chapter 2

THE EVOLUTION OF THE BRITISH UNIVERSITIES

Introduction

Our task now is to examine and explain the British case in the light of the history of British society. But we may briefly anticipate the outstanding characteristics of the present system of universities in Britain so as to order the comparative and historical sketch of their development which follows. First, this group of institutions is relatively small and slow in its rate of expansion: measured in terms of the number of graduates per 10,000 population in 1958 it was smaller than the U.S.A., the U.S.S.R., Canada or Japan.[1]

Second, the British universities have a strong centrifugal tendency evident in the comparable standard of their degrees which has been maintained hitherto by a voluntary system of external examining involving the interchange of staff between universities for examining purposes, by the role played by London in the development of provincial colleges and by the more diffuse influence of Oxford and Cambridge.

Third, there is concerted control over standards and numbers of entrants, partly through a national system of undergraduate and graduate scholarships, partly through a customarily agreed ratio of about one teacher to eight taught, partly through a linked system of secondary-school examining boards and, in recent years, through centralised inter-university machinery for undergraduate applications.

Fourth, there is an evolving standardisation of financial and administrative procedures which derives from the dependence of the universities on state finance. While this dependency is not unique to Britain, the method of organising the amount and distribution of

[1] See Joseph Ben-David, 'The Growth of the Professions and the Class System', in R. Bendix and S. M. Lipset (eds.), *Class, Status and Power*, 2nd ed., The Free Press, 1966.

resources through the University Grants Committee has been a distinctive feature of the British system and we shall examine it in detail in Chapter 4.

Finally, there is, as we shall try to show in Part II, an 'English Idea of the University' which gives a common stamp to universities in this country despite differences of age, size and location. In other words, there are norms in British universities which mark them as reflecting a more or less unified conception of university education.

British universities in the nineteenth century

The social and cultural unity of England and the political incorporation of Scotland and Wales into Great Britain are centuries old. They pre-date the Industrial Revolution and had already generated aristocratic and religious traditions which have acted as a powerful brake against movement towards the incorporation of the university into the service of the technological society. Modernisation began early in England, but the university response to it has been most strongly contained within an educational hierarchy corresponding to the structure of power and prestige of the wider society. The needs of the aristocracy, the gentry and the clergy (who were closely linked to them) were already provided for in Oxford and Cambridge, whose dominance over British university life was attained by the defeat of the migration to Stamford in 1334.[1] In the fourteenth century Oxford and Cambridge, backed by royal power, established themselves as national institutions with a monopoly over higher learning. The monopoly was challenged frequently but unsuccessfully until the rise of the universities in the industrial provincial cities of the nineteenth century, and even then monopoly only gave way to pre-eminence. The technical changes which precipitated the Industrial Revolution of the late eighteenth and early nineteenth centuries were linked to entrepreneurship rather than to the formal development of scientific research and the training of scientists and technologists in the manner of those countries, like Germany and France, whose industrialisation came later.[2] In Britain, the challenge of industrialism

[1] H. Rashdall, *The Universities of Europe in the Middle Ages*, Oxford, The Clarendon Press, 1936, Vol. 3, pp. 89–90.

[2] 'If the universities, through the persons of Grocyn, Colet and Erasmus and through Cranmer, Latimer and Ridley, had played a part in the Renaissance and the Reformation, they had little to do with the Scientific and still less with the Industrial Revolution. Trinity College, Cambridge, had offered house-room

and of religious non-conformity was met partly by reform and expansion of the ancient foundations, partly by assimilation of the sons of successful businessmen through the colleges and the public schools which supplied them, and partly by the movement of Oxford and Cambridge dons to teach in the newly created universities.

As a result, two university traditions emerged: Oxford and Cambridge were national universities connected with the national élites of politics, administration, business and the liberal professions offering a general education designed to mould character and prepare their students for a gentlemanly style of life: the rest were provincial, all of them, including London, addressed to the needs of the professional and industrial middle classes, taking most of their students from their own region[1] and offering them a more utilitarian training for middle-class careers in undergraduate courses typically concentrated on a single subject.[2]

Until the middle of the nineteenth century these two traditions existed side by side with little contact. But the assimilating processes of the latter half of that century resulted in the twentieth century in a two-tier structure with Oxford and Cambridge at the apex. In summary, then, what we have to analyse in Britain is the slow and faltering development of an élitist system of higher education during the course of the century which preceded the Robbins Report.

In 1850 there were four universities in England–Oxford, Cambridge, London and Durham. There were also four universities in Scotland but none in Wales. Owen's college in Manchester was about to be founded, representing the rising aspirations of the provincial industrial bourgeoisie, which were to gain expression in 'Redbrick'

---

to Newton, though even he, it is said, had worked out his main discoveries before he returned as a fellow. Glasgow University had lent working space to James Watt to save him from the restrictive regulations of the City Corporation. Apart from him, almost the only inventor connected with a university was the Rev. Edmund Cartwright, sometime fellow of Magdalen College, Oxford, and inventor of the power loom, a wool-combing machine, a precursor of the bicycle and even a form of internal combustion engine; but he resigned his fellowship to marry an heiress long before he turned his mind to mechanical invention.' H. J. Perkin, *Key Profession: The History of the Association of University Teachers*, Routledge and Kegan Paul, 1969, p. 4.

[1] The percentage of students drawn from within thirty miles in 1908–9 were, at Bristol 87 per cent, Leeds 78 per cent, Liverpool 75 per cent, Manchester 73 per cent, University College London, 66 per cent.

[2] These degree courses were, of course, directed especially towards the newer technological and professional occupations created by industrialism, such as chemistry, electrical engineering, state grammar school teaching and the scientific civil service.

civic universities at the end of the century. The University of London had been formed fourteen years earlier by a combination of University College and King's College but was itself only an examining body and was not to become a full teaching university for another half-century. Durham, like Owen's college and other provincial university centres, was scarcely viable in the 1850's, turning out only a handful of graduates. It was in any case an Anglican foundation concerned mainly with preparing young men for the ministry. The English scene was dominated by Oxford and Cambridge, ancient, rich and secure, but together admitting less than eight hundred students each year and providing an education for the upper classes and those intending to be ordained in the Anglican Church. Their traditions and curricula inhibited either concern with the technological requirements of industry or training for the new scientific professions, and in this respect they were less responsive to the new needs of the middle classes than they had been at earlier times. Compared with Germany, the major source of inspiration to those bent on university reform, England and Wales had roughly one-tenth as many university students per head of population.

The absence of competition indicated by Ben-David might have been reversed if there had been independent religious, regional or ethnic groups with the material resources and cultural tradition necessary to challenge the English aristocratic hierarchy. Scotland provided the only example of such conditions and the situation there was indeed very different. No religious tests were imposed on would-be entrants. There was already a long-standing tradition of broadly based secondary education, and of encouragement for clever boys to go to the university from the agricultural areas; the university year accommodated itself to the cycle of agriculture. 'While Oxford and Cambridge slept, insulated by Anglicanism from influences from abroad, the Scottish universities maintained a constant traffic of ideas especially with the universities of Holland . . . In philosophy, science and medicine, they provided an austere but healthy diet; moreover they precipitated the reform of higher education in England, for it was the immoderate animadversions of Sir William Hamilton in the *Edinburgh Review* which helped to stimulate Oxford and Cambridge to adapt themselves to the Victorian age.'[1]

[1] Eric Ashby, *op. cit.*, p. 7. Ashby also points out that all was not well with the Scottish universities, especially in their government and their adherence to out-dated curricula (see pp. 23–4).

Religion and the universities

The triumph of secular learning is now so complete that the English educational world of the 1850's seems almost inexplicably remote.[1] Religious thought was then still inextricably mixed with attempts to define the educational aims of a society recognised as changing; and Church interests were deeply entrenched in both schools and universities.

Here is John Sparrow's description of Oxford in the late 1840's. It was 'an entirely Anglican and largely clerical society: it contained no dissenters, no Roman Catholics and, among the Dons, a minority of laymen. Every undergraduate had to sign a declaration that he had read the XXXIX Articles and to subscribe to them in order to qualify for a degree. Most Fellowships required their holders to take Holy Orders, and for many undergraduates the degree was simply a step on the road to Ordination; it has been calculated that of rather over twenty-five thousand men who matriculated at Oxford in the first half of the century, about one thousand four hundred were called to the Bar and over ten thousand were Ordained; Oxford in other words, was turning out about two hundred Clergymen a year.'[2]

It is true that, in a Victorian context, Mark Pattison thought of Oxford as having undergone revolutionary change in its climate and preoccupations between 1840 and 1850: and there were indeed reformist stirrings against the Anglican establishment inside as well as outside the Colleges. Yet in Pattison's nearest neighbour college, Exeter, one of the tutors, William Sewell, had publicly burned Froude's *The Nemesis of Faith* only the year before. It is true too that Tractarianism was receding from the centre of debate at that time and that academic minds were turning to the challenge of the flourishing new scientific scholarship led by a distinguished professoriate in the German universities. Nevertheless, insofar as the country's need for new men in science, literature and the learned professions had been recognised at all, the new class had been identified by Coleridge as 'the Clerisy'.[3]

Moreover it was in the 1850's that Cardinal Newman began to

[1] A book like Sir Walter Moberly's *The Crisis in the University*, SCM Press, though published as recently as 1949, would almost never be mentioned as relevant to the 'crisis' as defined in contemporary discussion, precisely because of its preoccupation with the religious tradition of the universities.

[2] John Sparrow, *Mark Pattison and the Idea of the University*, Cambridge University Press, 1967, pp. 82–3.

[3] W. H. G. Armytage, *Civic Universities*, Ernest Benn, 1955, p. 167.

write the letters and discourses which he eventually published as *The Idea of a University*–a book which, for all its emancipated catholicism, embodied a conception of the essential place of religion in university institutions and a denial of the place of scientific research which would make nonsense of the actual development in British universities in this century. Newman's ideal was a fusion and preservation of classical and Christian knowledge. 'In the nineteenth century, in a country which looks out upon a new world, and anticipates a coming age, we have been engaged in opening the schools dedicated to the studies of polite literature and liberal science, or what are called the arts, as a first step towards the establishment on catholic ground of a Catholic university. And while we thus recur to Greece and Athens with pleasure and affection, and recognise in that famous land the source and the school of intellectual culture, it would be strange indeed if we forgot to look further south also, and there to bow before a more glorious luminary, and a more sacred oracle of truth, and the source of another sort of knowledge, high and supernatural, which is seated in Palestine. Jerusalem is the fountain-head of religious knowledge, as Athens is of secular.'[1]

But those who were to shape the future of higher education were already beginning to turn their eyes further north: and those who saw the vital reform as that of altering the character of Oxford and Cambridge colleges found themselves in direct conflict with Church interests. The Commissions set up in 1850 instantly roused theologians and ecclesiastics to resist the intrusion of Parliament into the affairs of the ancient universities. The Bishop of Exeter described the Commissions as having 'absolutely no parallel since the fatal attempt of King James II to subject them [Oxford and Cambridge] to his unhallowed control'.[2]

Parliamentary interest was in opening Oxford and Cambridge to dissenters–a debt owed by Russell to his supporters in the growing non-conformist middle class. But, backed by a small professorial group,[3] the attack was generalised into a campaign against the extensive decay of scholarship which was held to have afflicted Oxford and Cambridge over the past century and a half, and against the inadequacy of arrangements for the training of professional people. The Commissioners pointed, for example, to the complete

[1] John Henry Newman, *The Idea of a University*, Doubleday, 1959, p. 259.
[2] Quoted by Armytage, *op. cit.*, p. 147.
[3] There were about twenty-five professors in Oxford in 1850.

absence of a school of medicine in Oxford and its unsatisfactory connection with the profession of law.[1] They even charged Oxford with having 'no efficient means for teaching candidates for Holy Orders in those studies which belong particularly to their profession', and they complained of the rarity of learned theologians in the university.

In both the ancient foundations the struggle to establish higher standards of learning and teaching developed into a conflict over traditional forms of collegiate life and the relation of the colleges to the university. For learning the model was the German universities with their powerful professoriate. For teaching the problem was to get rid of closed fellowships which were linked to the distribution of Church employment and preferment. As Frederick Temple of Balliol put it to the Commissioners in discussing restrictions on election to fellowship, 'men who are naturally well fitted to be country clergymen are bribed, because they are born in some parish in Rutland, to remain in Oxford as Fellows, until they are not only unfit for that, but for everything else. The interests of learning are entrusted to those who have neither talents nor inclination for the subject. Fellowships are looked upon and used as mere stepping stones to a living. A large number of Fellows live away from the place and thus, in reality, convert the emoluments to a purpose quite alien from that for which they were intended.' Temple later became Archbishop of Canterbury, but his opinions were emphatically not those of the dominant Church party in Oxford. Dr. Pusey, who was their leader, was strenuously opposed to the introduction of a lay professoriate, seeing it as a threat to the traditional morals and religious life of the university. Armytage[2] quotes Henry Mansel to illustrate the prevailing animosity to secular and professorial development, and in particular to the supporters of the professorial interest who collaborated with the Royal Commissioners.

Professors we,
From over the sea
From the land where Professors in plenty be;
And we thrive and flourish, as well we may,
In the land that produced one Kant, with a K,
And many Cants with a C.

[1] 'It is true that before 1850 Cambridge had effectively lost contact with lawyers and doctors whose professional education took place elsewhere.' Sheldon Rothblatt, *The Revolution of the Dons: Cambridge and Society in Victorian England*, Faber and Faber, 1968, p. 249.

[2] W. H. G. Armytage, *op. cit.*, p. 202.

College fellows were celibate. Their fellowships were tenable for life but were forfeited on marriage or the taking up of a College living. The idea of university teaching, as a profession, secular and full-time as we now know it, had no place in Oxford or Cambridge in 1850. Only about a third of the fellows actually lived there. Tutors had yet to realise their interests in securing well-paid and permanent careers in their colleges, freed from Church connections. They sought control of colleges and of the university in order to create the conditions of appointment, teaching and examining which would make such careers possible. Meanwhile, as John Sparrow puts it, 'being a tutor was not well enough paid to be looked upon as a vocation or profession, or even a regular post; a tutorship was simply a perquisite, a job with which a junior fellow would occupy a year or two while he was waiting for a college living. When a tutorship became vacant, the head of the college would offer the post to the fellows in residence in order of seniority, without regard to their abilities, easily passing over those who were not in orders.'[1] All in all Oxford and Cambridge had changed little since the seventeenth century in their system of fellowships and selection of undergraduates until the 1850 Commissions and the reforming legislation of 1854 and 1856.

Outside Oxford and Cambridge the most important innovation in the first half of the nineteenth century was the secular foundation in London of University College. When a Bill of Incorporation was introduced by Brougham in the House of Commons in 1825, the established Church opposed the grant of a charter to what W. M. Praed satirically termed 'the radical infidel college'. When this failed Church interests turned instead to establishing a rival institution with the same function but under Anglican control. This led to the foundation of King's College. But the orthodox and the godless institutions had enough in common to combine and were given a charter as the University of London in 1836. This was the first non-sectarian university to be established in England with the power to grant degrees in Arts, Law and Medicine. But the battle over Church influence in London did not end there. Thus, Thomas Arnold resigned from the University senate in 1839 in protest against its refusal to make examination in scripture compulsory for undergraduates. Nevertheless, especially as an examining body and a centre for the affiliation of provincial institutions, the new University

[1] John Sparrow, *op. cit.*, pp. 66–7.

in London was an essential step in breaking the Anglican grip on university studies.

The other university in England at this time was at Durham.[1] It was concerned mostly with the training of the Anglican clergy, but also set out from the beginning to offer professional training of other kinds, including engineering. Durham university remained an unimportant and ailing institution in its early years, and by the end of the 1850's it had declined to the point of granting only a handful of degrees each year. It was rescued by parliamentary action in the 1860's, when new degrees in science and theology were established, along with new professorships in chemistry, geology and mining.

Social stratification and the universities

In nineteenth-century Britain, as elsewhere, access to the universities was almost wholly denied to the working classes. For the mass of the population there was no viable avenue from the primary and secondary schools to the colleges. Before 1870 even primary education was by no means universal. The existence of primary schools was dependent on local church and voluntary provision, which had an uncertain relation to the rapid movement of population out of agriculture into the industrial centres of the North and West. In 1841 nearly half the women and a third of the men who were married in England and Wales signed the register with a mark and the percentages were still 27 and 20 in 1870, when the Forster Act provided for a national system of state primary schools. It was not until 1880 that compulsory attendance was introduced, and then only up to the age of ten, the age being raised to eleven in 1893 and to fourteen in 1918.

The link to universities through secondary education was also almost non-existent for the working classes throughout the nineteenth century. A national system of secondary schools only began to develop

[1] There had been a college set up at Durham in 1656 by Cromwell, but it never obtained university powers, mainly because of Oxford and Cambridge opposition, and was swept away during the Restoration. Not until nearly two centuries later was the university founded, and then not without considerable Church opposition. The Bishop of Exeter, one of the wealthy oligarchs in the Chapter of Durham, held the view that 'to establish a university from the Chapter incomes was unwise, for it would only increase discontent in the country and add to the excess of educated people for whom there were already too few positions' (Armytage, p. 175). The Chapter did in the end co-operate by enfranchising their South Shields estates for £80,000 which enabled them to give the university £3,000 a year. A charter was granted empowering the new university to award degrees in 1837.

in the twentieth century after the 1902 Education Act. There were, of course, endowed and proprietary secondary schools including grammar schools of mediaeval origin, but even by the end of the century they contained no more than 100,000 children. And the public schools, though they grew rapidly during the nineteenth century in response to the needs of the upper and middle classes to prepare their sons for careers which increasingly demanded professional qualifications, were schools from which the mass of the public were excluded. In the main and throughout the century, elementary education was for 'workmen and servants', concerned not with the promotion of talented individuals but with inculcation among the masses of discipline, piety, and respect for private property and the existing social order.[1] There were some exceptions, some narrow channels through local grammar schools which carried poor boys into the universities. Nevertheless, their social isolation continued and they remained insulated from the kind of populist sentiment which contributed heavily to the expansion of the American universities in the second half of the nineteenth century.

The economy and the universities

The Great Exhibition of 1851 declared Britain's lead among the industrial countries. Yet, as we have seen, the universities were still more closely tied to the Church than to business. As D. S. Cardwell, referring to the 1840's, points out, 'professional studies, even at that late date, had no place in the university. Law was studied at the Inns of Court, Medicine at the London Hospitals and for the clergy, no special training was thought necessary. The Victorian engineer and his predecessors were trained in the old craft apprenticeship system . . . the universities were concerned with the liberal education of men of a privileged class who would later adopt suitable professions or else follow a life of leisure. The educational ideal was the Christian gentleman; if he was a scholar, then so much the better; if not, then he would benefit from the corporate life in the university.'[2]

Why was this so? Why was it that, in sharp contrast to Germany, Britain failed to develop university institutions for the training of

[1] Cf. D. V. Glass, 'Education and Social Change in Modern England', in M. Ginsberg (ed.), *Law and Opinion in England in the 20th Century*, Stephens, 1959.

[2] D. S. Cardwell, *The Organisation of Science in England*, Heinemann, 1951, p. 45.

scientists and technologists and the development of applied scientific research? Again the answer lies partly in the social isolation of the ancient English universities. Dons were not at all concerned to reduce the social distance between themselves and the Victorian business classes, while businessmen regarded colleges with the greatest suspicion.

> According to one estimate, only about 7 per cent of all Cambridge undergraduates entered business, to include banking, in the period 1800–99, or less than half the percentage of students coming from business backgrounds. . . . Leaders of commerce and industry returned the resentment. Not only were they reluctant to employ arts graduates, they saw little use for science and engineering graduates as well. For at least sixty years prominent intellectuals, parliamentary spokesmen, heads of scientific associations and institutions, government committees and royal commissions had urged the schools and the universities to produce scientists and technologists to staff industry and increase the importance of British manufacturing. University colleges, which grew into universities, and colleges of technology had been founded to help produce men of science and technology. Government had been used to establish adequate science teaching in schools. Voices demanding the union of science and industry had become more strident and occasionally hysterical with the rise of industrial Germany and America, but industrialists had not responded. The overwhelming majority of trained science and engineering graduates from all universities, chemists as well as physicists, were employed in teaching rather than in industry. Manufacturers continued to favour industrial chemists or engineers who had received their training essentially in the works itself. The attitude that college life ruins a man for a business career was still prevalent.[1]

Nor did it die with the nineteenth century.

There was support for, even idealisation of, the professional man among dons, but the word 'professional' had ethical and status as well as occupational connotations. 'The professional man, it was argued by those who distrusted and feared the ethical implications of the acquisitive aspects of industrialism, thought more of duty than of profit. The gratitude of his client rather than the market defined his reward, and technically he was not paid but granted an honorarium. He earned his reputation by discretion, tact and expert knowledge rather than by advertising and financial success. He was a learned man, and his education was broad and comprehensive. Unlike the

[1] Sheldon Rothblatt, *op. cit.*, p. 268.

businessman, who operated within an impersonal market situation, the professional man was involved with his clients at a personal, intimate level. Ideally he did not have to compete with others of the same profession, at least not to the same extent as the businessman. The professional society, with its principles of restricted entry, embodied in the professional examination and the *numerus clausus*, insulated him from the severer pressures of supply and demand. There was, therefore, a certain self-restraint in his manner, a gentlemanly quality which distinguished him from the brash and aggressive industrialists of the Midlands and the North.'[1]

Nor was there anything resembling the German demand from industrial employers for trained scientists and engineers or any appreciation of the contribution they could make to industrial efficiency. Most British employers did not think it worth while to make the necessary investment in training and research. On the contrary, as Landes has argued, 'they were convinced the whole thing was a fraud, that effective technical education was impossible, scientific instruction unnecessary. Their own careers were the best proof of that: most manufacturers had either begun with a minimum of formal education and come up through the ranks or had followed the traditional liberal curriculum in secondary and sometimes higher schools. Moreover, this lesson of personal experience was confirmed by the history of British industry. Here was a nation that had built its economic strength on practical tinkerers–on a barber like Arkwright, a clergyman like Cartwright, an instrument maker like Watt, a professional "amateur inventor" like Bessemer, and thousands of nameless mechanics who suggested and effected the kind of small improvements to machines and furnaces and tools that add up eventually to an Industrial Revolution.'[2] Britain thus paid the price of its historical precosity as an industrialising nation.

'In sum, job and promotion opportunities for graduates in science and technology were few and unattractive. The most remunerative field . . . was chemistry, and even there the best positions were often reserved for men trained abroad; undoubtedly the mediocre quality of many British graduates served to reinforce the scepticism of management.'[3]

Hitherto, science in England had not been a profession. It was in the hands of amateurs who could pursue their interests only on the

[1] *Ibid.*, pp. 91–2. [2] Landes, *op. cit.*, p. 345.
[3] *Ibid.*, p. 346.

basis of private means. In 1851 Charles Babbage could list only a small number of official scientific posts, including 'a few professorships; the Royal Astronomers; the Master of Mechanics to the Queen; the Conductor of the Nautical Almanac; the Director of the Museum of Economic Geology and of the Geological Survey; Officers of the same; Officers of the Natural History Museum'.[1]

Cardwell summarises the situation as follows:

> The mid-century was that time during which the beginning of the social organisation of science can first be seen. Primarily it took the form of the organisation of studies by the reform of the older universities in the matter of the inclusion of the progressive sciences in the examination syllabuses; by the foundation of the Government School of Science and the Owen's College; by the introduction of London Science degrees, and by the beginning of State aid to scientific education through the agency of the Science and Art Department. Perhaps the central fact of these reforms was the institution of examinations, for these . . . are associated with the 'expert', with discipline and, ultimately, with professionalism.[2]

We have noted the general lack of opportunity for children to go to universities and this of course also affected potential scientists.

> The major defect in the structure was the chaotic state of education; both primary and secondary. The public schools and the old endowed grammar schools were hardly touched by science. Only occasionally would a headmaster include science in his syllabus. Generally it occupied no place in the school; at Eton, in the early sixties there were twenty-four classical masters, eight mathematics masters and three to teach all other subjects. This meant that youths went up to the universities unprepared for science and even if inclined that way would be discouraged by the simple fact that there was little prospect of being able to make a living as a scientist; certainly not at the 'old school' at any rate.[3]

Social and educational stratification kept amateur science apart from industrial processes in nineteenth-century Britain. 'There was practically no exchange of ideas between the scientists and the designers of industrial processes. The very stratification of English society helped to keep science isolated from its applications: it was admitted that the study of science for its useful applications might be

[1] Charles Babbage, *The Exposition of 1851*, quoted by Cardwell, *op. cit.*, p. 60–1.
[2] D. S. Cardwell, *op. cit.*, pp. 80–1.
[3] *Ibid.*, p. 81.

appropriate to the labouring classes, but managers were not attracted to the study of science except as an agreeable occupation for their leisure.'[1] This social division has deeply affected the relation between the universities and industry down to the present day, despite the rise of the Redbrick universities in the industrial provinces, the government pressures generated by twentieth-century wars and the almost continuous alarms raised in Parliament and Press from the earlier years of the nineteenth century, with their theme that scientific and technological 'manpower' was the key to British survival in a modern internationally competitive industrial world.

This relation between university pure science and industrial technology, or rather the absence of it, is well illustrated in the history of the aniline dye industry. The first of the aniline dyes was discovered in 1856 by W. H. Perkin while working in the Royal College of Chemistry. Together with his father and brother he set up a manufacture of the new dye at Greenford Green, being aware of its commercial potentialities. The Perkin family soon made a fortune and retired. This new discovery was of immense potential importance to British industry in that it could be manufactured from coal and thus relieved the necessity to import dye-stuffs. The facts were recognised but it was the German chemical industry and not the British which took advantage of the possibilities of industrial exploitation, establishing dye factories at Höchst, Ludwigshafen, Elbefeld, Berlin and elsewhere. 'Although the actual discovery was made by an Englishman, many German scientists had worked and were working in that and collateral fields; . . . the Prussian government, having decided that the facilities for advanced chemistry were inadequate at the universities of Bonn and Berlin, resolved to erect new laboratories. These attracted wide attention all over Europe and with reason for, at a time when Owen's College was still installed in Cobden's old house, these laboratories were built on a palatial scale.'[2]

The Royal Commission on Technical Education of 1881–84 showed that the German organic chemical industry had taken a strong lead over Britain. The applied science laboratory was not yet a feature of British industry whereas in Germany and Switzerland close links had been established between chemists in the universities and technical

[1] Sir Eric Ashby, *Technology and the Academics*, London, Macmillan, 1958, Chapter 3.

[2] D. S. Cardwell, *op. cit.*, p. 80.

Hochschulen and research development laboratories in industrial firms. 'In the evidence given to the Commission, W. H. Perkin showed that Germany, in 1879, produced some £2-million worth of coal-tar colours and Britain some £450,000. There were seventeen colour works in Germany and five in this country. Thus the industry which it was anticipated in 1862 would render Britain independent of foreign dye-stuffs, an industry which originated in England and depended for raw material on England's greatest asset–coal–had been lost to Germany in less than thirty years from the date of original discovery.' By the end of the century the German aniline dye industries were supreme and the German universities were responsible for two-thirds of the world's annual output of original chemical research. Germany had four thousand trained chemists in industry and this 'had all begun in 1862 with the founding of the aniline dye industry' behind which was 'the educational system of the country, and not least, the original Giessen laboratory of 1825 and the vision of von Humboldt'.[1] Meanwhile in Britain the industrial research laboratories remained in their infancy.

The rise of the provincial universities

Nevertheless, the later years of the nineteenth century saw the beginnings of what may now be seen as a fundamental change in the relation of the university to the economy in Britain. Though modified at every point by the older Oxford and Cambridge ideals of a liberal education for gentlemen, this has gradually and belatedly widened the conception of admissible professions and vocations, and has come to some sort of terms with the applied sciences and business studies. At bottom, these changes, in Britain as elsewhere, represent the establishment of science as an institution, incorporated into the universities as an integral part of their life as teaching and research bodies, and into industry as a widening range of new professions concerned with the practical development of fundamental research in the sciences and its application to industrial processes.

The story is mainly a provincial one–provincial aspirations, provincial pressures and provincial responses. By the end of the century, after fifty years of fitful and transient attempts, there were universities firmly established in the provincial cities.

[1] *Ibid.*, p. 136.

Among the forces which led to this situation were the Mechanics Institutes. These had their origins in Glasgow in the eighteenth century and came to London in 1805 with George Birkbeck, the founder of the London Mechanics Institution whose name was subsequently given to one of the colleges of the University of London. The movement spread throughout the country during the first half of the century until in 1853, for example, there were no less than 100 branches of a union of Institutes in Yorkshire alone, with twenty thousand members. However, although the Institutes had begun as places for the further education of young artisans and ambitious young workers, they gradually fell into the hands of middle and lower-middle-class students, putting decreasing emphasis on technological instruction and more on 'liberal education'.

It was in the 1850's that a suggestion was made for a new national industrial university with the Mechanics Institutes as constituent colleges. It failed, but the underlying aim of providing for technological education did not exhaust itself and the needs of the provinces were becoming increasingly recognised. Thus, for example in the 1860's, Matthew Arnold was arguing that 'we must plant faculties in the eight or ten principal seats of population, and let the students follow lectures there from their own homes with whatever arrangements for their living they and their parents choose. It would be everything for the great seats of population to be thus made intellectual centres as well as mere places of business; for the want of this at present, Liverpool and Leeds are mere overgrown provincial towns, while Strasbourg and Lyons are European cities.'[1] And the reform movements in Oxford and Cambridge also led to attempts at colonisation of the provinces through the University Extension movement which has continued to the present day.

Nottingham and Sheffield both exemplified the influence of the Oxford and Cambridge Extension movements. Nottingham was the first town to run an extension course. It was organised in a re-built Mechanics Institute and held under the direction of Henry Sidgwick of the University of Cambridge. Out of this extension movement and with the support of trade unionists, private donors and the civic authorities (who levied a 1½d rate on the town for the purpose) a University College was founded in 1881. This, like Exeter, Southampton, Leicester and Hull, was a college which prepared students for the

[1] M. Arnold, *Schools and Universities on the Continent*, London, 1868, p. 276 (quoted by Armytage, *op. cit.*, p. 220).

examinations of the University of London until it received an independent charter after the Second World War.

But the main thrust came from the industrial cities themselves. In 1869 Leeds proposed to establish a college of science in Yorkshire, which was built by 1874. The Newcastle College of Physical Science dates from 1871. Josiah Mason College opened in Birmingham in 1880. A College of Science for the West of England was founded at the same time in Bristol and the University College of Liverpool began in 1882, according to Armytage 'in a disused lunatic asylum in the midst of a slum district'. In Manchester, Owen's College, which still had only 116 students in 1867, became the first constituent college of the new Victoria University in 1880 with the backing of its energetic professor of chemistry H. E. Roscoe and the powerful support of Mark Pattison of Oxford and Lyon Playfair. Liverpool joined in 1884 and Leeds (the Yorkshire College of Science) in 1887, both bringing with them a local medical school.

The character of the provincial universities thus derives from the convergence of two nineteenth-century movements. One was local–a desire to bring the perceived benefits of metropolitan liberal culture to civic life, and this was supported by the University Extension movements of the ancient English universities. The other was a national movement which aimed to bring higher technological education into the service of industry. It was inspired by fear of industrial competition from the Continent, appreciation of the industrial benefits gained by Germany, France and Switzerland from their polytechnics and admiration of the American land grant colleges.

The slow and tentative assimilation of an older aristocratic and gentlemanly conception of education with the newer and more practical orientations representing a response to industrial needs was therefore reflected in a fusion of contrary educational philosophies which gave technological study a place in university life. 'The leaders of educational thought in Britain were under the spell of Newman's lectures, Pattison's essays and Jowett's teaching. It is not surprising, therefore, that they opposed the segregation of technological education into separate institutions. The manager-technologist must receive not only a vocational training: he must enjoy also the benefits of a liberal education; or at least he must rub shoulders with students who are studying the humanities.'[1] On the other hand, there was also

[1] Eric Ashby, 'On Universities and the Scientific Revolution', in A. H. Halsey *et al.* (eds.), *op. cit.*, p. 220.

opposition in the same circles to the idea that the lower middle classes needed the cultural benefits of higher education and so, contrarily, 'the most powerful argument for the new university colleges was one based on their utilitarian value'.[1]

Thus technology established itself in the civic colleges in Scotland and in London and finally spread to the older English universities to become an integral part of the university curriculum. At the same time, however, technological and applied studies never gained the prestige accorded to them in either the separate technological institutions of Germany or France, or such American institutions as the Massachusetts Institute of Technology or 'Cal. Tech.'. Once established, the provincial universities tended everywhere to shift the scope and balance of their studies to resemble as closely as possible the norms set by Oxford and Cambridge. But they lacked the wealth,[2] the independence of cultural tradition, the social status and the political connections to offer a serious challenge to the entrenched position of the ancient foundations.

British universities in the twentieth century

We have tried to show that the British universities developed slowly in the nineteenth century and entered the twentieth century as a restricted and élitist group of institutions. In England Oxford and Cambridge stood at the centre, the University of London had emerged as a federation of heterogeneous colleges in the capital, and university charters were being granted to colleges in the major provincial cities. Scotland, meanwhile, had four well-established universities. The system as a whole mustered only 20,000 students out of a population of forty million.

In the twentieth century there has been more substantial growth from this tiny base. The number of students has risen from twenty-five thousand before the first war to twice as many between the wars and nearly eight times as many at the present time, so that in 1966–67

[1] *Ibid.* 'The utilitarian argument', he adds, 'was less persuasive in Wales. In Aberystwyth and Bangor it was the idea of a university as a place for liberal education which aroused public support.' See B. E. Evans, *The University of Wales: A Historical Sketch*, Cardiff, 1953.

[2] Their private endowments were modest and by the end of the First World War were negligible by comparison with governmental grants. The income from endowments in 1919–20 was, at Birmingham University £7,500, Bristol University £8,000, Leeds University £7,100, Manchester University £30,500. U.G.C. Returns, 1919–20, Cmd. 1263, H.M.S.O.

there were nearly one hundred and ninety thousand university students on full-time or 'sandwich' courses.[1]

The two wars stimulated this growth; partly because they created climates of opinion favourable to reform in general and to educational reform in particular and thus increased the effective demand for university places, and partly because they dramatised the utility of university research for military and industrial efficiency. Also underlying these accelerating forces of war there has been the steady pressure from beneath, made possible by the increase in the number of grammar schools which followed the creation of a national system of secondary schooling in 1902.[2] At the same time the demand for graduates has strengthened slowly as the managerial and professional occupations have expanded in government, in industry and in the educational system itself.[3] The universities, moreover, not only supply a larger market for graduate teachers; during the course of the century they have also increased their ratio of staff to students as they have become centres of every kind of research in the sciences and the arts.

Although the growth of the universities has been continuous throughout the century, and although the two wars accelerated the trends, it is clear that social and economic developments since the second war have surpassed all previous pressures towards expansion and will continue to do so. The change in opinion about the scale of provision of university and other forms of higher education since the mid-1950's is quite unprecedented.[4] At that time only a very small minority of radical expansionists were ready to contemplate 10 per cent of the age group in universities. By the time the Robbins Committee reported, middle-class opinion, including academic opinion, as we show in Chapter 11, had already shifted to accept the idea of educating some 20 per cent of the age group to this level by 1980. Behind this shift lie fundamental changes of political and social

[1] The latest official estimates, based on projections of recent numbers of qualified school leavers, anticipate four hundred and sixty thousand university students by 1981. *Student Numbers in Higher Education in England and Wales*, Education Planning Paper No. 2, H.M.S.O., 1970.

[2] The percentage of seventeen-year-olds in full-time education doubled from 2 per cent to 4 per cent between 1902 and 1938 and rose further to 15 per cent by 1962.

[3] The professional class grew from a little over 4 per cent in 1911 to a little under 8 per cent in 1959. See G. Routh, *Occupation and Pay in Great Britain, 1906–60*, Cambridge University Press, 1965.

[4] For a graphic description of the changing climate of opinion see Noel Annan, 'Higher Education', in B. Crick (ed.), *Essays on Reform 1967: A Centenary Tribute*, Oxford University Press, 1967.

outlook: aspirations to this higher standard of education are now taken for granted in the middle classes and are penetrating into working-class families, especially those in which the parents have themselves had some experience of education beyond the minimal school-leaving age. And the old fear of industrial decline, with its invidious international comparisons and its acceptance of the theory that skill and training make the largest marginal contributions to the productivity of the economy, have resulted in political support for the ever-growing higher education budget.

Moreover, the older class conceptions of education have been eroded rapidly in the post-war years. Statistics of inequality of educational opportunity have become popular knowledge and have turned access to the universities into an almost commonplace criterion of distributive justice. This motif has been strengthened by the economic aim of eliminating waste of potential talent in the work force and particularly by the insistent attack on the assumption of a restricted 'pool of ability' which has come to be seen as a rationalisation for preserving class privileges. In this process the ideological defence of an élite system of universities has been seriously undermined and policy for the development of higher education has come to be seen more in terms of economic feasibility.

The course of expansion has had three phases. The first began around the turn of the century with the foundation of the civic universities and continued after the First World War until the depression years of the 1930's. The second, which was more rapid, occurred after the Second World War. Unlike its predecessor, it did not fade out but instead has formed the basis for the third phase in the 1960's and 1970's. At the beginning of the first period Oxford and Cambridge were numerically, as well as academically and socially, preponderant. By the end of it, just before the second war, they had been surpassed in numbers of students and staff by the major Redbrick universities and overtaken by London. Within the first decade of the century Birmingham, Bristol, Leeds,[1] Manchester[2] and Sheffield[3] all gained charters as independent universities; together with Durham and its Newcastle constituent, they began to lead the expansion of the British university system and they have continued to do so ever since.

[1] A. H. Shimmin, *The University of Leeds*, Cambridge University Press, 1954.

[2] H. B. Charlton, *Portrait of a University 1851–1951*, Manchester University Press, 1951.

[3] A. D. Chapman, *The Story of a Modern University: A History of the University of Sheffield*, Oxford University Press, 1955.

The second period of growth after the second war included the granting of independent charters to the former provincial university colleges at Nottingham, Southampton, Hull, Exeter and Leicester.[1] The last-named became independent in 1957 bringing the total number of British universities to twenty-one. Meantime the establishment of the University College of North Staffordshire at Keele[2] without tutelage from London was the precursor of a much publicised movement at the end of the 1950's to found new universities with independence *ab initio*. The first of these, Sussex,[3] admitted its first students in 1961. Subsequently East Anglia, York, Essex,[4] Kent, Warwick and Lancaster have received charters and four new Scottish universities have been formed, one at Strathclyde (out of the Royal College of Science at Glasgow), one at Stirling, Heriot Watt in Edinburgh and one at Dundee. No doubt these new foundations will contribute greatly to the third phase of expansion. But in the second phase they counted for little. The bulk of the expansion between 1947 and 1964 was borne by the established universities in the industrial provincial cities, by London, by Wales and by the ancient universities in England and Scotland.

Numerically a more important addition has been the translation of nine English colleges of advanced technology to university status.[5] Their incorporation into the university system during the three or four years after the Robbins Report has produced a group which is larger than either the new English universities, the ancient English colleges or the University of Wales. Moreover, with their heavy concentration on engineering and the applied sciences and their keenness to develop the sandwich type of course, they have in some respects a greater claim to newness than the new universities. Academically the new universities have distinguished themselves from the older foundations in their attempts to move away from the dominant single-subject honours degree to wider and more flexible curricula and this has had its organisational counterpart in a blurring of the lines and reduction of the autonomy of disciplinary

[1] J. Simmonds, *New University*, Leicester University Press, 1958.

[2] W. B. Gillie, *A New University: A. D. Lindsay and the Keele Experiment*, Chatto and Windus, 1960.

[3] Sir John Fulton, *Experiment in Higher Education*, Tavistock Pamphlet No. 8, 1964; and David Daiches (ed.), *The Idea of a New University: An Experiment in Sussex*, André Deutsch, 1964.

[4] A. E. Sloman, *A University in the Making*, British Broadcasting Corporation, 1964.

[5] These are Aston, Bath, Bradford, Brunel, Chelsea, City, Loughborough, Salford and Surrey.

departments. But the new technological universities embody a no less radical departure in the stress which they put on co-operation with local industry and particularly the development of teaching arrangements interposed and in partnership with industrial experience.

With the establishment of engineering studies in Cambridge and London and the rise of the provincial universities at the end of the nineteenth century technological studies found their way into the British university system. But their scope was limited by the persistence of the older established ideas of liberal education, and technological education continued for the most part in sub-university institutions. In the twentieth century the struggle on behalf of technology has continued and a new chapter in the story opened with the Robbins proposals for expanding this sector of university life. The new group of technological universities also represents a radical departure from tradition in that the institutions concerned are specialised from the outset.[1]

The CATs were designated in 1957 (except for Bristol in 1960, and Brunel in 1962) and were taken from the control of the local education authorities, who had nurtured them from their nineteenth-century origins, to be given independent status under the direct control of the Ministry of Education in 1962. Robbins' recommendation that they be upgraded to university status was accepted (though not the linked proposal for the creation of five Special Institutions for Scientific and Technological Education and Research) and all except Chelsea, which has been absorbed into the University of London, now have an independent charter. Only two of them have retained the technological label in their titles–Loughborough University of Technology and Bath University of Technology. The Bradford Institute of Technology has become the University of Bradford, Northampton College of Advanced Technology has become the City University, Battersea College of Technology has become the University of Surrey and has moved to Guildford, Brunel College has moved ten miles away from Acton to a larger site near Uxbridge as Brunel University.[2]

[1] For a discussion of the technological universities see R. A. Buchanan, 'The Technological Universities', *Universities Quarterly*, December 1966. Mr. Buchanan discusses ten ex-CATs by excluding Scotland and Northern Ireland but including the Welsh College of Advanced Technology at Cardiff which has its origin in a science and arts school dating from 1866. It became a CAT in 1957.

[2] A discussion of the staff of the ex-CATs by Oliver Fulton is included in Appendix A below.

The State and the universities

The expansion of the universities in the twentieth century in Britain and the beginning, since the publication of the Robbins Report in 1963, of their incorporation into a emerging system of higher education, has involved massive government patronage of education of the kind which began much earlier in other countries. Higher education in Britain in the nineteenth century was largely a matter of private enterprise, though lacking the competitive character which resulted in the rapid expansion of the American system from the middle of that century. In the twentieth century the state has provided almost all of the resources for expansion.

Thus the role of the state has been transformed. For the Victorians the task was to re-examine and to widen narrow liberal definitions of state responsibility ('interference'). Now it is to manage purposeful social change, to administer development and to reconcile competing interest groups. Then the universities were small, private and inconsequential for the mass of the population, exercising the freedom of irrelevance. Now they are a crucial foundation of the economy, conceived since Robbins as integral to a higher education system which supplies scientific man-power and technological innovation for economic growth and widening opportunities to a rising proportion of the population. They are thus also of crucial political importance and are in any case pressed into responsibility, or at least responsiveness, to the state as the manager of economic growth, and the dispenser of individual opportunity for participation.

Increasing state control over higher education is the common theme of current discussion and, in his standard work on the modern history of the relation between the universities and government, Berdahl summarises the general tendency in Britain. 'From having almost no contact with the instruction of its citizens before the nineteenth century, the state has now reached a position in which it is necessarily interested in every facet of education from the primary school to the university.'[1] No doubt this is an over-simplification. For example, in explaining 'the low level of thought and life' characteristic of both Oxford and Cambridge in the seventeenth and eighteenth centuries G. M. Trevelyan attributes the major responsibility to the 'control and outside interference exercised by King and

[1] R. O. Berdahl, *British Universities and the State*, Cambridge University Press, 1959, p. 105.

Parliament'.[1] But, until at least the middle of the nineteenth century, positive state interference with the pre-industrial English universities was concerned with regulating their life and practices in the interests of Anglican religious orthodoxy. Freedom to develop non-conformist and industrial university institutions was negatively hampered, on the other hand, by a failure of state support which contrasts markedly with German and French experience. It was reluctant and niggardly in relation to industrial needs and, as we have seen, was confined largely to emancipating the don and his university from constricting clerical influences. However, it has become clear in the present century in Britain that the incorporation of the sciences and the adaptation of higher learning to an industrial, democratic and secular age involves much more than a dismissal of clerics. Whether necessary or not, the form of secondary education, the creation of industrial and military research organisations, the provision of student scholarships, academic salaries, and university buildings and research facilities have in fact transformed the scale and character of state intervention.

It would of course be highly misleading to suppose that the magnitude of this transformation was foreseen at the beginning of the century. What actually happened was that means were sought of channelling funds to the universities which paid every possible respect to the interests of both academic freedom and the tax-payer's pocket. The principle was that of the 'buffer or shock absorber': the mechanism, established in 1919, was the University Grants Committee.

The terms of reference of the U.G.C. as laid down in a Treasury minute in 1919 were 'to enquire into the financial needs of university education in the United Kingdom and to advise the government as to the application of any grants that may be made by Parliament to meet them'. In 1952 the following words were added, 'to collect, examine and make available information related to university education throughout the United Kingdom and to assist, in consultation with the universities and other bodies concerned, the preparation and execution of such plans for the development of the universities as may from time to time be required in order to ensure that they are fully adequate to national needs'.

This reformulation of U.G.C. functions raises at every point fundamental issues about the idea of a university, the meaning of phrases like 'academic freedom', 'national needs' and 'plans for

[1] G. M. Trevelyan, *British History in the Nineteenth Century*, Longmans, 1923.

development' which will form part of our discussion of the characteristics of British universities in the next chapter. Here we shall confine ourselves to the formal relations between the universities and the state.

A recent publication of the University Grants Committee contains a succinct description of the principle of these relations:

'There is no doubt that in the early days, when relationships between the Government and the universities were being tentatively and gradually established, the "buffer" concept was advantageous to both sides. It relieved the Government of assuming direct responsibility for the universities, and it safeguarded the universities from political interference. More positively, it was an earnest of the Government's willingness to provide money for the universities "without strings", and it enabled the universities to enjoy public funds without the fear that the gift might turn out to be a Greek one.'[1]

The key to the working of the principle is again accurately described in the Committee's passage on its relation to the Government:

'From 1919 until 1963 the University Grants Committee was the direct concern of the Treasury. Its staff consisted of Treasury Civil Servants. It was always clear, and totally accepted, that once they "came to the University Grants Committee" these Civil Servants were the servants of the Committee and not of the Treasury. But they knew the Treasury, its habits, its ways of thinking; and they knew personally the individual Treasury officials with whom they were dealing on the Committee's behalf.

'Not only was this fact a source of immense strength to the Committee, through its officials and their day-to-day dealings with their Treasury colleagues. More, the authority of the Treasury was behind the Committee in its dealings both with the Government and with, for example, the Public Accounts Committee. The Treasury was deeply committed to the "buffer" principle, and guarded most jealously the Committee's independent status. A succession of highly paid Treasury officials, among whom the most determined was Sir Edward (now Lord) Bridges, defended with all their acumen and experience the autonomy of the universities, and of the Committee, against every attack from whatever quarter.'[2]

What in short is being described here is an historical continuity,

[1] U.G.C., *University Development 1962–67*, Cmnd. 3820, H.M.S.O., 1968, para. 554.

[2] *Ibid.*, paras. 576–7.

within the framework of a recently completed parliamentary democracy of *de facto* control of élitist institutions by likeminded members of the élite. It has worked through fifty years of Conservative and Labour governments because, as the Committee put it, 'it has been rooted and grounded in one indispensable element, reciprocal confidence between the bodies concerned'.[1] The observer might specify the tribute more closely to the extraordinary stability of the British system of élite recruitment to positions of political, industrial or bureaucratic power.

The growth of state power expresses itself dramatically in Table 2.1 which shows the income of universities from 1920 to 1968 distributed by their source.

TABLE 2.1

Sources of university income, 1920–68

		Sources as percentage of total income					
Year	*Total income of universities* £	*Parliamentary grants*	*Grants from L.A.'s*	*Fees*	*Endowments*	*Donations and subscriptions*	*Other sources* (a)
1920–21	3,020,499	33·6	9·3	33·0	11·2	2·7	3·3
1923–24	3,587,366	35·5	12·0	33·6	11·6	2·5	4·8
1928–29	5,174,510	35·9	10·1	27·8	13·9	2·4	6·9
1933–34	5,593,320	35·1	9·2	32·8	13·7	2·4	6·8
1938–39	6,712,067	35·8	9·0	29·8	15·4	2·6	7·4
1946–47	13,043,541	52·7	5·6	23·2	9·3	2·2	7·0
1949–50	22,009,735	63·9	4·6	17·7	5·7	1·7	6·4
1953–54	31,112,024	70·5	3·6	12·0	4·3	1·6	8·0
1955–56	36,894,000	72·7	3·1	10·8	3·8	0·9	8·7
1961–62	74,113,000	76·5	2·1	9·0	2·7	0·9	8·9
1964–65	124,161,715	79·9	1·4	8·1	1·9	0·6	8·1
1967–68	216,204,321	72·9(b)	0·9	7·4	1·7		17·1(b)

(a) includes payment for research contracts from 1955–6.

(b) The amount of parliamentary grant shows an apparent drop in 1967–8 because for that year only grants from the Exchequer are distinguished in the statistics. Grants and payments for research from other government departments are included in 'other sources'. Previously all parliamentary grants had been grouped together.

Source: U.G.C. Returns and information.

Since the creation of the U.G.C. the total income of the universities on the grant list has risen from just over £3 million in 1920–21 to over £216 million in 1968: and these figures do not include non-recurrent grants by parliament for new building and equipment which in

[1] *Ibid.*, para. 555.

1966–67 amounted to a further £77·4 million[1] bringing total expenditure in that year to something near £270 million. There are two essential features of the statistics. First, the rate of growth in the 1960's, associated of course with the Robbins enquiry and the redefinition of higher education which has increased the number of universities from twenty-four to forty-four in the last ten years, dwarfs all previous experience. Second, an increasing proportion of this now vast income is provided by the state. Direct parliamentary grants alone account for 82·7 per cent. The local authorities contribute 0·2 per cent and in any case take out through rate charges more than they put in.[2] Oxford and Cambridge 'are still regarded as a source of revenue by local authorities'[3] and the nineteenth-century foundations now have a 'favourable balance of trade': for example the University of Birmingham in 1963–64 received £56,150 in contributions from the neighbouring cities and paid out £198,578 in rates.[4] Thus the expansion of university studies, especially in the natural and applied sciences (to which more recently must be added a tremendous growth of the social sciences[5]), has almost completely eroded the financial basis of autonomy, converting the universities to this extent into state dependencies and thus placing the burden of maintaining academic freedom on the beliefs and sentiments of those who wield power in the modern system of government and administration. The question therefore becomes: who are the power wielders and, more specifically, who exercises what kind of power in, over and through the University Grants Committee? We shall return to this question in Chapter 4.

[1] The total capital expenditure on buildings and equipment from public and private sources has risen from less than £30 millions in the 1952–7 quinquennium to £99 millions in 1957–62 and to £295 millions in 1962–7.

[2] See the figures compiled by the Estimates Committee in their Fifth Report for 1964–5, H.C.P. 283, H.M.S.O., 1965. As Lord Bowden has remarked, this report 'was a most important and illuminating document which has . . . been forgotten much too soon'.

[3] *Ibid.*, p. xxxvi.

[4] *Ibid.*, Appendix G, p. 275.

[5] Between the end of the last but one quinquennium (1961–2) and the end of the last (1966–7) undergraduates in faculties of social studies increased by 181·2 per cent and postgraduates by 149 per cent. Comparable increases for the total student body were 62·3 per cent and 65·1 per cent. The numbers were:

		1961–2	1966–7
Undergraduates	Social Studies	10,554	29,675
	Total	93,781	152,230
Graduates	Social Studies	1,907	4,749
	Total	19,362	31,973

Source: U.G.C., *op. cit.*, Table 5, p. 19.

PART II

THE ENGLISH IDEA OF A UNIVERSITY

In the four chapters which form Part II of this book we shall begin by arguing that in Britain there is a distinctive idea of the university which serves also as an ideal. It is a traditional conception derived from the Oxford and Cambridge colleges (though not necessarily a description of them now or at any time in the past). We shall then go on to describe the British universities against the yardstick of the traditional idea.

The argument, in other words, is that a university in Britain tends to be evaluated in terms of certain normative criteria. First, it should be ancient: second, it should draw its students, not from a restricted regional locality, but from the nation and internationally: third, its students, whatever their origins, should be carefully selected as likely to fit into and maintain the established life and character of the university: fourth, those who enter should be offered (to use a Victorian distinction) 'education' and not merely 'training'. This end necessitates, fifth, a small-scale residential community affording close contact of teachers with taught in a shared domestic life and, sixth, a high staff-student ratio for individualised teaching. These six aspects of the academic and social character of a university are examined in their relation to recent trends in the university system in Chapter 3.

A seventh criterion of the traditional ideal is that a university should be politically autonomous which tends to mean richly and independently endowed. We look at the British universities from this point of view in Chapter 4.

Eighth and finally the internal affairs of the ideal university should be governed by a democracy of its own academic members. This is our subject in Chapter 5.

Then, to conclude Part II, we include a brief note (Chapter 6) on a recent set of proposals for the modernisation of Oxford as the prototype of the collegiate university.

Chapter 3

IDEAS AND REALITIES[1]

Ideas, once built into a social organisation, tend to persist and to resist organisational change. Universities are no exception and indeed, despite the present clamour for expansion and change, it is worth emphasising that the university also has fundamentally conservative functions for the culture of the society of which it is part. It is the task of the university to preserve and hand on some of the most highly prized elements of knowledge and belief in the cultural tradition. A corresponding social function of the university–to prepare young men for élite positions in society–is similarly a conservative one. Nevertheless, throughout their history, the European universities have been under pressure to adapt both their cultural and their social functions to a changing society: and the form and strength of these pressures have changed with every new period of intellectual, religious, political or economic upheaval.

The British universities, in company with such institutions all over the industrialised and industrialising world, are in the process of adapting to expansion. We traced this process in the first chapter and argued there that a developing link to the economy is the crucial connection between education and society in the modern world. It defines the functions of the modern university. If the university has been traditionally conservative in its functions–'a place of teaching universal knowledge rather than the advancement of knowledge'[2]–it is now, in its modern context, one of the organisations through which the content of the culture is changed by research. Higher education has become an essential part of the apparatus through which the inevitability of future social change is built into present social structure. Thus the university, which has always played the uneasy

[1] We have incorporated in the following pages some revised extracts from A. H. Halsey, 'British Universities', *European Journal of Sociology*, Vol. 3 No. 1, 1962.

[2] John Henry Newman, *op. cit.*, Preface.

role of both guardian and critic, preserver and destroyer, becomes a sharp focus of the conflict between continuity and change.

The modern urge towards change, expressed particularly as a trend towards larger-scale universities, is partly due to the new form that the cultural function of the university must take. The growth of science implies a more elaborate and differentiated structure of knowledge and hence more specialist scholars. The nature of science implies research and therefore more members of the university who are not wholly or even primarily concerned with teaching. The application of science to industrial processes extends the social functions of the university. Scientific industrialism implies expansion of the professional classes: it usually also implies large-scale productive organisations and therefore expansion of the administrative classes:[1] in general it is associated with an extension of the tertiary sector of the economy which is itself partly constituted as a consumption demand for education.

These developments in the nature of the scientific culture and their social consequences need not, and in most countries do not, elicit a total response from the universities. Institutional adaptation to cultural and social change may take the form of increased functional specialisation. Thus teaching and research may be incorporated into new organisational forms. Advanced teaching and research may be segregated into quarternary institutions as in the great American graduate schools. Research may be concentrated in governmental or industrial institutes. Professional training may take place in non-university institutions, for example, school teaching in England or engineering in Russia. To a greater or lesser extent the rise of higher learning in industrial countries has resulted in the emergence of the university as a specialised organisation within a larger complex of institutions of advanced education.

In Britain this larger complex has been rationalised, following a now famous speech at Woolwich by the Secretary of State for Education in April 1965, as the binary system comprising the universities, or autonomous sector, and the institutions of 'further education', which he described as the 'public' sector. In his introduction to the 1968 edition of the *Commonwealth Universities Year Book*, W. H. G. Armytage has added a third sector which he calls the

[1] 'A society like ours today needs a far larger élite–in science, commerce, administration and in the professions–than it did at an earlier time.' Sir Edward Boyle, *Universities Quarterly*, March 1962, p. 129.

'extra-mural'. He points out that there were over thirty-one thousand external students registered in 1966/67 for degrees of the University of London. And he also includes the 'University of the Air' which has been discussed through the 1960's and is scheduled to begin operations in October 1970.[1] The rationale of the binary system, and the principle of pluralism in higher education which underlies it, need not concern us here.[2] But the second and third sectors embody an idea of the university which is in sharp contrast to the traditional English idea which we describe below. These departures spring from the need to adapt higher education to the growth of popular demand for it. But the process of adaptation is itself strongly conditioned by the traditional British notion of an ideal university.

The existence of collective representation is difficult to prove and shared notions are never fully shared. Yet few would deny that there is a distinctive English idea of a university. Cardinal Newman was acutely aware of it when he wrote (in 1852) that 'some persons may be tempted to complain that I have servilely followed the English idea of a university to the disparagement of that knowledge which I profess to be so strenuously upholding; and they may anticipate that an academical system, formed upon my model, will result in nothing better or higher than in the production of that antiquated variety of human nature and remnant of feudalism, as they consider it, called "a gentleman"'.[3]

Behind the traditional English conception there lies the conflict, which Max Weber identified as fundamental to educational theory, between the cultivated man and the specialist. In his remarks on a typology of educational systems Weber saw two opposite polar types, the one designed 'to awaken charisma' and the other 'to impart specialised expert training'.[4] He saw that, in modern Western, rational bureaucratic society, educational systems tend towards the latter type.

[1] The Planning Committee is under the Chairmanship of Sir Peter Venables, the retiring vice-chancellor of the University of Aston in Birmingham. This committee is commissioned to work out a comprehensive plan for the establishment of an 'open university'. It is intended that the new venture will be financed directly by the Department of Education and Science and will not fall under the U.G.C. system. It will use television, radio and programmed learning, reinforced by correspondence courses and tutorial meetings at selected centres. Degree courses, spread over four or five years, will be offered in a range of subjects. They will lead to general, not honours degrees.

[2] For a detailed analysis and critique see Martin Trow, 'Binary Dilemmas: an American View', *Higher Education Review*, Summer 1969.

[3] John Henry Newman, *op. cit.*, p. 7.

[4] H. Gerth and C. Wright Mills, *Essays from Max Weber*, Routledge and Kegan Paul, 1948, p. 426.

But between the two opposites he recognised many educational systems which aim at cultivating the student for a 'conduct of life', i.e. the style of life appropriate to the status group for which he is destined. Elements of training for an expertise as well as education for participation in the culture of a status group are present in all educational systems. However, the modern Western type of technological society maximises the former and minimises the latter. The traditional status functions of education have been heavily modified by the requirements of selection and of socialisation into particular professional groups. 'The modern development of full bureaucratisation brings the system of rational, specialised and expert examinations irresistibly to the fore.'[1] Educational qualifications are, as Weber emphasised, a status claim–a substitute for birth or ascription to a style of life.

It is in this sense that the rise of the university graduate in Britain since World War II is comparable to the rise of the gentry in the sixteenth century. In a country like Britain with a past 'structure of domination' other than the modern bureaucratic one, the expert examination meets resistance. The great period of the English universities as bodies distinguishing their students for a high place in a social hierarchy involving aristocratic domination is represented by Oxford and Cambridge in the century and a half before the reforms initiated by the Royal Commissions in 1850–a point which marks the beginning of the ascendancy of the examination principle in English public life. In this period the universities were 'seats in which the youth of the country could acquire a modicum of classical learning; they gave an intellectual sanction to the domination of the gentry and brought up the young men to be gentlemen, accepting and exemplifying the ideals of a class'.[2] Here is Lord David Cecil's description of life at Cambridge for a young Whig aristocrat, William Lamb (Lord Melbourne) between 1795 and 1799:

> For Cambridge, where he went at seventeen, he could never feel the same affection. He was even less industrious there than at Eton. Rich young men always find it hard to work at a university, especially if they have the Lamb gift for pleasure. It is only the poor-spirited or the morbidly conscientious who can go on doing lessons in the flush of their first appearance in the world as mature young men able to do whatever they please. William did not even trouble to follow the regular courses; along with the rest of the

[1] *Ibid.*, p. 241.

[2] W. Dibelius, *England*, trans. M. A. S. Hamilton, London, 1929, p. 409.

> gilded youth at Cambridge he spent the next four years revelling, talking and making friends, sauntering the streets by day and sitting up over the port at night. However, he was too active-minded to live without any intellectual occupation. He read a good deal in a desultory kind of way. And it is likely that he profited more by so doing than if he had kept himself to the narrow path of academic study. His strong young brain, rejoicing in its own activity, ranged over an enormous variety of subjects. Mathematics, indeed, he never cared for. They were too inhuman a science. But he read widely in the classics, ancient and modern, he devoured history books, he delved into the mysterious problems of ethical philosophy. With this intellectual development came a growing interest in public affairs.[1]

Industrialism may have changed the face of Britain since that time: certainly the primary and secondary school systems were invented much later, and nine-tenths of British university students now attend institutions of Victorian or post-Victorian foundation. Nevertheless 'the English idea' has manifested a stubborn resilience. It expresses itself partly in the conspicuousness of Oxford and Cambridge and the vagueness bordering on invisibility of 'Redbrick' universities. Oxford and Cambridge still stand in the public mind for the older social and educational ideals of the cultivated member of a governing class rather than the highly trained professional expert. They are thought to embody the pedagogical ideal of an intimate relation between the teacher and the taught through the tutorial method, through shared domestic life in a human-sized collegiate organisation, and through the separation of the role of teacher and examiner. They are held up as examples of democratic self-government by academics where the administration is either subservient to or is itself the don, individually or in committee. Above all they have the envied dignity of antiquity combined with riches and architectural splendour to produce a calm assurance of secure status for intellectual life no matter what political or economic vicissitudes assail the society of which they are an adornment. The ideal of a university in Britain is accordingly based on a conception, whether accurate or not, of the essential characteristics of Oxford or Cambridge.

In this chapter we describe the British universities with these

[1] Lord David Cecil, *Melbourne*, Grosset and Dunlop, 1954, p. 46. It may be added that at this period, the 'grand tour' being impracticable because of the Napoleonic Wars, some Whig families sent their cleverer sons for further education to the Scottish universities. Melbourne went to Glasgow and soon became aware of the danger to his position in aristocratic society of too serious or 'pedantic' an interest in intellectual matters.

criteria in mind on the basis of recent statistics, discussions, events and our own survey material. We want to discover how far the 'English idea of a university' underlies the current patterns of adaptation and growth in the university system. It should be clear, however, that we do not imagine ourselves to be describing a theory of university life which exactly coincides with current Oxford and Cambridge practices. On the contrary, the Franks Report[1] to which we refer in Chapter 6, is also evidence of adaptation to changing conditions, though heavily conditioned by the eight criteria which we have distinguished.

There is, in any case, no universal agreement about what exactly determines the pre-eminence of the ancient English foundations, nor how far this pre-eminence is being modified or perhaps even obliterated by developments since the Robbins Report.[2] Our own view of the situation immediately before the Robbins Report follows from the history of universities in Britain which we outlined in Chapter 2. Oxford and Cambridge prestige was based first and foremost on an enormous social prestige. 'She may not get into Oxford or Cambridge, but she can always go to London,' says an Iris Murdoch character. Oxford and Cambridge would come first to mind when English university education was mentioned so long as the sports correspondent of *The Times* could assume that there was only one university football match and a powerful therapy would be needed to cure this extraordinary national hallucination.

The luminosity of these two universities was strongly supported by their selection of students from the upper echelons of the class and status hierarchy of English society. Only one in ten of the Cambridge undergraduates in the 1950's came from the families of manual workers compared with one in three at universities like Manchester, Leeds and Birmingham. Oxford and Cambridge students had fathers who were predominantly well-to-do, southern, professional and managerial, conservative and Church of England. Three-quarters of the entrants at that time came from public or direct-grant schools, whereas two-thirds of the Redbrick entrants came

[1] University of Oxford, *Report of Commission of Inquiry*, Clarendon Press, 1966 (2 vols.).

[2] An illuminating symposium of views appeared in *Universities Quarterly*, September 1961, with contributions from Sir Charles Morris, then Vice-Chancellor of Leeds University, Noel Annan, then Provost of King's College, Cambridge, and Professor W. J. M. MacKenzie, then Professor of Politics at the University of Manchester.

from L.E.A. maintained schools. For most parents of public school boys a 'provincial' university was not considered.

Academic support also existed in that the self-respect of grammar schools was firmly tied to the annual scholarship stakes for places in Oxford and Cambridge which were thus associated with academic high flying and Redbrick with more pedestrian performances. Moreover, enquiring parents of sixth-formers soon discovered, if not from television programmes from King's College chapel then from headmasters and L.E.A. officers, that student life at Oxford and Cambridge was blessed with much superior amenities and that, for state scholars, the maintenance grant, in addition to tuition, might be up to £325 per annum while at Birmingham the maximum was £225. The cost of living, i.e. the standard of living, was higher in Cambridge. Similarly, half the Oxford undergraduates lived in college and the other half enjoyed dining rights. Only a quarter of the Redbrick students lived in and the boozy squalor to which Saturday night in the Union might sometimes descend, was no substitute for civilised collegiate life.

Finally, and no less important than the disparities of social and intellectual composition, public reputation and civil amenity, was the secure and comprehensive connection of Oxford and Cambridge with the world of 'top' people. The one hundred and fifteen thousand graduates (one-fifth of the total) of these two universities contributed half the entry to *Who's Who*,[1] three-quarters of graduate M.P.s, nearly all of those who entered the Administrative Class in the Civil Service and Foreign Service by Method II (which includes a series of personal interviews), and so on. And even where initial entry to professions, business and high scientific posts was open to all graduates, the freemasonry of school and college tended to publicise the abilities and accelerate the promotion of the public school and Oxford or Cambridge man.

It seemed at that time that if the Robbins enquiry into higher education and the demands for reform of the public and state schools were to produce a viable plan for an integrated school system or at least the transformation of the public schools into a small, socially innocuous private sector of education, then what Sir Charles Morris distinguished as the 'ancient' and the 'modern' universities might compete for public esteem on more level terms. A more gloomy view was that the prospects were more likely to be the emergence of a

[1] Excluding bearers of inherited titles and professional soldiers and sailors.

contained meritocracy–that reform would strengthen the existing social hierarchy of learning by the further legitimation of merit.

On the other hand, the amount of room at the top of the professional and scientific world would clearly expand faster than the output of Oxford and Cambridge, which produced a quarter of the graduates in England and Wales in 1938 but would produce as little as one-fifteenth in the 1970's. Sir Charles Morris believed that in graduate education the modern universities had already gone a long way towards establishing themselves as independently excellent–and certainly the idea of a university in terms of which the Victorian foundations were conceived made them admirably equipped for the education of research scholars and the pursuit of scientific research. But the primary emphasis of expansion, no doubt properly, was on undergraduate education in science and technology and the major burden of this training of the new white-collar classes was to be borne by Redbrick. Though the traditions of the modern universities might have fitted them better for graduate education, in fact Oxford and Cambridge had more graduate students (2,842) in 1959 than did Manchester, Birmingham and Leeds combined (2,426).

It seemed possible, then, that a score of competing educational principalities might emerge to replace the subservience of province to metropolis and so have an emancipating effect on English culture, liberating creative energy and providing a strong stimulus to modernity. Victorian and Edwardian expansion had established the universities in the industrial cities and reflected a serious, if passing challenge to the central, metropolitan aristocratic culture of England by the provincial, dissenting bourgeoisie. The new expansion held out the possibility of building a university system as the crowning edifice of a flourishing and diversified common culture. Perhaps the best measure of success would be a reduction in the relative popularity of Oxford and Cambridge.[1]

What in fact has been happening as the universities have expanded and added new institutions during the 1960's? We shall consider the six criteria of the traditional ideal which together express the social and educational character of the universities: antiquity, cosmopolitanism, selectivity, 'education', domesticity and intimacy.

[1] Cf. A. H. Halsey, 'A Pyramid of Prestige', *Universities Quarterly*, September 1961.

Antiquity

The criterion of antiquity literally cannot be met by most British universities. Apart from Oxford, Cambridge and the four oldest Scottish universities, none of the forty-four university institutions in Britain pre-date the rise of industrialism. The main burden of expansion has been carried by the English provincial universities, Liverpool, Sheffield, Manchester and the other industrial cities, and by the 'ex-colonies' of the University of London, such as Nottingham, Leicester, Exeter, Southampton and Hull. Moreover, the recent growth of degree candidates in 'public' and 'extra-mural' sectors of higher education still further reduces the numerical importance of the ancient foundations.

However, the 'English idea' has been sufficiently powerful to ensure that the new English foundations have been put down in ancient locations rather than, as the Victorian universities were, at the urban growing points of population. Professor Armytage proposed a university for Scunthorpe, but in the scramble for U.G.C. funds the cathedral town was preferred to the industrial area. Only two of the successful applicants were from the industrial North and both of these were in old, non-industrial towns–York and Lancaster.[1] The southern towns are all strongly associated with mediaeval or pre-industrial England: Brighton, Norwich, Colchester, Canterbury and Warwick. And the new technological universities have not all stayed close to urban industrial districts: as we noted in Chapter 2, there were movements outward from Battersea, Bristol and Acton. It has often been argued that a characteristic of British culture is to reject the urban industrialism which it invented.[2]

[1] The criteria used by the U.G.C. for selecting among applications for new universities are set out in their Report for 1959–60 (Cmnd. 1489), pp. 7–9. The Committee holds that increased student mobility has lessened the argument for location in densely populated catchment areas. Apart from this the Committee mentions (a) local enthusiasm, (b) the presence of industries in the area, (c) local financial support, (d) a site of no less than two hundred acres within two or three miles from the centre of a city or town, (e) a suitable supply of lodgings, and (f) attractive facilities for staff and their families.

[2] Cf. Ruth Glass, *Current Sociology*, Vol. IV, No. 4, 1955, for a brilliant critique of the anti-urban traditions of English social thought. Academic opinion on the location of universities is finely balanced in relation to this tradition. Our respondents were asked: 'Most of the new universities established since the war have been located in small towns or rural areas. Are you in favour of that policy, or do you favour locating new universities in the large cities?' There were 52 per cent of the votes in favour of the 'rural' policy.

Cosmopolitanism

The second normative criterion is that a university should be national rather than provincial. The nineteenth-century foundations in the industrial cities were avowedly provincial.

They were the creatures of a non-conformist and non-metropolitan culture, drawing their students, in the main, from the middle and lower middle classes of their own region, while Oxford and Cambridge drew from the sons of those families who were able to use the national public schools. In the twentieth century, however, and especially since 1945, the Redbrick universities have been attracting students from the whole country and also from abroad. About ten per cent of full-time students at British universities are from overseas and less than one fifth now live at home. These developments towards national status for every university have been strongly reinforced by government policy. A system of state scholarships frees the student from the necessity of earning and encourages him to live away from home by offering him a larger grant if he does so. Moreover, the new universities founded in the 1950's and 1960's have been free to choose a 'model' or 'image' with a less regional colouring than that which was possible for the Victorian and Edwardian foundations. They do not think of themselves as provincial and the term itself is now much less often heard in reference to any British university. Cosmopolitanism is pretty much taken for granted. Thus, of the eight criteria, this one is very fully shared by all the institutions in the university system.

Selectivity

Our third normative criterion is that an ideal university is exclusive to a carefully selected group rather than open to all who wish to attend. There is universal concern with maintaining a rigidly high standard for the Bachelor's degree and, traditionally, a widespread belief that the proportion of the population, or 'pool of ability', capable of reaching this standard is severely limited. The Robbins Report itself was in part the culmination of an attack on restrictive 'pool of ability' theories but the traditional sentiment remains deeply rooted. Selectivity is held to be essential to the maintenance of standards which in turn are guarded by the system of external examiners for Bachelors' degrees. A sharp contrast can be drawn here with the two thousand odd American degree-granting institutions in which the variation of student quality is such that the most able in some, by conventional measures of intelligence and attainment, are below the level of the least able in others. In Britain the straight and narrow path to a degree for the highly selected minority in full-time attendance is paralleled and shadowed by other routes to the same destination–part-time courses in technical and commercial colleges, and correspondence courses offering preparation for an external degree of the University of London. The London external degree and the 'extra-mural' sector generally acts as a safety valve against pressure for university education which cannot be satisfied in the 'normal' way.

The sponsorship process[1] of student selectivity is associated with low drop-out rates. These are lower in Britain than in either the Continental systems, which offer university places automatically to those who have a baccalaureat or Abitür qualification, or the less selective American institutions where appropriate high-school graduation is a claim on university entrance. Thus the junior colleges in America have an open door to high-school graduates and in the American system as a whole less than two-thirds of college entrants graduate, even when all delays and transfers are taken into account. By contrast, in any British university department, a drop-out rate of more than ten per cent is cause for alarm.[2]

Within the continuing high selectivity of the university sector of higher education as a whole, there are of course differences in the effectiveness of different institutions which continue to give Oxford and Cambridge an advantage in approximating to the traditional ideal. But these advantages are by no means clear-cut. Some of the London colleges, the University of Sussex and others enjoy severe competition for the places they offer. These differences in the attractiveness of particular institutions, and departments within institutions, are in any case over-shadowed by the selectivity of the university sector as a whole. Thus, again, in relation to this third criterion, the traditional ideal continues to exercise a dominant influence.

[1] Cf. R. H. Turner, 'Modes of Social Ascent through Education: Sponsored and Contest Mobility', in A. H. Halsey *et al.* (eds.), *Education, Economy and Society*.

[2] But the drop-out rates from highly selective American colleges and universities are comparable to those of the British universities.

Education rather than training

In Britain there is a long history of resistance to the expansion of vocational studies in the universities. Undergraduates in the technology faculties amounted to 10·4 per cent of the total in 1938/9 and had risen to 15·4 per cent by 1959/60. In the following year (1961/2) these undergraduates numbered 14,240 and in the following five years, with the granting of charters to the former Colleges of Advanced Technology, their numbers rose to 31,362 (1966/7), an increase of 120 per cent compared with the general increase in undergraduate numbers over the same five years of 62 per cent. Nevertheless, the arts, social studies and pure science faculties between them still accounted for two-thirds of all the undergraduates in 1966/7 (101,546 out of a total of 152,230). These undergraduates moreover still make up the great bulk of the total student body. There were 31,973 post-graduate students in 1966/7. And only a quarter of these (7,926) were studying applied science, engineering, technology, medicine, dentistry, agriculture, forestry or veterinary science. The other three-quarters were in the arts, social studies and pure sciences.

Thus for the university sector as a whole the emphasis remains in the arts and pure sciences with a pronounced recent shift towards the social studies. However, there is a compromise with traditional notions in the case of the former colleges of advanced technology whose students are almost wholly in engineering, technology and applied science, though they too are developing the social studies. Without the ex-CATs and Heriot-Watt College the percentage increase in students of applied science, engineering and techology would have been 33·1 per cent instead of 120·2 per cent; on the other hand these colleges were responsible for only 27 per cent of the overall increase in the university student population.

Domesticity

'Education' is thought in Britain to need a domestic milieu. And perhaps the most significant characteristic of the institutional setting of British university life is its small scale. Only London University is large by modern standards and, quite apart from its modest size by comparison with Berkeley or the Sorbonne, its staff of 6,138 was divided among forty-five more or less autonomous institutions in 1968, i.e. into groups of teachers and research workers numbering typically less than one hundred. Again, Oxford and Cambridge, though of medium size in the range of universities all over the world, each has its one thousand academic members divided into small collegiate societies. The largest universities with unitary organisation are Leeds, Manchester, Birmingham, Edinburgh and Glasgow. In 1968/9 their staff numbered 1,218, 1,302, 1,200, 1,288 and 1,269 respectively, and it is precisely in these universities that there is some uneasiness about size, especially in relation to maintaining the traditionally peaceable relation between staff and students in Britain.

The relatively rapid expansion of the 1960's has done little to modify the teaching milieu. The typical university department has no more than ten academic members and the situation remains, in this respect at least, perfectly compatible with the distinctive English idea of a university which provides for maximum solidarity between teachers and taught through the absence of a separate administration and an emphasis on close personal relations, achieved by means of tutorial teaching, high staff/student ratios, and shared domestic life. Even the collegiate form of domesticity which characterises Oxford and Cambridge has been incorporated in some of the new universities, for example at York and Canterbury. Elsewhere the hall of residence has developed as a way of preserving some of the advantages of the college system. The number of university students rose from fifty thousand to nearly one hundred and sixty-seven thousand between 1938 and 1965 but in spite of this increase in numbers the proportion in residence also rose from 25 per cent to 33 per cent and to 36 per cent in 1968. This reflects the widespread view, only seriously challenged during the 1960's, that residential halls are the best kind of accommodation; a valuable means of bringing students and their teachers together and of fostering academic and scholarly values.

Both the Vice-Chancellors' Committee and the University Grants Committee have endorsed the building of halls of residence, the former suggesting at the end of the 1940's that the best size would be establishments for about one hundred and fifty people. In its report for 1959/60 the U.G.C. welcomed 'the widespread and deeply held conviction in all the universities of the role that university residence can play in university education'.[1] And the Robbins Committee supported the general policy, recommending that universities should aim to have two-thirds of their students in residence. More recently,

[1] Cmnd. 1489, p. 15.

however, this policy has been questioned, partly on economic grounds, partly through recognition of its function as a brake on the expansion of the university system and partly for more general reasons. Certainly it hardly seems practical to aim to accommodate two-thirds of all students on the estimate that this would involve providing two hundred and twenty thousand places or more by 1980. But the more general objections are that halls of residence do not in practice do much to foster academic and scholarly values and that they create an artificial and sheltered environment. The Vice-Chancellor of Essex has argued that they are costly, that they cater only for a minority of students, that few senior members have the capacity to make a success of running a hall, that most modern halls are too big for necessary economic reasons and therefore no longer meaningful communities, and that students should be encouraged to lead more independent and responsible lives.[1]

In fact, in 1967, roughly half the universities had less than 40 per cent of students in residence.[2] A number of surveys in the 1960's have shown that the proportion of students in hall or college varies a great deal between institutions: 15 per cent of all students at Sheffield in 1961, 99 per cent of all students at Loughborough in 1963, 61 per cent of third-year students at Cambridge in 1962, 51 per cent of third-year students at Southampton in 1962, 81 per cent of second-year students at Exeter in 1964, but only 36 per cent of those at University College, London, and there were no students at all living in at Bath. That the University of Bath lacks residential students is understandable enough. The Colleges of Advanced Technology were traditionally local, and only as they develop as national institutions, drawing students from outside their immediate area, will the accommodation problem become pressing.

The growing criticism of the residential halls has led to a number of new developments. In some places old houses have been converted into bedsitting-rooms with a communal kitchen. Some universities have provided specially built blocks of flats. On the other hand, three of the new universities have chosen to establish colleges, which although lacking the autonomy of the Oxford and Cambridge institutions, yet reflect the conviction of the educational and social value of a residential community. While the proportion of students

[1] Albert Sloman, *A University in the Making*, B.B.C., 1964.

[2] Joan Brothers and Michael Kendal, 'Student Residential Policies, Provisions and Regulations', 1967, quoted by the Committee of Vice-Chancellors and Principals, *Interim Report on Student Accommodation*, 1968.

in colleges or halls of residence in 1968 had risen to 36·5 per cent compared with 25·1 per cent in 1938/9, the proportion living at home had fallen to 17·2 per cent, and the remaining 46·3 per cent were in lodgings. The differences between types of institution in the accommodation of their students are shown in Table 3.1.

TABLE 3.1

Residence of students by type of institution, December 1968

	Colleges or halls of residence		*Lodgings*		*At home*		*Total*	
	No.	%	*No.*	%	*No.*	%	*No.*	%
Cambridge and Oxford	12,857	61·5	7,802	37·3	239	1·1	20,898	100
London	8,184	25·9	16,253	51·5	7,111	22·5	31,548	100
Other universities in England and Wales (excluding former CATs)	43,608	41·0	51,951	48·9	10,703	10·1	106,262	100
Scotland	7,166	21·2	12,396	36·7	14,255	42·1	33,817	100
Former CATs	4,445	27·0	8,451	51·3	3,581	21·7	16,477	100
Great Britain	76,260	36·5	96,853	46·3	35,889	17·2	209,002	100

Source: Information from the U.G.C.

Intimacy

The continued insistence on small residential communities is also relevant to this criterion, but there is too the tradition of high staff/student ratios. By all international standards the ratio of staff to students in Britain's universities is extraordinarily favourable. The conventional figure is 1:8. Before the Robbins Report (in 1961/2) it was 1:7·9[1] and in the continuing expansion of the five following years it *improved* to 1:7·8. Moreover, this calculation only includes those full-time academic staff who are wholly paid from the general university funds. They numbered 23,609 in 1966/7 and to these must be added a further 3,862 who were not wholly paid from these funds. The continuation of this favourable ratio, which does not vary unduly between institutions, is clearly a contribution to maintaining in practice the principle of close teaching contact through tutorial methods, but it must also be recognised as a built-in constraint to

[1] It was about 1:10 between the wars.

rapid expansion. On this, the sixth criterion, the traditional idea of a university has continued without check in the expansion which has taken place since the Robbins Report. So far, then, the expansion of the 1960's has been strongly contained within the English idea of a university. We must now look at the other two criteria–self-government and wealth–and this we do in the following two chapters.

Chapter 4
UNIVERSITY AUTONOMY

Until at least the early 1960's there was no more congratulated body than the British University Grants Committee. Robert Berdahl ended his study of the relation between the British universities and the state in 1959 with an enthusiastic salute 'although the social institutions and traditions of other democracies may preclude their creating exact replicas of the University Grants Committee with its peculiarly informal modes of operation, the general applicability of the principles enumerated above could lead to Britain's ultimately being regarded not only as the home of the Mother of Parliament, but also as the progenitor of the most enlightened principles of state conduct towards universities'.[1]

By the end of the 1960's however, all was turmoil and doubt. The government's acceptance of the Robbins Report led to the transfer of the U.G.C. from the Treasury to the Department of Education and Science: the Public Accounts Committee's special report for January 1967 led to the opening of the books and records of the U.G.C. and the universities to the inspection of the Comptroller and Auditor General: and the report of the Prices and Incomes Board of December 1968 on academic salaries seemed to herald the possibility of direct intrusion into university affairs by an instrument of government which is outside the control of the U.G.C. or the D.E.S.

Yet our seventh and eighth criteria, set by the English idea of a university, were that it should be financially rich and autonomous and governed by a democracy of its own academic members. There is a double problem here; one is the question of autonomy or external control, the other is the problem of the distribution of power within the university. We must now take up these problems where we left them at the end of Chapter 2.

The traditional ideal of self-government by an autonomous guild

[1] R. O. Berdahl, *op. cit.*, p. 194.

of dons persists strongly both in the formal constitutions of Oxford and Cambridge and in the customs and usages of all British universities. Nevertheless, autonomy is widely felt to be threatened. The reasons lie basically in the universities' increasing reliance on the financial support of the state and the need for the University Grants Committee to become something more than a buffer. The U.G.C. has so far, throughout its history, protected the universities from public debate, while at the same time acting as an agent of government policy. The rising financial importance of the U.G.C. with an associated decline in power of local finance has also, in the case especially of the Victorian foundations, served to protect the universities from interference on the part of local laymen to whom a crucial place is given in the formal constitutions of modern universities. The 'correlation of status with self-government was a constant theme of the U.G.C. (between the wars) and ran directly counter to the local government traditions of the founders of the civic universities'.[1]

Nevertheless, the central government is now almost completely the universities' paymaster and whatever this may imply for the calling of the tune it raises the issue of financial pluralism more seriously than ever before. The U.G.C. sees itself as on the side of neither the universities nor the state. 'We are concerned to ensure that a vigorous and creative university life prospers in this country without interference from the government of the day and at the same time to ensure that the tax-paying community, represented by Parliament and the Government, gets a proper return for its money in this field of considerable public expenditure.'[2] But critics like Professor Max Beloff are quick to comment that in accepting a definition of this kind, 'the U.G.C. is in no sense a body representative of the universities it claims to serve but in fact controls',[3] and go on to argue that 'although the state can and must be a principal source of supply, it is essential that there be private funds outside its control'.[4]

Although dependence on state funds is now overwhelming there are other ways of financing the universities[5]–student fees, private

[1] John Vaizey, 'The Finance of Higher Education in the United Kingdom', *Year Book of Education 1959*, Evans, 1960, p. 302. It may be added that the role of the D.E.S. in the development of technical colleges and colleges of education has also worked in the direction of increasing their autonomy *vis-à-vis* local authorities.

[2] U.G.C., *University Development 1962–67*, para. 611.

[3] Max Beloff, 'British Universities and the Public Purse', *Minerva*, Summer 1967, p. 527.

[4] *Ibid.*, p. 530.

[5] For a recent discussion see Sir Sidney Caine, *British Universities: Purpose and Prospects*, Bodley Head, 1969, Chapter 11.

donations and endowments and research contracts. Private gifts are now negligible. Perhaps the most important reason is the cost of new foundations which typically require a wholly different scale of donations than that which permitted the foundation of small institutions in the nineteenth century. A second factor is high taxation and the character of the British tax laws. In this connection there has been some advocacy in recent years of a change in the tax laws on the American model by which charitable gifts up to a proportion of a man's income are tax-deductible. But apart from the amount of money required and the disincentive to private generosity, there is the growth of state finance itself which adds further discouragement. The British universities are therefore denied a source of income which has been crucial to the expansion of the American universities and colleges.[1]

Student fees as a method of university finance have also been eroded during the course of the present century, mainly by inflation. They are, in any case, almost wholly paid by the state under the present grant system. As Sir Sidney Caine has pointed out, the cost of fees and maintenance for a university student are now of the order of £1,500 a year and a sudden switch to complete reliance on this source would result in a sharp reduction in the total number of students, especially those from the poorer families. Such a switch is not in prospect, but there is active discussion of the possibility of raising fees to make them a much larger proportion of total university income and so provide an important alternative channel for the flow of state funds to the universities. It has also been suggested that this proposal could be carried further and that the total state budget allocated to student grants might be paid to students with adjustments according to personal and family circumstances and then in the form of a realistically costed fee by individual students to universities. Another alternative would be for the state to make grants to the universities based on a strict *per capita* calculation and this again is under discussion among the Vice-Chancellors, the U.G.C. and the Government.

Neither of these ideas, however, represent a serious departure from

[1] Alarm about this state of affairs has gone far enough in some quarters to generate a movement for the creation of a new university which would aim to be entirely independent of state support. Sir Sidney Caine is the Chairman of the Development Group. The idea was formulated by Professor H. Ferns of the University of Birmingham in a pamphlet of the Institute of Economic Affairs. The proposal has given rise to a good deal of barbed discussion. See, for example, *The Listener*, 29 May 1969.

government maintenance of the student population. More radical liberal opinion advocates the use of student loans–a scheme which offers the advantages of 'giving to the student himself (and no doubt his parents and advisers) a vital share in the decision about the direction of higher education and what it is worth paying for it; and the placing of greater responsibility on the student himself for the cost of his privileged position as a recipient of a university education'.[1]

This last point makes it clear that the fundamental argument is not about finance as such but about power. Those who oppose the resuscitation and development of private sources for university money are questioning the autonomy of the universities as institutions. The government insists on its right to determine the strategic allocation of resources according to social priorities which are legitimised for them by the democratic process and not by the distribution of private wealth. There are, it is insisted, priorities to be decided within the educational system as a whole, for example between slum primary schools and graduate science, which cannot be left to private decisions. The transfer of responsibility from the Treasury to the D.E.S. is an assertion of the existence of education as a system of related parts which requires central planning and decision-making. The U.G.C., in this sense, accepts a 'socialist' rather than a liberal role. It takes for granted the claims of government to ensure that an appropriate service to 'national needs' in the shape of qualified professional people and 'useful' knowledge is forthcoming from the universities. It accepts that these services must submit to tests of efficiency. It recognises that 'the Public, the Press, Parliament show a deep and almost daily concern not simply with student behaviour but with the place of the universities in discussion about skilled manpower, with the "brain drain" and with the proper adjustment of the provision of university places to student demand at the one end and national needs at the other'.[2]

These views imply 'making positive judgements, an activity which goes far beyond the capacity of a buffer or a shock absorber':[3] they mean, in other words, positive direction of resources by the U.G.C. between different universities. The Committee apologises for the word 'rationalisation' but nevertheless uses it to describe its respon-

[1] Sir Sidney Caine, *op. cit.*, p. 238.
[2] U.G.C., *University Development 1962–67*, para. 556.
[3] *Ibid.*, para. 564.

sibilities. Only within this framework can the U.G.C. see itself as a defender of academic freedom – a term which can now have meaning only in the light of a distinction between 'the intellectual freedom of the individual academic and the institutional autonomy of an academic society'.[1] The latter is now strongly curtailed by governmental power and the Committee believes that university opinion has acquiesced. They do not deny the dangers. 'The dilemma is clear. On the one hand if each university does that which is right in its own eyes, with no regard for the totality of university provision or for national needs, there is a clear danger that anarchy and licence, under the universally respected name of academic freedom, will result. On the other hand, if the Committee becomes too *dirigiste*, too tidy-minded and too much concerned with overall planning, there is an equally clear danger that the free growth of academic institutions will be stunted by excessive control.'[2] 'We have not permitted ourselves to be frightened by charges of our becoming more *dirigiste*.'[3]

This official formulation of the issues may be contrasted with Ben-David's analysis of the development of university systems in the nineteenth century and with the liberal criticism of the role of the U.G.C. which we discuss below. On Ben-David's view the shortcomings of British university achievement stem from the absence of competitive relations between independent institutions and the control of the system from a metropolitan centre under the guidance of constricted class and governmental interests. The dangers, it would be argued, are not 'anarchy and licence' but lack of vigour and creativity. The liberal critique is also less concerned with anarchy and licence: it fears instead that 'dirigism' will supplant university autonomy and thus stifle academic initiative.

The extent of 'dirigism' is partly determined by the availability of private funds and therefore is more threatening to some institutions than to others. Variations in sources and amounts of income in 1967–68 are set out in Table 4.1. Apart from St. David's, Lampeter, only Oxford and Cambridge universities have more than 5 per cent of their incomes from endowments, donations and subscriptions. Next comes Hull with 3·4 per cent and Southampton and Warwick with 3.2 per cent. Some, like Bath, Salford and other ex-CATs, have no endowments at all and elsewhere, except in the ancient English foundations, the sums are negligible.

The Oxford and Cambridge figures do not include the colleges and

[1] *Ibid.*, para. 574. [2] *Ibid.*, para. 566. [3] *Ibid.*, para. 574.

this is crucial. The Franks Commissioners estimated for 1963–64 that, including the colleges, the income per student from endowments was £222 compared with a figure for all universities in Great Britain (except for Cambridge, East Anglia and York) of £13. Oxford's total income per student from all sources in that year was £967 compared with £840 for the other universities, an excess of £127.[1]

The advantage thus given to Oxford and Cambridge must contribute powerfully to their capacity to approximate more closely than others to the English idea of a university–and not only in respect of autonomy. It makes it easier to improve salaries for dons and to provide better amenities for teaching and research. An important illustration of this advantage is library provision, as may be seen from Table 4.2 (p. 92). The Oxford and Cambridge figures again exclude college libraries. Yet still there is a clear diminution in the number of books and reading places per student from the ancient foundations at one end through London, the major Redbricks, Scotland and Wales, the minor Redbricks and the new English universities to the ex-CATs at the other. At one extreme Cambridge has forty volumes per student and at the other Salford has one.

The spectrum of opinion

Within the wide spectrum of opinion on the relation of the university to the modern British state five articulate points of view may be distinguished from current discussion. None of them appear in pure

[1] University of Oxford, Report of Commission of Inquiry (Franks Report), Vol. 1, Table 1, p. 157. 'But it should be observed that roughly half of this endowment income is used to make up for the lower level of public grants which Oxford receives as compared with other universities, that is, half its endowment income is used to meet academic costs which would otherwise fall on the public purse.' In para. 366, p. 159, it is stated that 'Oxford has a higher income available for academic purposes than the established civic universities. The main source of this difference arises from Oxford's level of endowment income per student. In 1963–4 it was £209 a year greater than the average endowment income of the other universities. Oxford's fees for tuition and other academic purposes, now largely paid by local education authorities, was also higher than in other universities by £47 per student. But as against this last figure the other universities received £148 more per student in direct grants from the Exchequer and local authorities than did Oxford. It follows from this that Oxford spent £101 per student out of its endowment income to make up the deficiency, as compared with other universities, in financial assistance from public authorities; this is about 48 per cent of the amount by which Oxford's endowment income exceeded that of other universities. This is only another way of saying that the higher costs of Oxford, which are made possible by its endowments, use up little more than half of the income derived from them, the remainder . . . being used in relief of the taxpayer.'

TABL[E]

Summary of incon[e]

	Endowments and donations		Grants from local authorities		Excheque[r] grants
	Amount (1)	*Percent-age of total income* (2)	*Amount* (3)	*Percent-age of total income* (4)	*Amount* (5)
	£		£		£
1 Aston	4,844	0·1	—	—	3,181,726
2 Bath	—	—	—	—	1,413,333
3 Birmingham	106,901	1·4	39,167	0·5	5,635,718
4 Bradford	—	—	3,290	0·1	2,908,044
5 Bristol	114,973	2·1	24,450	0·4	3,915,437
6 Brunel	10,079	0·6	3,000	0·2	1,329,963
7 Cambridge (b)	550,874	5·4	—	—	6,613,640
8 City	133	—	—	—	1,849,396
9 Durham	59,169	2·3	27,030	1·1	1,920,846
10 East Anglia	111	—	60,000	4·1	1,120,901
11 Essex	—	—	123,750	9·9	815,160
12 Exeter	4,724	0·2	19,217	0·9	1,626,122
13 Hull	88,479	3·4	30,000	1·1	1,982,132
14 Keele	22,818	1·5	60,112	4·0	1,100,730
15 Kent	—	—	10,000	0·8	1,021,431
16 Lancaster	20,826	1·4	56,350	3·8	1,040,458
17 Leeds	94,361	1·2	66,273	0·9	5,679,817
18 Leicester	18,692	0·8	17,425	0·7	1,739,617
19 Liverpool	97,522	1·5	70,905	1·1	4,829,095
20 London, including the colleges and schools	665,875	1·4	483,376	1·0	33,609,636
21 London Business School	—	—	—	—	120,792
22 Loughborough	2,024	0·1	—	—	1,883,273
23 Manchester	181,043	2·3	36,010	0·5	5,879,592
24 Manchester Business School	8,590	2·8	—	—	103,677
25 University of Manchester Institute of Science and Technology	8,311	0·2	45,700	1·2	2,990,747
26 Newcastle	26,993	0·5	59,763	1·0	4,275,337
27 Nottingham	41,508	1·0	87,675	2·1	2,974,766
28 Oxford (*b*)	679,112	7·1	—	—	6,183,830
29 Reading	30,872	0·8	12,350	0·3	2,664,870
30 Salford	—	—	10,000	0·3	3,035,096
31 Sheffield	89,504	1·6	36,510	0·7	4,175,418
32 Southampton	129,409	3·2	34,550	0·9	2,706,594
33 Surrey	—	—	—	—	2,079,273
34 Sussex	4,060	0·1	38,600	1·3	1,991,735
35 Warwick	47,433	3·2	—	—	1,104,557
36 York	18,584	1·1	39,800	2·5	1,159,321
37 **Total England**	3,127,824	1·8	1,495,303	0·9	126,662,080
38 **Total University of Wales**	70,187	0·6	169,060	1·5	8,654,328
39 Aberdeen	68,555	1·7	23,500	0·6	2,917,999
40 Dundee	21,774	1·0	—	—	1,833,050
41 Edinburgh	170,392	2·0	50,800	0·6	5,890,530
42 Glasgow	178,114	2·3	48,700	0·6	5,806,179
43 Heriot-Watt	3,057	0·3	—	—	838,872
44 St. Andrews	24,527	1·4	4,500	0·3	1,396,231
45 Stirling	—	—	80,734	16·8	349,409
46 Strathclyde	10,611	0·3	—	—	3,348,911
47 **Total Scotland**	477,030	1·6	208,234	0·7	22,381,181
48 **Total Great Britain**	3,675,041	1·7	1,872,597	0·9	157,697,589

Source: Information from U.G.C.

the year 1967–68

ition, exami- n, graduation, riculation and istration fees		Research grants and contracts		Grants and payments for other specific purposes		Miscellaneous income		Total income (15)	
ount 7)	Percent-age of total income (8)	Amount (9)	Percent-age of total income (10)	Amount (11)	Percent-age of total income (12)	Amount (13)	Percent-age of total income (14)		
£		£		£		£		£	
29,955	6·1	132,389	3·5	50,853	1·4	159,326	4·2	3,759,093	1
9,579	7·4	71,190	4·4	11,372	0·7	4,911	0·3	1,620,385	2
21,940	6·6	1,219,231	15·4	138,291	1·7	254,285	3·2	7,915,533	3
98,707	5·9	143,734	4·2	8,034	0·2	131,790	3·9	3,393,599	4
99,818	7·2	858,351	15·4	92,205	1·7	159,757	2·9	5,564,991	5
98,446	6·3	61,288	3·9	52	—	49,882	3·2	1,552,710	6
88,190	6·7	1,582,910	15·4	240,312	2·3	598,658	5·8	10,274,584	7
50,086	7·5	85,793	4·0	22,150	1·0	25,859	1·2	2,143,417	8
21,834	8·7	233,338	9·1	40,755	1·6	51,629	2·0	2,554,601	9
35,583	9·2	84,918	5·8	13,892	0·9	56,757	3·9	1,472,162	10
91,618	7·4	167,492	13·4	8,220	0·7	39,199	3·1	1,245,439	11
2,515	9·8	109,088	5·0	92,582	4·3	101,345	4·7	2,165,593	12
34,668	9·0	170,031	6·5	22,566	0·9	84,858	3·2	2,612,734	13
4,633	7·6	139,159	9·2	—	—	75,741	5·0	1,513,193	14
7,044	9·2	73,991	5·8	238	—	50,074	3·9	1,272,778	15
27,661	8·7	108,896	7·4	66,745	4·6	44,926	3·1	1,465,862	16
7,597	7·8	903,711	11·6	188,347	2·4	236,038	3·0	7,776,144	17
8,768	8·7	277,610	11·5	54,133	2·2	96,032	4·0	2,412,277	18
6,596	7·3	694,567	10·7	107,360	1·7	226,870	3·5	6,502,915	19
3,987	6·7	6,534,752	13·6	1,929,814	4·0	1,752,256	3·6	48,209,696	20
3,175	16·2	21,807	6·7	—	—	131,776	40·2	327,550	21
2,381	6·5	145,824	6·2	29,937	1·3	122,371	5·2	2,335,810	22
7,801	7·6	720,960	9·2	151,722	1·9	282,217	3·6	7,849,345	23
6,393	15·3	36,591	12·1	—	—	107,961	35·6	303,212	24
3,910	6·1	453,178	11·9	28,732	0·8	47,199	1·2	3,807,777	25
3,005	7·0	765,191	12·9	143,835	2·4	237,383	4·0	5,921,507	26
1,452	7·9	386,437	9·3	188,844	4·5	159,268	3·8	4,169,950	27
3,795	5·2	1,649,202	17·3	121,347	1·3	402,924	4·2	9,530,210	28
8,597	7·3	323,868	8·2	520,488	13·2	109,187	2·8	3,950,232	29
9,318	6·8	98,326	2·8	19,111	0·5	109,327	3·1	3,511,178	30
6,876	7·3	542,412	9·9	62,308	1·1	166,113	3·0	5,469,141	31
0,723	7·5	662,382	16·5	159,971	4·0	13,756	0·3	4,007,385	32
2,306	7·1	91,793	3·8	12,784	0·5	79,104	3·2	2,435,260	33
0,817	8·5	586,035	19·8	33,063	1·1	51,155	1·7	2,955,465	34
6,154	7·2	128,438	8·7	14,236	1·0	71,357	4·8	1,472,175	35
3,604	8·2	212,039	13·1	6,788	0·4	51,391	3·2	1,621,527	36
9,532	7·1	20,476,922	11·7	4,581,087	2·6	6,342,682	3·6	175,095,430	37
2,750	8·5	737,169	6·5	331,586	2·9	381,248	3·4	11,296,328	38
4,045	9·6	307,542	7·7	167,969	4·2	111,833	2·8	3,981,443	39
0,457	7·9	93,102	4·3	38,362	1·8	822	—	2,157,567	40
3,832	8·0	1,062,896	12·4	395,071	4·6	298,072	3·5	8,551,550	41
1,843	8·2	681,113	8·9	84,660	1·1	209,001	2·7	7,629,610	42
7,634	12·9	46,833	4·4	1,040	0·1	36,135	3·4	1,063,571	43
5,030	8·5	70,227	4·1	17,500	1·0	57,805	3·4	1,715,820	44
3,942	2·9	17,526	3·6	6,564	1·4	13,732	2·8	481,907	45
5,824	10·3	276,113	6·5	36,575	0·9	123,061	2·9	4,231,095	46
2,607	8·7	2,555,352	8·6	747,741	2·5	850,418	2·9	29,812,563	47
4,889	7·4	23,769,443	11·0	5,660,414	2·6	7,574,348	3·5	216,204,321	48

TABLE 4.2

Library provision, 1965–66

University	*Bound volumes* (000,*s*) (1)	*Places for readers* (2)	*Students* (a) (3)	*Volumes per student* (4)	*Places per student* (5)
Cambridge	4,017	3,061	9,943	40·4	0·31
Oxford	3,321	3,389	9,808	33·8	0·35
London	4,122	8,348	31,586	13·0	0·26
Birmingham	680	1,299	6,060	11·2	0·21
Leeds	638	1,425	7,047	9·0	0·20
Leicester	216	564	2,478	8·7	0·23
Sussex	158	850	2,133	7·4	0·40
York	84	300	1,000	8·4	0·30
Aston	78	250	3,093	2·5	0·08
Salford	35	102	3,463	1·0	0·03
Scotland	2,954	6,830	30,188	9·7	0·23
Wales	918	3,189	9,992	9·1	0·32
Great Britain	22,063	46,461	184,354	11·9	0·25

Notes: (a) Includes full-time and part-time students.
Source: Calculated from U.G.C. Returns, 1965–6, Cmnd. 3586.

ideological form and all are in any case fused and confused with a larger body of more or less inarticulate sentiment. But all take up a position on the claims of the state to control in the interests of 'national needs' and towards the rights of institutional autonomy. (Perhaps the first and most important fact is that the question of individual right to free doctrinal expression is nowhere in question.) Articulate opinion is usually the proponent of a particular interest group, and the five identified here may be labelled (1) liberal, (2) revolutionary, (3) retreatist, (4) donnish, and (5) parliamentary.

The classical liberal ideologue would conduct a revolution backwards. For him the autonomy of private organisations in general and universities in particular is paramount. The strength and appeal of this view lies in its forthright championing of an academic freedom which is derived and justified by a political theory of pluralism and an economic theory of free markets. Its weakness is not that its origins are historically bourgeois–though they certainly are that–but that as a practical strategy it has become irrelevant. This is not to say that criticism of the role of the U.G.C. cannot be effectively deployed from this direction. There is force, for example, in Professor Beloff's argument, illustrated by the case of Latin American studies in Oxford, that the freedom promoted by the U.G.C.'s 'block grant' principle is often nullified by earmarked grants. Similarly, his argument that 'the only effect of raising private money for universities is to help the taxpayer: it is in the end bound to be set off against what they get from public sources'[1] is conceded by the U.G.C. whose rules are in any case open to criticisms of rigidity of the kind illustrated in their objection to lavish bathrooms at private expense in the London and Manchester Business Schools.[2] The essential argument is that if there is to be 'any real measure of university autonomy in this country, the important thing is to increase the proportion of money obtained through private endowments and fees and lessen that which comes directly from the state'.[3] But what is perhaps the most noteworthy feature of Professor Beloff's advocacy is the assumption that the state '*must be* a principal source of supply'[4] of university finances whereas a thoroughgoing liberalism would confine the role of the state to guardianship of the ring for competing private interests. Professor Beloff's liberalism is more modern and more realistic than this: nevertheless his argument that 'the other great advantage of private endowments is that they permit proper forward planning' is a direct challenge to the legitimacy and/or practicality of government planning of the system of higher education as a whole.

Paradoxically the views of the liberals are by no means wholly in conflict with those of another minority–the student revolutionaries. This group also rejects the legitimacy of state management of the universities. Their reasons are, of course, different. For them the universities are primarily a part of the apparatus of state capitalism. They argue that 'modern capitalism is characterised by particularly great educational needs. The ruling class has an ever greater need for an educated work force. The directing élite needs more technical knowledge to rule and the armies of intermediaries between the élite and the work force–the vast industrial bureaucracies above all–are expanding.'[5] The analysis of the relation between university and state here begins by recognising the official ideology of academic freedom but, so the argument runs, 'even in terms of direct financing, the U.G.C. is far from the harmless body it is often credited to be. The majority of the Committee consists of people actively engaged in university teaching or research; the rest are drawn at present from other forms of education, from industry and from research establish-

[1] Max Beloff, *loc. cit.*, p. 530.
[2] *Ibid.*, p. 523.
[3] *Ibid.*, p. 530.
[4] The italics are ours.
[5] Chris Harman *et al.*, *Education, Capitalism and the Student Revolt*, an International Socialism publication, 1968, p. 8.

ments. In fact of the twenty members in 1963 four, including the chairman, held directorships of private industry, one being chairman of Mobil Oil and director of nine other companies, another ex-chairman of Unilever. Two other members held appointments in the nationalised industries. The recent freeze on the university building programme by the U.G.C. is an indication of the gross external constraints within which the universities operate.'[1] Moreover, it is asserted, the apparatus of court, council and professorial senate which rules individual universities ensures that 'the values of the ruling class permeate down from the top. Individual ruling-class interests do not in the main direct particular courses or spheres of research; rather the values of the ruling class determine what is to be considered academically permissible and relevant as areas of debate and research. But this overall hegemony does leave room for other interests and aspirations to make themselves felt at lower levels. Here traditions of academic style and classical conceptions of what a university is, or even very occasionally the demands of science or scholarship, continue to play an important and independent role. Within an overall bias (which means that a chair of "industrial relations" is taken for granted, while one in revolutionary agitation is inconceivable) there is considerable leeway. By ruling a whole range of considerations out of order a suffocating negative sanction is operated: within the area left for debate there is freedom for considerable and immensely valuable academic "freedom" – such freedom is, of course, "academic".'[2]

This point of view may be criticised for the overriding importance it gives to interests as against ideologies. But, from this point of view at least, it is a relevant and salutary reminder of the fact that university teaching and research reflect class interests and that no one, not even the academic himself, is guided only by the demands of science and scholarship. This view is valuable too in casting a hostile light on the possibility of a triumphant bureaucratic power. The Labour Government, it is argued, committed itself after the Robbins Report to major expansion of higher education outside the universities and 'within the other institutions of the "binary" system the situation is not in the least obscured by any liberal metaphysics'.[3] There is no U.G.C. buffer but bureaucratic rule from the D.E.S. and the local authorities representing local business interest. Fundamentally, however, these views are unacceptable to the majority, including the

[1] *Ibid.*, p. 11. [2] *Ibid.*, p. 14. [3] *Ibid.*, p. 15.

majority of students, because of their denial of the possibility of worthwhile university reform except in the context of social revolution. Beyond demonstrating that the university and the educational system are subject to the general control of a capitalist ruling class the university becomes of interest to the student revolutionary only as a focus of the wider class struggle.

There is a third view which has even fewer adherents. Nevertheless, we include it, not only because we ourselves have considerable sympathy with it, but also because we believe it to have relevance to the future of the university as a special type of institution within an expanded system of higher education. This view shares with the first two a rejection of the kind of society in which the university now exists. It seizes on a strand in the ideological tradition of universities, which one of us has referred to elsewhere as the alliance of the Franciscan with the aristocrat,[1] a university in which the scholar is free to pursue 'useless' knowledge at the cost of other-worldly abstinence from the material rewards available to him as a middle-class professional in the existing academic system. This view can be dismissed as retreatist in that it would rescue the universities as a small appendage of the higher education system. It would leave the U.G.C. problem unsolved, along with the industrial society which created it, while the university would become a minor charge of some sort of state or private charity.

Though the retreatist view could be caricatured in this way, it nonetheless bears an essential truth which cannot be so lightly dismissed. Even without a commitment to something less than the normal academic salary levels we see no evidence that more than a tiny minority wish to belong to a purely academic university either as teachers or as learners. If this is so, then it will indeed be the case that the university, in this sense, will have to become a small appendage of the system of higher education. Indeed we would say that if universities tried to approximate to what we have characterised as the English idea of a university and at the same time tried to accommodate forty, fifty or sixty per cent of the relevant age group then they would cease to be universities.

In any case, it can surely be argued that a system of higher education does not have to have one characteristic but can have many, and that there may be a place in the differentiated system for a few institutions which are small and 'retreatist' by choice. This is not to argue that the

[1] See A. H. Halsey, 'Holy Erudition', *New Society*, 26 December 1968.

university system as a whole could or should cut itself off from the demands of society for its products, and particularly for trained professional people. Nor is it an argument in support of those who simply want to recreate the unreformed ancient universities as they conceive of them. It is rather to suggest that within the form and structure of a large system of higher education there should be a place for a great variety of institutions including a few which make no attempt to meet the legitimate demand for mass higher education. There is no intention here to deny the claims of distributive justice nor to oppose a society based on egalitarian relationships. Nevertheless, a central problem for democrats to work out is how to preserve the best of the élite values expressed in university life while at the same time, within the context of a system of higher education, meeting modern social demands for both high educational standards and an intellectual service for society's productive and administrative needs.

In their different ways all of these three views are fundamentalist and, in that sense, unrealistic. A fourth view which accepts in principle the right of the state to determine strategies and, though not uncritically, the role of the U.G.C. in translating them into university management has been put forward by Sir Eric Ashby. He challenges the interpretation of current realities by Professor Beloff and by David Thompson[1] in which the bureaucratic hand of the D.E.S. and the U.G.C. are identified as undesirable controllers of the universities. Ashby is more impressed by the concern of the U.G.C. to protect than that of the universities themselves to defend academic freedom.

'Hands of some sort will inevitably be laid upon the universities. . . . They should be, as they are already, predominantly the hands of other dons. Why other dons? Why not politicians and civil servants? Have I forgotten that reform in universities has almost invariably had to wait upon the pressures of Royal Commissions? No, I have not. The interesting fact about Royal Commissions on universities is that it has been the academic members who have exerted the greatest influence. (Haldane was perhaps an exception, but he was a don *malgré lui*.) But there is a valid reason why the hands should be the hands of dons. University teaching is as highly technical as is the practice of medicine. It is right that the layman should say what society expects from its professors and its medical practitioners. It would be crazy for the layman to tell the professor how to teach

[1] See *The Listener*, January 1966.

or the doctor how to prescribe. So government influence on the movement of universities must be confined to overall social policy (such as the proportion of the age group to receive post-secondary education). Apart from this, the hands must remain the hands of other dons. To safeguard this I am sure that dons themselves will have to be willing to adapt for the 1970s their traditional ideas of what constitutes university autonomy.'[1] This view may be taken to represent the enlightened and judicious elements in university senior common rooms.

Finally, there is a parliamentary reformist view expressed cogently by Lord Bowden.[2] Here there is wholehearted acceptance of governmental responsibility for university development: the problem is to make it work with maximum efficiency. Public accountability is welcomed and academic autonomy is held not to be threatened by it. For example, German universities are subject to government audit and German university professors are all civil servants, yet 'German universities and their staff preserve a degree of academic freedom and individual autonomy which is in some ways more absolute than anything we know in England'.[3] Lord Bowden's fear is not this but that the Accountant General may not be competent to do anything for academic efficiency. This is partly because the status and career prospects of his staff are worse in Britain than in any other major western country. Nor does Lord Bowden fear that the examination of university accounts would reveal anything but the most impeccable proprieties. The problem, in his view, is rather that we do not keep proper 'management accounts' which would make efficiency tests possible. To this end, and more generally in order to bring 'mutual understanding between the universities and the educational system on the one hand and the entire machinery of government (including the Houses of Parliament) on the other' a new parliamentary committee on the model of American congressional committees and with a reformed Comptroller and Auditor-General's department at its disposal is urgently necessary.

This is a serious vote of no confidence in the U.G.C. which opposed the step already taken in this direction by Mr. Crosland following the report of the Public Accounts Committee. Lord

[1] Eric Ashby, *Hands off the Universities?*, The Foundation Oration, Birkbeck College, 1968.

[2] Lord Bowden, 'The University, the Government and the Public Accounts Committee', *Minerva*, Autumn 1967.

[3] *Ibid.*, p. 30.

Bowden's general view represents the modernising and technocratic elements among parliamentarians. It is not without support in academic circles. Lord James, the Vice-Chancellor of York University, and Mr. C. F. Carter, the Vice-Chancellor of Lancaster, welcomed the powers of inspection given to the Comptroller and Auditor-General, both believing that efficiency is essential, that accountability to Parliament is an obligation and that enquiry would yield favourable comparison against the control and economy exercised in other public enterprises.

Some kind of accommodation between Lord Bowden's position and that expressed by Sir Eric Ashby is probably the best guess for the next ten years. It leaves the fate of the U.G.C. in delicate balance. Accommodation between the 'donnish' and 'Parliamentary' view could mean the formal disappearance of the U.G.C. buffer and its replacement by direct confrontation between, on the one hand, a single body representing all the institutions of higher education and, on the other hand, a re-modelled and expanded Universities branch of the D.E.S. An alternative, closer to Ashby's position, might be the retention of the buffer type of organisation but with a reformed structure including full-time membership, further expansion of the Committee's secretariat and provision for much more contact with individual universities.

Meanwhile, the U.G.C. as at present constituted, with or without the modest reforms now in train, is unlikely to retain 'reciprocal confidence between the bodies concerned'. University opinion has been shifting greatly under the pressure of economic stringency imposed by the Government as well as pressures from both staff and students towards a demand for open and direct relations with the central administration. The U.G.C., fairly or unfairly, is now commonly seen to wear the outmoded imperial clothing of an Edwardian club, conducting its business in diplomatic secrecy and perpetuating itself by co-optation of carefully selected and safe 'establishment' members. Modernisers and revolutionaries alike are unsympathetic to what has traditionally been a characteristic feature of British society–respect for the private autonomy of governing institutions. Provincial suspicion of the metropolitan inner circle has its manifestations not only in remote Welsh and Scottish political constituencies, but also, more mildly, among university staffs on campuses remote from London. The present quinquennial visits are widely seen as bordering on the farcical and the proposed extension of them is unlikely to be an adequate antidote to these growing sentiments.

Above all, the increased number of institutions and their growing internal complexity makes the university system, and still more the higher education system, a colossal organisation. It surely cannot be effectively managed by part-time dons, and while this continues to be attempted, power will inevitably gravitate to the full-time officials–and all the more so as expansion leads to increased Parliamentary demands for economical operation. Given that financial autonomy has gone, 'the hands of other dons' have to be recognised as the principal defence of academic freedom. The outstanding question is whether these hands are likely to be impotent if they continue to be laid on an unreformed U.G.C.

Chapter 5
UNIVERSITY GOVERNMENT

> The choice is only between bureaucracy and dilettantism in the field of administration. (Max Weber)

In Chapter 4 we discussed the question of university autonomy. We turn now, within this framework of the relations between the universities and the state, to look at internal government and so to examine the eighth and final criterion of the English idea of a university. We shall describe the formal constitutions of the British universities and discuss their customs, usages and recent innovations.

We have emphasised the strong traditions of self-government which had their origins in the collegiate guilds of Oxford and Cambridge and which, at least for the professoriate, led very quickly to substantive academic self-government if not academic democracy in the Victorian foundations. But we are now considering a period of expansion which involves not only a growth in the university system as a whole but an increase in the size of particular institutions. We discussed in the last chapter the implications for autonomy of the growing and now overwhelming reliance of universities on the state for funds. The growth of the universities themselves is, in any case, a separate factor likely to set problems for the type of academic democracy which was developed in societies comprising no more than a handful of dons. Enough is known, and much more surmised, about the power of administrators in the large American universities for size to be regarded as a threat to the control of their institutions by university teachers. We must consider the practices of internal government and in later chapters we shall look in detail at the attitudes which academics bring to the problems of administration and power. But first we must examine the constitutional framework in which attitudes and behaviour are placed.

Most British universities exercise their powers, rights and duties by virtue of a charter establishing their major responsibilities: only three of the Scottish universities, St. Andrews, Glasgow and Aberdeen, have constitutions defined by Act of Parliament without charter. Less important matters are dealt with under the universities' own statutes which must be approved by the sovereign and may also have to be laid before Parliament. Day-to-day affairs such as the conferring of degrees and the determination of entrance requirements are regulated by the ordinances, decrees, graces and regulations promulgated by the universities themselves in accordance with their charters and statutes.

Individual systems of government vary within this common constitutional framework. There are marked differences in structure with more or less loose federations of colleges (Oxford, Cambridge, London, Wales, Durham) contrasting with the monolithic organisation typical of the major civic universities (Birmingham, Leeds, Liverpool, Manchester, Sheffield, Newcastle). There are also marked differences in the way in which power to take policy and administrative decisions is distributed among academics, administrators and laymen on the one hand and between different ranks within the academic professions on the other. This second point is of great significance, for the degree of power which university teachers have to govern themselves and to plan their own work is crucial for the questions of autonomy and academic freedom which are central issues in university affairs.

The most obvious difference in formal government structure is between the federal college systems of Oxford and Cambridge and the unitary administration of the Redbrick universities. The University of London and the University of Wales are also federations of colleges and some of the new universities have devised a collegiate structure. Nevertheless, all of these modern universities as well as the older universities of Scotland have a closer resemblance to one another than to the ancient English foundations. This is not to say that there are no features common to all, over and above establishment by royal charter. For example, each university has an organised body of its own graduates. This is usually called 'Convocation' though it is known as the General Council in Scotland and as the Senate in Cambridge.[1]

[1] Normally Convocation has no authority; in some universities it elects the Rector or Chancellor and may present views to the university as a whole. In Oxford and Cambridge it has certain powers in some circumstances to confirm or reverse the decisions of Congregation or of Regent House, though in practice these powers are very rarely used.

It is, however, the financial and organisational independence of the Oxford and Cambridge colleges which allows greater powers and participation to academics of all grades and over practically all aspects of university affairs than in other institutions. The universities as such in Oxford and Cambridge are relatively weak. Nevertheless, the extent of democratic control, at least in Oxford, is presently being modified to some degree in the interests of speed and efficiency of administration.[1]

Oxford and Cambridge

Perhaps the most remarkable feature of Oxford and Cambridge is that the government of these universities is entirely in the hands of their academic members. The colleges are self-governing, financed by fees and endowments, and they control the admission and teaching of their undergraduate students. Most college tutors also hold university teaching appointments and the university provides certain lectures, classes, seminars, libraries, laboratories and other facilities. It is also the university that conducts examinations and awards degrees. Some of the academic staff hold university appointments without having college fellowships, but recent changes in Oxford have meant that all university appointees become entitled to a college fellowship after a qualifying period of five years. While the colleges manage their own affairs, the boards and committees that govern the university are also elected from college fellows and Heads of Houses, and it is in this way that the interests of the individual colleges are powerfully represented in the management of the university as a whole.

At both universities ultimate authority rests with all academic staff who are actively engaged in teaching or research. In Oxford this body of resident Masters of Arts is known as Congregation, in Cambridge it is called Regent House. Measures may be submitted for approval only by the Hebdomadal Council in Oxford or the Council of the Senate in Cambridge. Both these bodies are composed of the Chancellor and Vice-Chancellor, and in Oxford certain other university officers who sit *ex officio*, and eighteen or more further members who are elected by the academic staff. Financial administration, though not policy, is managed in Oxford by the Curators of the University Chest and in Cambridge by the Financial Board, both

[1] See below, Chapter 6.

of which include the Vice-Chancellor and other members nominated by Congregation, the colleges or some other university body. Academic matters are the responsibility of the General Board and the faculty boards where questions of policy and planning are debated before proposals are submitted to the General Board and thence to Congregation or to Regent House. In Oxford the faculty boards have half their members elected by and from the whole faculty and half elected by the faculty from professors and readers. In Cambridge faculty boards include all professors, readers who are heads of departments, co-opted members and members nominated by Council as well as those who are elected by the faculty. The General Board of the Faculties in Oxford is mainly an elected body though a third of its members are nominated or serve *ex officio*. In Cambridge the composition of the Board is similar, though it is only half the size of its Oxford counterpart.

Thus, in both ancient universities, policy and administration are controlled by academics who are at the same time pursuing their professional activities.[1] There seems, however, to be a slightly different degree of democracy between the two institutions. Unlike Cambridge, no individual professor or reader in Oxford holds a place on a faculty board by virtue of his position; and while professors account for nearly a quarter of the members of the chief administrative bodies in Cambridge, they amount to only an eighth in Oxford.[2]

London

London, too, has a collegiate structure though the autonomy of the colleges is less complete than in Oxford and Cambridge largely because they are not individually so well endowed and depend more on government money which is distributed among the schools by the university Court. Nor is the degree of control by the academics anything like so great as in Oxford or Cambridge. Overall responsibility for the property and financial affairs of the university rests with the Court, a body whose seventeen members include six appointed by the university Senate, four by the sovereign and three by the local authority–the L.C.C., as it was in 1961. In this way

[1] There is a minor exception in some of the college heads who may no longer be engaged in academic work and in a few who never have been.

[2] *Higher Education*, Appendix Four, p. 41, Tables 14 and 15.

university and outside interests are almost evenly balanced. There are no members who are elected by the general body of the academic staff, though the six Senate nominees are normally university teachers. The final authority for all academic matters rests with the Senate, which appoints all professors and readers and 'recognises' other teachers. One-third of its 59 members are elected from and by the faculties and another third are graduates of the university (who may be university teachers) elected by Convocation. Faculty boards and boards of studies have the usual deliberative and advisory functions.

The mechanics of election to the Senate are formidable in such a large organisation, especially as Convocation, which consists of graduates of the university and which in recent months has abolished the age limit of 21, is involved in the election of members. These elections by Convocation to the Senate are on a faculty basis; for example the Faculties of Arts and Science each elect five members whereas the Faculty of Law elects one member. Elections are by postal vote of members of Convocation in each group or faculty. Thus, if there is a vacancy in the Faculty of Law and more than one candidate is nominated, then voting papers are sent to every member of Convocation who is a graduate in that group. A member of the Senate elected by Convocation serves for a term of four years, when he must retire, but he is eligible for re-election. A member seeking election to the Senate must be nominated by at least ten members of Convocation.[1]

In London, then, the Court and Senate are the major university bodies but the colleges[2] have their individual councils or academic boards and two of them have a governing body of their own corresponding roughly to the Court of the Redbrick university. College councils may have anything from fourteen to over fifty members composed in varying proportions of academics, laymen[3] and administrators. In all cases, however, laymen are in the great majority. Academics from the institutions concerned very rarely form more than a quarter of the membership of the councils and in

[1] The Standing Orders provide that, in contested elections, a candidate may submit an autobiography not exceeding 100 words for circulation with the order of business and voting papers to the electors concerned, and he is also entitled, subject to payment of a prescribed fee, to submit an election address not exceeding 500 words for circulation in the same manner. Voting is in effect on a proportional representative basis, each voter indicating on his voting paper his votes in order of preference.

[2] The medical schools are not included in this description.

[3] Laymen may include representatives of other universities or colleges.

some cases a very much smaller proportion.[1] The colleges vary in their practice of including or excluding academics below the rank of professor on their councils. The academic boards, by contrast, all include non-professorial members, some sitting *ex officio*, some elected and some nominated. The professors outnumber other academics on the Boards of exactly half the colleges–often by more than four to one, but none of the Academic Boards has more than three administrative members. There is enormous variation in size; the smallest has twelve and the largest one hundred and thirty-five persons.

Wales

The Welsh situation is similar though the University of Wales, its four constituent colleges and the Welsh National School of Medicine each has a Charter, Court, Council and Senate of its own. The Principals of the four colleges act in turn as Vice-Chancellor of the University for a period of two years. The University Court is a mixture of laymen and academics with the latter in a minority of under ten per cent: there are seventeen professors and only two more junior university teachers. All academic members are elected by the Senates of the constituent colleges and the School of Medicine. The Council controls finance, approves the estimates and distributes the U.G.C. funds among the constituent institutions. The only representatives of the colleges to sit on Council are the Principals and the Provost of the Medical School. The Academic Board is composed mainly of professors. The five college heads serve *ex officio* and there are three co-opted members, but the remaining eighteen seats are filled by election by the faculties. Professors dominate the academic representation by five to one.

The college governing bodies follow the same pattern. The Courts have a very large preponderance of lay members with professors forming a large majority of the academics who are sometimes elected and sometimes sit *ex officio*. The Councils are also heavily dominated by laymen with professors still in the majority among the academics. The Senates are composed of professional members with a few administrators but no laymen, and professorial domination is again evident, professors sometimes outnumbering other academics by as many as seven to one as at Aberystwyth. In general all university

[1] *Higher Education*, p. 25, Table 7.

teachers who have permanent full-time jobs are faculty board members.

The Redbrick universities

Thus the two essential differences between London and Wales on the one hand and Oxford and Cambridge on the other are in respect of the formal degree of control given to laymen and to professors in academic government. The two modern universities have laymen on their governing bodies and relatively far more professors than do the older foundations. The Redbrick universities are even further removed from the ideal of democratic self-government in an academic guild.

For all of the Redbrick universities the Court, Council and Senate are the chief statutory governing bodies. The Court is in theory the supreme authority but in practice its powers are restricted to formalities–particularly over academic matters. It meets regularly only once or twice a year to review accounts and other reports of university work, though special meetings may be held at other times. The size of the Court varies apparently arbitrarily from one hundred and twenty-nine members at Manchester to sixty-five at Sheffield. Academics are invariably a small minority, rarely representing a third, and in the case of the Manchester College of Science and Technology only eight out of one hundred and twenty-seven, of the total membership.[1] Laymen make up the great majority and are selected by a variety of methods including enumeration, nomination, appointment and election.[2]

The university Council of a Redbrick university is responsible for financial matters and, formally at least, for all policy decisions. It formally approves the proposals or decisions of the Senate in

[1] *Ibid.*, Appendix Four, p. 20, Table 4.

[2] To take an example, the Court of the University of Liverpool has seventeen different classes of members of the Court. All the professors of the University are *ex officio* members. The Members of Parliament elected for the divisions of Liverpool, Birkenhead, Bootle and Wallasey are enumerated as are the Earl of Derby, the Lord Mayor of Liverpool, the Roman Catholic Archbishop of Liverpool, the Liverpool and District Rabbi, the Chairman of the Mersey Docks and Harbour Board, the Secretary of the Liverpool Trades Council and Labour Party and many others. Some are appointed by such bodies as the Royal Society of London, the British Academy, the General Medical Council, or the Royal Institution of Naval Architects. Other persons are appointed by various City and County Councils in the region as well as by County Boroughs, Urban Districts and Rural Districts. Others are elected from the non-professorial staff, from the Guild of Undergraduates, or from Convocation itself. And others are co-opted, for example, heads of schools to a number not exceeding twenty-five on the nomination of the Court.

respect of academic policy, though custom decrees that the Senate in practice rules such matters. Generally, Council chooses the Vice-Chancellor in co-operation with the Senate.[1] And it, again formally, authorises all academic appointments. It usually has between thirty and fifty members, the majority of whom are laymen, either nominated by local authorities or appointed by the Court and who, on average, outnumber the academics by four to one. Professors have more seats than their junior colleagues and are usually elected by and from the Senate or hold their seats by virtue of some other office. The other university teachers on the Council are occasionally elected by all nonprofessorial academic staff but more usually by the Senate or the Faculties.

In the Redbrick university, Senate is the chief academic body and in practice the centre of university power, sanctioning and co-ordinating the work of the faculties and taking overall responsibility for the teaching and discipline of students. Senates vary in size from thirty to one hundred and nine members and are made up exclusively of university teachers with the Vice-Chancellor as chairman and generally including all professors, a handful of more junior academic staff, the university Registrar, the Librarian and the wardens of halls of residence. Subject to Senatorial approval the faculties regulate and discuss academic affairs relating to their special group of studies and consider questions referred to them by the Senate, though in some cases these responsibilities are delegated to faculty boards. Faculty board membership for teachers other than professors is, however, restricted though the practice varies not only between universities but also between faculties of the same institution.

Scotland

The constitution of the Scottish universities is not dissimilar to that of the English Redbricks. Indeed, Scotland provided a model for the Victorian foundations. In Scotland, however, similar bodies sometimes go by different names. The final authority is the Court, which is similar in power and functions to the Councils of the English civic universities. It is responsible for property and finance,

[1] For example, in the statutes of the University of Liverpool it is stated that 'the Vice-Chancellor shall be appointed by the Council after consideration of the report of the joint committee of which the President of the Council shall be a member *ex officio* and chairman and the other members whereof shall be nominated in equal numbers by the Council and the Senate'.

makes academic appointments and can review Senate decisions. It contains fourteen or eighteen members partly nominated, partly elected by the Senate and General Council, with the Rector as Chairman and including in some cases the Lord Provost of the city. Lay members predominate, and academic representation was confined to professors in 1961 except at St. Andrews where two seats were reserved for university teachers below professorial rank. The General Council in the Scottish universities is an enormous body consisting of all graduates, the Court and the academic staff. It may make representations to the Court on any matters to do with university affairs and it also elects the Rector who serves for three years. Responsibility for academic questions rests with the Senate, a body of between fifty and one hundred members which includes all professors *ex officio* with the Principal as Chairman and other university teachers who must not number more than a quarter of the professors.

The new English universities

The new English universities have the same kind of autonomy as the older institutions but their systems of government have been modified in some ways to reduce formal local lay control, to increase participation by non-professorial staff and to allow students some voice in university government. The U.G.C. regarded the new universities as an opportunity for experiment but appears to have been disappointed in the actual constitutions adopted. 'On the whole . . . we should have welcomed in the statutes of the new universities some greater changes in the system of university government.'[1]

What is the extent of the innovations which have been made?[2] All of the new universities have a very large Court, but few have retained it as the supreme governing body; it is generally restricted to receiving and discussing reports on university affairs and submitting its opinions to the Council and Senate. It is not properly a governing body at all but one in which the work of the university can be explained and discussed and through which it can be interpreted to the community. In this sense the Court forms a link between the university and the outside world with the job of maintaining good relations and of winning support.

[1] U.G.C., *University Development 1957–62*, Cmnd. 2267, H.M.S.O., 1964, p. 105.

[2] The following description is based on H. J. Perkin, *Innovation in Higher Education: New Universities of the United Kingdom*, O.E.C.D., 1969.

In most of the new universities it is the Council that thus becomes the ultimate governing authority responsible for property and finance, for academic appointments and for control of university affairs generally, apart from such purely academic matters as planning courses. The Councils have up to forty members including the important university officers, a majority of lay members representing outside bodies and the Court, and a minority of academics, dominated by professors. Some academics, mindful of the Oxford and Cambridge model, argue that they should themselves form a majority on the governing body but the preponderance of laymen is seen by others as necessary to ensure that universities serve the public interest, and also have a stock of disinterested and knowledgeable opinion at their disposal.

All but one of the new universities also have a Senate but in some cases there is a departure from the older practice of including all professors and membership is restricted to only a proportion who are elected. Academics below professorial rank are also more generously represented, having a third as many seats as the professors. York is an exception with a two-tier academic authority, a professorial board and a general academic board, no more than a fifth of whom need be professors. This arrangement is intended to limit professorial authority to the appointment and promotion of academic staff while the general board deals with all other matters of policy and has its decisions automatically endorsed by the professors.

So far as the actual organisation of studies is concerned the new universities have adopted a variety of arrangements. Faculties have been largely abandoned, at any rate in name, and schools or boards of studies introduced in a search for more flexibility. It is difficult to see how successful such innovations are and to some extent at any rate the old rigidities of faculty and departmental structure seem to be reproduced in a new form. Three of the new universities have set up general boards or assemblies of all academic staff to improve communications among university teachers of all grades and subjects. These bodies generally meet once a year to discuss academic matters, express opinions and raise grievances.

Changes in form, however, are less important than, though they may be associated with, changes in power. And here the two crucial issues re-emerge. How far are academics responsible for managing their own affairs and how far do the different grades of academics take part in the process of government? The new universities have preserved the principle of academic control of administration and thus perpetuate the old dilemma–that high academic position won through professional merit also often involves heavy administrative duties which necessarily divert some of the most able men from teaching and research. The new arrangements seem to have done little to resolve this problem and some of the deans of the different schools spend as much as fifty per cent of their time on administration. The second issue of democracy within the academic profession seems to have been pretty much neglected. Professors remain a substantial majority on the Council and Senate though non-professorial representation has been increased, particularly on Senate, and there have been some attempts to extend committee membership to more junior university teachers.

The technological universities

Finally, there are the new technological universities or ex-CATs. One of these institutions (Chelsea) acquired its new status as a member of London University but the others transformed themselves into independent universities. At the time of their formation the whole matter of university government had developed into a political issue, so much so that the Privy Council recommended a number of provisions to be included in the new charters, one of the most important being that Council and Senate should be able to establish joint committees of themselves and student representatives.[1] Otherwise the ex-CATs have followed the traditional pattern of government in civic universities with a Council responsible for financial affairs and general matters of university policy and administration and composed of a majority of laymen and a Senate dealing with academic questions and including non-professorial members. The colleges agreed, at the suggestion of the U.G.C., to set up academic advisory committees to advise them on the transition to university status. The work of the committees included consideration of the academic and governmental structure, of the procedure for granting degrees, and the drafting of charters. The committees were small bodies of six or seven members who were, for the most part, academics from other universities but also included some representatives from industry.

[1] U.G.C., *University Development 1962–67*, p. 62.

The university department

So much, then, for Court, Senate, Council and committees. These are established bodies, but, to repeat and re-emphasise, not too much must be made of formal constitutions. In practice the effective ruling body of all the modern universities is the Senate and this is, in every case, a committee of academic persons dominated by professorial heads of departments. There is, in this sense, a well-established tradition of academic self-government and, formalities and legalities notwithstanding, a trend, which set in early after the Victorian universities were founded, towards reducing local lay influence. Thus, the problem of academic freedom is increasingly a problem of the relation between the universities and central government and the problem of academic democracy is increasingly internal to the university organisation itself, which is in turn related to the structure of the university professions. These professions, and therefore the organisation of the universities, have become larger, in a special sense more bureaucratised, and in an unambiguous sense more specialised. In consequence, the power of the professor in the modern British university is crucial to the whole question of academic democracy and we shall return to it in Chapter 14, below.

It is notable that the department as such has no place in the formal constitutions of the British universities. It is an organisational product of specialisation, reinforced by the requirements of research in the sciences and also by the English tradition of single-subject honours degrees. Though in Oxford and Cambridge the collegiate structure has inhibited departmentalism in the arts, the demand for laboratories in the sciences has long since given departmentally based power to professors as heads of science departments which sharply distinguishes their position from that of their colleagues in the humanities. Specialisation and increasing size in the Redbrick universities has led to increased separation of faculties and departments. For example, the social studies were once typically organised as parts of the arts faculties but in most universities have been separated into independent faculties since the war. Each department typically has a professorial head who sits on the Senate. Expansion therefore has had the unintended consequences of producing both a professorial oligarchy and Senates so unwieldy as to give rise on the one hand to smaller circles of power within the Senate and fragmentation of power to 'barons' who run departments. It is not too fanciful to see the modern university as a federation of departments each facing outwards towards the research councils for research funds and towards schools and other universities for students and staff while at the same time living together on a campus with faculty boards and the Senate as mechanisms for negotiation and arbitration of their divergent interests. This type of development resembles much more an American campus than the collegiate federation of the English ideal. As it develops it will put great strain on the tradition of academic control of internal administration if a separate and perhaps dominating administration is not to emerge. Departmentalism also threatens the 'English idea' of gentlemanly 'all round' education as opposed to training for a specialised professional role. The new universities were highly conscious of the separatist and narrowing dangers of powerful and isolated departments when they experimented with new school and faculty structures. The emphasis on residence, the importance attached to high staff/student ratios, the encouragement of undergraduate societies concerned with every conceivable cultural pursuit and the determination in general not to have 'nine-to-five' institutions have been no less noticeable in recent years than they ever were. In part they are a response to the threat posed by departmentalism to the traditional ideals of university education.

Student participation

In this description of academic self-government we have not so far referred to students who have traditionally been excluded from serious participation in university government outside the affairs of the student unions. Students nowadays however appear as an unenfranchised group in the university polity, demanding various degrees of participation. Both old and new universities are now taking steps to meet the students' demands for more power, but student participation in government is still minimal and representation on the powerful university committees is rare.[1] In 1968 out of forty-seven universities or colleges only six had students on Council and the same number admitted students to Senate. A few others had student committees that make recommendations to Council and Senate, but in general students are most often represented on catering, sports, library and accommodation committees or on the university

[1] John Pratt, 'How Much Power', *Higher Education Review*, Spring 1969.

Court. The universities which do have students on their policy-making bodies are a mixed group. Three of the new universities, one ex-CAT and two of the civic universities have students on Council and two new universities, two former CATs and one London college have students on Senate. These arrangements for student participation have developed very recently, mainly over the past three or four years, and it is too early yet to be able to judge the results.

Potentially, of course, the student power movement is deeply threatening to accepted traditions of *academic* self-government. We do not pretend to give it serious consideration in this book,[1] though in recent years it has occupied a sharply increased, if undocumented, proportion of the time and energy of many university teachers especially at the London School of Economics and more spasmodically in other institutions where there have been disturbances.

However, the traditional conception of a university which we have been discussing is one which provides for maximum solidarity between teachers and taught through the absence of a separate administration and an emphasis on close personal relations, achieved by means of tutorial teaching methods, generous staffing and shared domestic life. We have seen that recent expansion has involved some movement towards larger scale, more specialisation, more impersonal instruction. But the traditional norms remain strong and the students' role defined in terms of them promotes a close identification with the college. Moreover 'meritocratic' tendencies in selection for the universities with the highest prestige have also served to merge college identification with adherence to the intellectual purposes of the university and, in this way, to heighten identification with the don. There are, to be sure, counter pressures towards generational solidarity, and academics may be distracted from teaching by other career interests. Nevertheless the organisational changes associated with mass higher education are scarcely in evidence in Britain yet. Staff–student relations remain peaceable by contemporary international standards and the joint 'ten point' programme made in 1968[2] by the Vice-Chancellors' Committee and the N.U.S. is a landmark of co-operative compromise. Whether and how long this position can be maintained is an open question. The student reaction to evidence and rumour about the keeping of political files which began at Warwick

[1] For a short account see A. H. Halsey and S. Marks, 'British Student Politics', *Daedalus*, Winter 1968. A recent and excellent book is E. Ashby and M. Anderson, *The Rise of the Student Estate in Britain*, Macmillan, 1970.

[2] The text is published in *Minerva*, Vol. VII (1967–68), pp. 67–72.

early in 1970 was widespread and, for the first time, appeared to threaten quite directly the traditional fiduciary relations between university teachers and students. There are those who believe that the relation of trust has been destroyed by the rise of the youth culture and the expansion of higher education.[1]

The university administration

Given the increased size of universities, the large amount of money they control and the growing pressure on them to co-ordinate their activities and work in accordance with government plans, it is predictable that there will be a growth in the apparatus of internal university administration. This is indeed the case, though so far administrative staff have not apparently increased proportionately more than academic staff.[2]

The administrative staff of the British universities appears, by contrast with American universities, to be small in number and strongly conditioned to subservience to the academic will. The key administrative figures are chairmen of committees and deans of faculties who are always part-time academics and not bureaucrats. The secretary to such bodies is typically a full-time member of the

[1] For an argued pessimism of this kind see B. Wilson, *The Youth Culture and the Universities*, Faber and Faber, 1970. But for a no less realistic and more sanguine view see Ashby and Anderson (1970), *op. cit*.

[2] According to Mr. Rowland Eustace, who is involved in a study of university government at the University of York, 'The growth of administration has indeed been great (though not faster than that of the universities) so that a whole new profession is emerging, sustaining several national conferences a year. (Over two hundred representatives attended the 1968 conference for junior non-financial administrators.) The academic who not so long ago was used to checking at coffee that the seminar room was free at noon, now finds that he should have applied to a central office ten weeks ago; and he asks himself why all these intelligent graduates, many back from high responsibilities in the Colonies (where would universities be without the collapse of empire?), why did they take up this career if it does not carry the satisfaction of power?' R. B. Eustace, 'The Government of Scholars', in David Martin (ed.), *Anarchy and Culture: the Problem of the Contemporary University*, Routledge and Kegan Paul, 1969, p. 55.

We have no exact figures on the growth of administrative staff in British universities but we would be surprised if close study did not show that these staffs are growing more rapidly than the size of the universities. And certainly we would suspect that this will be a trend in the future and carry with it a developing set of problems of the relation between administrators and academics similar to those already found in the larger American universities. Our view is that academic self-government works more securely under stable or very slowly changing conditions. The faster the rate of change and the more problematic the relations both within and without the university, the more likely is it that the administrative and executive branch of university government will enhance its strength. It is rate of change as much as size that makes administrative staffs so relatively powerful in American universities.

registry staff who characteristically sees the committee rather than the registry as the object of his first loyalty. Whatever these attitudes may imply for efficiency in the management of increasingly large organisations they have so far not represented any serious threat to academic control within the organisation. As Mr. Eustace has put it, 'It is not merely the restricted function of the administrator that is important: attitudes are equally so. Some of the younger recruits to administration are apt to be impatient of the perversities and delays no doubt inseparable from endless consultation and committee government, but they are not encouraged by their elders. Even those senior administrators still wielding real influence through their unique knowledge, believe sincerely and deeply, and to the outsider almost contradictorily, in the supremacy of the academic will. It may surprise how rapidly the ex-colonial officer, though probably a little surprised at what he may have been accustomed to regard as inefficiency, absorbs the academic ethos and accepts the need for collective decision-making. This is not something that shows up from outside; and it is noticeable that as academics move further into the decision-making process, they drop their stereotyped dislike of a stereotyped bureaucrat. They begin to appreciate, with surprise, the bureaucrats' ready acceptance of the role of midwife, not progenitor. Moreover, the university bureaucracy differs from the Civil Service in that it works much closer to its master. Its characteristic job is to service committees on which serve, as it were, Members of Parliament. As a result, the administrator seems frequently to identify with his committee rather than with his profession; and to tend to put the committee's interests first. He may even be instructed by its chairman (an academic) not to consult his administrative superiors.'[1]

Then, however, the question arises of the power of the Vice-Chancellor and his relation to academic self-government. The Vice-Chancellor is both the chief academic and the chief administrative officer of the university and he stands at the centre of a web of communications both within the university and between the university and outside bodies which must inevitably give him the opportunity of exercising crucial influence. At the same time the Vice-Chancellor can be outvoted in the decision-making committees, particularly Senate and Council. In fact his position is that he can do nothing unless he is able to persuade a majority of his senior academic

[1] *Ibid.*, p. 56.

colleagues. Senates can and occasionally do over-ride the wishes of their chief officer.

There can be little doubt that self-administration by the academics is a reality in the British universities. But it has its costs. University administration is commonly criticised now for its amateur quality. It is often suggested that the permanent officers, as well as the Vice-Chancellor himself, are gravely over-worked, and that university constitutions generally fail to provide for any effective delegation of responsibility.[1] Mr. Eustace has argued that administrative initiative increasingly requires knowledge and that recently this has resulted in increased use of development committees of Senates. These committees require more sophisticated information about the operation of the university than has traditionally been available and has called for the appointment of statistical officers and the like to provide such information. This does not mean, however, that the power of the Vice-Chancellor is thereby necessarily increased 'if a Vice-Chancellor's sources of administrative leverage rest heavily on his command of information, then the more sophisticated techniques now being introduced may be beginning to transfer some of this leverage to committees of Senate which have access to the results'.[2]

However, if academic self-government remains assured there is the separate problem of academic democracy. Amateur government is sometimes thought of as the concentration of very heavy administrative duties among a comparatively small number of senior academics. This may or may not be inefficient; it certainly leads to oligarchy within the university professions. One way of reducing the administrative responsibilities of senior academic staff is to allow junior university teachers a greater part in the work of internal government. As Sir Eric Ashby has pointed out, the concentration of power in professorial hands reflects a situation which no longer exists. In the nineteenth century academic self-government was guaranteed by giving control to the professors, who constituted the majority of the permanent academic staff. Today, however, as we show in detail in Chapter 7, the academic professions have elongated and professors make up less than an eighth of the full-time university teachers. The constitutions of the modern universities have not adapted to this change with the result that power is still concentrated

[1] Rose and Ziman, *op. cit.*, p. 215.
[2] R. Eustace, *loc. cit.*, p. 58.

with the professors who form a minority of academic staff.[1] It remains to be seen how far the newer institutions will in practice be more democratic in their internal government.

Attitudes of university teachers

The attitudes of university teachers to the basic ideal of academic self-government is, in one sense at least, easy to describe. There has always been strong support for autonomy combined with an assumption that control implies day-to-day administrative duties. However, these attitudes are part of a wider set involving even more strongly held commitments to academic freedom and, more contentiously, beliefs about the appropriate degree of academic democracy. Academic freedom, of course, is a wide and elusive notion. As regards freedom to follow and express political and social views in opposition to government or convention there has never been any serious question. Nor is there any formal obstacle to a pursuit of research and intellectual interests determined by the individual university teacher for himself. Indeed, it is hard to imagine a more privileged life of freedom than that enjoyed by the average British university teacher from these two points of view. Again, freedom in the sense of institutional autonomy, for all the threats of difficulties which loom in the future for a system so heavily dependent on state funds, has hitherto been as respected in lay and parliamentary opinion as it has been assumed by the academics themselves. The widespread suspicion of government which is part and parcel of American tradition is almost totally absent in Britain and both attitudes may be said to have good reason.

However, academic freedom in the sense of democratic participation is inevitably a problem for any organisation which attains a certain size, and similarly for any organisation which has a hierarchy of rank, authority and security. The informal democracy of a small academic community, and the small scale of British academic institutions in the past must be remembered here, inevitably comes under pressure with increasing size. We may therefore appropriately glance at our survey results in order to examine university teachers' views about the size of their institutions in 1964. Nearly half of all

[1] Eric Ashby and Mary Anderson, 'Autonomy and Academic Freedom in Britain and in English-speaking Countries of Tropical Africa', *Minerva*, Spring 1966.

university teachers at that time and, significantly, three-quarters of those at Oxford and Cambridge, were satisfied with the size of their universities.[1] Dissatisfaction was most apparent in London, Wales and the minor Redbricks; in London, because the university was too big, and in the others because it was too small. One inference is that the college structure in London has apparently not mitigated the disadvantages of large size (at least in the eyes of the academic members) as it has in Oxford and Cambridge. The distribution of opinion about size shows the correlation between satisfaction with the milieu and smallness of scale.

A more direct approach to views about administration was made in our questions on handicaps experienced by university teachers in carrying on research.[2] We included a category of 'other commitments' among the responses and we knew from our interviews that these were chiefly academic administration. These other commitments were mentioned by 50 per cent of the respondents as being a handicap to research but it is notable that academics in Oxford and Cambridge, where government is relatively democratic, felt no more hampered from this point of view than teachers in other universities. There were however considerable differences in the experiences of men of different ranks. As many as 82 per cent of the professors compared with 50 per cent of all university teachers mentioned this handicap.

Attitudes towards academic democracy irrespective of rank were covered in our survey by questions on professorial power and are discussed in detail in Chapter 14 below.

Over a third of all university teachers fully agreed with the suggestion that 'a serious disadvantage of Redbrick universities is that all too often they are run by a professorial oligarchy'.

[1] The question was: 'Do you think your present university as it is now organised is too big/about right/too small?'

[2] The question was: 'What are the major handicaps you experience in carrying on research?

Teaching commitments
Other commitments
Insufficient finance
Slowness in getting equipment
Insufficient contact with other workers
Deficient libraries
Unresponsive university administration
Unresponsive department or college.'

The views of the A.U.T.

Finally we may look at the views expressed by the university teachers through their union–the A.U.T.[1] The general policy of the A.U.T. directly expresses support for democratic self-government. The union believes that academic policy in universities should be controlled by academic staff. All members should take part in deciding policy at some level and should be eligible to serve on statutory bodies and their sub-committees. The A.U.T. also believes that the burden of administrative work should never be so heavy for any individual as to interfere with his primary academic activities. The burden should be lightened by being shared as widely as possible.

The A.U.T. is especially concerned with the increasing size of Senates given the present formal constitutions. They see the consequences as, first, that more power passes into the hands of administrative staff, and, second, that Senates become less efficient because of having less time for discussing serious and urgent issues. And they point to the further consequence which we have already mentioned, i.e. the development of an inner executive body within the Senate in which power is concentrated in a professorial oligarchy. The A.U.T. therefore argues that professors should not automatically be made members of Senate, and also that the size of Senate should be limited by abandoning departmental representation in favour of *ex officio* seats for the main faculty officers and other members who should be elected by Boards of Faculties and the whole academic staff. In this way Senates might be reduced to about forty members. It should be noted in this connection that some of the new universities (Sussex, Lancaster and Kent) have kept automatic professorial membership of Senate, while East Anglia and Essex have abandoned it. In the constitutions of the ex-CATs professors are not *ex officio* members of their Senates. In general the constitutions of the new technological universities provide for a quarter to a third non-professorial membership.

The A.U.T. also believes that Councils should be reduced in size to a total membership of twenty or thirty. A majority of these members should be laymen, but nearly half should be academics including non-professorial representatives. They endorse the custom that Senate should have full control of academic affairs and that the

[1] See the policy statement by the A.U.T., 'University Government and Organisation', published in January 1965.

powers of Council should be limited to either accepting or referring back recommendations from the Senate.

But the main concern of the A.U.T. is with departmental government. As departments grow in size they tend to become isolated from wider academic affairs and so the A.U.T. sees a need to develop within departments machinery for discussing general academic issues as well as matters concerning the work and management of the department. The growth in size of universities is such that details of courses cannot be discussed in Senate or even in the faculty boards and therefore must be left to departmental scrutiny. One A.U.T. voice[1] has queried whether the free expression of opinion on academic matters is encouraged within departments. W. B. Palmer points to the very hierarchical structure of departments and the fact that professors control equipment, money and research students. The degree of communication and debate within departments is extremely variable and efforts by professors to promote genuine discussion may easily fail because of the departmental structure. 'It takes a very exceptional man as head of department to lead but not to dominate to the exclusion of healthy discussion.'[2] Growth in size means there is need for more formality in conducting departmental business. The A.U.T. view is therefore that provision for departmental government should be made in university constitutions. All members of the academic staff of a department should be members of a departmental board. This would make it possible for departmental policy to exist rather than a policy which simply expressed the professor's views.

Conclusion

Academic self-government is strongly entrenched in the British universities, constitutionally in Oxford and Cambridge and by custom elsewhere. The constitutions of the Victorian foundations, which resemble those of the Scottish universities, are formally vulnerable to lay control through Councils and Courts, and the same is true to a lesser extent in London and the new universities: but *de facto* self-government was quickly established in the Redbrick universities and the subsequent trend has been towards formalisation of established practice. Lay members are valued for their expertise but not feared for their voting power.

[1] W. B. Palmer, 'University Government and Organisation', *British Universities Annual*, 1966. [2] *Ibid.*

Academic self-government, however, is not academic democracy. The nearest approach to democracy is to be found in Oxford and Cambridge but even there the representation of the professoriate is safeguarded by a double election system (Oxford) or *ex officio* membership of faculty boards (Cambridge). The colleges are primitive democracies: the principle that 'a fellow is a fellow is a fellow' is infrequently broken so that all fellows are voting members of their college governing bodies: and the colleges in effect rule the university. In the Redbrick universities, Scotland and Wales, by contrast, self-government means professorial oligarchy and the democratic ideal has made only modest and recent advances. Nor is the situation drastically different in the new universities.

Moreover, the democracy to which we refer is a democracy of academics, not of all teachers and learners. Student enfranchisement was never considered before the mid-1960's; concessions to it are recent and severely limited.

The potential threat to self-government *internally* is not, so far, from the university administration. Vice-Chancellors can vote but can be outvoted, other senior administrators are either academics with part-time duties as committee chairmen or full-time non-academic, non-voting servants of the committee apparatus. The traditions of collective self-rule through committee, defined in this way, amateur and conservative as they may be, are virtually unquestioned. The strains of large-scale organisation have not, or at least not yet, disturbed them. With the qualifications which we have made in considering the details of constitutions and conventions it can be said that the universities have changed and developed so far in faithful conformity to the ideal of academic self-government.

Chapter 6

TRADITION REVIEWED: A CASE STUDY OF OXFORD

This chapter ends Part II of the book by looking at the proposals of the Commission of Inquiry under Lord Franks[1] which reported in 1966 with recommendations which aimed to adapt the organisation of Oxford to modern conditions while still maintaining the essentials of what we have described as the English idea of a university. Oxford had not been thoroughly investigated since the 1870's.[2] Since that time there had been the gradual development of the universities in provincial industrial cities, the growth of London University and (more recently) the new English universities and the incorporation of the colleges of advanced technology. Universities, not excluding Oxford, had grown in size, had incorporated science into their curricula, had begun to increase their graduate students and to acquire larger, more specialised and more elaborately organised teaching and research staffs. The growth of state interest in the universities in the twentieth century and the emergence of government as overwhelmingly the most important source of funds had slowly produced a structure of universities and colleges which Robbins explicitly recognised as a national system of higher education. Oxford had to have a defined place within this system. The problem therefore was to state the essential nature of Oxford in twentieth or even twenty-first century terms.

From our point of view the proposals put forward by Lord Franks and his colleagues illustrate a coherent approach to each of the eight major elements in the traditional ideal which we have discussed in this part of the book. But they also raise issues about the character of the British system of higher education – the place of the universities

[1] For a brief comparative review outlining parallel developments in Cambridge see Lord Annan, 'The Franks Report from the Nearside', *Universities Quarterly*, September 1966.

[2] The Royal Commission of 1922 did not undertake a comprehensive enquiry.

within it, the viability of traditional conceptions and the position of Oxford and Cambridge *vis-à-vis* the other university groups in England, Scotland and Wales.

The Franks Committee followed a firm line. Oxford was an ancient, and still perhaps *the* collegiate university. It drew its students nationally and internationally, selected them carefully and from the type of school and social background which had hitherto maintained the established life and character of the university; it offered them education and not merely training through entry into a small-scale residential community affording close contact of teachers with taught, a shared domestic life, and a high staff/student ratio for individualised teaching.[1] The university remained financially rich, autonomous and governed by a democracy of its own academic members. In short, Oxford met the eight major criteria which we distinguished in Chapter 3 as the hallmarks of an ideal university.

Nevertheless, modern conditions meant that the criteria had to be re-interpreted. New academic subjects and new methods of scientific research had called for new buildings, new equipment and new organisations. New professions, new vocationalisms, and even the academic succession itself, had led to the development of graduate studies and hence to the appearance of the unfamiliar graduate student. New conceptions of social justice and new demands for educational opportunity had resulted in both expansion and competition for entry from new types of school and increasingly from children with working-class backgrounds. The riches of the colleges (though not all colleges were rich) had been increasingly augmented by state funds channelled through the university. The consequent involvement of Oxford with Government departments, the U.G.C. and the Committee of Vice-Chancellors and Principals had put great pressure on the traditional forms of administration. The inherently centrifugal tendencies of modern teaching and research, which had elsewhere produced the 'multiversity', were beginning to threaten the capacities of colleges to maintain their high teaching standards and their attractive careers for the college tutor. But the most difficult and delicate of all the issues was to reconcile the claims of Oxford (and Cambridge) to international standing with the claims of

[1] But the Commission pointed out that the staff/student ratio compared unfavourably with other British universities. In 1964/5 it was 1:12·3 while for all the universities in Great Britain except for Oxford, Cambridge and the six newest, it was 1:9·9. The Commission therefore argued that a 20 per cent increase in staff was needed to bring Oxford into line with other universities.

other universities for equable treatment within the national system of higher education.

The Committee therefore set out to produce a plan in which new developments would be made to fit into or revolve around a modernised and federated college system. They recognised all the modern threats to the viability of collegiate organisation and attempted to produce solutions making Oxford safe for commensality. The graduate student was to be incorporated and to be tutored by dons in his college, the university was to complement the federated colleges, there was to be redistribution of income from the richer to the poorer colleges and at the same time the university would streamline its administration and government and explain itself more quickly and more clearly to the U.G.C. and the outer world by better statistical services. Oxford would justify itself to an egalitarian age by a reformed procedure for admissions, the abolition of closed scholarships, the encouragement of more women students, and the rationalisation of dons' incomes.[1] These measures were aimed to ensure the continuing reality of the collegiate ideal in which teaching is linked harmoniously to research and administration gives unobtrusive direction to both.

At the same time the claim to international standing was plainly asserted. 'Oxford is an international university with a higher than average concentration of talent, and . . . it is reasonable that this should be reflected in a higher than average salary, age for age, than is to be found in British universities taken as a whole.' It was accordingly recommended that Oxford salaries should be fixed at 10 per cent above the national average. The Commissioners did not accept the idea, put forward by Peter Laslett and others, of making Oxford and Cambridge international graduate universities.[2] On the other hand, they were not prepared to abandon the position of great prestige already attained in making necessary adjustments to the emerging post-Robbins system of universities.

The collegiate conception

The Commissioners envisaged Oxford as a medium-size university growing in the 1970's and 1980's to accommodate 13,000 students,

[1] See Chapter 9, pp. 195–8.

[2] See Peter Laslett, 'The University in High Industrial Society', in Bernard Crick (ed.), *op. cit.*

including 3,500 to 4,000 graduates.[1] In the course of expansion greater emphasis was to be placed on the applied sciences–engineering, clinical medicine and social studies. More generally the natural and social sciences were to be encouraged with 'compensating contractions', presumably in the arts.

The question was therefore raised as to how increased numbers were to be fitted into the colleges. For their part, the Commissioners did not baulk at the prospect of creating one or two new colleges, recognising that 'in the collegiate university those who are not fully brought into college life inevitably suffer'. It is, however, debatable how far graduate students can and should be integrated into a fully collegiate organisation. Many would argue that the teaching and research of graduates, who must be specialised and may be married, is best organised through departments. The doubters, who presented evidence to the Commissioners in open hearings, included the students themselves as represented by the Student Council,[2] the economists as represented by their sub-faculty,[3] and some scientists who would similarly transfer teaching responsibilities from college to university in the case of undergraduates.

The nub of this problem is to ensure a proper distribution of students and staff between colleges. The difficulties here are most acute in the case of graduates, but they also affect the undergraduates in so far as the need to concentrate specialist dons for specialist graduates is combined with the aim of involving all dons in both undergraduate and graduate teaching so as to avoid the American experience of steady devaluation of the former as the latter expands. To incorporate the graduate fully into the intellectual and the social life of the colleges was a novel, large and complicated task. The Commissioners did not exaggerate when they said that 'if postgraduate training is to be brought into the system of college education and made part of the balance of life of the fellow-lecturer, the consequence will be a fundamental change in the nature of Oxford, and the magnitude of this change should not be underestimated'.[4]

The advantage of the traditional undergraduate college is that it brings together a comprehensive range of scholarship among the dons

[1] The total number of matriculated students in the Michaelmas term of 1964 was 9,313 of whom 2,018 were graduates. By the beginning of 1970 the number of students had risen to 10,500 and a figure of 11,500 in 1977 was mentioned in the Vice-Chancellor's letter (26 January 1970) replying to a letter from the Chairman of the U.G.C. on the question of university development in the seventies.

[2] *Franks Report, Evidence,* Vol. III, p. 77.

[3] *Ibid.*, p. 70.

[4] *Ibid.*, para. 256.

who then pass on a wide cultivation to their students through the close personal contacts of college residence and the tutorial system. Intimacy plus breadth necessitate small numbers of dons in any particular subject. But as the boundaries of knowledge widen, conversation at lengthening high tables narrows. Nevertheless, for the undergraduate, or at least for the arts undergraduate, the educational advantages remain immense.

However, the traditional college had hitherto made no serious attempt to teach graduates and, with a few recent exceptions, very inadequate efforts to offer them social amenities. If college teaching was now to be offered to graduates at least one of the arguments for the traditional college had to be abandoned. One logical solution was to forsake breadth of studies and specialise. Nuffield College is a highly successful venture along these lines. The concentration on the social sciences gives it unity; there is genuine academic discussion among colleagues and comprehensive teaching for students which is clearly related to the research interests of the dons. On the other hand, this same college has preserved intimacy at the expense of excluding all the undergraduates and the majority of graduate students in Oxford who are working in the fields of special interest to the college. Except in very small schools, the 'college-department' would tend to be either too big or to fail to meet the requirement that a college is a microcosm of a wide range of studies.

There seems to be no obvious way out of this dilemma which is intrinsic to the modern university as graduate students and research proliferate. All solutions are imperfect be they on the model of Berkeley or of Claremont. Given Oxford's collegiate history, the proposals of the Franks Commission cannot cause surprise, though equally they may not convince the critics that the graduate can be wholly incorporated into the college system. Implicitly the Commission acknowledged this. They not only left graduate admissions in the hands of the university but they also proposed to leave the general organisation of studies to the faculties and recommended the setting up of faculty centres to fulfil the same functions for graduate studies in arts as do the science departments for science subjects. They regarded 'the establishment of these centres as essential'. Most graduates, however, would continue to belong to the traditional undergraduate colleges. The Commission recommended that no college be allowed to admit a graduate unless someone could look after him academically. Specialisation was recommended but its extent must be limited by both the practical size of a college and by the requirements of undergraduate teaching. There will therefore be awkward problems of duplication in the larger subjects and co-operation between colleges in the smaller and more specialised fields. The colleges of Oxford, if they follow the lead of the Commission, are in for a long period of adaptation and expansion which would call for much energy and more artfulness.

The implications were just as fundamental for the academic staff as for the students. As we shall try to show in the next chapter, the central core of Victorian Oxford was a group of working tutorial fellows to which the growth of the university added professors, readers and lecturers. The modernised collegiate conception would produce further convergence of the older structure of academic staff to the hierarchy of ranks which characterises the Scottish and the English Redbrick universities. Until recently the Oxford academic staff were divided between the colleges and the university with most wearing two hats, either as university men with college fellowships or as college men with part-time university posts.[1] Under the new proposals two hats were to become standard issue.

A special place in the system

One longstanding criticism of Oxford and Cambridge has been that their selectivity has a class bias: undergraduate places have been given disproportionately to public school boys and too little to the able sixth-formers of grammar and, more recently, comprehensive schools. The result, as recently as 1956, was that while 26 per cent of all British undergraduates had working class origins, in Oxford there were only 12 per cent. The wider problems of establishing equality of educational opportunity and recognising talented individuals begin, of course, before children enter primary schools. They could not have been solved unaided by any reform of university admissions. The realistic question was how to reform admissions so as to encourage and accommodate the most able potential applicants from the existing secondary schools. To this end the Commission proposed the abolition of closed scholarships, the restriction of open scholarships to 10 per cent in any particular college and the limitation of

[1] I.e. statutory obligations to lecture in the university (typically sixteen lectures a year) as C.U.F. lecturers paid from a common university fund supplied by the U.G.C.

prizes to £50 per annum, awarded for only one year either at entry or during residence, and only to be renewed on evidence of satisfactory work.[1] The Commissioners also urged Oxford to take the lead in working out a new national scheme for admissions and then to end its own special entrance examinations with, or if necessary without, the co-operation of Cambridge. They also proposed a single entrance examination to redress some of the advantages now enjoyed by the major public schools.[2]

The admissions question was, however, relatively unimportant by comparison with the claim to special consideration as a university of international standing which was heard with much misgiving and some hostility by academics in other institutions. One of the more articulate voices was that of C. F. Carter, the Vice-Chancellor of the new University of Lancaster. 'Certainly we must not level the universities down to a dull mediocrity. But, before we can allow Oxford to get away with the argument, there are some awkward questions to be answered–to which the Report gives no attention at all. What is meant by calling Oxford an "international university"? Taking a broad view of her activities, is she contributing more (per head of staff) to civilisation than Manchester, or (dare we say it) Sussex? There are subjects to which Oxford, though apparently having a "higher than average concentration of talent", is contributing little. There are important areas of study which Oxford has neglected. If the state is to be asked to use public money to maintain, say, two

[1] As the Commissioners argued, 'the original eleemosynary purpose of college scholarships and exhibitions was finally removed by the Education Act, 1962, which requires all local education authorities to make grants, graded according to the income of the parents, to all university entrants' (Vol. I, para. 187). They recognised that closed awards were an anomaly and that they had favoured boys wishing to enter from the public schools. They added, however, that there had been no monopoly of this kind. 'Of the closed awards made for entry in 1965–6, only 45 per cent went to boys from independent boarding schools' (Vol. I, para. 189). As to open scholarships, the limitation to £50 per annum was in recognition of their prestige value rather than as a substitute for state grants. The Commission wished to keep them in order to provide academic incentive to the schools and to spread them out over the period of undergraduate residence as further prizes for distinguished work.

[2] The Commissioners saw that, educationally, the relevant distinction was not between public and maintained schools but between schools which could and schools which could not provide a fast stream to a three-year sixth form. They therefore proposed to divide the papers into two parts. Those who had had the advantage of a fast track to seven terms of sixth-form teaching would have to answer their questions from the first part. The others–typically from the small and maintained grammar schools, comprehensive schools and especially girls' schools of all types–would be able, if they wished, to choose from the second part in which the questions would assume no more knowledge than could be reasonably expected after four terms of post-'O'-level work.

privileged centres of excellence, does it follow that the two should be sited at Oxford and Cambridge? May it not be that minds responsive to the true needs of the advancement of knowledge and the training of young people will be found in London, the centre of so much of our culture, or among the independent people of the North?

'The "centres of excellence" argument', Mr. Carter argued, 'itself is suspect. The activities of a university grow, not like a single tree, but like a forest, with some fine and vigorous specimens and others stunted or in decay. It is not reasonable to expect that all will be vigorous at once, and a given sum of money may be better used in encouraging vigour wherever it is found in the university system, rather than in trying to raise the average quality of the single university.'

Mr. Carter's is an ultra-modern voice, speaking in terms not of separate universities but of a national system with the implication that some form of central planning is desirable which would treat faculties, departments or even smaller teaching and research groups as its units. The logic of this view, like that of Peter Laslett and the proponents of the graduate scheme for Oxford and Cambridge mentioned above, is that there has to be one national university, or better one university system, on the grounds that 'in the contemporary and coming world no university or institution of higher education of any other kind can be looked upon as an independent unit. Each and every one of them must be regarded as belonging to a network, a national network for the most part but one which has increasing connections and extensions abroad.'[1]

The response

Just as the proposals put forward by the Franks Commission can best be seen as an adaptation to changing conditions of the traditional English idea of a university, so too can the response. The main forum of discussion has been Congregation, i.e. the assembled resident Masters of Arts, constituting a body of 1,600 each with one vote and the central instrument of academic democracy in Oxford. The report came before Congregation on 31 May 1966 as a resolution to take note of the Commission's findings and as a signal of the beginning of a process of legislating changes in the Statutes of the University. In the following two years Congregation approved all the titles of a

[1] See Peter Laslett, *loc. cit.*, p. 125.

corpus of new statutes arising out of the Report. Congregation, like the Commission, was mindful of the criticism made by the Robbins Committee of 'the difficulty Oxford has in reaching rapid decisions on matters of policy with its present constitutional arrangements, and the general obscurity in which so many of its administrative and financial arrangements are shrouded'. The need for administrative reform was generally accepted. All the powers of Convocation were abolished with the single exception of its power to elect the Chancellor. The Hebdomadal Council became established by statute as the chief administrative body of the University. The central administrative services were unified under the Registrar and additional statistical information and liaison services on a professional basis were established. And, most important, a four-year Vice-Chancellorship was instituted beginning with the tenure of Alan Bullock, the Master of St. Catherine's, in 1969. The Vice-Chancellor henceforth was to be elected by Congregation (on the nomination of a committee consisting of the Chancellor or Vice-Chancellor, and representatives of Council, Congregation, and the colleges) from among the members of Congregation.

These administrative changes had been proposed by the Franks Commission in order to arrive at an optimal combination of democracy with decision. But acceptance was mediated through the characteristically cautious outlook of the main body of Oxford dons which, while responsive to the need for clear relations with the U.G.C. and other outside bodies, was at the same time jealous of ancient and established forms of democratic academic government. In the event, the Commission's plan for modifying the democratic but slow-moving machinery of decision in traditional Oxford was seen as too radical and accordingly defeated at a crucial point. Congregation refused to give Council power to make decrees. Instead it retained the power to annul, amend, or repeal decrees and regulations made by Council and reserved its right to pass resolutions which, if carried with at least seventy-five members voting in favour, would require Council to promote legislation giving effect to them.[1]

The Commission had also proposed a new constitution of faculty

[1] A system was also introduced under which any decision taken on a division at a meeting of Congregation could be submitted, if Council so decides or if at least fifty members of Congregation so require, for rejection or confirmation to a postal vote of all the members of Congregation. This procedure was followed for the first time in 1969 when opposition to the setting up of a new Human Sciences degree was finally overcome through a postal vote.

boards grouping the existing sixteen faculties into five 'super faculties' with up to eight sub-faculties under each faculty board. Professor Beloff argued before Congregation that the super faculties would find it impossible to draft a sensible agenda. Lord Franks argued in reply that 'seventeen bodies reporting to the General Board . . . is an administrative nonsense, as much of a nonsense as thirty-one colleges being in correspondence with the Hebdomadal Council'. Congregation approved the Commission's recommendation by a margin of only two votes but both the Hebdomadal Council and the General Board were opposed 'mainly because it seemed to them that the new faculty boards would have no clear function to perform and that the new sub-faculty boards (up to forty in number) would fragment academic administration too greatly'.[1] In consequence these bodies advised rejection of the new statute and Congregation approved by 179 votes to 115.[2]

In presenting the Report of the Commission to Congregation Lord Franks had been explicit about two principles which had guided him and his colleagues concerning the internal government and colleagiate character of Oxford. 'Of course, Oxford, like all other universities, is preoccupied with teaching and research, but here we carry out these activities in our own characteristic style, and we thought that in this characteristic style there were perhaps two things which stood out, and which, taken together, make Oxford nearly unique. They are our democratic form of government, whereby academics govern themselves, and the college system. Both are old. The first, I suppose, goes back to the very origins of Oxford itself, and the second is many centuries old.'[3] For these reasons the Commission had envisaged a medium-sized university for the future and its proposals as to size and shape were approved. Lord Franks

[1] Annual Report, 1966–7, *University Gazette*, 5 October 1967, pp. 51–2.

[2] This involved amending the Commission's proposed composition for the General Board. The new composition agreed by Congregation was that the Board should consist of the Vice-Chancellor, the Proctors, the Assessor, a representative of Council, six members elected by Congregation from the members of the faculties of Theology, Law, Literae Humaniores, Modern History, English Language and Literature, Medieval and Modern Languages, Oriental Studies, Social Studies and Music; six members elected by Congregation from the members of the faculties of Medicine, Physical Sciences, Biological Sciences, Anthropology and Geography, Agriculture and Forestry, Psychological Studies and Mathematics; and up to two co-opted members. This was carried by 124 votes to 67. A further amendment that the members to be elected from the two groups of faculties should each be eight instead of six was carried *nem. con.*

[3] *Oxford University Gazette*, 20 July 1966, p. 1486.

and his colleagues had also noticed that the expansion of Harvard and other leading American universities had involved the creation of large graduate schools and research centres, more or less separated from undergraduate schools. But in rejecting this strategy of expansion they correctly anticipated college opinion in Oxford. 'Our reasons,' Lord Franks told Congregation, 'were that we thought, first, that if they came into being in Oxford, undergraduate education would almost certainly be devalued. Secondly, it leads to a division in the academic staff between those who do research and teach graduates, and those who teach undergraduates. We believe that this would be a bad thing in that society of equals to which Oxford aspires.' It was feared that the development of post-graduate schools would drive the colleges into a secondary place in Oxford 'but since it was our purpose to preserve the life, the enterprise, the initiative, and the responsibility of the colleges, we therefore turned away from separate great graduate schools'.

Even so the Commission was less cautious than Congregation. Defence of college autonomy is probably the most strongly held interest in Oxford. Under the Commission's recommendations a Council of Colleges would have been set up, under a statute of the University, having power to bind colleges by the votes of a majority of its members. This would have been a major constitutional change in the relationship between the University and the colleges, moving the balance of power towards the centre. Congregation would not have it and substituted a Conference of Colleges with no formal powers but providing a forum for the exchange of information and opinions. However, the Commission's scheme for internal taxation aimed at redistributing income between the richer and the poorer colleges was accepted along with a series of proposals for rationalising the keeping of college accounts.

The scheme for fellow-lecturers, which is essential to the full participation of colleges in expanded graduate work, involved the proposal that all appointments should be advertised and then made jointly by the University and a college. This again is in effect to propose greater university control over the internal affairs of colleges. It is not yet instituted but is about to be considered (1970). Similarly faculty centres for the arts and social studies, which were seen by the Commission as essential to the development of collegiate participation in graduate teaching and research, are now under active consideration.

Conclusion

The outcome of both the Franks proposals for a modernised collegiate Oxford and the continuing discussion of the position of Oxford or any other university as one with special claims to extra resources in order to maintain an international standing thus show themselves to be tests of the adaptability of the English idea of a university. The changes we have discussed in this chapter at Oxford will result in a closer approximation of university organisation to the patterns of the British universities in general. The reformed administration will be more like that of the new universities. The further development of applied sciences will involve more extensive departmental organisation and the proposed faculty centres in social studies and the arts may shift the academic centre of gravity somewhat further away from the colleges, particularly those which are least successful in some kind of specialisation or focus of studies at the graduate level.

In the case of Oxford and in our general discussion of the evolution of the British universities we have repeatedly stressed the pervasive influence of an ideology of education which goes back to the pre-industrial period when Oxford and Cambridge were patronised largely by the aristocracy and the gentry. The influence of this idea of a university, with its strong orientation towards the social role and culture of the gentleman, may be traced throughout the modern history of Britain and is reflected to a greater or lesser degree in our description of the present universities as social systems. It has expressed itself in strong support to the humanities and resistance to the displacement of fundamental by applied disciplines. It has manifestations in the history of the machinery for relating the universities to the state through the University Grants Committee as a mediator or buffer. It is reflected in the desired pattern of internal organisation of teaching and residence and even in the siting of the post-war foundations. Above all the English idea of a university has contained the pressure for a high rate of expansion, restricting numbers to a minority of highly selected entrants. As we shall see in Chapter 11, the Robbins Committee's modest proposals for further expansion were supported with some apprehension by the main body of university teachers. Expansion has taken place and will continue, but it emerges in the form of a developing hierarchy of institutions with somewhat specialised functions for the changing culture of scientific industrialism and the changing occupational structure of its élite positions. Oxford and Cambridge have become numerically less and less important but they retain a leading position in the academic hierarchy as the nearest approximation to a deeply entrenched ideal.

PART III

THE ACADEMIC CAREER

We have now reached the point at which we can concentrate directly on the university teacher. In Part I we traced the main changes in the relationship of higher education to society in the Western industrial countries and sketched the evolution of the British universities in these terms from the middle of the nineteenth century. The British experience, in our view, has resulted in the development of a distinctive *institutional* setting–the outcome of a complex adaptation of ideas and ideals to a changing set of social pressures and organisational requirements.

The role of the university teacher has been redefined at every stage of institutional evolution. In the following chapters, making up Part III, we describe the developing characteristics of the university professions, the growing division of academic labour associated with the expansion and elaboration of academic work and the changing conditions under which academics pursue their careers. In this way we trace the evolution of the academic professions in relation to institutional and social change.

We shall then, in Part IV, be in a position to analyse the ambitions, opinions and self-conceptions of university teachers of the present.

Chapter 7

THE EVOLUTION OF THE UNIVERSITY TEACHING PROFESSIONS

There were 31,476 full-time academic members[1] of the staff of British universities in 1968–69. In Part II of this book we have described the social and institutional context in which they work. The task now is to describe the professional life of this large, growing and heterogeneous group.

The academic professions, like the institutions in which they serve, have evolved in response to the changing structure of society. We see them broadly as having developed from the pre-industrial traditions of Oxford and Cambridge, where they constituted a tiny group oriented to the customs and demands of the clerical and aristocratic classes to which, at least by the seventeenth century, they largely owed their existence. In Chapter 2 we sketched an outline of Oxford in the first part of the nineteenth century and referred to Rothblatt's description of gentlemanly donnishness in Cambridge. As Professor Perkin has put it:

> Before the reforms of the early nineteenth century, in fact, it is doubtful whether there was a university teaching profession in any meaningful sense, at least in England. At Oxford and Cambridge the dons – strictly, the fellows of the colleges – were not, except occasionally and by accident, permanent members of a profession with a recognisable function and an articulated career structure. They were privileged but for the most part temporary members of a corporate, self-perpetuating, property-owning society, enjoying their 'dividends' in return for the moral rather than the intellectual supervision of a small number of mostly wealthy young men only slightly younger than themselves. . . . In short, university dons were leisured gentlemen by appointment rather than inheritance, and, saving the rule of celibacy, were as free to do what they pleased with their time and resources, to teach or not to teach, to work or

[1] Including all teaching and research staff irrespective of the source of finance.

not to work, as were the rest of the leisured, but not necessarily idle class.[1]

The academic career began to change in the second half of the nineteenth century with the development of professionalism, specialisation and expansion. Adaptation to these processes, while transforming the role of the university teacher, has been influenced at every step by the traditional conception of a gentlemanly guild which was cradled in the English foundations and which is congruent with the English idea of a university which we have used to describe the evolution of the institutional setting of university teaching and research in the preceding chapters.

The nineteenth-century developments were of small numerical importance. At the end of the century there were about eight hundred Oxford and Cambridge dons, five hundred teachers in the provincial Redbrick universities, a similar number in Scotland and less than two hundred and fifty in London. Nevertheless, the pattern of adaptation of the traditional conceptions may already be seen in the qualitative changes which took place after 1850. Perkin has neatly identified them as the creation of two distinct ideals which still struggle for ascendancy. He points, on the one hand, to the notion of the professor primarily concerned with lecturing and research who was particularly in evidence in London and the civic universities and, on the other hand, to the idea of the college tutor concerned also with the pastoral care of his undergraduates who was particularly strong in Oxford and Cambridge. The first characterisation of university teaching emphasises expert knowledge and implies hierarchical organisation; the second stresses service to students and equality of status if not expertise among colleagues. Both forms were to be found, Perkin continues, in both kinds of university and in particular the claims of assistants in the provincial universities to better pay and a share in university government expressed aspirations to a degree of equality with the professors. The two traditions were not entirely incompatible, he points out, in that both professors and non-professors and, later, Oxford and Cambridge as well as the civic universities were represented in the professional association. But nevertheless the greatest support for the Association of University Teachers has come from the non-collegiate universities where, Perkin suggests, professors

[1] H. J. Perkin, *Key Profession*, pp. 3 and 7. Chapter 1 of this book is an illuminating summary of the history of the university teaching profession in Britain. We shall trace the changing class position of university teachers in the twentieth century in Chapter 9 and their changing status position in Chapter 10.

support its professionalism and other staff its egalitarianism. By contrast, the principle of equality which is observed at the collegiate universities makes the professional association less relevant and support for the A.U.T. is consequently weak.[1]

But, though the struggle for ascendancy began in the nineteenth century, the major battles have been joined in the twentieth. We have therefore concentrated on the development of the university teaching professions over the past seventy years. In the remainder of this chapter we give a numerical outline of the distribution of university teachers between different types of university, different grades or academic ranks, and different faculties or subjects. In this way we are able to demonstrate the shift away from the traditional conception, the elongation of the professions and their increasing specialisation.

As may be seen from Graph 7.A. the number of university teachers in Britain has grown from rather under 2,000 at the beginning of the

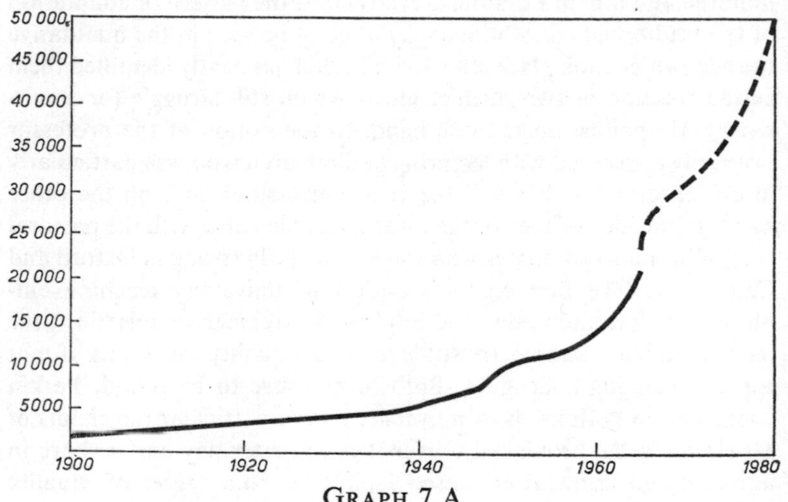

GRAPH 7.A

Number of university teachers in Great Britain, 1900–80

Note: The figures from 1938–9 and 1962–3 are taken from the Robbins Report, Appendix 3, Table 1, p. 4. Those for 1965–6 and 1966–7 are from the U.G.C. Returns and include all staff in all universities irrespective of their sources of financial support. The figures for 1971–2 and for 1980 are estimates which assume that the present official target for the former year of 225,000 student places in universities will be met and that a new estimate of 400,000 for 1980 will also be met and that both will be subject to present staff/student ratios. The break in the curve between 1965 and 1966 results from a change in the official statistical figures for the later dates include all university staff whether or not they are paid from university funds.

[1] *Ibid.*, pp. 14–15. We discuss the A.U.T. in Chapter 9 below.

century to over 30,000 at the present day.[1] The growth has been continuous but it accelerated sharply in the 1960's following acceptance of the Robbins Report. The latest estimate (1970) for university student numbers in 1980 is over 400,000 which, given a continuation of the present staff/student ratios, means that there will be 50,000 university teachers in this country at the end of the seventies.[2] The figures for December 1968 showing the number of staff in each university institution according to academic rank and source of financial support are reproduced in Table 7.1. We have further divided the universities into eight groups, each group different according to its character, age and location. These groups are derived from our analysis of the pattern of development of the universities and have significance for the life and career of the university teachers in them.

In 1968 the largest group, employing more than a quarter of all university teachers, was made up of the major Redbrick universities in the larger provincial industrial cities.[3] The second largest group, with a fifth of the university teachers, was formed by the constituent colleges of the University of London.[4] Third in order, and accounting for 15·5 per cent of all university teachers, were the seven Scottish institutions.[5] Fourth came the minor Redbrick universities[6] which

[1] The statistics, however, are unusually imperfect because of changes in administrative habits during the course of the century and especially because of the vagaries of Oxford and Cambridge records. The main source from 1919 is the U.G.C. in its Annual and Quinquennial Returns. Only for 1965–6 (Cmnd. 3586) is it possible, for the first time, to discover an exact count of the number of university teachers irrespective of the source of funds for their employment. The effect in Graph 7.A is to produce a jump in the numbers at this point through the inclusion for the first time of staff paid from other than general university funds. They numbered 3,429 out of the total of 25,294 in 1965–6.

[2] The estimate of student numbers has since been revised to 460,000 in 1981, so that the number of university teachers may well exceed 50,000, at any rate by the beginning of the nineteen eighties. See note 3, p. 55 above.

[3] These were Birmingham, Bristol, Durham, Leeds, Liverpool, Manchester (including the School of Business Studies and the Institute of Technology), Newcastle and Sheffield, most of which received their charters within a few years of the turn of the nineteenth and twentieth centuries.

[4] London received its charter in 1836, mainly on the basis of the recently-formed University and King's colleges; in 1968 it was composed of thirty-one self-governing schools and fourteen institutes directly controlled by the university. We also include the Graduate School of Business Studies.

[5] Aberdeen, Edinburgh, Glasgow, Heriot-Watt, St. Andrews, Strathclyde and Stirling. St. Andrews, founded in 1410, was the oldest of these, with an additional college at Dundee founded in 1881. Aberdeen, Edinburgh, and Glasgow were fifteenth- and sixteenth-century foundations. The Royal College of Science and Technology at Glasgow goes back to 1796 but received a charter as the University of Strathclyde in 1964. Stirling was new, admitting its first (107) students in 1967.

[6] Exeter, Hull, Leicester, Nottingham, Reading and Southampton. With the exception of Reading all were at one time provincial colleges preparing students for the examinations of the University of London. They received their charters between 1948 and 1957. Reading was founded in 1926.

T

Full-time teaching and re
partly financed a

At 31 December 1968

		Professors			Readers and lecture.	
		Wholly fin-anced	*Partly fin-anced*	*Not fin-anced*	*Wholly fin-anced*	*Partl, fin-ance*
1	Aston	30	—	1	71	—
2	Bath	19	—	—	50	—
3	Birmingham	117	—	1	196	9
4	Bradford	29	—	—	63	—
5	Bristol	75	1	4	123	6
6	Brunel	13	—	2	33	—
7	Cambridge	120	4	2	85	1
8	City	18	—	—	60	—
9	Durham	41	2	—	54	1
10	East Anglia	29	—	—	29	—
11	Essex	23	—	2	22	—
12	Exeter	36	1	1	54	1
13	Hull	35	—	—	78	—
14	Keele	21	—	—	33	—
15	Kent	27	—	—	30	—
16	Lancaster	25	1	—	29	3
17	Leeds	101	3	1	205	8
18	Leicester	42	—	1	53	—
19	Liverpool	87	—	—	183	—
20	London Graduate School of Business Studies	6	—	—	8	—
21	London University	743	10	29	1,255	17
22	Loughborough	20	—	—	45	—
23	Manchester School of Business Studies	4	—	—	9	—
24	Manchester University	124	1	1	189	8
25	Manchester Institute of Science and Technology	28	—	1	70	—
26	Newcastle	85	4	—	138	8
27	Nottingham	58	1	2	95	1
28	Oxford	114	—	3	77	—
29	Reading	52	1	15	72	—
30	Salford	21	—	—	67	—
31	Sheffield	84	—	—	142	—
32	Southampton	53	1	1	75	—
33	Surrey	20	2	—	53	1
34	Sussex	48	1	5	57	3
35	Warwick	19	4	—	30	1
36	York	22	—	1	34	—
37	**Total England**	**2,389**	**37**	**73**	**3,867**	**68**
38	Aberystwyth University College	28	1	1	53	6
39	Bangor University College	33	—	1	52	—
40	Cardiff University College	40	—	—	71	—
41	St. David's, Lampeter	6	—	—	3	—
42	Swansea University College	34	1	—	58	3
43	Welsh National School of Medicine	13	—	—	35	—
44	University of Wales Institute of Science and Technology	14	—	—	31	—
45	**Total Wales**	**168**	**2**	**2**	**303**	**9**
46	**Total England and Wales**	**2,557**	**39**	**75**	**4,170**	**77**
47	Aberdeen	52	2	—	95	—
48	Dundee	36	—	—	78	—
49	Edinburgh	118	5	3	240	2
50	Glasgow	114	—	—	226	4
51	Heriot-Watt	16	—	—	32	—
52	St. Andrews	32	—	—	57	—
53	Stirling	14	—	—	10	—
54	Strathclyde	45	1	1	151	—
55	**Total Scotland**	**427**	**8**	**4**	**889**	**6**
56	**Total Great Britain**	**2,984**	**47**	**79**	**5,059**	**83**

Source: Information supplied by the U.G.C.

in posts wholly financed,
ıced from university income

At 31 December 1968

cturers		Assistant lecturers			Others			Total				
Partly fin-anced	Not fin-adced	Wholly fin-anced	Partly fin-anced	Not fin-anced	Wholly fin-anced	Partly fin-anced	Not fin-anced	Wholly fin-anced	Partly fin-anced	Not fin-anced	Total	
—	15	12	—	9	—	—	—	358	—	25	383	1
—	5	5	—	4	—	—	—	243	—	9	252	2
20	99	64	1	33	39	2	84	942	32	226	1,200	3
—	3	19	—	—	—	—	—	374	—	3	377	4
12	74	85	1	27	10	—	—	676	20	125	821	5
—	8	12	—	7	—	—	—	183	—	18	201	6
60	38	180	14	9	—	—	—	1,025	79	49	1,153	7
—	—	24	—	—	—	—	—	295	—	—	295	8
6	6	32	—	8	9	—	43	337	9	57	403	9
—	7	48	—	20	7	—	5	220	—	33	253	10
—	22	23	—	—	4	2	1	167	2	28	197	11
5	14	43	—	10	22	—	—	332	7	26	365	12
1	3	74	—	21	5	—	—	418	1	24	443	13
1	19	28	—	3	36	—	11	233	1	34	268	14
1	1	32	2	15	7	—	8	222	3	25	250	15
7	16	40	2	10	3	—	3	191	13	30	234	16
36	58	83	7	48	73	7	79	964	61	193	1,218	17
—	17	39	—	—	—	—	—	318	—	18	336	18
2	35	90	1	27	19	1	32	805	4	95	904	19
—	4	3	—	1	2	—	3	28	—	9	37	20
32	533	470	5	398	107	—	202	4,801	64	1,273	6,138	21
1	17	10	—	—	—	—	—	228	1	18	247	22
—	6	7	—	10	—	—	—	29	—	20	49	23
15	55	178	3	43	70	—	31	1,134	27	141	1,302	24
—	—	22	—	—	73	—	—	446	—	1	447	25
13	83	65	10	57	25	3	49	668	38	194	900	26
8	35	41	1	34	33	—	39	517	11	114	642	27
—	126	53	1	64	15	—	28	1,121	1	223	1,345	28
—	71	52	—	70	39	—	31	491	1	216	708	29
—	4	29	—	8	6	—	—	421	—	12	433	30
—	—	80	—	—	41	—	—	712	—	—	712	31
5	10	28	—	2	8	—	—	459	6	16	481	32
—	—	8	—	—	—	—	—	262	3	—	265	33
2	40	35	1	38	—	—	9	356	7	108	471	34
2	8	22	—	26	3	—	—	158	7	34	199	35
2	14	15	—	18	3	—	9	186	2	45	233	36
231	**1,446**	**2,051**	**49**	**1,020**	**659**	**15**	**667**	**20,320**	**400**	**3,442**	**24,162**	37
7	—	35	1	—	29	—	—	292	15	1	308	38
—	13	28	—	10	18	1	13	310	1	38	349	39
—	13	40	1	14	17	—	11	352	1	40	393	40
—	—	11	—	—	2	—	—	40	—	—	40	41
5	15	44	—	25	30	—	27	350	9	68	427	42
—	—	2	—	—	—	—	—	73	—	—	73	43
—	2	21	—	1	1	—	—	219	—	3	222	44
12	**43**	**181**	**2**	**50**	**97**	**1**	**51**	**1,636**	**26**	**150**	**1,812**	45
243	**1,489**	**2,232**	**51**	**1,070**	**756**	**16**	**718**	**21,956**	**426**	**3,592**	**25,974**	46
—	26	67	—	30	23	—	25	538	2	86	626	47
—	13	35	—	9	8	—	21	334	—	43	377	48
2	118	57	1	59	48	1	71	1,007	11	270	1,288	49
2	72	244	1	51	32	—	45	1,087	7	175	1,269	50
1	—	21	—	—	1	—	—	169	1	—	170	51
1	3	38	—	—	7	—	—	276	1	3	280	52
—	1	17	—	8	4	—	1	79	—	10	89	53
2	25	57	—	27	9	—	5	621	3	58	682	54
8	**258**	**536**	**2**	**184**	**132**	**1**	**168**	**4,111**	**25**	**645**	**4,781**	55
251	**1,747**	**2,768**	**53**	**1,254**	**888**	**17**	**886**	**26,067**	**451**	**4,237**	**30,755**	56

between them employed 9·7 per cent of all university teachers. Oxford and Cambridge came next with 8·1 per cent and they were closely followed by the former English colleges of advanced technology.[1] The new English universities occupied the seventh place[2] with 6·8 per cent of all academic staff and last came the University of Wales[3] accounting for 5·9 per cent of university teachers.

The distribution of university teachers among these groups in 1968 is set out, again in order of numerical importance, in Table 7.2 and is

TABLE 7.2

Distribution of full-time staff among university groups, 1961–68 (per cent)

	Full-time staff		
University group	*1961–62*	*1964–65*	*December 1968*
Major Redbrick	32·4	32·7	25·9
London	23·6	21·7	20·1
Scotland	15·5	16·2	15·5
Minor Redbrick	10·2	10·6	9·7
Ancient English	10·4	8·6	8·1
Ex-CATs	—	—	8·0
New English	1·0	3·2	6·8
Wales	6·9	6·9	5·9
Total Great Britain	100	100	100
Total number	14,276	18,352	30,755

Source: Calculated from U.G.C. Returns and information from the U.G.C. The two earlier years include staff at Oxford and Cambridge who were paid only partly from university funds since they also did college work. The 1968 figures include those not financed at all from university funds–223 at Oxford and 49 at Cambridge.

compared with the situation for earlier years. The group of universities which were formerly colleges of advanced technology is, by definition, excluded from the earlier figures but in the years after the Robbins Report the institutional pattern shows a shift away from Oxford, Cambridge, London and the Victorian foundations to the new and the new technological universities.

The pattern of growth from 1910 in each of the seven university groups in existence before 1963 is plotted in Graph 7.B. Though they have changed their relative numerical positions, every group has

[1] Aston, Bath, Bradford, Brunel, Chelsea, City, Loughborough, Salford and Surrey.

[2] East Anglia, Keele, Sussex, York, Lancaster, Kent, Essex and Warwick.

[3] It received its charter in 1893 though several of its constituent colleges dated from earlier in the nineteenth century. Aberystwyth was founded in 1859, Bangor in 1885, Cardiff in 1885 and Swansea in the 1920's. St. David's, Lampeter, also received grants from the University Grants Committee under a scheme agreed in 1961 through the University College of South Wales, Cardiff.

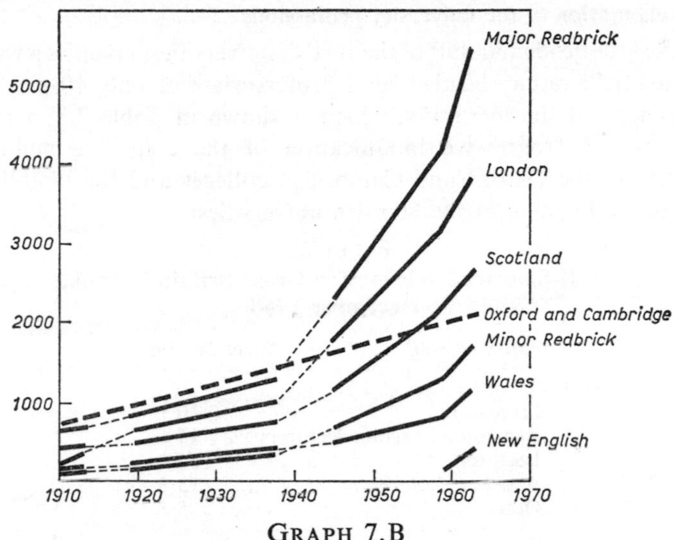

GRAPH 7.B

Number of university teachers in Great Britain by university group, 1910–64

increased its numbers. The exact number of dons at Oxford and Cambridge at the beginning of the century is not known but there were probably about eight hundred including all university teachers and college fellows. There were 471 resident MAs at Oxford in 1900 and 3,446 undergraduates. Oxford's total academic staff in 1922 was 357 rising to 1,127 in 1964–65[1] with 9,450 students. At Cambridge the number of dons primarily engaged in teaching and research, with or without college fellowships, rose from 458 in 1928 to 1,001 in 1959 when there were 8,997 students. The Scottish full-time academic staff numbered 498 in 1920 and 2,600 in 1963–64.

At the beginning of the century Oxford and Cambridge, quite apart from their overwhelming academic and social importance, were numerically the strongest group. But by the Second World War they had been surpassed by the major Redbrick universities and overtaken by London. Our estimate is that academic staff at Oxford and Cambridge increased from 800 at the beginning of the century to something like 1,000 in the 1930's. In the major Redbrick universities the increase was from 626 in 1910 to 1,349 in 1938–39 and in London from 202 to 1,057.

[1] These were the members of Congregation. They numbered 1,358 in 1963–64.

The elongation of the university professions

By 1968 the academic staff of the British universities, taken as a whole, formed a hierarchy headed by a professoriate of only 10 per cent. The shape of the hierarchy, which is shown in Table 7.3, was the outcome of progressive modification of the collegiate guilds of masters in the Oxford and Cambridge colleges and the established professorial system of the Scottish universities.

TABLE 7.3

Full-time academic staff in Great Britain by rank, December 1968

Full-time staff	*December 1968*
	%
Professors	10·1
Readers and senior lecturers	17·6
Lecturers	53·2
Assistant lecturers	13·3
Others	5·8
Total	100
Total number	30,755

Source: Information from the U.G.C.

Nevertheless the power of the college teaching fellow remains central even today in Cambridge and especially in Oxford. It is therefore worth while to glance back at the development of this situation in Oxford in the nineteenth century. There was, of course, an increase in the professoriate there as in other growing universities.[1] In 1800 there were nineteen Oxford professorships which had increased to twenty-four by 1852. In the second half of the century, however, the numbers doubled to 47 in 1892. These were responses to the reform of the examination system and the development of scientific research but they left the dominant power over the life of the university in the hands of the college fellows.[2]

In order to understand how this came about, it is necessary first to recognise that the Royal Commission on Oxford of 1850–52 was not the official non-partisan body which it has often been supposed to have been. The appointment of the Commission itself was opposed

[1] And the professional classes generally were expanding–in government administration, the law, medicine, the clergy, the armed forces and engineering. See W. J. Reader, *Profession Men: The Rise of the Professional Classes in Nineteenth-Century England*, Weidenfeld and Nicolson, 1966.

[2] We owe the following account of Oxford developments to Mr. Arthur Engel of Wadham College, Oxford and Princeton University, who is preparing a thesis on academic careers in Oxford in the nineteenth century.

by virtually all elements within the University with the exception of a small group of reformers who were interested in raising the position of the professoriate within the University. As a result the Commission became a partisan body composed of this small group of reformers since no one else would serve on it. In this situation, two other groups within the University also published reports which were modelled on the form of the Royal Commission's blue book in that they, too, printed evidence submitted by interested parties and invited witnesses and wrote reports based on that evidence. One of these groups was the Hebdomadal Council itself. The other was the Tutors' Association, an unofficial organisation composed of most college tutors and other college officers resident in Oxford. This group opposed both the existing order, as represented by the Hebdomadal Council, and the proposed reforms of the Royal Commission.

There was thus a struggle for power between the supporters of the professoriate, the tutors, and the heads of houses. In regard to University government, the Royal Commission proposed that the authority for University legislation be removed from the Hebdomadal Council and vested in a new body to be composed of the heads of houses and the senior tutors of each college together with all the professors. Thus the subsequent expansion of the professoriate would have carried with it access to power.

The significance of this proposal was not lost on the Tutors' Association. They attacked the Royal Commission's plan in their report explicitly on the ground that it would give the professoriate a dominant position in the University. The Royal Commission's plan, they argued,

> gives an indefinite, but palpably a very undue predominance to the professorial element, which would not only predominate in the 'remodelled Congregation', but would have the entire control of all its votes and proceedings. This would be an enormous change from the present state of things, in which professors, *as such*, have neither place nor influence; and would, almost of necessity, lead, within a short time, to such further alterations as would amount to a complete revolution in our existing system. . . . We speak from no jealousy of professorial teaching, which we wish to see made more effective in Oxford, but as it is in no way desirable that the instruction of professors should ever become the main instruction of the place, so it seems unfit that its dispensers should have the chief influence in University legislation.[1]

[1] 'No. 2. Recommendations respecting the Constitution of the University of Oxford, as adopted by the Tutors' Association, April 1853', Oxford, 1853, pp. 41–2.

As an alternative the Tutors' Association proposed that the new legislative board consist of 27 members, 9 elected from the heads of houses, nine elected from the professors and nine elected by the resident MAs, i.e. by the college tutors and officers. This scheme would reduce the professorial element to one-third and give a safe majority to college interests.

The committee appointed by the Hebdomadal Council also condemned the plan of the Royal Commissioners, but it had little more enthusiasm for the Tutors' recommendation. Instead, it argued that the existing system had in fact operated well. But, to silence discontent, the heads of houses were willing to accept a plan for enlarging the existing Hebdomadal Council of 24 heads of houses and two proctors by an addition of twelve MAs elected by Convocation. The committee took special pains to attack the professorial plans of the Royal Commission,

> . . . the system of the Commissioners, with its ample staff of well-endowed professors, its array of lecturers . . . is one which this University never knew, and, we may be permitted to hope, will never know.[1]

The Council's plan was of course unacceptable either to the tutors or to the Royal Commission–it was in fact a plan to retain power in the hands of heads of houses.

Meanwhile, between the setting up of the Royal Commission and the consideration of a Bill by Parliament in 1854, Lord Aberdeen had replaced Lord John Russell as Prime Minister. His government was, on the one hand, too weak to ignore the desire of the dissenters for university reform and, on the other hand, too indifferent to the issue of reforming the universities to propose a strong or consistent Bill. The result was a Bill, discussed and passed by a half-empty House, which did little more than abolish the requirements of subscription to the XXXIX Articles for matriculation and for the BA, thus opening the University to dissenters.

As to university government the Bill was vague, though in the end of great importance. It gave to Congregation the right to initiate and amend legislation alongside the unreformed Hebdomadal Council. Furthermore, each college was given the right to alter its own statutes. The effect of these reforms was to increase greatly the powers of

[1] *Report and evidence upon the recommendations of Her Majesty's Commissioners for inquiring into the state of the University of Oxford, presented to the board of Heads of Houses and Proctors, December 1, 1853.* Oxford, 1853, Part I, pp. 59–60.

the college tutors and other college officers. Under the terms of the subsequent Reform Act, they gained great power in legislating for the University and dominating power within their own colleges. These changes were crucial, in that they ensured the victory of the tutors over both the proponents of the professorial system and the heads of houses. Since 1800, the tutors had already greatly improved their position through the increasingly important examination system. Strengthening the examination system enhanced the position of the tutor by making his role more important. In the years after 1854, the tutors managed to restrict membership in Congregation to resident college fellows fulfilling college tutorial or other administrative duties. They also secured the election of their own members to the Hebdomadal Council and to the Delegacies which were being created to take up the administration of an expanding university. By the 1880's, when the academic management of the University was first divided into faculty boards, the victory of the tutors was so complete that they were able to dominate these boards as well. The professors were, of course, included, but the tutors were certain of a clear majority. Thus whereas before 1850 the University of Oxford had been dominated by an oligarchy of heads of houses, after 1850 it was run by college dons.

In the new Victorian foundations in London and the provinces the professors initially constituted the academic staff[1] but in order to carry on their work they had to appoint assistants. Before the end of the century these junior men and women, with their ill-defined status, their low salaries and typically temporary conditions of employment, on *ad hoc* contracts either with the institution or with the professor himself, had come to outnumber the professors. For example, in Manchester, the original six professors of 1851 had increased by 1900 to 24, but meanwhile 43 non-professorial teachers had been appointed, only seven of whom had permanent tenure.[2] In this way an under-privileged teaching class was formed which became a permanent feature of the academic structure. Subsequently the academic hierarchy has been elaborated and regularised[3] and its changing shape is

[1] They often had to engage in struggles with local trustees to establish the elements of academic freedom and self-government which they held to be appropriate to their professional status and which many of them had brought to their new universities from the traditional academic guilds of Oxford and Cambridge. They quickly won academic freedom in practice, if not in formal constitutions.

[2] H. B. Charlton, *op. cit.*, p. 183.

[3] We deal with the establishment of salaries and tenure in Chapter 9 below.

shown in Table 7.4. The sharpest drop in the proportion of professors took place during the 1920's (from nearly a third to little more than a fifth) though the fall has been continuous throughout the period and for all the groups included in the statistics.

Before 1920 the ranks below the professorship were neither equivalent from one university to another, nor distinguished in the Board of Education statistics. Many of them carried low status and low pay, but, as may be seen in the table, the proportion in the main career grade – the lectureship – has risen. Thus there have been two rather conflicting processes at work. On the one hand the hierarchy has been lengthened with the creation of a non-professorial staff and a corresponding decrease in the proportion of chairs. On the other hand, within the non-professorial ranks there has been a tendency towards up-grading with a corresponding decrease in the proportion of assistant lecturers.

In recent years there has been renewed pressure to increase the proportion of senior posts. The Association of University Teachers has successfully advocated the abolition of the assistant lecturer grade, to which in any case recruitment is more difficult in periods of expansion. The Association also supported a suggestion of the Vice-Chancellors' Committee in 1962 that the restriction of readers and senior lecturers to two-ninths of all non-professorial posts should be revised to one-third. And in 1967 the U.G.C. announced that, in any given university, senior posts (including professorships, senior lectureships and readerships) could be filled to a maximum of 35 per cent of the total academic staff.[1]

Thus by the sixties the structure of ranks outside Oxford and Cambridge developed into a hierarchy with four levels. At the bottom, and for most recruits the beginning, there was a grade of assistant lecturer which carried probationary status though promotion from it was in practice almost always given. This grade is now to disappear. Next is the main career grade of lecturer which is sub-divided by an efficiency bar, reached after six or seven years' service in the grade, and passed after review of the individual's competence and performance as a university teacher by his faculty board.[2] Third are posts of

[1] 'The ratio is to be applied to the total numbers of full-time academic staff wholly paid from general university funds. . . . The ratio is calculated for each university "across the board". . . . The actual distribution of the number of senior posts within each university between the different faculties and departments is entirely a matter for the university itself to decide.' U.G.C., *University Development 1962–67*, para. 77.

[2] This is largely a formality; it is extremely rare for an individual to be denied promotion because of unsatisfactory performance.

Full-time academic staff in Great Britain by university group and rank 1910–68 (per cent)

	*1910–11**	*1919–20†*	*1929–30*	*1938–39*	*1949–50*	*1959–60*	*1963–64*	*1965–66¶*	*Dec. 1968*
A. *Major Redbrick*									
Professors	30	28	21·4	18	13	11	10	9·6	9·6
Readers									
Assistant professors			6·3	6	5	4	5		
Independent lecturers								17·0	17·7
Senior lecturers	70	72	—	—	9	12	12		
Lecturers			41·0	48	42	52	48	50·1	51·1
Assistant lecturers			22·0	18	18	9	8	17·2	12·3
Others			9·1	10	13	12	17	6·2	8·7
TOTAL	(626)	(849)	(1,031)	(1,349)	(2,743)	(4,148)	(5,456)	(6,754)	(7,956)
B. *London*									
Professors	31	31	21	19	14	13	14	12·7	12·7
Readers									
Assistant professors			16	16	12	15	14		
Independent lecturers								24·0	22·5
Senior lecturers	69	69	—	—	10	11	12		
Lecturers			29	31	34	42	40	41·5	45·4
Assistant lecturers			27	26	21	12	11	16·5	14·2
Others			7	8	9	7	9	5·3	5·1
TOTAL	(202)	(601)	(856)	(1,057)	(2,146)	(3,072)	(3,750)	(5,205)	(6,175)
C. *Minor Redbrick*									
Professors	27	31	20·5	16	12	11·3	11	10	10·1
Readers									
Assistant professors			10·0	8	4	2·0	4		
Independent lecturers								16	15·7
Senior lecturers	73	69	—	—	3	6·3	10		
Lecturers			43·0	39	43	54·0	48	50	54·4
Assistant lecturers			18·0	20	22	10·4	11	17	13·9
Others			8·5	17	16	16·0	16	7	5·9
TOTAL	(104)	(151)	(258)	(324)	(842)	(1,236)	(1,669)	(2,344)	(2,975)

TABLE 7.4 *continued*

	1910–11	1919–20	1929–30	1938–39	1949–50	1959–60	1963–64	1965–66	Dec. 1968
D. *Wales*									
Professors	42	37	25	23	17	13·9	11·7	9·4	9·4
Readers, Assistant professors, Independent lecturers			6	12	8	0·3	2·4		
(Readers … Senior lecturers combined)								15·5	17·4
Senior lecturers	58	63	—	—	14	13·9	13·1		
Lecturers			26	35	39	47·0	47·3	50·9	52·0
Assistant lecturers			28	23	21	12·8	10·3	13·9	12·9
Others			15	16	7	12·1	15·2	10·3	8·2
TOTAL	(143)	(178)	(301)	(371)	(512)	(799)	(1,121)	(1,649)	(1,812)
E. *Scotland*§									
Professors	32	35	23	22	13	11·1	10	8·8	9·2
Readers, Assistant professors, Independent lecturers			8	7	5	3·0	3		
(Readers … Senior lecturers combined)								19·7	19·4
Senior lecturers	68	65	—	—	10	16·5	18		
Lecturers			41	44	46	50·0	49	47·2	50·1
Assistant lecturers			27	25	19	15·6	15	19·6	15·1
Others			1	2	7	3·8	5	4·7	6·3
TOTAL	(403)	(498)	(553)	(718)	(1,439)	(2,120)	(2,600)	(3,759)	(4,781)
F. *English new universities*									
Professors						13·9	14	13·4	10·8
Readers, Assistant professors, Independent lecturers						0·9	3		
(Readers … Senior lecturers combined)								13·7	14·1
Senior lecturers						2·8	10		
Lecturers						55·6	42	43·2	51·8
Assistant lecturers						24·0	18	21·4	18·0
Others						2·8	13	8·3	5·3
TOTAL						(108)	(331)	(1,107)	(2,105)

G. *Oxford and Cambridge*									
Professors								9·4	9·7
Readers and senior lecturers								7·5	6·6
Lecturers								65·8	69·1
Assistant lecturers								17·4	12·9
Others								—	1·7
TOTAL								(2,287)	(2,498)
H. *Ex-CATs*									
Professors								4·3	7·1
Readers and senior lecturers								14·5	18·1
Lecturers								65·3	68·5
Assistant lecturers								11·1	6·1
Others								4·8	0·2
TOTAL								(2,189)	(2,453)
I. *All universities in Great Britain except Oxford and Cambridge*									
Professors	31·4	31·4	21·8	19·6	13·4	12·0	11·5	9·8	10·1
Readers }									
Assistant professors }			9·6	8·8	6·4	6·2	6·5 }		
Independent lecturers }								17·4	17·6
Senior lecturers	68·6	68·6	—	—	9·5	12·0	12·8 }		
Lecturers			36·2	40·4	40·4	48·6	46·0	50·4	53·2
Assistant lecturers			24·6	22·4	19·6	11·6	10·5	16·8	13·2
Others			7·8	8·8	10·7	9·6	12·7	5·6	5·8
TOTALS	(1,478)	(2,277)	(3,049)	(3,819)	(7,682)	(11,483)	(14,927)	(25,294)	(30,755)

Source: U.G.C. *Returns*, information from the U.G.C. and *Statistics of Education*.

* Figures in Group A for these years include the staff of the Merchant Venturers' Technical College, formed as part of Bristol University 'to afford preparation for an industrial or commercial career'.

† For 1919–20 Heads of Departments are counted as professors. The numbers may then include some non-professorial Heads of Departments.

§ The Board of Education Report for 1910–11 gives only staff numbers at Dundee University College. Staff numbers for Scotland have been calculated from the calendars of the Scottish Universities for 1910–11.

¶ 1965–66 and 1968 include Oxford, Cambridge and ex-CATs and are based on all teaching and research staff irrespective of source of financial support.

seniority but without professorial rank–the reader and the senior lecturer. Promotion to this level is by individual selection. In some universities the distinction between readers and senior lecturers is a horizontal one: readers are recognised primarily for research and senior lecturers for teaching. In other universities the division constitutes a further elaboration of the hierarchy, the readers having higher rank. At the top are the professors, though here again the beginning of further elongation of the pyramid is to be seen in the distinction between professorial heads of departments and other professors not adorned (or burdened) with this authority.

Moving down the ranks, the numerical proportions for all universities in 1968 were, professors 10·1 per cent, readers and senior lecturers 17·6 per cent, lecturers 53·2 per cent and assistant lecturers 13·2 per cent, leaving 5·8 per cent in posts of various kinds outside the main hierarchy (Table 7.4).

These figures include Oxford and Cambridge whose staffs are classified in the same terms as those for other universities. This means that the great bulk are classified as lecturers (988 out of 1,345 in Oxford and 738 out of 1,153 in Cambridge) which is misleading in that many college teaching fellows have a salary and status superior to that of lecturers elsewhere. Moreover, the fact that Oxford and Cambridge have no senior lectureships is of no significance in the context of the collegiate staff structure. The proportion of professors and readers is relatively low, partly because some college dons have equivalent positions. Nevertheless, it should be noted that the Franks Report recommended that Oxford seek more professorships.

London has a higher proportion of professors and readers, partly because of the strength of the medical faculty, while the new English universities have a high proportion of professors as 'founder members'. Scotland and Wales have relatively few readerships though the former has a compensating high proportion of senior lectureships. The minor Redbricks have fewer staff of senior rank than the major Redbricks. Apart from London the differences in the proportion of senior staff among the several types of university institution are quite small. It is very close to 26 per cent or 27 per cent for all universities except London, Oxford and Cambridge. However, the figures for 1965–66 show that the ex-CATs were exceptional in their low proportion of professors; they had only 4·3 per cent in that year. This reflected the recent promotion of these institutions from the ranks of the technical colleges where professorships do not exist and where staffing is different in both nomenclature and structure.[1] The distribution of ranks in the former colleges of advanced technology had moved much closer to those in the other types of university by 1968 (Table 7.4).

The long-run decline in the proportion of professors among all academic staff must both reflect and reinforce the status and power of the professoriate in the universities. It also means that, as the universities have expanded, authority and responsibility has been increasingly carried by a decreasing minority of the academic staff. This may account for the rather common complaint, which we heard in our interviews, that administrative responsibilities were too great bearing in mind that professors are primarily selected for their reputation as researchers and teachers. We shall return to both these points in Chapters 12 and 14.

Specialisation and the changing balance of studies

University studies in the twentieth century have widened in scope and the balance between the faculties has also shifted. The first change, however, has been continuous while the second has fluctuated. Widening the scope of studies has meant that university teachers have specialised increasingly in their academic interests, between research and teaching, and between undergraduate and graduate supervision. One crude but dramatic illustration of the widening range of specialisms may be derived from the U.G.C.'s statistics on the branches of study pursued by advanced students. In 1928, 123 subjects were distinguished: a quarter of a century later there were 382. In the meantime, economics had been divided into economics, industrial economics, econometrics and econometric history; the number of branches of engineering had risen from seven to twenty-two and such subjects as Ethiopic, fruit nutrition, immunology, personnel management, medical jurisprudence and space science had appeared.

The changing balance of studies since the First World War is shown in Table 7.5. After the First World War the arts faculties expanded, especially at the expense of medicine and the applied sciences. These developments were remarked by the U.G.C. in their

[1] For a detailed comparison of academic salaries and ranks in the various institutions of higher education see Eric E. Robinson and David Jaynes, 'Pay and the Academics', *Higher Education Review*, Autumn 1968.

TABLE 7.5

Academic staff or students, by faculty, 1919–68

	*1919–20**	*1928–29*	*1938–39*	*1949–50*	*1961–62*	*1964–65*	*Dec. 1968*
	%	%	%	%	%	%	%
Arts	38·7	53·3	44·8	43·6	25·5	25·5	16·7
Social studies†	—	—	—	—	8·4	10·5	14·6
Pure science	18·3	16·7	15·5	19·8	26·3	28·3	28·9
Applied science, Technology, Agriculture, Forestry	16·4	11·1	12·6	16·0	19·5	17·0	39·8
Medicine, Dentistry, Veterinary science	26·6	18·9	27·1	20·6	20·2	18·6	
TOTAL	(43,018)	(44,309)	(50,246)	(85,421)	(13,104)	(17,117)	(30,755)

Source: U.G.C. *Returns.*

* Oxford and Cambridge student numbers were not included in U.G.C. *Returns* for 1919–20. These numbers were taken from the *Returns* for 1922–23, the first year they were included, and added to the numbers for other universities given in the 1919–20 *Returns.*

† Including Education.

Note: Student numbers are given for the years 1919–20, 1928–9, 1938–9 and 1949–50 and *include* Oxford and Cambridge. Staff numbers are given for the years 1961–2 and 1964–5 and *exclude* Oxford and Cambridge lecturers and below. For 1968 all staff are included who were wholly paid from general university funds including Oxford and Cambridge.

report for 1928–29 and attributed to 'the attraction exercised during a period of bad trade and restricted opportunities in other professions, by the securer and greatly improved prospect of the profession of teaching; in Scotland, the general tendency [was] intensified by the official requirement that only graduates [could] now normally be admitted to the provincial centres for training as men teachers.'[1] Nevertheless, despite the continuation of 'bad trade' in the 1930's, the trend was reversed and the arts faculties have declined ever since. By the end of the 1920's they constituted half of the academic staff; they now account for only one-sixth.[2] The social studies, as we noted earlier,[3] have expanded much more rapidly than

[1] U.G.C. Report for 1928–29.

[2] It should be noticed, however, that the decline was not as marked after 1950 as may appear from Table 7.5 since before 1959 the social studies were included with arts subjects.

[3] See above, p. 79.

the other faculties in the 1960's. Between 1961–62 social studies teachers increased by 155 per cent compared with 46·5 per cent for university staff as a whole. The pure science faculties declined during the inter-war period but have risen steadily since the Second World War to become the largest faculty group in 1966–67. Medicine has declined throughout the period, sharply in the 1920's with a recovery at the end of the 1930's and with a further decline since the Second World War. The applied sciences and technology were proportionately more significant after the First World War than at any subsequent point until 1950 and even with the incorporation of the former CATs these subjects still accounted for less than a fifth of all academic staff in 1966–67.[1]

None the less, it is clear from the figures for 1968 that the traditional stereotype of the academic as an arts don is seriously inaccurate: and this was already so at the turning point of British higher education which was marked by the Robbins Report. In 1968 the arts faculties made up only one-sixth of the total. The largest single faculty was pure science (29 per cent); the remainder, in descending order of size, were medicine and dentistry, applied science, social studies, education and last agriculture, forestry and veterinary science. Thus even assuming that half the social scientists were 'pure', nearly 50 per cent of academics worked in some kind of natural or social-science-based technology. The technologist, thus broadly defined, has the most plausible claim to be thought of as the typical university teacher, despite what we have said earlier about the characteristic resistance of the British system to the intrusion of vocational studies.

Age and sex

We have not been able to reconstruct the history of the age structure of the university professions. Presumably the celibacy rule in Oxford and Cambridge, which continued into the 1860's, must have distorted the age structure to produce a relatively old group of bachelor dons and a younger group of unmarried fellows with comparatively few in their late thirties and forties.

Expansion also disturbs the age structure of any profession. In 1952 the U.G.C. thought that, because of expansion, the average age

[1] The figures in Table 7.5 up to 1950 are based on the distribution of students and therefore since we have used them to represent staff, the assumption is made that staff/student ratios were equal between faculties.

had probably never been lower than it then was. However, the renewed rise in the rate of expansion in the early 1960's resulted in a further reduction in the average age of the university teacher. The age distributions in 1961–62, 1964–65 and 1968 are shown in Table 7.6.

TABLE 7.6

Age distribution of university teaching staff, 1961–62, 1964–65 and December 1968

Age	*1961–62*	*1964–65*	*December 1968**
	%	%	%
–25	5·3	6·6	2·6
26–30	17·2	21·8	17·7
31–5	20·6	18·1	21·0
36–40	20·7	18·3	16·4
41–5	12·4	13·8	14·7
46–50	9·5	8·1	11·2
51–5	6·6	6·2	6·7
56–60	4·7	4·2	9·7 (56–60, 61–5, 66+)
61–5	2·6	2·6	
66+	0·4	0·3	
TOTAL	8,269	9,779	25,179

Source: A.U.T. Surveys, 1961–62 and 1964–65. See *The Remuneration of University Teachers 1961–62* and *The Remuneration of University Teachers 1964–65* published by the A.U.T. in December 1962 and December 1965 respectively. Information from the U.G.C. for 1968.

* The percentages for 1968 refer to slightly different age groups: under 25, 25–29, 30–34, 35–39, 40–44, 45–49, 50–54, and over 55.

The increased rate of expansion is reflected in the greater proportion of younger staff in 1965 than at the earlier date. The over-forties counted for almost the same proportion as they had in 1962, so that there had been a relative decline in the numbers between age thirty and forty. Just under 65 per cent of all university teachers were forty years old or younger. The smaller proportion of young staff in 1968 no doubt reflects the fall in the rate of expansion in the second half of the 1960's. In 1968 only 58 per cent of university teachers were under forty. The proportion of women academics has probably risen slightly during the century as more women have entered the universities but they still constitute a small minority of 10 per cent who tend to concentrate in the lower ranks and in the faculties of arts and social studies.[1]

[1] See Ingrid Sommerkorn, *The Position of Women in the University Teaching Profession in England*–a thesis presented for the Ph.D. degree for the University of London, 1966.

Conclusion

It appears then that, out of dual 'collegiate' and 'professorial' origins in the nineteenth century, the academic professions in Britain are passing through a period of expansion which has accelerated especially in the sixties and will go on through the seventies until there are 50,000 university teachers in 1980. Expansion has meant more university institutions of larger size and has drastically reduced the numerical importance of Oxford and Cambridge. At the same time it has elongated the academic hierarchy in the sense of reducing the proportion of professorships and, as we shall see in Chapter 10, also in the sense of a pyramid of prestige for the different university groups.

Expansion from another point of view means increasing specialisation–a proliferation of subjects and research interests. A shifting balance of faculties has arisen from uneven rates of subject development and has resulted in a larger place for the social and applied sciences.

Chapter 8
VICE-CHANCELLORS AND PRINCIPALS

Chancellors of universities are ceremonial figureheads drawn from the Royal Family or other elevated circles of political and public life. The office thus symbolises the dignity of the institutions but in other respects is unimportant. Vice-chancellors and principals are in fact the academic and administrative heads of the universities and colleges. Historically the pre-eminent position of the office of vice-chancellor seems to have derived from the successful movement in Oxford in the thirteenth century to gain autonomy for dons by having the highest administrative officer of the university elected from their own membership. In more recent centuries the office has, as we shall see, frequently been held by an Oxford or Cambridge man in universities of more recent foundation. At all events the vice-chancellors have to be regarded as a special group at the summit of the academic professions. Indeed, they are typically notable members of the British 'establishment' as may be illustrated from the *Who's Who* entry of two of them, one recently retired from a new English and the other at an ancient Scottish university.[1]

[1] (i) Chairman of British Council since 1968 (Member Exec. Cttee. since 1964; a Governor and Vice-Chairman of B.B.C. 1965–67. Educ.: Dundee High School; St. Andrews University; Balliol College Oxford (Exhibitioner). Assistant in Logic and Scientific Method, L.S.E., 1926–28; Fellow, 1928–47, Balliol Coll. Oxford; Tutor in Philosophy 1928–35; Tutor in Politics 1935–47; Jowett Lecturer 1935–38; Jowett Fellow 1945–47; Rockefeller Fellow 1936–37; Faculty Fellow, Nuffield Coll. 1939–47; Principal, Univ. of Swansea 1947–59; Vice-Chancellor, Univ. of Wales 1952–54 and 1958–59; Univ. of Sussex 1959–67; Principal and Assistant Secretary Mines Department 1940–42; Principal Assist. Sec. Min. of Fuel and Power 1942–44. Director Wales and Mon'shire Industrial Estates Ltd. 1948–54; Board of Mining Qualifications 1950–62; Universities Council for Adult Education 1952–5; Council of Nat. Inst. of Adult Educ. 1952–55; Commn. on educ. requirements of Sierra Leone 1954; Selection Cttee. for Miners' Welfare Nat. Scholarships 1949–59; Nat. Adv. Coun. on the Training and Supply of Teachers 1959–63; U.C.C.A. 1961–64; Commn. on establishment of a second Univ. in Hong Kong 1962; Inter Univ. Coun. for Higher Educ. Overseas 1964–; B.B.C. Liaison Adv. Cttee. on Adult Educ. Progs. 1962–65; B.B.C. Further Educ. Adv. Coun. for U.K. 1965; Inst. Development Studies 1966–67; Cttee. on Civil Services 1966–; I.T.A. Adult

Vice-chancellors are distinguished from the rest of the university professions by the extent of the influence they can exert both on developments within their own institutions and on the general pattern and direction of higher education in the country as a whole. On the one hand, they have a voice in all decisions to do with the administrative and academic affairs of their university or college, though the weight of their opinions and influence inevitably varies both with the personality of the individual and the constitution and traditions of the institution. Where academic and administrative matters are the responsibility of different hierarchies, the vice-chancellor or principal is the most important official link between the two. On the other hand, they also have special opportunities to influence national policy. The Committee of Vice-Chancellors and Principals is a deliberative body whose opinions inevitably help to shape Government plans and actions; and at the same time individual men, whether they are members of the Committee or not, may play a significant part in shaping the relations of the state and the universities either through their own personal acquaintance with politicians and civil servants or through their connections with relevant bodies such as the U.G.C.

The potentially powerful and influential positions of the vice-chancellors and principals might have justified a special enquiry to try to establish how far they are men and women with special characteristics who are likely to hold certain kinds of attitudes and beliefs about the most desirable system of higher education for this country. Although vice-chancellors and principals generally have a background of university teaching and research they are unlikely to

---

Educ. Adv. Cttee. 1962–65; Coun. of Inst. of Educ., Univ. of London, 1967–; Coun. of Tavistock Inst. of Human Relations 1968–; Member: Commn. of Royal Univ. of Malta 1957 (Chm. 1962–); National Reference Tribunal for Coal Industry of G.B. 1957–; Cttee. on Univ. Teaching Methods 1961–64; President, Society for Research into Higher Educ. 1964–; Hon. LL.D.: Chinese Univ. of Hong Kong 1964; California 1966; Yale 1967; Sussex 1967; Hon D.Litt., Ife 1967.

(ii) Educ. Winchester, Gonville and Caius Coll. Cambridge. Fellow of Gonville and Caius Coll. Cambridge 1946–52; Univ. Demonstrator of Zoology, Cambridge 1946–52; Prof. Natural History, Univ. Edinburgh, 1952–65; Mem. Adv. Cttee. on Educ. in Scotland 1957–61; Mem. Fisheries Adv. Cttee. Development Commn. 1957–65; Mem. Council St. George's School for Girls 1959–; Mem. Edinburgh Univ. Court 1959–62; Mem. Medical Research Council 1962–65; Mem. Cttee. on Manpower Resources 1963–; Mem. Council for Scientific Policy 1965–; Chairman, Nuffield Foundation Biology Project 1962–65; Dean of the Faculty of Science, Edinburgh Univ. 1963–65; Hon. LL.D. Aberdeen 1967.

be typical of the profession as a whole. We did not ourselves attempt a special enquiry but a number of independent studies have recently been completed and we use these as a basis for our following observations.[1]

In 1967 one hundred and sixteen men and women held appointments as vice-chancellors or principals of British universities or their constituent colleges. The two positions are rather different; vice-chancellors are full-time paid officials with tenure until retirement (except in the cases of London, Oxford and Cambridge) and present (1970) salaries at provincial universities are round about £7,500. The heads of Oxford and Cambridge colleges receive smaller salaries than vice-chancellors and the job is obviously less important in the sense of attaching to a much smaller institution. Nevertheless, it can carry great prestige and provincial vice-chancellors have moved to become college principals in Oxford or Cambridge. The latter job is almost certainly more flexible in permitting a man to carry on with his own academic work or to engage in other public affairs if he so wishes.[2]

The great majority of these posts are held by men; there were only ten women in office in 1967 and all of them were heads of institutions which were exclusively for women. Practically all vice-chancellors and principals are between fifty and seventy years of age and the majority were appointed in their fifties.

The appointment procedures vary but in no case are positions publicly advertised. Names are proposed by a special university committee or by members of college governing bodies,[3] enquiries are generally made privately as to the suitability of prospective candidates and their willingness to stand and elections then take place. In Oxford and Cambridge all the fellows of a college vote in

[1] S. Szreter, 'An Academic Patriciate–Vice-Chancellors 1966–68', *Universities Quarterly*, Winter 1968. Peter Collison and James Millan, 'University Chancellors, Vice-Chancellors and College Principals: a Social Profile', *Sociology*, January 1969.

[2] For example, one master of an Oxford college has been the Chairman of the Royal Commission on Local Government which reported in 1969. Another was Chairman of the Schools Council, and another recently chaired a national enquiry set up by the Department of Education and Science into Association Football. These are but three examples of a characteristic pattern of engagement in public life which is not exclusive to the heads of houses but which is clearly facilitated by their office and enables them to perform social functions which in other ages would have depended on the existence of a leisured aristocratic class.

[3] For an account of a nineteenth-century Oxford election see Mark Pattison's *Memoirs*. For a fictional account of a twentieth-century Cambridge election see C. P. Snow, *The Masters*, Macmillan, 1951.

the election of their head of house but in other universities the selection of a vice-chancellor is normally in the hands of Council but with the advice of Senate (usually a sub-committee of senior members) so that the great majority of university teachers play no direct part. In Cambridge the office of vice-chancellor is held in turn by college principals for three years and in Oxford this office was similarly held for two years until 1969. A new procedure was then introduced on the recommendation of the Franks Committee whereby the vice-chancellor is elected by a special committee and holds office for a period of four years.[1]

Who are the men and women who occupy these responsible and potentially very influential positions in academic life? In 1967 36 per cent of vice-chancellors and principals had been educated at independent boarding schools and 22 per cent in day schools whose heads were members of the Headmasters' Conference,[2] while a further 27 per cent came from other grammar schools.[3] In 1935, by contrast, 56 per cent came from independent boarding schools and 19 per cent each from Headmasters' Conference day schools and from other grammar schools. Just as the proportion of men and women coming from the public schools has fallen, so has the proportion who were undergraduates at Oxford or Cambridge. In 1935 two-thirds of vice-chancellors and principals came from these two institutions, 18 per cent from Scotland, 5 per cent from the major provincial universities and 5 per cent from London. In 1967 a rather lower proportion came from Oxford and Cambridge (59 per cent) and from Scotland (15 per cent) and rather more, 10 per cent, from the major provincial universities.

There is a strong tendency for Oxford and Cambridge colleges to choose men who have been undergraduates of their respective universities as college heads. This was true for twenty-four of the twenty-nine Oxford colleges and twelve of the twenty-one Cambridge colleges in 1935, and for twenty-five of the thirty-four Oxford and sixteen of the twenty-six Cambridge colleges in 1967. This kind of internal recruitment is less evident in most other institutions which, like the Oxford and Cambridge colleges themselves, tend to draw their heads from the same two universities. In 1935 four of the eight

[1] See above, Chapter 6, p. 130.

[2] H.M.C. membership is the conventional criterion in Britain for defining a 'public' school.

[3] These proportions are based on an analysis of 109 of the 116 vice-chancellors and principals holding office in 1967.

major provincial universities had vice-chancellors from Oxford and only two had appointed men from within their own group. Among the principals of the London colleges, an equal number (just over a third) had been undergraduates at Oxford or Cambridge as at London. The minor provincial universities drew more of their vice-chancellors from among their own undergraduates but still half of them from Oxford and Cambridge. Only the Scottish universities recruited entirely from their own ranks. In 1967 the pattern was similar. Five of the major provincial universities had vice-chancellors from Oxford or Cambridge and only one from within the group. Among the London colleges more principals had been undergraduates at Oxford or Cambridge than at London. The minor provincial universities still drew nearly half of their vice-chancellors from Oxford and Cambridge and in 1967 this was also true of the Scottish universities. In the new universities five out of ten vice-chancellors came from Oxford and Cambridge. The ex-CATs, however, were a marked exception to the general pattern with only one vice-chancellor out of ten from either Oxford or Cambridge and the majority coming from the Scottish or major provincial universities. There can be no clearer evidence of the continued pre-eminence of Oxford and Cambridge than the recruitment of vice-chancellors and principals to other universities. The slight decline–7 per cent over thirty years–in the proportion coming from the ancient foundations with their traditional roots in the arts subjects may be linked with greater readiness to elect scientists to these positions. Certainly it would be understandable if the ex-CATs, with their interest in science and technology, were predisposed in this direction. And this seems indeed to be the case. Between 1935 and 1967 there was a drop in the proportion of vice-chancellors and principals who had read arts subjects from 68 per cent to 48 per cent and an increase from 19 per cent to 41 per cent in the scientists. In 1967 all of the ex-CATs had either scientists or technologists as vice-chancellors while Oxford and Cambridge colleges, and especially the former, still showed a strong preference for arts graduates.

We suggested earlier that while vice-chancellors and principals were not likely to be typical of the profession many had at some time been university teachers. In fact 88 per cent of vice-chancellors in 1967 had a previous academic career while 8 per cent came from the Civil Service or diplomatic service. An analysis of activities of vice-chancellors and principals outside their main career shows nearly a third–a growing proportion–who have experience as civil servants or diplomats and another third who have been members of Royal Commissions or government advisory bodies. This reflects, no doubt, the general increase in government activity since the Second World War and the increasingly close and complex relations between the Government and the universities.

Within his university the vice-chancellor is *primus inter pares*. He is influential but not in the position of an autocrat. As we pointed out in Chapter 6,[1] his influence stems from a position at the head of both the academic and the administrative hierarchies of the university. In small organisations–and most universities in Britain have hitherto had less than three thousand students–he could carry the whole organisation 'in his head' and thus by dint of personality could make or break a university. Thus, the new universities have been heavily stamped by the character and outlook of their founding vice-chancellors–Sloman at Essex, Fulton at Sussex or James at York. We must re-emphasise that the Senate or its equivalent is the effective central power in a British university: it both can and sometimes does overrule its vice-chancellor. We must also again emphasise the tradition of self-government by academics entrenched in the British universities and the absence there of the American tradition of the administrative-cum-entrepreneurial President with his separate and powerful bureaucracy.

Vice-chancellors can be and have been innovators even in the face of conservatism among their senior academic colleagues. Nevertheless, what we have seen in the foregoing pages of the pattern of recruitment to vice-chancellorships, dominated by Oxford and Cambridge and with manifold connections to the establishment, strongly suggests that the direction of the interests of the vice-chancellors have been along common traditional lines to perpetuate traditional conceptions of British university life.

Vice-chancellors and principals are important figures not only in the internal affairs of their own institutions, but also in the more public sphere of national policy, and here the Committee of Vice-Chancellors and Principals is especially significant in providing an obvious link between the Government and the universities. The Vice-Chancellors' Committee is also a characteristic example of the British way of adapting to changing situations by creating private bodies to exercise public functions which rest not on constitutions

[1] See Chapter 6, pp. 115–16.

but on pragmatically developed conventions. This body grew out of the first Congress of the Universities of the British Empire which was convened in 1912.[1] Originally the Committee had neither a constitution nor any formal powers to speak for the institutions it represented, forming only a part of the executive council of the Universities Bureau of the British Empire and meeting after imperial business had been dispatched. Nevertheless, even in the early stages it was important in drawing the British universities closer together and was consulted by the Government about university affairs. During and after the First World War the vice-chancellors were having regular quarterly meetings to discuss matters of general university concern.

In 1931 the Committee adopted a formal constitution which was approved by the Courts and Councils of all the relevant universities who then appointed the vice-chancellors as their representatives. This marked a change in status rather than in power; the Committee remained a consultative body without any authority to commit the universities it represented to any decision or course of action. From 1939 onwards, however, there seems to have been increasing pressure for the Committee to assume powers which it might not formally possess. 'With war impending, the Government sought the advice of the Committee on many issues affecting the universities which were then invested with a high degree of secrecy . . . There was no answer to the Government view that they must have some organisation able to speak for the universities as a whole, and able to keep silence when silence was called for.'[2]

At the end of the 1940's the Committee of Vice-Chancellors and Principals was strengthened by an increased grant which its member institutions agreed to provide and its activities began to grow. It undertook enquiries and recommended the universities themselves to undertake enquiries into a number of matters including the planning of university halls of residence and university entrance requirements. It also joined the Federation of British Industries in sponsoring conferences on the university and industry and it has played a significant part in salary negotiations for university staff. In spite of its growing activities the Committee remains an informal consultative body without executive authority but with an increasingly important co-ordinating function and a vital role in presenting university opinion to the Government.

[1] R. O. Berdahl, *op. cit.*, p. 47.
[2] Sir Hector Hetherington, quoted in Berdahl, *op. cit.*, p. 68.

VICE-CHANCELLORS AND PRINCIPALS

All vice-chancellors of universities of the United Kingdom are members together with the principal and four heads of colleges in London, the principal of two of the Welsh colleges and the head of the Manchester Institute of Science and Technology. The Registrar of Oxford and the Registrar of Cambridge also attend meetings.

In its *Report on University Development 1967*, the U.G.C. refers to its numerous contacts with individual vice-chancellors and other administrative officers of the various universities and then goes on to stress the importance of consultations with the Committee of Vice-Chancellors and Principals in reaching decisions on matters of general policy affecting all universities. 'They [the Committee of Vice-Chancellors and Principals] are in no way to be held responsible for the decisions we have reached; but it is certainly true that the form and content of many of those decisions have been greatly influenced by their advice.'[1]

The Report also points to the way in which the Committee has changed 'almost beyond recognition'. Beginning in the second decade of the century as a small informal gathering meeting four times a year for the exchange of information and views, with no claims to policy-making, the Committee has gradually come to be regarded as a body voicing university opinion and over the past few years it has deliberately aimed to present the university view to the Government and to the outside world. It was responsible, for example, for the setting up of a national scheme for student admissions in 1961.

The report of the Robbins Committee was, of course, a strong impetus to increased activity. There followed an unprecedented growth of student numbers, the founding of new universities, the granting of university status to the former Colleges of Advanced Technology and, above all, the re-organisation and augmentation of state support for higher education which we have discussed in earlier chapters. The increased public and parliamentary interest in the universities, the economising pressures generated by the new scale of the system of higher education and the complexities of policy formation and executive management have substantially raised the importance of the role of the vice-chancellor in his own university and have forced re-organisation of the body of vice-chancellors in order to speak for the universities and respond to the pressures brought to bear upon them. Hence the Committee's secretariat has been strengthened and the Committee meets six times a year. It has

[1] Cmnd. 3820, para. 607.

now over sixty members, having nearly trebled in size over the past ten years, and, in order to increase its efficiency, has organised itself into five divisions,[1] to allow more time for consideration and discussion of particular problems than would be available in the meetings of the full committee. Apart from the five main divisions there are *ad-hoc* sub-committees to deal with current problems and also a consultative committee intended to give quick access to academic opinion in the universities beyond the vice-chancellorial circle.

The future role of the Committee of Vice-Chancellors and Principals is unclear: however it develops it is bound to be affected by the changing nature of the relation between the universities and the state on the one hand, and on the other, the non-university sector of the higher educational system. Over the years the Committee proceedings have become increasingly formal and authoritative. With increasing Government interest in university affairs and increasing awareness within the universities of their dependence on the state and their somewhat less secure place in the system of higher education as a whole, it seems likely that this trend will continue.

[1] Division A is concerned with university development, student numbers, capital grants, university building and use of plant. Division B deals with recurrent finance (research grants, fees and costs). Division C deals with staff and student affairs. Division D deals with external relations (to Government establishments, other institutes of higher education, industry, schools, etc.). Division E looks after relations with Commonwealth and foreign universities.

Chapter 9
ACADEMICS AS A CLASS

Lead Man holler, All men foller, Down you go
For a working dollar (*West Indian work song*)

A vicarious leisure class. . . . They have entered on the academic career to find time, place, facilities and congenial environment for the pursuit of knowledge, and under pressure they presently settle down to a round of perfunctory labour by means of which to simulate the life of gentlemen. THORSTEIN VEBLEN (1918)

The social composition of the academic group, together with its economic status . . . makes for strongly democratic-minded faculties, typically plebeian cultural interests outside the field of specialisation, and a generally philistine style of life. LOGAN WILSON (1942)

In this chapter we deal with the class aspects of the academic career: the discussion of status belongs to Chapter 10 but the maintenance of a style of life depends, at least in the long run, on a set of material conditions. For academics these include 'time, place, facilities and congenial environment for the pursuit of knowledge' whether provided institutionally or indirectly through an appropriate income.

The conditions of academic work are especially noteworthy in this respect. Staff/student ratios in British universities are high and formal obligations light. There is freedom in the sense of personal autonomy of an order to be found rarely, if at all, in other occupational groups. These conditions permit the essential elements of what is considered a 'gentlemanly' way of life. They also make professionalism possible in that, with assured income, both the self-respect of the university teacher and the pressure on him to work beyond the unexacting minimum of his formal duties derive in large measure from his reputation among his colleagues. Reputation largely, though not wholly, depends on professional standards. At the same time the material conditions permit yet a third possibility–entrepreneurship: the academic may use his freedom to conduct in effect a private business within the framework of resources afforded by his university post. The nature of the business may mean that what is essentially entrepreneurship is indistinguishable from professionalism. Overt use of time and resources for profitable activity unrelated to a man's academic work is judged scandalous. Idleness is also an offence against professional codes and it is frequently the ambiguous relation between indolence and the leisure necessary for intellectual activity which may create tension between the gentlemanly and the professional elements in the academic style of life.

A gentleman is not subjected to wages, hours and conditions of work. He has no employer, no trade union and no machinery of negotiation, arbitration and conciliation. He may receive remuneration but never a rate of pay. He may follow a career or vocation, or better still dedicate himself to a hobby, but he does not have a job. A profession is, ideally, a self-governing body possessing and practising a civilised branch of knowledge or expertise: it serves the public interest according to high standards set and protected by itself in corporation. Our thesis about the evolution of British university teaching is that it is a traditionally gentlemanly profession informed by the norms of a democratically self-governing guild which is in process of adapting itself to internal and external pressures towards bureaucracy and specialisation. The nature and determinants of academic incomes, promotions and careers must now be shown to accord with this pattern of development.

We are dealing, of course, with a very small segment of the working population. The professional classes as a whole have remained a numerically insignificant proportion throughout the history of industrial development: they made up little more than 4 per cent in 1911 and still only 9·5 per cent in 1966.[1] Most men are manual workers. There has been a slow and steady shift towards non-manual work, but in 1966 the manual worker still constituted exactly two-thirds of the total of economically active men in England and Wales. Nevertheless, though the changes in the general character of the work force have been slow and small, the expansion of professional work is an important feature of the occupational history of this country. The impact of this growth is negligible for the composition of the labour force as a whole but is, at the same time, a dramatic transformation for the professions themselves. The socio-economic group

[1] Guy Routh, *op. cit.*, p. 13, gives the following comparison between Great Britain and the United States (excluding farming) for the proportions in professional work:

	G.B.	U.S.A.
1910 or 1911	4·4	5·8
1950 or 1951	6·35	8·4

of male professional workers in which university teachers are included[1] numbered 541,000 in 1961 and 709,000 in 1966, an average annual increase as a proportion of all employed men of 3·5 per cent.[2] We have already noted the accelerated growth of university teaching posts during the 1960's from 13,000 in 1959 to 31,000 in 1969 and towards a total of perhaps 50,000 by 1980 compared with 2,000 at the beginning of the century. Thus the increase in the number of academics in recent years is part of a larger professionalisation of the work force.

Academic salaries in perspective

Discussion of a general level of salaries implies, however misleadingly, the notion of a typical academic. This fabricated creature emerges from the statistical tables as a scientist aged 36, married with two children and holding a lectureship at a major Redbrick university. He is at the top, or near the top, of the lecturer grade and is a candidate for promotion to one of the senior posts–a chair, a readership or a senior lectureship. His salary scale in 1970 ran up to £3,105 a year and promotion may carry him beyond £5,000.

He is comfortably inside the top ten per cent of earners, a secure member of the British middle classes. Disregarding the 'extras' he gets more than twice as much as the average man who is a manual worker in manufacturing industry.[3] Comparison with the pay and hours of the British worker plainly establishes the material position of the don as high in one of the richest countries of the world.

Dons, of course, do not normally compare their lot with that of the bus driver or, far less, the Indian peasant. If they did they might be alarmed to notice a deterioration of relative advantage over the past generation, an illustration of the general proposition that the position of a professor in the scale of income is inversely proportional to the

[1] That is by the Registrar General for purposes of analysing the Census of Population.

[2] See C. Holmes, 'Changes in the Working Population in England and Wales', *Journal of the Market Research Society*, Vol. 11, No. 3.

[3] It may be added that on his collective say-so the British academic works a 40½-hour week during term (*Higher Education*, Appendix Three, Table 60, p. 56) compared with the average manual worker in manufacturing industry who puts in 44·2 hours. But this comparison has been hotly disputed. 'Yet not only are these hours longer than the normal hours of other brain workers–now about 37½ a week for most office workers–but they are *actual hours worked*, deducting all times for tea breaks . . . etc. Academics are here the victims of their own honesty . . . as for holidays, I have yet to meet the academic who takes more than a month, and a fortnight is the most usual.' H. J. Perkin, *Key Profession*, p. 30.

wealth of his nation (to which, ironically, education is commonly held to be a major modern contributor). 'Thus a university professor in India, with an annual salary of, say, seven to eight thousand rupees is receiving an income which is in absolute terms much lower than the seven to eight thousand dollars received by the university professor in the United States. But since per-worker income in India is not much more than 100 rupees, the Indian professor's salary is from seven to eight times the countrywide average; whereas with per-worker income in the United States close to 5,000 dollars, the professor's salary in that country is less than twice the countrywide average.'[1]

The position of the British university teacher is intermediate in international comparisons of this type. He has more than twice the national average income but absolutely much more than his Indian and less than his American colleague. The average salary for British university teachers in 1966–67 was £2,368 per annum compared with £1,102 for adult male workers in manufacturing industry. The average academic salary in ten major American universities in 1955 among associate professors was $6,500.[2] Though in absolute terms more than one and a half times as much as that of the British academic ($3,704 in 1956–57), the American stipend compared unfavourably with the income of American railroad engineers and firemen.[3] On the basis of the comparisons over time which are shown in Table 9.1 it can be seen that the position of academic salaries in Britain relative to national normal earnings has deteriorated since before the war, i.e. it has moved away from the 'Indian' towards the 'American' position. In 1928–29 the academic was nearly four times better off than the average manual worker: he is now hardly more than twice as well off.

In the case of the professors this trend has meant a reduction from nearly eight times the average manual income before the First World War to three and a half times by the mid-1950's. For the assistant lecturer the same trend brought him, in the 1950's, to an absolutely lower annual income than the average manual worker whereas in 1910 he was twice as highly paid. Thus the assistant lectureship is an example of one of the middle-class occupations which, in the general 'concertina' effect of income differentials, compares unfavourably with many manual jobs. It is important to

[1] S. Kuznets, *Six Lectures on Economic Growth*, Free Press, 1959, p. 65. The figures refer to the mid-fifties.

[2] T. Caplow and R. C. McGee, *The Academic Marketplace*, Basic Books, 1958, p. 99.

[3] *Ibid.*, p. 23

TABLE 9.1

Average salaries of academic staff, 1910–67

	*1910–11**	*1928–29†*	*1938–39*	*1951–52*	*1956–57*	*1966–67*
	£	£	£	£	£	£
Professor	600	1,082	1,115	2,041	2,303	
Reader / Assistant professor / Independent lecturer	250	632	671	1,468	1,760	
Senior lecturer	250	632	477	1,380	1,653	
Lecturer	250	461	477	863	1,061	
Assistant lecturer	150	311	313	533	600	
Others		354				
All university teachers average earnings (A)		584	612	1,091	1,323	2,368
Average earnings in manufacturing industries (B)‡	78	156	184	455	648	1,102
$\frac{A}{B}$		3·7	3·3	2·4	2·0	2·1

Notes: Oxford and Cambridge staff other than professors and readers are excluded throughout.

* Rough estimate from Board of Education Reports for 1910–11 from Universities and University Colleges in receipt of grant. Cd. 6245.

† 1928–29 figures exclude the university colleges (Nottingham, Southampton and Exeter) which had lower scales.

‡ Calculated from average weekly earnings from *London and Cambridge Economic Bulletin—The British Economy Key Statistics 1900–1964*, London and Cambridge Economic Service, 1966, and from A. L. Bowley, *Wages and Income in the United Kingdom Since 1860*, C.U.P., 1937.

remember however that these comparisons are between *annual* and not *life* earnings. The assistant lecturer is on three years' probation to a profession in which his salary will rise until it at least doubles itself in the next thirteen years and will probably rise still further by promotion to senior rank. The typical manual worker, meanwhile, is already at or near peak earnings.

However the university teacher usually compares himself with either the administrative civil servant or the industrial manager or scientist. In recent salary claims the Association of University Teachers has used these two reference groups explicitly in application of its doctrine of 'fair comparison'.[1] The industrial comparison is held to be between professors and higher business management; between senior lecturers, readers and lecturers and senior and middle

[1] This principle had been elaborated by the Royal Commission on the Civil Service, 1953–55 (see Cmnd. 9613) in relation to Civil Service salaries.

management; and between assistant lecturers and junior management. In the case of the Civil Service the comparison again is between professors in the universities and deputy secretaries and under-secretaries in Whitehall; between readers and senior lecturers and assistant secretaries; and between lecturers and principals.

A rough comparison of the history of relevant professional incomes is shown in graph 9.A. Over the course of the century the professors appear to have narrowed the gap between themselves and deputy secretaries and assistant secretaries in the Civil Service while losing their comparative advantage over other professions. The lecturers have similarly narrowed the differential between themselves and civil service principals but have maintained a relatively stable relation to general professional earnings.

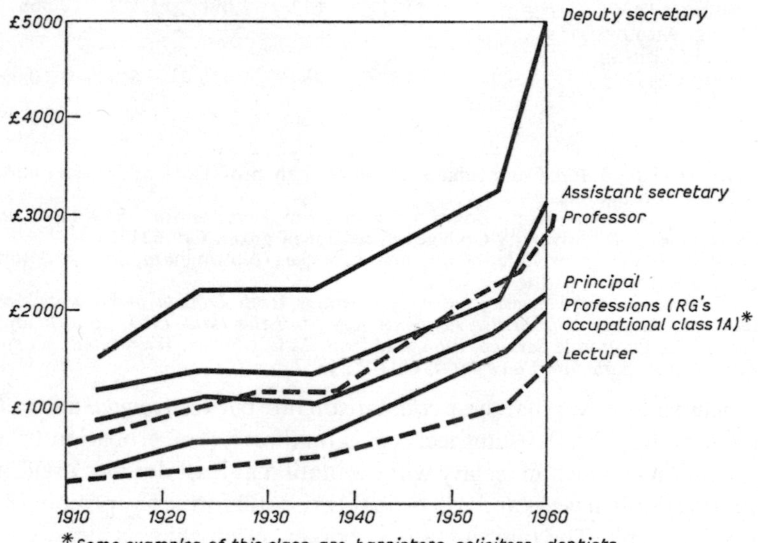

GRAPH 9.A
Academic, Civil Service (admin.) and professional salaries, 1910–61

The history of academic salaries in the period of rapid expansion associated with the Robbins Report begins in the early summer of 1962 when the Association of University Teachers was claiming that university salaries were about 25 per cent below comparable jobs in industry and in the Civil Service and it was on this sort of comparison that they made their case to the National Incomes

Commission. The Commission for its part rejected the comparisons made by the Association. They argued that 'university teaching is a single and unified profession. It is incapable of comparison in terms of functional content with any other calling',[1] though they clearly had competition from the Civil Service and industry in mind in fixing the new scale of salaries. They took the view that over recent years there had been a decline in the position occupied by university salaries in the 'overall pattern of relativities'. The salary scales recommended by them in 1964 were based on the view that 'the expansion of the universities does not and should not require, so far as recruitment and retention of staff are concerned, that they should be put in a prominent position in relation to their competitors. Equally they should not be asked to enter the critical period immediately in front of them from a position of relative disadvantage: or, to put this aspect of the matter in more positive form, they should be enabled to face the strains and difficulties of the next few years with a feeling of confidence that they have been treated fairly. "Fairly" in this context means that they stand on a competitive footing with other services and occupations seeking the best academic talent, and that if the community calls for expansion it will not attempt to secure it by taking advantage of established loyalties.'[2]

Argument over the meaning of job comparability did not end there and will doubtless continue. Meantime, whatever the technicalities of salary negotiation may be, it is clear that the middle-class careers of administrators and scientists in industry and the Civil Service are the reference groups to which academic salaries are related by all the interested parties. In support of its claim to the Prices and Incomes Board in 1968 the A.U.T. argued for a general increase of 15 per cent for all non-medical staff 'to restore that competitive equivalence between salaries and prospects in the universities and in other occupations drawing on the same pool of recruits which your predecessors, the National Incomes Commission ... judged to be in the national interest. We estimate the increase needed for this purpose in all the grades covered by this claim at 15 per cent by December 1967'[3] and they documented their case by

[1] National Incomes Commission, Report No. 3, *Remuneration of Academic Staff in Universities and Colleges of Advanced Technology*, Cmnd. 2317, H.M.S.O., 1964, p. 26, para. 79.

[2] *Ibid.*, p. 20, para. 63.

[3] National Board for Prices and Incomes, Report No. 98, *Standing Reference on the Pay of University Teachers in Great Britain*, First Report, Cmnd. 3866, H.M.S.O., 1968, p. 8.

details of rises in pay among industrial managers and the graduate professions generally.[1]

The P.I.B. rejected the argument but on new grounds:

> The claim for an all-round increase is based on a need, so it is contended, to restore a competitive equivalence with other salaries. In recent years the movement in salaries in general has been faster than the movement in national productivity and has therefore been inflationary. An all-round percentage claim based on this movement would, if conceded, add to the inflation. The resulting rise in the index of salaries could cause groups which earlier obtained increases to seek to maintain their differential, and so on *ad infinitum*. While we would not contend that general comparisons of pay are the sole cause of cost inflation, they play a contributory part. To cut the chain is, we recognise, hard on those waiting at the point where the chain is broken. Not to seek to cut it, however, would help to perpetuate the national situation of recurring financial crises arising in large part from a growth in money incomes relative to productivity greater than elsewhere.[2]

The most disturbing feature of this argument, in the light of the increasing dependence of the universities on state funds, is that academics are in a peculiarly vulnerable position in relation to government economic policy. Being directly dependent on government grants they are especially likely to be at the point where 'the chain is broken'. If salaries were not to be maintained at a level comparable with those of other professions competing for graduates, the quality of recruits would probably eventually fall. It is therefore all the more significant that the P.I.B. also produced evidence that the quality of recruits had declined in recent years.[3]

The report of the Prices and Incomes Board was in any case given a most hostile reception by the universities. According to the official historian of the A.U.T. it was 'greeted with astonishment and derision by most university teachers. . . . These extraordinary arguments, that the chain of inflationary increases could somehow be broken, and the equilibrium of the national economy restored, by attacking not only the smallest and weakest but the *last* link in the chain, a tiny profession whose salary increases always came too late to affect anyone else's, and that the morale, efficiency and competitive position of a profession can be gauged by the maintenance of an abstract staffing ratio based on an expectation that the profession would in the

[1] *Ibid.*, Appendix D.1, p. 56. [2] *Ibid.*, p. 28.
[3] See below, Chapter 10.

long term be treated fairly in comparison with competing professions, would have been labelled specious and callous if they had been put forward by an ordinary employer.'[1]

So far then we see that the British university teacher stands high in the income scale of his compatriots but with increasing uncertainty about his relation to other professional incomes as expansion increases the pressure on government to economise. Against this background we can now examine the income structure of the academic professions.

The salary framework

The salary framework for university teachers in 1970 in Britain is set out in Table 9.2 and its previous history from 1949 in Table 9.3.

TABLE 9.2

Academic salaries from October 1969 (excluding clinical teachers)

Professor	Average salary at each institution not to exceed £5,100. Minimum £4,120.
Reader and senior lecturer	Range with varying maxima up to £4,000.
Lecturer	£1,355 × £115 (13 increments) to £3,105.

The 1964 scales were proposed after special enquiry by the National Incomes Commission[2] and reviewed by its successor, the National Board for Prices and Incomes, which reported in December 1968 and again in April 1970.[3] The resulting recommendations raised several important issues which cannot be fully appreciated except in the light of the more general discussion of the material conditions of university teachers which we undertake in this chapter.

It will be seen from the tables that the grading structure of the university teaching professions in 1968 began with the assistant lectureship which, in practice, was probationary for the first three years, though promotion to the next grade–that of lecturer–was almost automatic. The P.I.B. recommended in 1968 that all university teachers, apart from clinical staff, who joined the profession either at

[1] H. J. Perkin, *Key Profession*, p. 190.

[2] National Incomes Commission, *op. cit.* (A summary of the history of university salaries from the point of view of the U.G.C. may be found in Chapter 6 of the U.G.C.'s *University Development 1957–62.*)

[3] National Board for Prices and Incomes Report No. 145, April 1970, Cmnd. 4334.

TABLE 9.3

Academic salary framework, 1949–68*

	1949	*1954*	*1957*	*1960*	*1962*	*1963*	*1964*	*1966*	*1968*
1. *Non-medical posts*	£	£	£	£	£	£	£	£	£
Professors: salaries ranging from	1,600	1,900	2,300	2,600	2,600	2,900	3,400	3,570	3,780
to	2,500	2,850	3,000	3,600	3,600	4,000	4,445	4,990	4,675
Readers and senior lecturers: a range of									(average)
salaries with varying maximum up to	1,600	1,850	2,150	2,425	2,425	2,700	3,250	3,415	3,670
or in special cases to	—	—	2,250	2,525	2,525	2,800			
Lecturers: scales rising generally from	500	650	900	1,050	1,150	1,250	1,400	1,470	
to a maximum of	1,100	1,350	1,650	1,850	1,950	2,150	1,505	1,630	2,850
or in a limited number of cases to	—	—	—	2,000	2,100	2,300	—	—	—
Assistant lecturers: salaries ranging from	400	550	700	800	900	1,000	1,050	1,105	—
to	500	650	850	950	1,050	1,150	1,275	1,340	—
B. *Pre-clinical posts*									
Professors: salaries ranging from	2,000	2,250	2,300	2,600	2,600	2,900	3,400	3,570	3,780
to	2,500	2,850	3,000	3,600	3,600	4,000	4,200	4,990	4,675
Readers, senior lecturers and lecturers:									(average)
scales rising from	600	700	900	1,050	1,150	1,250			
to maxima ranging from	1,200	1,450	1,650	1,850	1,950	2,150	up to 3,250	up to 3,415	up to 3,670
to	1,800	2,050	2,250	2,525	2,525	2,800			
C. *Clinical posts*									
Professors: salaries ranging from	2,250	2,500	2,500	2,800	2,800	3,150	3,500	3,465	
to	2,750	2,850	3,000	3,900	3,900	4,445	4,445	4,885	
or in certain cases to	—	3,100	3,250	—	—	—	—	—	
Readers, senior lecturers and lecturers:									
scales rising from	600	700	900	1,050	1,150	1,250	1,400	1,470	
to maxima ranging from	1,500	1,750	1,750	2,200	2,200	2,500	2,500	2,800	
to	2,200	2,400	2,550	3,200	3,200	3,600	3,600	3,950	
or in cases of special responsibility to	2,500	2,750	2,900	3,500	3,500	3,990	3,990	4,380	

Source: U.G.C. *Reports.*

* From 1957 allowances of £100 for professors, £80 for readers and senior lecturers and £60 for others in the pre-clinical and non-medical staffs of London University were payable. These are known as London Allowances. In earlier years £50 was payable to non-medical staffs, but in the case of professors only within the maximum of the scale. With effect from October 1969 the London Allowance became £100 p.a. irrespective of grade.

the grade of assistant lecturer or lecturer, should be required to serve a probationary period of four to five years. They also suggested that passage beyond probation should be rigorously controlled, instead of being automatic as it now is in many places. The lecturer grade is the main career grade and before 1966 it had thirteen annual salary increases with an efficiency bar at a point which varied from institution to institution. Crossing the merit bar involved a review of the university teachers' performance and competence. The P.I.B. suggested that the efficiency bar should be more rigorously controlled. Following the advocacy of the Association of University Teachers, the Board recommended a combination of the assistant lecturer and lecturer scales. It also wanted the combined new scale to be shorter than the previous two scales with consequently larger jumps. The object of the larger annual increment was to compensate for the 'deteriorating prospects of promotion in the system subject to increasing financial tightness and to weaken the case for claims for general salary increases'.[1]

Promotion beyond the lecturer grade to the ranks of senior lecturer, reader or professor is by individual selection. In the past, however, there has been a limit on the proportion of non-professorial posts with senior status. In its quinquennial report for 1942–47, the U.G.C. suggested that one-fifth would be an appropriate proportion of senior appointments. In 1959 this quota became two-ninths and in its report the National Incomes Commission stated that the U.G.C. were then about to consider a suggestion of the Committee of Vice-Chancellors that the ratio should be changed to one-quarter. In 1967 the permitted proportion of senior appointments, including professors as well as readers and senior lecturers, was fixed at 35 per cent. In fact the percentage for 1969–70 was 28 and had been 32 in 1961–62. Moreover, these figures are for all faculties whereas the medical faculties have always been exempted from the quota requirements. Non-medical faculties have lower salary scales than those of the clinical staff of the medical faculties. A range of salaries has been permitted for professors but no institution could have an average exceeding £5,100 from October 1969.[2]

[1] *Ibid.*, p. 29.

[2] In addition to the basic salaries there was once a system of family allowances which began at the London School of Economics before the war and was nationalised immediately after the war. These allowances of £50 per child were, however, discontinued from January 1965 following the N.I.C. report. Teachers already entitled to these allowances retain them for as long as their appointment lasts, but they are not given to new entrants to the profession or to those who are promoted to a higher grade.

With minor variations these scales are national but the collegiate complications at Oxford and Cambridge produce a distinctive structure with a number of peculiarities. First, all non-clinical professors are paid the same, though some also receive allowances for departmental responsibilities. Second, there is no grade of senior lecturer but the lecturer scale rises three increments above the national maximum. Third, the lecturers' scale is a rigid age-wage scale irrespective of length of service or subject. Fourth, any university post, save that of professor, may be held together with a paid college post, and there are a considerable number of part-time university posts which are tenable only by those who also hold a paid college post. And finally, some members of the academic staff are employed only by the colleges and hold no university post. These college teaching fellowships typically carry higher pay than that of lectureships elsewhere.

The academic marketplace

It is therefore less easy to explain what is the structure of British academic salaries than to describe what it is not. It is not the outcome of an individual competitive market of buyers and sellers. On the contrary it reflects primarily a unified profession organised as if it were a national bureaucracy. Perhaps not quite a unified profession for there are medical differentials and perhaps not quite a national bureaucracy while Oxford and Cambridge are not wholly assimilated to it: but the recent changes all illustrate a trend towards rationalisation and standardisation. In any case the system differs fundamentally from a perfectly competitive market: on the demand side it is arguable that, though there are seventy-six colleges[1] there is only one buyer; and on both the demand and supply sides there is a strongly and widely held conception of university teaching as a single vocation which stems from the mediaeval guild but which now also reflects the hierarchy of professional expertise. The expansion of the universities outside Oxford and Cambridge has relied increasingly on state funds with the result that now the essential fact is that academic salaries are fixed by the Chancellor of the Exchequer.[2] The limited power of

[1] Counting the individual colleges of the Universities of London and Wales.

[2] The following extract from *The London Gazette*, 2 November 1967, expressed the formal position.

PRICES AND INCOMES ACT 1966

Instruction under Section 3(2) to the National Board for Prices and Incomes

The last full review of the remuneration of the academic staff of universities in Great Britain was undertaken in 1963–64 by the National Incomes Com-

universities to vary the conditions of individual members of their staff is less significant than the trend away from university independence which has followed the expansion of higher education in this century. In their early years the modern universities assumed their freedom to fix salaries (and tenure), and it is noticeable that this went along with a frank employer–employee relationship between the civic universities and their professors.[1] There was little uniformity of staff structure and salary levels were roughly correlated with the size of endowments. Thus one effect of financial dependency on the state has been to move the salary variations of independent guilds (or, in the case of the Victorian foundations, local academic corporations) towards the uniformity of a national bureaucracy.

From its formation after the First World War until the end of the second war the U.G.C. largely confined itself to advocating general rises in academic salaries in order to maintain the quality of recruits and to allow university teachers to pursue 'their intellectual ideal under conditions which do not make this impossible of attainment'. These conditions were thought of as 'the prospect of marrying and maintaining himself and his family in such material comforts as are enjoyed by moderately successful members of other learned professions, and of providing satisfactorily for the education of his children.'[2] But the U.G.C. certainly never advocated standardisation of academic salaries. Thus in 1930 they were insisting on the opinion 'which we have expressed on previous occasions, adverse to any general scheme applicable to all university institutions and providing for uniform fixed salary scales with automatic increments. Each university or college must be free to decide for itself what is best

---

mission. Since that time the procedure has reverted to the arrangement under which increases are awarded directly by the Government after consultation with the University Grants Committee, which in turn is responsible for consulting the Committee of Vice-Chancellors and Principals and the Association of University Teachers.

1 Sir Eric Ashby and Mary Anderson, 'Autonomy and Academic Freedom in Britain and in English-Speaking Countries of Tropical Africa', *Minerva*, Spring 1966, p. 325. 'The original pattern was very simple, higher education in the industrial cities of Victorian England began as private enterprise, financed by a joint stock company, as was University College, London; or by individual benefactors, as were Owens College, Manchester and Mason College, Birmingham; or by groups of citizens, as were the colleges in Leeds and Liverpool. The trustees for the endowments and subscriptions acted as governing bodies; they began by regarding the professors as employees and they considered it as part of their duty as trustees to decide policy in the colleges they governed.'

2 U.G.C. *Report*, 1928–29, H.M.S.O., 1930, p. 23. 'We are convinced', said the U.G.C., 'that it would be a national calamity if university teaching became a preponderantly celibate profession.'

suited to its own needs and resources and it is not only natural but desirable that the size, wealth and standing of different institutions should be reflected in differences of salary.'[1]

And they were. In the year before the U.G.C. expressed this opinion, the salaries of British university professors were scattered over a range as great proportionately as that which now covers the great majority of all university teachers. Of the seven hundred and forty-seven professors fourteen had stipends of £700 a year or less and twelve received £2,000 a year. The range among readers and assistant professors was from £350 to £1,100 and among lecturers from £250 to £1,000.

Within twenty years both the facts and U.G.C. opinion had been transformed. After the second war the universities could not expand to meet the growing demand either for graduates or for research without more money from the state. As we saw in Chapter 4, before the war about a third of university income came from government grants (£2·4 million in 1938–39). By the 1960's the proportion was over two-thirds (£52·2 million in 1961–62) and in the meantime total university incomes multiplied more than twenty times from £6 million to £190 million a year.[2] Since over a third of the income of the universities (£83 million in 1969–70) is spent on academic salaries it is not surprising to find that government control has penetrated into what was once a matter for independent negotiation.

Two particular circumstances led to formal intervention by the Treasury through the U.G.C. There was a sharp increase in the cost of living at the end of the war and the poorer universities were unable to raise salaries sufficiently without government help. Matters came to a head in 1946. Knowing that there was no uniformity in the proposals of different universities and that government grants would be necessary, the U.G.C. consulted the Treasury and laid down a standard rate of professorial salary. The universities were at first left to decide for themselves on the salary scales of non-professorial staff in relation to the standard professorial rate: but by 1949 this flexibility also ended. Salary increases were needed in that year and the U.G.C. concluded that 'since this readjustment of salary levels was only made possible by Exchequer assistance it was necessary to ensure that the universities observed a certain measure of uniformity in the treatment of their staffs, and the additional grants were given

[1] *Ibid.*, p. 29.
[2] These figures do not include non-recurrent capital grants.

on the condition that the new scales to be introduced would not exceed certain specified limits'.[1]

There was no public battle. The strength of the forces involved was effectively illustrated by the firm suppression of the only rebel–the University of Cambridge–which proposed to raise its standard professorial rate to £250 per annum above the national level. The U.G.C. informed Cambridge that it had '. . . raised an issue of utmost gravity which affects not Cambridge alone, but all the university institutions which participate in the Exchequer grant. Both the committee and, as they believe, the Treasury are anxious to maintain the principle of academic autonomy to the fullest possible extent, and it is with that object in view that the present system of administering the general recurrent grant has been devised. But that system can only be maintained on the footing that the recipients of the grants can be relied upon to respect the express views of the government on a matter which passes the bounds of purely academic concern. There is no doubt in the minds of the committee that the fixing of standards of academic remuneration must be regarded as such a matter . . . there can, in the judgment of the committee, be no justification for the utilisation by a university of the largely increased Exchequer grant for the purpose of raising salaries beyond the level which the Treasury are prepared to subsidise.'[2] There has been no recurrence of rebellion since that time. State finance has brought with it uniformity of salary scales between institutions.

This is not to say, however, that university autonomy, or far less academic freedom, is undermined by government control of the salary structure. The vital questions of who is appointed or promoted, and to do what, are completely in the hands of individual universities. But national salary scales do, nevertheless, reduce the scope of competition between institutions, or at least change its character.

The academic guild

The concept of the academic profession as a unitary guild also restricts competition and dampens the effects of neighbouring markets for educated or professional men outside the universities where job comparability might lead to differentiation between faculties in favour of, for example, applied scientists. Before making

[1] U.G.C., *University Development 1947–52*, p. 38.
[2] U.G.C., *University Development 1957–62*, p. 137.

its recommendations for academic salaries, in 1964 the N.I.C. took evidence from the Treasury, the U.G.C., the Committee of Vice-Chancellors and Principals, the A.U.T. and a number of sectional interests among university teachers including the British Medical Association, the Royal Veterinary College, the Royal Society and the Society of Public Teachers of Law. In its written evidence the Treasury referred to 'the tradition of the unity of the academic profession' and the N.I.C. reported 'that eventually none of those whom we questioned in oral evidence really pressed for an extension of the system of differentials by faculties or subjects beyond the present scope of the medical teachers. Those of them who, at first sight, might appear to have been proposing further differentials by faculties and subjects, and in particular the Council of the Royal Society, were in fact asking for further flexibility within salary scales, not confined to any faculty or subject, to overcome difficulties of recruiting and retaining university teachers wherever and whenever such difficulties occur.'[1]

The academic union

It is mainly through the A.U.T. that the profession expresses its unity. Some 60 per cent of British university teachers (16,500 in 1968) belong to the A.U.T. Membership is less strong in the ancient universities and the higher ranks but, apart from the Universitas Belgica, the A.U.T. is probably the strongest and most prestigious national association of academics of its kind.

The tension between gentlemanly conceptions of a learned body of academics and the pressure towards organised adaptation to the emerging national system of higher education is evident at every point in the history of the A.U.T.–in its origins, preoccupations and activities. It is and it is not a trade union just as the Committee of Vice-Chancellors and Principals and the U.G.C., which was also formed immediately after the first war, are and are not employers' associations.

The formation of the A.U.T. represented the first victory of unity over sectional interests despite its origins before the first war in sectional discontent among the non-professorial staff of the new civic universities led by Manchester men like J. S. B. Stopford and J. E. Myers. When the Victorian universities were founded the staff were the professors aided by their assistants. 'By the First World War

[1] National Incomes Commission, *op. cit.*, p. 42, para. 127.

the universities and colleges were still tiny by modern standards–the non-professorial staff of fifteen of them in 1917–18 averaged only twenty-two members, while Manchester with forty-eight (excluding demonstrators etc.) was one of the largest–but the assistants now outnumbered the professors and did a large part of the work. Meanwhile their status remained low, there was no uniform system of grading to distinguish those with high academic attainments or long experience and their salaries were exiguous.'[1]

The first war had cut short negotiations with Council at Manchester on behalf of the assistants. There was a conference of university lecturers at Liverpool in December 1917 which decided to appeal directly to the Board of Education to provide money for increased salaries and improved superannuation. The conference adopted the provisional title of an Association of University Lecturers. But unity was advocated by the Manchester delegates–they wanted to act only in concert with the university Senates and Councils. The Manchester view, helped perhaps by the decision of H. A. L. Fisher at the Board of Education to see a Deputation of Governing Bodies rather than a sectional 'Deputation from the Assistant Lecturers,' finally prevailed in 1919. The non-professorial delegates to a joint conference on superannuation held at Sheffield reported back to their Senate at Manchester: 'We are convinced that further opposition on our part to the formation of an association will have the effect of giving the association which will be formed a sectional and partisan character. On the other hand we are of opinion that a wide association, open to all members of University staffs, might prove to be of great value as a medium of intercourse and for the more effective formulation of general university ideals. We therefore appeal for the approval of the Senate to the foundation and trial of such an association.'[2] The A.U.T. was formed nationally later that year. A parallel Scottish association was formed in 1922 and the two organizations formed a single union in 1949.[3]

Salary negotiation

Outside the Oxford and Cambridge colleges salaries are negotiated

[1] H. J. Perkin, 'Manchester and the Origins of the A.U.T.', *British Universities Annual*, 1964, pp. 88–91. 'The average for 330 lecturers in 15 institutions in 1918 was £206.'

[2] *Ibid.*, p. 90.

[3] T. R. Bolam, 'The Scottish Association of University Teachers', *loc. cit.*, 1964, pp. 77–87.

at two levels: the scales nationally and individual positions locally. We have already described how nineteenth-century autonomy, and therefore variation in salaries between universities, was gradually modified during the twentieth century by increasing reliance on state finance until, in 1949, the U.G.C. set standard national scales. Before that time the A.U.T. had no recognised position in the determination of salary scales, though the U.G.C. received deputations and memoranda from, and occasionally held discussions with, representatives of the Association. After 1949 the A.U.T. pressed repeatedly for the establishment of a clear system of negotiation. It had to wait for success until 1970.

The course of events again illustrates the peculiar organisation of university teachers as neither a self-governing guild nor a trade union, neither self-employed nor employees. As the then Mr. Butler, Chancellor of the Exchequer, put it in 1959, '. . . the relationship between the governing bodies and academic staffs of the universities is in important respects different from that between employers and employees. This relationship is unique, and I should be sorry to see any attempt to change it. Its effect is to make inappropriate the development of negotiating machinery of the normal type.'[1]

Butler's view was that of Whitehall and the U.G.C. It was based on two arguments. First there was no clearly defined employer–employee relationship. Neither the Treasury nor the U.G.C. nor the Committee of Vice-Chancellors and Principals were employers. Nor were the university teachers employees: they were members of a society called a university and therefore determined corporately their individual pay and conditions of service. Second, there should be no direct negotiation along employer–employee lines because this would destroy university autonomy, impose rigid salary scales and establishments and result in detailed governmental scrutiny of university accounts.

On a strict interpretation of this view there is no justification for the existence of the A.U.T. The university is the collective organisation of the academics and as such it needs no further organisation as a trade union. However, the fact of the existence of the A.U.T. has come to carry greater weight than the logic of a guild conception of the universities and after 1949 the U.G.C. recognised 'a growing feeling that the views of the Association should be taken into consideration when the basic salary framework was being revised.' From 1954 the Association along with the Committee of Vice-

[1] Quoted in U.G.C., *University Development 1957–62*, p. 141.

Chancellors and Principals was given a formal right of approach to the U.G.C. on questions of changing the basic salary framework. Though this by no means amounted to recognition of the A.U.T. as a negotiating body (and significantly the sectional interests of the B.M.A. were also recognised) it none the less was a first step, and it was formalised in 1960 into a procedure for salary discussions which was described by the U.G.C. as follows:

(1) Upon the initiation of a salaries review the Association of University Teachers will begin the preparation of detailed salary proposals. While the A.U.T. is preparing proposals,
  (a) there will be consultations between the Vice-Chancellors' Committee and the University Grants Committee about the general considerations involved;
  (b) the Committee of Vice-Chancellors and Principals will make themselves freely available to the Association's Executive for confidential consultation, exchange of views and the provision of such background information as they can supply, including some indication of the extent to which they are able to support the Association's proposals.

(2) The Association will complete their proposals and formally submit them to our Committee in writing.

(3) The Committee of Vice-Chancellors and Principals will be asked to advise us on the basic salary framework and will discuss this with us.

(4) We will meet representatives of the Association to discuss their proposals and any major points of difference or difficulty. We will not disclose the source of these major points, i.e. whether they came originally from the Vice-Chancellors' Committee or from ourselves. These major points of difference or difficulty, together with such evidence as is available, will be made known to the Association's representatives in advance of discussion.

(5) We will, if necessary, arrange a further meeting with the Committee of Vice-Chancellors and Principals before making our submission to the Chancellor of the Exchequer, and if some fresh consideration should have arisen after our meeting with representatives of the Association, we will see their representatives a second time.

(6) After the Chancellor's decision has been taken and made known, we will give to the Committee of Vice-Chancellors and Principals and to the Association the 'considered reply' promised in the then Chancellor's announcement in Parliament on 29th July, 1955. It is understood that in so doing we cannot disclose the advice that we have given to the Chancellor.[1]

The U.G.C. pronounced itself satisfied that 'by and large, this

[1] U.G.C., *ibid.*, p. 142.

procedure seems to have worked well . . .' The A.U.T. on the other hand remained far from satisfied. It is true that opinion among university teachers has always been in principle in favour of university autonomy and against overt trade unionism. And A.U.T. officials often comment wryly on the frequency with which members at local meetings or in the press will deprecate too much discussion of the sordid business of pay or even highmindedly declare themselves and their colleagues to be overpaid.[1] Nevertheless the essential role of the Association has always been to protect the material conditions of its members and to this end it has constantly sought an employer with whom it could establish the right to negotiate. Before 1953 the U.G.C. appeared to the A.U.T. to be taking on, if not the role of employer then at least that of a recognised independent review body in the determination of salary scales. Of course the Government exercised ultimate financial control, but it seemed that U.G.C. recommendations on salaries were more or less automatically accepted. After 1953 however the situation seemed to change: as the position of the U.G.C. weakened the employer became more elusive and decisions appeared to be taken behind the scenes in Whitehall. Discontent in A.U.T. circles and among academics generally gradually increased and was partly responsible for the referral of the salaries question to the N.I.C.

The recommendations of the Commission did nothing to allay A.U.T. discontent which was expressed sharply by Professor Michael Fogarty, the convenor of the Association's Salaries and Grading Committee, in the following terms in 1965.

> Behind the scenes; that is the point. Now as before N.I.C., the effective decisions about the terms and conditions of employment of university staff are taken behind closed doors, by ministers and civil servants whom we have no right to meet and who deny (as implicitly the Treasury did to N.I.C.) that their exercise of the power of employers entails accepting the ordinary obligation of an employer to negotiate openly, in good faith, and with the careful preparation which in the Civil Service's own negotiations is taken for granted. The grounds of decision are not revealed in public or to our Association, and do not have to be justified: they cannot be challenged or cross-examined. Those whom we meet in negotiation have no power; those who have power are carefully kept from

[1] B.U.A., 1963, p. 89. 'Thus in the presidential address for 1963, Professor W. W. Chambers remarked "as salaries are in question, some of our colleagues are invariably prompted by their conscience of stating with cheerful altruism or moralising stoicism that they feel they are too well paid already".'

> meeting us. It cannot be said too often that N.I.C. is the one occasion when those who actually determine university salaries have had to appear in public and explain and justify what they have been doing or at any rate to try to justify it, since N.I.C. after all ruled that their view of salary levels fell short of justification by margins of up to twenty per cent. In any negotiation the solution arrived at may deviate from the ideal. . . .
>
> As an Association, we need not much mind what form future salary review procedure takes, so long as those who actually decide university salaries have under it to justify their decision in the first place, in discussion with us, and then, if agreement cannot be reached, before an independent tribunal. After discussion with the Vice-Chancellors and the U.G.C., we put forward a plan by which a panel of the U.G.C. would act as a conciliation commission, bringing the parties – ourselves, the Department of Education and Science, which has the money, and the Vice-Chancellors – together for discussion and trying to secure agreement between them. If agreement was secured, that would be that. If not, the disputed points would go to the Industrial Court. But we would equally accept an independent review body like that for the Higher Civil Service (Franks Committee) or the medical profession (Kindersley Committee), as proposed by the Robbins Commission, provided that the procedure brought all parties into the open and permitted discussion and cross-examination between them, and that the review body's decision was formally or by custom final, or, if the Government insisted on challenging it, could be taken to another tribunal for final decision.[1]

A.U.T. experience with the round of negotiations with the P.I.B. in 1968 did nothing to engender satisfaction either with salary levels or with the machinery for their determination. Nevertheless in both its 1968 and 1970 reports the P.I.B. expressed sympathy with the A.U.T.'s demand for negotiating machinery. Later in 1970 the Government agreed to a scheme submitted by the A.U.T., the U.G.C. and the Committee of Vice-Chancellors and Principals. At the first stage in future negotiations the A.U.T. would bargain with a body called the University Authorities which represents the universities as employers under the general guidance of the Vice-Chancellors' Committee. There was to be an independent chairman to conciliate and arbitrate between the 'employees' (A.U.T.) and 'employers' (university authorities). This is Committee A. At the second stage, Committee B, the agreed proposals were to be negotiated with the Government. Failure to agree would be dealt with by arbitration.

[1] *British Universities Annual 1965*, pp. 84–86.

Salary differentials

Too much must not be made of the principle of guild unity. Sectional interests exist; and though only medical trade unionism, taking the opportunity of the creation of the National Health Service, has been strong enough to get and keep formal differentials, claims for special treatment are advanced by nearly all faculties except arts and may be largely mutually cancelling. Moreover, though N.I.C. endorsed the sentiment of unity and reduced the size of medical differentials it made its recommendations more on grounds of practicality than of principle. Differentials applied to categories of academics cannot work. 'Within any faculty or department, be it one of science, technology or arts . . . it would not be possible to match outside market values by a university salary scale applying to the faculty or department. At the end of the day it comes down to individual subjects and that very often means individual men . . . and individual men cannot be graded or classified according to arts or science or technology.'[1] Furthermore if guild unity restricts market forces so too, in a different way, does the formal differential by creating a vested interest irrespective of subsequent changes in market conditions.

What happens in practice, what gives substance to university autonomy and at the same time permits some adjustment to the play of the market on a heterogeneous profession, is that universities take advantage of the flexibility of the scales for non-professorial grades and the provision for a range of professorial stipends. Some latitude is possible in the point of seniority at which appointments are made: promotion is possible from grade to grade within the limits of the ratio laid down of senior to junior non-professorial posts; acceleration of salary increase is possible within grades by 'merit increments' and the professorial 'spread' is used in part to reward and retain brilliant individuals and also shield the universities against outside competition.

The result is that faculty differentials exist in practice but in a form which is both flexible and consistent with the unity principle. The extent of these differences in 1966–67 is shown in Table 9.4. The figures exclude Oxford and Cambridge. Because of the formal differential and higher proportions of senior staff, salaries were higher in medical than in non-medical faculties. Median salaries among

[1] National Incomes Commission, *op. cit.*, p. 42, para. 128.

TABLE 9.4

Average (median) salaries of university teachers: by age and subject, G.B. (excluding Oxford and Cambridge), 1966–67

	Under 25	*25–29*	*30–34*	*35–39*	*40–44*	*45–49*	*50–54*	*Over 54*	*All age groups*
	£	£	£	£	£	£	£	£	£
Humanities	1,292	1,451	1,738	2,167	2,678	2,968	3,304	3,397	2,058
Education	1,500	1,602	1,875	2,255	2,525	2,552	2,604	2,964	2,513
Social studies	1,317	1,526	1,857	2,392	2,669	3,113	3,272	3,337	2,123
Pure science	1,308	1,542	1,924	2,473	3,006	3,253	3,317	3,369	2,191
Applied science	1,309	1,609	2,041	2,482	2,626	3,068	3,199	3,309	2,455
Agriculture	1,345	1,451	1,828	2,355	2,622	3,180	3,283	3,376	2,450
Clinical medicine and dentistry	1,339	1,974	2,298	2,629	3,510	4,047	4,112	4,615	2,794
Non-clinical medicine and dentistry	1,302	1,420	2,039	2,564	3,049	3,286	3,331	3,406	2,095
Total non-medical	1,341	1,518	1,903	2,411	2,728	3,100	3,262	3,344	2,277

Source: National Board for Prices and Incomes, Cmnd. 4334, p. 33.

clinical medical staff were between 15 and 30 per cent higher than the next highest group for all ages over 25. Salary differences among the non-medical faculties were relatively smaller, the main feature being that scientists and applied scientists and social scientists under fifty earned more than arts men. These differences presumably reflect the 'flexibility' of merit increments and early promotion to the senior ranks.

The P.I.B. analysed figures for 1966–67 in arriving at their 1968 recommendations. They showed the existence of informal differentials among the non-medical faculties but found them of no great importance. A graph of the subject groups which diverged most widely from the median salary of all university teachers, outside the medical faculties, is reproduced below (Graph 9.B). The medians are fairly close together at all ages. At no point do they diverge by much more than £500. But the picture of advantage among the younger scientists appears in more detail. Applied scientists tend to start higher but to lose their lead and fall slightly behind after their mid-thirties. A considerable part of the differences are in any case to be explained by differences in the age compositions of the different faculties. The physical, biological and social sciences have relatively lower proportions aged over forty, promotion prospects are thereby relatively good and the older staff in these subjects consequently rather better paid.

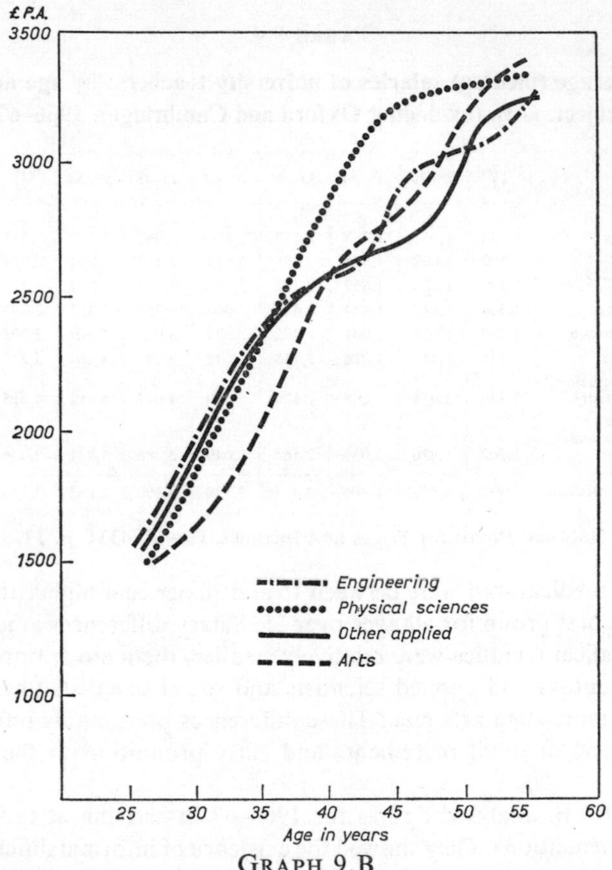

GRAPH 9.B

Median salaries of certain subject groups: by age, 1966–67

Moreover, age also largely explains the small informal differentials in the professoriate and between universities.[1]

Supplementary earnings

Apart from salary differences, supplementary earnings must also be taken into account. On the whole these tend to reflect opportunities for careers outside the universities and are to that extent a substitute for salary differentials. According to enquiries made in 1962–63 and in 1969 for the median man they do not amount to much because they

[1] National Board for Prices and Incomes, *First Report*, pp. 39–41 and *Second Report* pp. 22–24.

TABLE 9.5

Average total supplementary earnings of university teachers by grade and subject, 1968–69

All Universities

Subject	*Professors*		*Readers and sen. lecturers*		*Lecturers*		*Others*		*Total*		
	Median	*Mean*	*Median*	*Mean*	*Median*	*Mean*	*Median*	*Mean*	*Median*	*Mean*	
	£	£	£	£	£	£	£	£	£	£	£
Humanities	367	498	173	287	142	325	50	(220)	13	339	(448)
Education	514	(569)	189	(310)	114	351	25	(148)	138	347	(100)
Social studies	752	1,195	222	412	140	357	135	(275)	133	450	(439)
Pure science	370	653	143	379	65	191	17	87	97	255	(784)
Applied science	532	983	180	332	75	224	57	(89)	100	311	(433)
Agriculture	307	(373)	175	(552)	54	179	0	(15)	72	249	(93)
Total (excluding medicine)	455	772	170	362	96	265	36	131	119	324	(2,297)
Medicine	323	441	121	195	77	166	0	(8)	54	203	(370)
Total (including medicine)	..	..	..	..	..	..	..	..	107	306	(2,667)

Note: '..' means 'not available'. *Source:* Higher Education Research Unit, November 1969 Survey Preliminary Results

are only high for a small minority. The chief beneficiaries are the applied scientists and the social scientists as may be seen from Table 9.5 which is taken from the P.I.B. (1970) Report and was provided by the Higher Education Research Unit at the London School of Economics.

TABLE 9.6

Total income by age and university type, 1968–69

All subjects excluding medicine

Age	*London*		*Oxford and Cambridge*		*Other*	
	Median	*Arith-metic mean*	*Median*	*Arith-metic mean*	*Median*	*Arith-metic mean*
	£	£	£	£	£	£
24 or less	1,274	(1,328)	1,250	(1,410)	1,314	1,391
25–29	1,537	1,547	1,543	(1,672)	1,524	1,573
30–34	2,182	2,150	2,833	(3,243)	2,226	2,168
35–39	2,878	3,305	3,241	(3,868)	2,710	2,882
40–44	3,568	3,661	3,500	(4,349)	3,143	3,277
45–49	3,963	4,108	3,750	(4,196)	3,622	3,649
50–54	4,658	(4,536)	4,377	(4,416)	3,513	3,621
55+	4,182	(4,380)	4,654	(4,746)	3,784	4,016
Not known	2,254	(2,075)	2,980	(4,819)	2,833	(2,864)
Total	2,667	2,961 (334)	3,304	3,556 (170)	2,529	2,663 (1,794)

Source: Higher Education Research Unit, November 1969 Survey Preliminary Results. P.I.B. Report (1970), p. 46.

Nevertheless supplementary earnings must remain a problem given the circumstances of academic employment which have to permit the possibility of entrepreneurial activity in order to safeguard the pre-conditions of intellectual enquiry. A fine balance has to be drawn and complete codification is impossible. Moreover the opportunities for lucrative extra-mural earnings tend to increase more for the applied sciences and the social studies which are growing faster inside the universities than are other disciplines. Consequently extra-mural earnings in part serve the function of protecting the universities from their competitors for the services of these men in industry and the mass media. In practice the universities have some formal requirements concerning the reporting of outside earnings: but the main sanction is moral consensus about what is owed to the institution and to the academic calling.

University differences

Small differences in supplementary earnings also favour Oxford and Cambridge and to a lesser extent London as against the Scottish, Welsh and English provincial universities. The overall picture of total earnings is shown in Table 9.6. Average income in Oxford and Cambridge in 1968–69 was £3,556, in London £2,961 and elsewhere £2,663.

The Oxford differential

To complete the picture of variation we must look more closely at Oxford and Cambridge. Both the N.I.C. survey in 1962–63 and the H.E.R.U. survey showed that Oxford and Cambridge dons earned more in the way of supplementary earnings than did their colleagues elsewhere. But this is neither the whole nor the beginning of the story. A minor controversy was generated by the following remarks of the Robbins Committee in 1963: 'Since the Oxford and Cambridge colleges do not make detailed returns of their outlays, it is extraordinarily difficult to estimate the emoluments of college fellows and teachers, and we have not conceived it to be our business to make a special inquiry into the matter. But the evidence in Appendix Three suggests that there is substance in the assertion that in one, at any rate, of these universities teachers of a given seniority receive higher emoluments than their colleagues elsewhere and that there is also a higher proportion of senior posts. We believe any such disparity between the incomes and prospects of persons doing similar work in different universities, which are all in receipt of public funds, to be unjust; and we consider its effects to be harmful. By adding financial attraction to the already great attractiveness of Oxford and Cambridge it leads to too great a concentration of talent there and it militates against desirable movement between universities.'[1]

The Robbins Committee was aware that the National Incomes Commission was considering the university salaries and left the problem with the remark that 'if it is established that there are serious anomalies, these should be removed.' The N.I.C. refused to be drawn into the larger issues but formed some conclusions from its own inquiries. As far as full-time university teachers at the universities of

[1] *Higher Education,* para. 542. These remarks may be contrasted with the quoted opinion of the U.G.C. in 1930.

Oxford and Cambridge were concerned, the N.I.C. took the view that, taking account of the difference in staff structure which distinguishes a collegiate university from the unitary structure of other universities, neither at Oxford nor at Cambridge could the rates of salary be regarded as anything but a reasonable adaptation of the approved rates. On the other hand the question of college emoluments baffled them. Earnings at Oxford and Cambridge among college men are inextricably bound up with teaching methods and the Commission had insufficient evidence on which to base any recommendations. They believed 'that it is for each university authority to control and to set such limits as it thinks fit to external activities to prevent these activities from encroaching on academic duties. We think that the same principles should be applied by the universities of Oxford and Cambridge in relation to work done for colleges by the holders of university appointments.'[1]

The representatives of both Oxford and Cambridge assured the N.I.C. that college teaching is done without any reduction in the work which the teacher is required to do in respect of his university office; that those who do it carry a heavier load than those who do not; that sometimes it is undertaken at the sacrifice of alternatives personally more advantageous and that the remuneration for it is always paid on the footing that the work and duties involved are external to the demands of a full-time university appointment. Spokesmen for the A.U.T. agreed that there is often an overtime element in Oxford and Cambridge tutorial work which ought to be recognised by extra pay. But they added 'that there was a certain amount of "mythology" attached to the matter; that if extra payment were not made for college supervision the work would get done in the same way as it gets done in other universities, namely as part of the job; and that if lecture and supervision loads were added to tutorial loads the differences between Oxford and Cambridge and other universities were perhaps rather less striking than had been suggested.'[2]

The discussion was taken further by the Franks Commission which collected full information on salaries and earnings of Oxford dons[3] in 1964–65. The Commission calculated that the average salary in Oxford (including both university and college stipends) was about

[1] National Incomes Commission, *op. cit.*, p. 87, para. 262.
[2] *Ibid.*, p. 89, para. 265.
[3] Full details are in the *Oxford University Gazette*, Vol. XCV, p. 1077, and in the *Report of Commission of Inquiry*, Vol. II, Tables 334–51.

15 per cent above the national average[1] but allowing for the fact that Oxford dons are, on average, considerably older than their colleagues elsewhere,[2] recalculation gave an Oxford advantage of only 4 per cent over the national average. This, the Commission thought, was too low. They then went on to consider the other emoluments which are a frequent target of criticism, especially since the publication of the Robbins Report, including payments for tutorial work in the colleges and supervision of graduate students in the university. All of the latter and that part of the former which involves teaching members of other colleges is paid at piece-rates. Colleges also provide fellows with various fringe benefits such as housing allowances, private medicine through BUPA, meals and entertainment allowances. The total bill for these emoluments in 1964–65 was £360,000. Adding these extras the Oxford average salary was 18 per cent above the national figure. No doubt some equivalent payments were made elsewhere, but the Commission concluded that the Oxford advantage was nearer to the upper (18 per cent) than to the lower (4 per cent) limit. The Franks Commission proposed the abolition of piece-rate teaching and the reduction and rationalisation of fringe benefits. At the same time, however, they recommended, presumably to the U.G.C., that Oxford salaries, age for age, should be 10 per cent higher than the average for all British universities. This figure of 10 per cent is arbitrary–a guess by the Commissioners as to what was likely to be politically viable. Some, following the mood of the authors of the Robbins Report, reject the claim as an affront to the principle of guild unity which would proscribe unequal pay for equal work. Lord Franks and his colleagues justify their proposal on the grounds of Oxford's status as an international university of the first rank. Others for both this reason and because of the higher qualifications, longer hours and higher quality of Oxford teaching argue that the differential represents unequal pay for unequal work. The fate of the Franks proposals is not yet completely settled (1970). Meanwhile the Oxford and Cambridge differential remains shrouded

[1] Clinical medical staff are left out of this calculation.

[2] This is partly because other universities are expanding and appointing younger people but also because of the different staff structure. The college fellow in arts, usually with a part-time university lectureship, has no equivalent elsewhere except at Cambridge. His post is not equivalent to a lectureship but is thought of as a permanent career of sufficient attractiveness, at least in some colleges, to retain some highly distinguished scholars. College dons often leave to take chairs in the modern universities. But it is not uncommon for the reverse to take place.

in the complications and partial obscurity of their collegiate organisation. Perhaps it could not continue in any other form; it is difficult to imagine a visible and rationalised differential agreed by the other universities on the grounds of the superior quality of Oxford and Cambridge staff. And perhaps it is unnecessary. There is evidence that recruitment to the ancient foundations depends more on their other attractions and would not be greatly affected by salary equalisation.

Promotion

The differentials are small enough to validate the view that guild unity has fairly successfully contained the pressures in an expanding system towards permitting the play of market forces to distinguish institutions and subject groups as they do in the United States. The question, therefore, arises of how flexibility between individuals is secured in the academic career. The answer lies in the freedom of universities to offer promotion and of individuals to move from one institution to another.

As we have seen, the proportion of senior to junior posts is limited to 35 per cent, apart from medical staff, at any particular university. The actual percentage for all staff in all universities in 1966–67 was 31 per cent, though in London it was slightly higher. What then are the promotion chances? The P.I.B. tried to answer this question and reported as follows:

> To estimate the chances of promotion we have made a detailed projection on the basis of the information about recruits and leavers in 1965–66 provided by the U.G.C. This shows that, given the same pattern of recruitment as in 1965–66, if no staff were promoted between 1966–67 and 1971–72 the proportion by age group of senior staff in 1971–72 in all universities would be approximately as follows:

	%
50 and over	65
40–9	35
30–9	3
Under 30	—
All	22

> Thus it should be possible to promote 9 per cent of staff to senior posts without raising the overall proportion of senior staff above the 1966–67 level. This will not, however, quite suffice to raise the proportion within each age group to the level of 1966–67. To do

this the overall proportion of senior staff would have to rise to about 33 per cent. The modest nature of this increase over 1966–67 suggests that retention of the existing senior staff ratio will not have a particularly dampening effect on prospects. It might in fact raise the average age of promotion by about one year between 1966 and 1972. We should perhaps add that the calculations refer to all staff; within particular universities, notably those with the slowest expansion rate, the situation may be worse. After 1971–72, the rate of promotion will be powerfully affected by Government decisions on the future pattern of higher education.[1]

This analysis treats the British university system as a unitary structure of opportunities. In fact internal promotion is more common, as judged by figures for the period 1957–61, in Oxford and Cambridge (75 per cent), London (72 per cent), and the Redbrick universities (69 per cent) than in Wales (63 per cent) or Scotland (59 per cent).[2] Promotion may, however, involve movement for the individual between institutions. In principle and nearly always in practice, appointments to vacant posts are made in open competition after national advertisement. This is especially so in the case of professorships and for initial appointments at the junior levels: it is less so for senior lectureships and readerships which are often awarded to existing members of the staff of a particular university for meritorious service. Thus the pattern of promotion for those appointed to new posts (other than initial posts) in 1960 and 1961 was that 59 per cent of the chairs and 60 per cent of the lectureships were filled from inside the university concerned compared with 74 per cent of readerships and 72 per cent of senior lectureships.[3]

Taking the evidence all together–an emerging national system of universities with a distinctive tradition and a standardised structure of career opportunities and rewards–there are consequences for the character of British academic life which may be contrasted with the typical conditions of university professors in the United States. In particular energetic and competitive research activity may be relatively subordinate to those norms of academic life which place

[1] National Board for Prices and Incomes, *op. cit.*, p. 43. There is a complication in the case of medical staff. The fixed ratio of senior staff does not apply to them and their rate of wastage is rather higher. They comprised 41 per cent of all staff in 1966–67 and the effect of their inclusion is to make overall promotion prospects appear slightly more favourable than would otherwise be the case. Even this, however, does not alter significantly the magnitude of the projected change in promotion prospects.

[2] *Higher Education*, Appendix Three, Table 49, p. 43.

[3] *Ibid.*, Table 47, p. 42.

heavy emphasis on teaching and devotion to students–activities which do not necessarily enhance professional reputations.

Perhaps the outstanding difficulty of such a system is to maintain a high level of creativity. Both internal promotion opportunities and competition between departments in different universities are muted. Expansion itself, of course, releases some of the pressure by creating new posts. This has been the opportunity for the new universities. But already there are signs that they too, where they have been successful in gathering together able groups of young people, will suffer from the constraining effects of a rigid structure of ranks and a rather inflexible salary scale. Recruitment tends to result in 'bunching' by age so that a talented group of young lecturers find themselves, after perhaps four or five years, in intense competition for a limited number of senior posts. It is, as we have seen, possible for the university to vary the ratio of senior to junior posts within the university but such variation tends in practice to be blocked by the internal distribution of power between faculties. The rising young man therefore may face the dilemma of choosing between personal promotion elsewhere into a department of lesser intellectual standing as against remaining in a preferred academic milieu with lower status and lower rank. There is in other words a tendency in the British system for small centres of excellence to have only a temporary character and to be vulnerable either to dispersion through individual promotion or to the pull from Oxford, Cambridge and London with their general attractiveness at the top of the pyramid of institutional prestige. This pyramid–a hierarchy of status and styles of academic life–must now be the focus of our attention.

Chapter 10

STATUS AND STYLE OF LIFE

> The life of a well-established, middle-aged professor in the Arts faculty of a modern university can, if he likes to make it so, be one of the softest jobs to be found on the earth's surface. He may live ten, twenty, or sometimes even fifty miles from his work, and come in for only two or three days a week; he may have a cottage in the country and run down to it at irregular intervals for two or three days at a stretch; or he may even have his house and family at the distant seaside, go home on Friday afternoons for long weekends, return on Tuesday evenings, and spend the rest of the week between bachelor flat, lodgings, or club and the University.
>
> BRUCE TRUSCOT (1951)

> As professorships in so small a country are not numerous, the inducement to enter academic life is not powerful. But there is fortunately an academic way of life – simple, dignified, unworldly, so that, especially in the professorial grade, the amenities of life are not lacking and reliance on industry for additional income is distinctly 'bad form' – and, in consequence, very unusual.
>
> ABRAHAM FLEXNER (1930)

Writing by sociologists about social stratification is so voluminous that laymen may be forgiven for thinking sometimes that sociology is about nothing else. Yet a direct discussion of the status of the university teacher is necessary to illustrate an important aspect of our general thesis that the self-conception of academic men is predominantly gentlemanly in tradition and is changing, in Britain with more reluctance than rapidity, under modern conditions.

With the aid of a sociologically commonplace distinction between class and status we have examined various aspects of class including incomes, hours of work, terms of employment, and career opportunities. We saw in the last chapter that the typical life earnings of university teachers in Britain, in a context of diminishing differentials between professional and manual incomes, remains securely on the comfortable side of middle-class privilege. But neither class nor status is completely described or solely determined by income. The material conditions of the university teacher have to be interpreted in a context of historical development from varied and tenuously related local determination to an emerging national quasi-bureaucracy strongly influenced by conceptions of guild unity and of 'fair comparison' with other professions, especially the higher classes of the Civil Service. Another approach to all this is to be found in the various elements of status; and this is our purpose in the present chapter.

Status, as Max Weber distinguished it, refers to 'every typical component of the life fate of men that is determined by a specific, positive, or negative, social estimation of *honour* . . . Status honour is normally expressed by the fact that above all else a specific *style of life* can be expected from all those who wish to belong to the circle.'[1] Thus in describing the status of the university teacher we must first try to identify his general prestige as expressed by the typical degree of deference or respect accorded to academics by laymen: and, second, we must describe the content of the particular style of life which is expected of those who belong to the academic community. Neither task is simple. The 'social honour' or prestige of academic life has changed with the expanded functions of universities since the second half of the nineteenth century; like academic income, it may have undergone relative decline and has certainly become more differentiated. Expansion and specialisation have produced internal status divisions within the academic style of life. In England especially there is a characteristic tension between the gentlemanly style with its centre in the traditional idealised pattern of life of the Oxford arts don and the newer professional style with technocratic and 'classless' overtones which are associated with applied science and Redbrick.

Nor do the difficulties end here. Though Weber distinguished between class and status fundamentally on the basis of economic interest as opposed to social honour, the distinction is in fact ambiguous. Although status often takes the form of a claim against market determination of life chances, there is always some transferability of status into market claims, as well as the more obvious long-run dependence of status on successful maintenance of market opportunities. This is especially so in a modern industrial society in which occupational roles are at once the basis for economic interests and the major reference in social evaluation. Certainly life chances are determined by both status and class factors but the process is one

[1] H. Gerth and C. Wright Mills, *op. cit.*, p. 187. By contrast, Weber's definition of class is 'the typical chance for a supply of goods, external living conditions and personal life experiences in so far as this chance is determined by the amount and kind of power, or lack of such, to dispose of goods or skills for the sake of income in a given economic order' (p. 181).

of continuous interaction. The N.I.C. enquiry into academic salaries, or the revision made by its successor, the P.I.B., illustrates this interaction process–a complex compromise between prestige and market assessments of the value and price of intellectual labour.

Prestige

That the British university teacher enjoys high prestige can be deduced from the high value put upon occupational achievement in industrial countries with their characteristic tendency towards open competition for entry into a hierarchy of professions and trades arranged according to skill and tested by formal qualifications. The university, as Professor Talcott Parsons puts it, is now 'the keystone of the profession arch'. Underlying the prestige of intellectual disciplines is a generalised value of the cultural system of the modern world to which Parsons gives the label 'cognitive rationality'.[1]

Thus in occupational prestige scales based on popular surveys[2] the university teacher always appears alongside the major professions in the topmost group. But this is the crudest of truths. It does not identify the special quality of academic as against other professional prestige: it obscures the differences in relative prestige of British compared with, say, German or American academics; and it throws no light on the question of whether, as many fear, academic prestige has declined in this century. To answer such questions it is necessary to see how the prestige enjoyed by an occupational group in a particular country at a particular time reflects the class and status factors which have determined its composition, its functions, its autonomy and its remuneration.

[1] Talcott Parsons and Gerald M. Platt, *The American Academic Profession: A Pilot Study* (duplicated for private circulation), March 1968. See pp. 1–3. 'The American academic system has institutionalised a high level of primacy of one set of cultural values and interests, those in *cognitive rationality*. It is from the institutionalisation of this value that the resulting importance of systematic knowledge, for its own sake and for the practical benefits, has developed as the principal standard for evaluation and for orienting action in academia. Most immediately, this refers to a rather special branch of the culture we call the "intellectual disciplines". There has been a long and complex history of their differentiation from religion, the arts, and in certain respects other evaluative aspects of culture.'

[2] For example the British 'Hall-Jones' or the American N.O.R.C. scales which produce remarkably similar rankings in all industrial countries. See A. Inkeles and P. H. Rossi, 'National Comparisons of Occupational Prestige', *American Journal of Sociology*, 61 (1956), pp. 329–39. Also R. W. Hodge, D. J. Treiman and P. H. Rossi, 'A Comparative Study of Occupational Prestige', in Bendix and Lipset, *op. cit.* (1966).

Three particular aspects of academic status may be noted which give it a different quality from that of the other professions. First, the academic represents most directly the central criterion of achievement on which occupational prestige is based. Occupational selection in modern society takes place for the most part through educational selection and university teachers are not only themselves selected from those with the highest educational attainments but are also the custodians of the selection process itself. Moreover, as the link between education and occupation tightens in modern society, as education expands and qualifications to enter an increasingly wide range of employment are formalised, so the teacher generally and the university teacher especially becomes a more significant figure in the evaluations made by individuals of their own worth. In this sense, therefore, the prestige of the university teacher tends to be strengthened by his increasing role in determining the life chances of others.

This coin however has its other side. The custodian is necessarily set apart from the 'real' participants. The university teacher is a rather ambiguous figure–one who could have entered the competition for outstanding success in the professions or in industry but has not actually done so. He tends to be seen, as all teachers are seen, as sheltered from the rigours of the real world, as a 'theoretical' rather than a practical man, as in some way not a serious man. He is to ordinary men also a vaguely threatening figure, a reproach to the educational failures and intellectual shortcomings of their own youth; one who may be a source of embarrassment because of his knowledge yet one who at the same time has never been put to the harsh test of 'doing a real job'.

On the other hand the separation from practising professions which modifies academic prestige must be distinguished from the tradition of 'apart-ness' which is part of the history of the scholar. In the modern world as knowledge is secular rather than sacred, intellectual institutions open rather than closed, the university teacher has lost his affinity with the priest and become more involved with the world of practical actions. This development has profound implications for the style of life of the university teacher in recent times as well as for his role as a teacher and scholar.[1] His assimilation

[1] The trends are expressed by A. N. L. Munby as follows:

Remote and ineffectual Don,
Where have you gone, where have you gone?

to the life patterns of professional people in industry and public service has proceeded *pari passu* with the erosion of clearly demarcated functions between universities, government departments, industrial research bodies and other organisations in which intellectual or professional activity is pursued. The significant consequence of these two different trends in the development of the academic role is the differing social prestige of research as opposed to teaching, and of subjects having a visible utility or relevance to the practical spheres of technology, politics, war or industry as opposed to those subjects which are pursued 'for their own sake'.

It is obvious that in the twentieth century the boundaries of academic and non-academic life have faded, not only through the connection with the liberal professions, for which the universities have traditionally offered a preparation, but also through the involvement of academics in the machinery of government, and above all through the vast expansion of research activity having practical applications in industry, administration or government. Broadly this has raised the prestige of the scientist and the research man whose functions are rewarded not only as an expression of the fundamental values of the academic community but also in society generally. This is partly a matter of market opportunities and access to power, and in

---

Don in scarlet, Don in tails,
Don advertising Daily Mails,
Don in Office, Don in power,
Don talking on the Woman's Hour,
Don knocking up a constitution,
Don with ideas on prostitution,
Don who is permanently plussed,
Don floating an Investment Trust,
Don judging jive at barbecue,
Don dressing down the E.T.U.,
Don architecturally brash,
Don not afraid to have a bash,
Don with Bentley, Don with Rolls,
Don organising Gallup Polls,
Don back from Russia, off to Rome,
Don on the Third, the Light, the Home,
Don recently ennobled Peer,
Don Minister, Don Brigadier,
Don brassy, Don belligerent,
Don tipping off for ten per cent,
Don christian-naming with the Stars,
Don talking loud in public bars,
Remote and ineffectual Don,
Where have you gone, where have you gone?

Thoughts on re-reading Belloc's famous lines on Dons. A. N. L. Munby, quoted in Rose and Ziman, *op. cit.*, p. 216.

this way status is reinforced by the other two main elements of the complex stratification systems of an advanced industrial society.

In the case of academics this pattern partially integrates the status of individuals within the academic community with their more general status in society. Nevertheless, it is only a partial integration in that status discrepancies may arise between a man's internal and external role. This is further complicated by the existence of prestige markets other than those connected directly with excellence in research–for example, popularity or notoriety as an expositor in the mass media. Professor C. E. M. Joad would perhaps be the archetypal case here. In Oxford and Cambridge especially there is something paradoxical in that participation in the 'entertainment' industry is numerically concentrated among the dons at these universities[1] and at the same time is almost defined as a demonstration of academic inferiority within the same universities. Nevertheless, connection with these sources of economic gain or popular prestige outside the universities remains an important differentiating element between university teachers.

The third aspect of academic prestige is its connection with aristocratic and élite status. This has special significance in Britain because of the unique place held historically by Oxford and Cambridge in the education of the British upper classes and the career connections of Oxford and Cambridge men with the centres of power in Whitehall, the Church, the Courts and the boardrooms of major industrial concerns. The British university teacher everywhere carries with him something of the dignity of the gentleman, but again this is also a differentiating factor–in this case especially as between Oxford and Cambridge dons and the academic staff of the modern universities. This distinctive element in the prestige of British academics with its divisive and hierarchical effects within the university system is reinforced in the daily experience of newspaper readers, in the model of educational achievement held up to ambitious schoolboys, in novels about university life, among which those by C. P. Snow are only the most recent of a long-standing genre,[2] and in the biographies and memoirs of eminent persons.[3] The 'magic' of Oxford and

[1] This is reflected in higher supplementary earnings. See above, pp. 195–8.

[2] See Mortimer R. Proctor, *The English University Novel*, University of California Press, Berkeley and Los Angeles, 1957.

[3] Two recently published examples are: John Sparrow, *Mark Pattison and the Idea of a University*, Cambridge University Press, 1967; C. M. Bowra, *Memories 1898–1939*, Weidenfeld and Nicolson, 1966.

Cambridge is an essential part of the status symbolism of British élites.

American academic visitors commonly remark on the relatively higher prestige of university teachers in European countries compared with their own. The legendary respect accorded to the professor in pre-Nazi Germany was only the extreme example of a generally invidious comparison of academic status in the old and the new world. Oxford and Cambridge have long been the symbol of the most desirable social position for academic men. Abraham Flexner, writing in 1930, offers an eloquent expression of this view: 'I as an American profoundly envy them. Only the foreigner who has grown up in the glare and newness of a new world, be it America or Australia, can do full justice to the charm and educative value of the quiet quadrangles, the college libraries, the Bodleian rich in treasures and associations, the fellows' gardens–the strange intermingling of democracy and traditions, of asceticism and dignified luxury. No American or German institution of any kind enjoys, as do Oxford and Cambridge, the inestimable advantage of possessing ample means of associating in worthy scholarly fashion with men of learning and distinction–not only an amenity but a source of profound spiritual stimulus. However modest the means of the Oxford or Cambridge scholar, he can without effort or sacrifice be host to a Minister of State, a great scientist or philosopher.'[1]

These three aspects of academic status and style of life–its competitive achievement, its assimilation to non-academic professionalism and its connection with the leisurely dignity of aristocracy–are changing with the expansion of higher education. We must therefore explore the extent to which recent developments have encouraged different ways of life among the different faculties and at different levels in the hierarchy of institutions and academic ranks.

Academics as achievers

The university teacher is and is seen as a clever man. He is not only a graduate, but typically one with good-class honours and a higher degree. Moreover, if he had wanted more money or more technical or secretarial assistance he might well have been able to find them in business or medicine or the Civil Service or America. The survey of

[1] Abraham Flexner, *Universities: American, English, German*, New York, Oxford University Press, 1930, p. 288.

university teachers conducted by the Robbins Committee in the spring of 1962[1] showed that 81 per cent of the graduate university teachers held an honours degree from a British University; 16 per cent had pass or ordinary degrees, but more than half of these were in medical subjects, where honours are not usually awarded except as a mark of distinction. Higher degrees had also been taken by 60 per cent; 40 per cent having doctoral and 13 per cent masters' degrees.

But it is a serious question how far this high scholarly calibre can be maintained in the expanded system of higher education which is now developing, and dilution would have implications for many aspects of the academic role, apart from its status. At first glance the recent trends revealed in the 1962 survey of the universities as then constituted were alarming. Of honours graduates recruited between 1959 and 1961, 52 per cent had taken first class degrees compared with 61 per cent of the recruits in earlier years. The authors of the Robbins study offered two reassurances on these statistics–that wastage is heavy among young recruits and perhaps those who are least able are squeezed out, and that degree standards may have risen since before the war. It could be added that the Robbins Committee, along with others inside and outside the universities, make the dubious assumption that the first class degree is a perfect indicator of ability in teaching and research. Clearly this is not so. Some with high seconds, or even lesser degrees show themselves subsequently to be more productive academically than some with the highest honours.[2]

Nevertheless more recent statistics of this indicator of quality do not reinforce the earlier re-assurances. It is clear from Table 10.1 that recent recruits have relatively fewer among them who have first class degrees compared with all university teachers holding honours degrees in 1961–62.[3] Moreover, in the arts subjects, the biological sciences, engineering, technology and pre-clinical medicine they are less well qualified in this respect than those leaving in the same year.[4] On the other hand there is no serious evidence of deterioration on the criterion of the percentage holding higher degrees. The differences

[1] *Higher Education*, Appendix Three, p. 19.

[2] See L. Hudson, 'Degree Class and Attainment in Scientific Research', *British Journal of Psychology*, 1960.

[3] It should be noted, however, that 25 per cent of university teachers in 1961–62 did not hold honours degrees and this proportion may since have declined.

[4] It should be borne in mind that these figures (supplied by the U.G.C. to the P.I.B.) include only about half of the total number of recruits in 1965–66. If the excluded recruits were included the deterioration in quality might be reduced but would not be removed.

TABLE 10.1

Quality of university teachers: recruits and leavers, 1965–66, compared with all staff in 1961–62

	Percentage of those with honours degree with first class			*Percentage with higher degree*		
	1965–66		1961–62	1965–66		1961–62
	Recruits	*Leavers*	*All staff*	*Recruits*	*Leavers*	*All staff*
Arts	44	58	68	48	56	48
Social studies	32	31	47	38	39	44
Phys. science	57	46	63	80	69	79
Biol. science	30	48		84	86	
Engineering	45	55	56	48	44	62
Other technology	25	28		59	73	
Preclinical	24	33	39	39	38	57
Clinical	24	14		25	37	
TOTALS	(846)	(398)		(1,307)	(672)	

Source: National Board for Prices and Incomes, *op. cit.*, p. 46, Table 9. Note that the discrepant totals are accounted for by 461 recruits and 274 leavers without honours or with overseas degrees. (About half of these are medical.)

between those recruited in 1965–66 and all university staff in 1961–62 are small, and indeed the newly recruited scientists had proportionately more higher degrees. Moreover, it is reasonable to suppose that 1965–66 recruits are more likely to obtain higher degrees in post than the general body of university teachers who are, of course, older people.

Another way of looking at the problem is to note that those appointed in 1959–61 accounted for 22 per cent of home graduates with firsts or upper seconds. On the Robbins expansion plan this proportion had to rise to 34 per cent.

Admittedly later in the sixties the proportionate demand of this 'ploughing back' of highly talented people into the education system slackened and the demands of colleges and universities for a share in their own total output of graduates will not, in the long run, rise. However, two important qualifications to this forecast have to be made in the light of more recent events and discussion. First, the calculation by the Robbins Committee of the probable future demand for university teachers was based on a percentage of all graduates three years before the demand arose, and also on an estimate of the probable future number of students qualified for university entrance which was deliberately determined on minimum assumptions at the time and which now has to be revised upwards by perhaps 20 per cent.[1] But if the second qualification is ignored and the figures are taken as they stand but re-stated, as the A.U.T. insists, as a proportion of the top quarter of all graduates, it then appears that even on a minimum estimate for the period 1967–72, during which university expansion has been held back, it will be necessary to recruit into the universities 15 to 20 per cent of the top graduates of each year.

The revised plans for university expansion in the period up to 1980 must also be borne in mind together with the increasing competition for its services of high-honours graduates from other expanding elements of the profession. The statistical evidence of declining quality during its most recent period of expansion is not absolutely conclusive: but the possibility or even probability is clearly there.

The question then arises, which is very important for academic prestige, of how quality is distributed institutionally in the expanded system of higher education. Perhaps the most dramatic findings in Appendix Three of the Robbins Report were those relating to the difference in the quality of staff between the institutions already in existence. Some of them are put together in Table 10.2. The differences between university teachers and the staff of other institutions are not surprising. But the evidence of a steep descent in average quality within the university system from Oxford down through London and the Redbricks to the CATs is more impressive than might have been anticipated.[2] It certainly would not have been predicted from the accepted traditions of national salary scales, equal treatment from the U.G.C. and open competition for jobs nationally advertised. Moreover, it seems clear that past expansion had already had the effect of increasing the range in quality. The outstanding exceptions to the evidence that the quality of recent recruits had declined were Oxford and Cambridge, where the proportion of graduate

[1] On these two points see Association of University Teachers, *Memorandum on Salaries in Universities*, submitted to the National Board for Prices and Incomes, 1967, p. 3, and Committee of Vice-Chancellors and Principals, Quinquennial Memorandum to the Secretary of State for Education and Science, 24 February 1967. Also see the summary of recent statistics in *New Society*, 18 May 1967, p. 729.

[2] The award of academic honours is also given (i.e. Fellowships of the Royal Society and the British Academy) but it is not thereby suggested that class of first degree is the sole determinant of academic recognition.

TABLE 10.2

Quality of teaching staff at various institutions of higher education, 1961–62 (per cent)

	Oxford and Cambridge	*London*	*Redbrick*	*CAT*	*Teacher-training colleges*
(a) Proportion of all full-time teachers who are graduates	—	100–95	—	81	58
(b) Proportion of (a) with 1st class honours	76	54	52–59	33	17
(c) Proportion of relevant staff who are Fellows of the Royal Society	11·6	3·7	1·8	—	—
(d) Proportion of relevant staff who are Fellows of the British Academy	8·9	3·5	0·2	—	—
(e) Proportion of staff with senior posts	40+*	40	27–23	—	—
(f) Percentage contribution of this group's graduates to teaching staff of other groups	23·7	14·2	10·7	Not applicable	

Source: Higher Education, Appendix Three.

* Senior posts include professorships, readerships and senior lectureships. It seems reasonable to regard Oxford and Cambridge staff with both university posts and college fellowships as at least the equivalent of senior lectureships elsewhere. On this basis the proportion of senior posts is at Cambridge 45 per cent and at Oxford 55 per cent.

newcomers with firsts actually rose from 76 per cent to 78 per cent for the period 1959 to 1961 compared with earlier years while the national proportion fell from 61 per cent to 52 per cent.[1]

Robbins' conception of future development widened the definition of university institutions but continued to acknowledge the distinction between university and other forms of higher education. The plan envisaged a wide field of higher education in which 'there is a need for a variety of institutions whose functions differ.'[2] Institutions with the same functions were to have the same titles, but again even within the same category, differences of eminence were likely to emerge from competition. 'Where famous intellectual exploits take place, there should develop some concentration of staff and students

[1] *Higher Education*, Appendix Three, Table 19. [2] *Ibid.*, p. 8.

especially interested in the subjects concerned. Moreover such concentrations are not only probable but also desirable. What is important is that what differences there are should rest clearly on differences of function on the one hand, and on acknowledged excellence in the discharge of functions on the other. There should be no freezing of institutions into established hierarchies.'[1]

All this was most encouraging. It evoked the image of sturdy struggle for places in an informal league table of the kind that has always given life and promise to the American colleges. It resuscitated the hopes for escape from provincial nonentity for which the Victorian foundations temporarily and unsuccessfully fought at the turn of the century.[2] But would it work?

Clearly competitive advantages were most unequally divided between, say, Churchill College, Cambridge, and the Birmingham CAT, and something more than the granting of university status to the latter institution as the University of Aston would be required to redress the balance. The Robbins Committee looked for especially generous capital grants from the state to new and expanding institutions. Nevertheless their advocacy of a competitive system fell far short of American practice. For example, they interpreted the evidence of the A.U.T. survey reported in Appendix III to mean that Oxford and Cambridge dons were paid more than people in comparable posts elsewhere which they thought 'unjust', and led 'to too great a concentration of talent there.'[3]

This must mean that they regarded their earlier principle of competition for excellence as subordinate to the principle of equal pay for equal work.[4] But, supposing the equality principle is being violated at Oxford, it must also be noted that the same principle would restrict a new foundation from using financial inducements to build up a strong team in a particular branch of learning by the market methods which are taken for granted between American universities. Indeed it is difficult to see how equality principles in relation to staff salaries can do anything but protect the competitive advantages of Oxford and Cambridge. Similarly the widening of

[1] *Ibid.*, p. 9.

[2] Cf. the discussion of 'The Popularity of Oxford and Cambridge' in *Universities Quarterly*, September 1961.

[3] *Higher Education*, p. 178. See also our discussion in the previous chapter.

[4] The principle of equal pay for equal work was avoided by the medical fraternity. No possible interpretation of the evidence in Appendix Three could attribute the medical differentials to merit. Yet oddly enough the Committee let this go unremarked.

contacts between the two universities and state schools advocated elsewhere in the Report, and especially the entry of the former into the national clearing house scheme which subsequently took place will tend to raise the quality of their undergraduates and hence their attractiveness to the most able university teachers.

The conclusion seems to be inescapable that competition for excellence in the wider system of higher education proposed by the Robbins Committee can take place only within strata of the stable pyramid of institutions which has already emerged in Britain. The career patterns of university teachers and the distribution of quality may be expected to reflect this hierarchical structure. Some see this as a desirable result–a spur to individual competition and a recognition of different educational functions within the university system. Others seek ways to realise the declared aims of the Report–equality and fluidity. The hierarchy might be flattened by great generosity in salary scales, senior posts and capital grants to Redbrick coupled with drastic meanness to Oxford and Cambridge. The Robbins proposals pointed very mildly in this direction. Alternatively mobility could be maximised by the development of an academic market place of the American type. The current search for staff tends to move in this direction within the constraints of the national salary scales and 'U.G.C. rules'. But neither tendency seems sufficiently strong to move the system from its half-way house of a stable institutional hierarchy, and the prestige of academic posts is increasingly and accordingly graded.

The Oxford and Cambridge connection

The connection with aristocratic and élite circles, institutionally associated with Oxford and Cambridge, seems to be a very important element in their high status and prestige. Writing just before the second war, Bruce Truscott (in reality a professor of languages in the University of Liverpool) wrote wryly as follows:

> For to Oxbridge all the best people eventually gravitate, whereas to Redbrick no-one, if he can help it, ever comes at all. . . . If a learned society is looking for persons on whom to bestow one of its coveted fellowships, it may perfectly well ignore Redbrick altogether, but it will certainly begin by asking: 'Well, now, first of all, who is there at Oxford and Cambridge?' A Cabinet Minister may need an educationist for a Royal Commission; a foreign statesman may want to recommend some English scholar for a

decoration; an Eastern potentate may be seeking a temporary home for his son. Each of these, except for some rare and particular reason, will look first to Oxbridge and as likely as not there will be no need to look farther.[1]

In the same vein, in 1955, Edward Shils referred to 'the Oxford–Cambridge–London axis' to denote an inner circle of prestigious connections between the ancient universities and higher officialdom in London. His article merits extended quotation.

The movement towards London in the twenties and thirties was not merely a demographic fact. It was associated with the assertion of the cultural supremacy of London society – and with it, of Oxford and Cambridge – over the provincial centres. The aristocratic-gentry culture has now come back into the saddle, and with little to dispute its dominion. The twenties and thirties which did it so much damage, did even more damage to the provincial bourgeois culture. The rebellion of the intellectuals was rather against bourgeois culture than against the aristocratic-gentry culture. The latter never abdicated. Some of its offspring might revolt against it, but they could not find anything to substitute for it except Bohemianism and an utterly spurious proletarianism, both completely unviable. Bourgeois culture on the other hand, as soon as it came freely into contact with aristocratic-gentry culture, lost its self-esteem and its spiritual autonomy. It could not win the youth, even those brought up in its own atmosphere. It seemed paltry and mean alongside aristocratic-gentry culture.

This is not relevant solely to the description of the class structure of contemporary Britain. It has the most significant consequences for the development of the British intellectuals because the change in the status and self-esteem of the classes was paralleled by changes in the status and self-esteem of the cultural institutions patronised by the classes. I shall illustrate with reference to the relations between the ancient and modern universities.

The modern British universities, which in scholarship and science take second place to none in the world, have – despite efforts of the University Grants Committee and many worthy men who have loved them – been belittled in their own eyes. They have never had a place in that image of the right life which has evolved from the aristocratic, squirearchal, and higher official culture. To those who accept this image, modern universities are facts but not realities. They would not deny that Manchester, Liverpool, Birmingham, and the other urban universities actually exist and yet they do not easily admit them to their minds. Oxford and Cambridge are thought of spontaneously when universities are mentioned. If a young man, talking to an educated stranger, refers to his university studies, he is asked 'Oxford or Cambridge?' And

[1] B. Truscott, *Redbrick University*, Penguin, 1951, p. 44.

if he says Aberystwyth or Nottingham, there is disappointment on the one side and embarrassment on the other. It has always been that way.

True, very many more persons are now factually aware of the modern universities than, say, thirty years ago. They have established themselves as bulwarks of research in science and scholarship, and without them Great Britain would be poorer in every respect. None the less, fundamentally, the situation has scarcely improved. It has perhaps become even worse. The deterioration is revealed in the diminution in self-esteem which these universities have undergone among their own staff, graduates and patrons.

The modern universities have by no means declined in relative intellectual stature. On the contrary, in some subjects the modern universities now take the lead. The differences in prestige, however, have probably been accentuated. There is less contentment now in being in a modern university than there used to be. It is becoming more difficult to get first-class younger men to leave Oxford and Cambridge – and London – for professorships in the provincial universities, however superior the traditions of the chair to be filled. It is more difficult to keep young men in the provinces; they are less contented with the prospect of a career in one of the great provincial universities, and look at them instead as jumping-off places, as places where they can keep alive and wait until something better comes along. They are moreover even quite open in disclosing their motives, as if that were and always had been quite the normal thing. And the writers of the present day who are setting out to show the humanity and vitality of provincial life – particularly Mr. William Cooper, Mr. Kingsley Amis, and Mr. John Wain – do not their heroes, on different levels of talent, find their appropriate salvation in Oxford and London? Does not Dr. C. P. Snow's chronicle of the world of Lewis Eliot move southward and reach its plateau in the professional class in London and Cambridge, where over sunlit polished tables on which stand old silver milk jugs, few appear to do any hard work and all live graciously and spaciously?[1]

Shils' characterisation of British intellectual and academic culture has remained broadly valid through the sixties and into the seventies, despite expansion of the professional classes, the rise of new academic institutions in both the metropolis and the provinces, and the vogue of radical and iconoclastic movements. University students challenge many things from the institutions of property to sexual mores, but there has been little serious attack on the institutional hierarchy of British universities.

From our own studies in the mid-sixties we can add three quan-

[1] *Encounter*, April 1955.

titative indications of the status differences between Oxford and Cambridge and the other British universities. First, university teachers at Oxford and Cambridge are marked off from the rest in being more likely to come from the professional, managerial and white-collar classes (Table 10.3). Second, as is shown in Table 10.4,

TABLE 10.3

Social origins of university teachers: by university group (per cent)

	University group						
Father's occupation	*Oxford and Cambridge*	*London*	*Scotland*	*Major Redbrick*	*Minor Redbrick*	*Wales*	*All*
I Professional	29	21	19	18	20	15	20
	}72	}68	}59	}56	}54	}53	
II Lower professional and white collar	43	47	40	38	34	38	40
III Skilled manual	23	26	34	34	37	38	32
IV and V Semi-skilled and unskilled manual	2	4	8	8	7	9	6
Others	4	3	0	2	2	0	2
TOTALS	(161)	(238)	(247)	(469)	(160)	(117)	(1,392)

Source: 1964 Survey.

TABLE 10.4

Educational origins of university teachers: by university group (per cent)

	Oxford and Cambridge	*London*	*Scotland*	*Major Redbrick*	*Minor Redbrick*	*Wales*	*All*
Public schools	45	25	18	15	17	17	21
Direct-grant schools	9	8	13	11	11	5	10
Grammar schools	29	49	53	63	59	72	55
Others	18	18	15	11	13	6	14
TOTALS	(161)	(233)	(245)	(467)	(160)	(118)	(1,384)

Source: 1964 Survey.

Oxford and Cambridge dons are more likely to have been educated in public schools; a majority of them come from the public and direct-grant schools compared with less than a third of university teachers in London, Scotland and the minor Redbricks and a quarter of those in the major Redbricks and Wales. Under a third of the Oxford and Cambridge dons have been educated at the maintained grammar schools whereas at other universities a clear majority are ex-grammar school boys. Our survey also showed that whereas 14 per cent of the Oxford and Cambridge staff have fathers who themselves had attended either Oxford or Cambridge the proportions are negligible in all the other university groups.

Third, and a more direct indicator of élite connections, the distribution of fellowships of the Royal Society and the British Academy (Tables 10.5 and 10.6) show that well over a third of the Fellows of the

TABLE 10.5

Fellows of the Royal Society, 1900–60: by university group (per cent)

University group	1900	1910	1920	1930	1940	1950	1960
Oxford and Cambridge	35·6	37·6	37	37	34	36	39
London	31·8	31·7	33	30	34	21	26
Civic	16	15·6	15	20	21	25	25
Scotland	14·6	13·6	14	11	9	11	8
Wales	2	1·5	1	2	2	2	2
TOTALS	(445)	(464)	(463)	(447)	(463)	(509)	(594)

Source: Year Books of the Royal Society.

Note: Physicians, Consulting Physicians etc. attached to hospitals associated with the University of London have been counted with London. Those who gave an Oxford or Cambridge college or departmental address, although no university post was specified, have been counted with Oxford and Cambridge. Those described as Fellows of Colleges or a University have been counted with that College or University only if no other position either in another university or elsewhere was specified. Honorary Professors and Professors Emeriti have been counted.

Royal Society in 1960 were at Oxford or Cambridge and that this high proportion has been stable throughout the century despite the very marked diminution in the proportion of all scientists who are employed in these two universities. In this connection it is worth remembering that, while the balance between humanities and pure science was much the same in each group of universities before the changes initiated by the Robbins Report the place of Oxford and

TABLE 10.6
Fellows of the British Academy, 1910–62: by university group (per cent)

University group	1910	1930	1961–62
Oxford and Cambridge	74	62	63
London	8	16	24
Civic	6	7	3
Scotland	12	11	7
Wales	0	4	2
TOTALS	(99)	(133)	(230)

Source: Proceedings of the British Academy and *Who's Who.*

Cambridge in numerical terms has declined throughout the century.[1] The pattern for fellowships of the British Academy is even more accentuated. Oxford and Cambridge held no less than 63 per cent of all such fellowships in 1961–62. However, over the course of the century there has been a tendency for London University to take an increased share in this particular group of honorific awards. Meanwhile, Scotland seems to have received a decreasing share of Royal Society and British Academy fellowships.

But Oxford and Cambridge influences are not confined within the walls of their colleges. A third of all British university teachers have at some time studied or taught in the two universities. It therefore seems worth while to examine differences between those with varying degrees of contact with Oxford and Cambridge at some point in their student or teaching career and those who have none. For this purpose we distinguish the following six groups.

I. Those who presently teach at Oxford or Cambridge and had also studied there as undergraduates (118 cases or 8 per cent of the sample).

II. Those presently teaching at Oxford or Cambridge who had not studied there as undergraduates (43 cases or 3 per cent of the sample).

III. Those who now teach elsewhere but who had both studied and taught at Oxford or Cambridge in the past (70 cases or 5 per cent of the sample).

[1] See above, Chapter 4. *Higher Education*, Appendix Two (A), Table 2, p. 18, shows that whereas Oxford and Cambridge had 22 per cent of the students in Great Britain in 1938–39, by 1963–64 they had only 14 per cent.

IV. Those teaching elsewhere who had studied at Oxford or Cambridge but never taught there (226 cases or 16 per cent of the sample).
V. Those teaching elsewhere who had not studied at Oxford or Cambridge but had taught there in the past (45 cases or 3 per cent of the sample).
VI. Those teaching elsewhere who had never had any contact with Oxford or Cambridge at any point in their student or teaching careers (891 cases or 63 per cent of the sample).

The class origins of these six categories are shown in Table 10.7.

TABLE 10.7

Class origins (father's occupation) of various groups of university teachers (per cent)

	Oxford and Cambridge teachers			*Non-Oxford and Cambridge teachers*								
Father's occupation	Studied at Oxford or Cambridge I		Did not study at Oxford or Cambridge II		Have studied and taught at Oxford or Cambridge III		Have studied, never taught at Oxford or Cambridge IV		Have taught, never studied at Oxford or Cambridge V		No contact with Oxford or Cambridge VI	
Professional	30	76	26	60	25	61	24	71	9	56	17	55
Intermediate	46		35		35		46		47		38	
Skilled	20		33		35		23		36		36	
Semi-skilled	1	1	5	5	3	3	3	3	4	8	7	9
Manual	0		0		0		0		4		2	
Forces	4		2		3		3		0		1	
TOTALS	(118)		(43)		(70)		(226)		(45)		(891)	

Source: 1964 Survey.

It can be seen that members of groups I and IV come more frequently from middle class backgrounds, nearly three-quarters of their fathers having held white-collar jobs. These are the two main groups of those who have studied at Oxford or Cambridge and this distribution is similar to that of many national studies showing that Oxford and Cambridge students come from a rather higher social background than students at other universities.

The secondary schools attended by the six groups are shown in Table 10.8. The proportion of grammar school boys rises in each

TABLE 10.8

Secondary schooling of various groups of university teachers (per cent)

	Oxford and Cambridge teachers		*Non-Oxford and Cambridge teachers*			
Secondary schooling	Studied at Oxford or Cambridge I	Did not study at Oxford or Cambridge II	Have studied and taught at Oxford or Cambridge III	Have studied, never taught at Oxford or Cambridge IV	Have taught, never studied at Oxford or Cambridge V	No contact with Oxford or Cambridge VI
Grammar	26	37	41	48	59	63
Direct-grant	8	9	13	16	2	9
Public	52	26	38	31	16	14
Other	13	28	9	5	23	14
None	1	0	0	0	0	1
TOTALS	(118)	(43)	(70)	(226)	(45)	(891)

Source: 1964 Survey.

group from I to VI. Similarly the proportion who attended public schools decreases from half of group I to one-seventh of group VI with the exception of those in group II (who did not study at Oxford or Cambridge but teach there now) of whom over a quarter attended other (mostly foreign) secondary schools.

In Table 10.9 we turn from secondary education, which is, of course, closely related to social origins, to class of degree. Here a rather different pattern emerges. The group with the highest proportion of firsts is group I–those who both took their undergraduate degrees and now teach at Oxford or Cambridge. Nearly three-quarters of them have firsts. Next come three other groups who have

TABLE 10.9

Class of degree of various groups of university teachers (per cent)

	Oxford and Cambridge teachers		*Non-Oxford and Cambridge teachers*			
Class of first degree	Studied at Oxford or Cambridge	Did not study at Oxford or Cambridge	Have studied and taught at Oxford or Cambridge	Have studied, never taught at Oxford or Cambridge	Have taught, never studied at Oxford or Cambridge	No contact with Oxford or Cambridge
	I	II	III	IV	V	VI
1st class honours	70	60	59	41	58	47
TOTALS	(118)	(43)	(70)	(226)	(45)	(891)

Source: 1964 Survey.

taught at Oxford or Cambridge at some time (groups II, III and V), each of which includes 58 per cent to 60 per cent who hold firsts. Those who have never had any contact with the two universities (group VI) come next, with almost half who have firsts. And the last group is those who began in Oxford or Cambridge as students but have never taught there (group IV): of these 41 per cent have firsts. Thus we again see that Oxford and Cambridge have considerable attractive power for the most able university teachers as measured by this criterion, and they are particularly successful in keeping their own best graduates. But the low proportion in group IV is also interesting: it suggests that graduates without a first class degree stand a slightly better chance of employment as university teachers if they come from Oxford or Cambridge than if they come from one of the other universities.

Superficially the pattern of higher degree qualifications is rather different (Table 10.10). As before the group with the lowest proportion of Ph.D.s (and the highest proportion with no higher degree) is group IV, which suggests that this group may consist in part of men who gained moderate degrees at the ancient universities and then

TABLE 10.10

Higher degrees obtained by various groups of university teachers (per cent)

	Oxford and Cambridge teachers		*Non-Oxford and Cambridge teachers*			
Higher degree	Studied at Oxford or Cambridge I	Did not study at Oxford or Cambridge II	Have studied and taught at Oxford or Cambridge III	Have studied, never taught at Oxford or Cambridge IV	Have taught, never studied at Oxford or Cambridge V	No contact with Oxford or Cambridge VI
Ph.D.	40	56	47	33	64	49
M.A. only	8	12	4	8	11	16
None	53	33	49	58	24	36
TOTALS	(118)	(43)	(70)	(226)	(45)	(891)

Source: 1964 Survey.

retired to other universities, perhaps to teach, without so much interest in research or in further mobility. We shall explore this question later. The next group, however, is group I, roughly half of whom did not take higher degrees. This may be explained by the custom, especially at Oxford and Cambridge, of appointing a university's or college's own best students to fill teaching positions and fellowships immediately or soon after the bachelor's degree without requiring further academic certification. Next comes group III, those who have both studied and taught at Oxford and Cambridge but now teach elsewhere. About half of them hold Ph.D.s as do those in group VI; but in group VI 16 per cent hold M.A.s. Groups II and V show the highest percentage with Ph.D.s (56 per cent and 54 per cent respectively): group II represents those who gained their undergraduate degrees elsewhere but now teach at Oxford or Cambridge and it seems that the Ph.D. may be a useful passport for entry for those who are, so to say, not native of either of the two universities. The doctorate also seems to be especially useful to those who have been doubly mobile, group V, who have both moved into and then out of the Oxford and Cambridge world.

Table 10.11 shows the distribution of ranks. As we saw in Chapter

TABLE 10.11

Academic rank of various groups of university teachers (per cent)

	Oxford and Cambridge teachers		*Non-Oxford and Cambridge teachers*			
Academic rank	Studied at Oxford or Cambridge I	Did not study at Oxford or Cambridge II	Have studied and taught at Oxford or Cambridge III	Have studied, never taught at Oxford or Cambridge IV	Have taught, never studied at Oxford or Cambridge V	No contact with Oxford or Cambridge VI
Professor	12 } 22	5 } 12	33 } 39	20 } 28	24 } 42	11 } 20
Reader	10	7	6	8	18	9
Senior lecturer	0	2	11	14	7	20
Lecturer	67	58	43	53	47	53
Others	11	28	7	6	4	7
TOTALS	(118)	(43)	(70)	(226)	(45)	(891)

Source: 1964 Survey.

7, the structure of university ranks at Oxford and Cambridge is rather different from that at other universities, with no senior lecturer grade; and consequently the proportion of those formally placed in 'senior grades' (professor, reader, senior lecturer) is much smaller for both groups I and II than the average of 38 per cent for the whole sample. These groups therefore should not be compared with the other four; but there is a notable internal difference between the two: a considerably higher proportion of those who took their undergraduate degrees at Oxford or Cambridge are professors or readers, while over a quarter of those who were undergraduates elsewhere are to be found in the 'other' grade, which includes assistant lecturers, demonstrators, etc. Similarly, in the same table, those who have ever had any contact with Oxford or Cambridge seem to be markedly more likely to become professors. This is especially true of group III, those who have both studied and taught at one or other of the two universities and then moved out; no less than a third of them are professors, and half are in senior grades. These men are, among those who do not now teach at Oxford or Cambridge, the ones who have had most contact in the past, and could therefore be seen as the most significant members of a 'colonising' force. If they have succeeded in establishing themselves in professorships to such a large extent then colonisation is more than a phase. But before drawing conclusions from Table 10.11 we must control for age, since any marked age difference between the categories would affect the distribution of senior ranks. Similarly the proportion of students educated by other universities has been steadily increasing for the past hundred years, and Oxford and Cambridge graduates in our sample may therefore very well have the advantage of greater age. If we control for age (Table 10.12)[1] the picture is more, not less,

TABLE 10.12

Proportion of professors by age among various groups of university teachers (per cent)

	Oxford and Cambridge teachers		*Non-Oxford and Cambridge teachers*			
Age	Studied at Oxford or Cambridge I	Did not study at Oxford or Cambridge II	Have studied and taught at Oxford or Cambridge III	Have studied, never taught at Oxford or Cambridge IV	Have taught, never studied at Oxford or Cambridge V	No contact with Oxford or Cambridge VI
Under 40	0	0	7	3	12	3
40–9	19	18	54	33	31	19
50 and over	25	*	81	47	*	31
TOTALS	(118)	(43)	(70)	(226)	(45)	(891)

Source: 1964 Survey.
* Numbers too small to warrant reporting.

[1] This table presents the relation between three variables–rank, age and mobility between institutions. Therefore the columns do not add to 100 per cent, i.e. this is an economical way of presenting a larger table in which each figure would be a column distinguishing professors from those holding a lower rank.

striking though some of the sample numbers are very small, and should be taken as showing rather general tendencies. Among those presently teaching at Oxford or Cambridge the proportions of professors at each age are less than the national average for our sample–but this is the result of the actual proportions at these two universities. In any event there now seems to be no appreciable difference between groups I and II. It is in the other groups that the large differences appear. Those in group III, 'the colonial spearhead', are remarkably successful in gaining professorships: over half of those between forty and forty-nine are already professors, and for those of fifty or over more than four-fifths are professors. The only other group with even nearly half its members professors is the over-fifty section of group IV. Both groups IV and V also show a high percentage of professors, higher at least than group VI; and in general it is clear that any contact with Oxford or Cambridge improves the chances of reaching the highest academic rank elsewhere.

Mobility between universities

Mobility then, which we looked at in Chapter 9 in terms of the chances for individual promotion and the description of academic career patterns, also has consequences for the character of institutions and for the status structure of the universities as a system. Movement of men also implies movement of ideas. Mobility is not wholly inspired by the search for higher salary or rank. Departments differ in their resources, research and teaching interests and intellectual styles and these differences presumably attract and repel men of different aspirations, tastes and needs. The interaction of these factors, within the framework of university finance and government, determine the intellectual division of labour between universities and their departments. The analysis of mobility can accordingly afford insight into both the academic career and its institutional setting.

We can ask first about where university teachers are 'produced', or where they graduate, in the system. In 1961–62 the Robbins survey showed that the producers in descending order of importance were Oxford and Cambridge, contributing 31 per cent of all university teachers at that time, Redbricks providing 23 per cent, London supplying 22 per cent, Scotland 13 per cent and Wales 5 per cent; the remaining 5 per cent came from foreign (including Commonwealth) universities. These overall figures, however, disguise differences between faculties. Oxford and Cambridge have been even more dominant in the arts and social studies (48 per cent and 37 per cent respectively) while London has contributed substantially to medicine (30 per cent) and the Redbrick universities to applied science (35 per cent).

But none of the figures take account of the changing relative size of the university groups. We saw in Chapter 7 that over the course of the century, Oxford and Cambridge have dropped from first to fourth place among the five university groups we have mentioned here. This trend is reflected in the relation between 'production' and age. As the Redbrick universities have grown they have increased their contribution to the academic profession; 18 per cent of university teachers aged fifty and over come from Redbrick universities but 29 per cent of those aged under thirty. The opposite trend appears for Oxford and Cambridge, though a particularly high proportion of the graduates of those two universities and of London have become university teachers. By the end of the 1950's Oxford and Cambridge were turning out barely a fifth of all graduates while Redbrick universities were producing 40 per cent; yet 25 per cent of university teachers under thirty came from the former compared with 29 per cent from the latter.[1] London University, however, seems to have been proportionately the most productive in the 1950's. 'The number of university teachers in 1961–62 who had graduated from London University in 1952 or later was equivalent to 3·2 per cent of all London students who graduated in the same period. The comparable percentage for Oxford and Cambridge graduates over this period is 2·5 per cent; for Scotland 2·2 per cent, for Wales 1·9 per cent and for civic universities 1·8 per cent. These figures do not, of course, indicate the total percentage of graduates who are recruited as university teachers, since they exclude those who have already left the profession and those who have not yet joined. But they give a reasonable picture of the differences between university groups.'[2]

Second, the same statistics may be viewed the other way round by asking where universities recruit their staff. This reveals a measure of self-recruitment which shows that Oxford and Cambridge in 1961–62

[1] According to a sample survey carried out in 1968 and reported in H. J. Perkin, *Key Profession*, 24·5 per cent of all university teachers recruited since 1960 were Oxford and Cambridge graduates. *Op. cit.*, p. 37.

[2] *Higher Education*, Appendix Three, p. 37.

had drawn 78 per cent of their staff from their own graduates, Scotland 51 per cent, London 48 per cent, Wales 40 per cent and the Redbrick universities 40 per cent.

However, for a better perspective on relative mobility, 'production' and 'consumption' must be combined. Column (3) in Table 10.13 gives an index of the degree to which graduates who become university teachers tend to teach in their own group, making allowance for the varying sizes of the groups. The tendency not to move is greatest in Wales and Scotland: outward mobility is highest for Oxford and Cambridge (as is the tendency to self-recruitment). London graduates also show a high relative tendency to move out to teaching jobs in other groups.

TABLE 10.13

Relative mobility of graduates from different university groups, 1961–62

Present university group	*Percentage of teachers in this group who graduated in this group* (1)	*Percentage of teachers in all other groups who graduated in this group* (2)	*Column* (1) *divided by column* (2) (3)
Oxford and Cambridge	78·1	23·7	3·3
London	47·6	14·2	3·4
Civic universities	40·2	10·7	3·8
Wales	40·0	2·8	14·3
Scotland	51·1	5·4	9·5

Source: Higher Education, Appendix Three, Table L.2, p. 182.

An alternative way of gauging the mobility of academics within the system is to ask in how many universities have they held posts. In 1961–62 58 per cent had taught in only one university (i.e. where they were), 27 per cent had taught in two universities and 14 per cent in three or more.

These figures suggest only limited movement between different institutions. They refer of course to the period before rapid expansion which has certainly created, at least temporarily, a marked increase in the amount of migration from the older established to the new foundations.

In order to assess what changes have taken place in the volume of mobility between universities as they have grown and multiplied we have looked at a random sample of university staff in 1937 and 1938 and in 1967 and 1968. Between the two earlier years we estimate that 94 per cent stayed in the same university, 5 per cent left university teaching (through death, retirement etc.) and only 1·3 per cent translated to another British university. The comparable figures for 1967 to 1968 were 92 per cent, 6 per cent and 1·7 per cent. The differences are not statistically significant and they indicate that, despite the intervening growth in the academic professions from 5,000 to 30,000, mobility between universities has remained small.[1] But, what is most crucial to know is not the overall volume of mobility but the element in it which causes or reflects the variations in the reputations, styles, orientations and sizes of particular departments. The function of mobility in encouraging innovation and creativity is a neglected aspect of the planning of universities. Illustrations of it can be found[2] but it can hardly be said to have been a strong preoccupation of the U.G.C. The way in which the state allocates money and the 'nationalisation' of salaries combined with the idea of the *universitas* and the typical balance of power between the faculties inhibit the capacity of particular universities to invest dramatically in particular specialisms or branches of research. Nevertheless the system does not proscribe such developments: some recent examples are the social sciences at the new University of Essex, English studies at Birmingham or the recent blossoming of mathematical economics at the London School of Economics.

Mobility preferences

Again statistics on movement through the ranks and between institutions tell us nothing about the preference of university teachers

We propose to extend this analysis, which is based on the entries in the Commonwealth Universities Year Books, to include measures at other points of time and the pattern of movement between university groups and academic ranks.

Our 1967 sample of 1,853 university teachers included thirty-five who had moved by 1968. Of these twenty-four were promoted in the process, ten moved to a post of the same status and one dropped rank to move from Oxford to Cambridge.

[2] See, for example, J. D. Watson, *The Double Helix*, Atheneum Press, 1968, which gives an account of work on the DNA code at Cambridge but which also points to the complex and partly accidental nature of creative intellectual milieux.

for posts in different universities. We can throw some light on this aspect of mobility from our own survey.

We asked our national sample in 1964 how they felt about their present university. The responses for the different university groups are set out in Table 10.14. There are striking differences. Satisfaction

TABLE 10.14

University teachers' attitudes to present university: by university group (per cent)

In general, how do you feel about your present university?	*Oxford and Cambridge*	*Wales*	*Scotland*	*Major Redbrick*	*Minor Redbrick*	*London*	*Total*
It is a very good place for me	66	28	44	39	36	48	43
It is a fairly good place for me	31	64	54	54	56	44	50
It is not a good place for me	3	9	2	8	8	8	6
TOTALS	(159)	(116)	(248)	(469)	(158)	(233)	(1,383)

Source: 1964 Survey.

is high in Oxford and Cambridge where two-thirds described their university as 'a very good place for me'. But there is a sharp fall through London, with a comparable proportion of 48 per cent, to Scotland, 44 per cent, the major Redbrick universities, 39 per cent, the minor Redbricks, 36 per cent, and finally to Wales with 28 per cent. We further asked our respondents whether there was any other British university in which they would prefer to hold a post roughly equivalent to the one already held. On this measure only 8 per cent of the Oxford and Cambridge dons wanted to move and the pattern repeated itself with comparable proportions of 37 per cent and 38 per cent in Wales and the minor Redbrick universities (Table 10.15). These would-be movers were then asked about where they wanted to go. As may be seen from Table 10.16, 47 per cent of them preferred either Oxford or Cambridge. The major Redbricks attracted 14 per cent, London and the new universities 12 per cent each and Scotland 9 per cent.

As another indication of desire to move there was a question asking whether the respondents anticipated applying for a post at

TABLE 10.15

University teachers' preferences for another university: by university group (per cent)

Is there any other British university in which you would prefer to hold a post roughly equivalent to the one you hold here?	*Oxford and Cambridge*	*Wales*	*Scotland*	*Major Redbrick*	*Minor Redbrick*	*London*	*Total*
Yes	8	37	23	37	38	24	29
No	85	48	62	47	42	66	57
Don't know	7	15	16	16	20	10	14
TOTALS	(161)	(113)	(248)	(470)	(158)	(237)	(1,387)

Source: 1964 Survey.

TABLE 10.16

Preferred destination of university teachers who want to move (per cent)

Oxford and Cambridge	47
London	12
Major Redbrick	14
Minor Redbrick	3
New English	12
Scotland	9
Wales	2
Foreign	1
TOTAL	(387)

Source: 1964 Survey.

another university in the course of the next three years. The main difference again is between Oxford and Cambridge at one end and the Redbrick universities at the other with London in between (Table 10.17).

These responses suggest that, over and above a fairly high degree of satisfaction with present positions, the attractions of different institutions are not randomly distributed but form a definite hierarchy with Oxford and Cambridge at the apex, followed by London and the Redbrick universities. Scotland is a partially separate system but it too feels the pull of the old English universities (twenty-three of the

TABLE 10.17

University teachers' anticipations of applying for other posts: by university group (per cent)

Do you anticipate applying for a post at another university in the next three years?	*Oxford and Cambridge*	*Wales*	*Scotland*	*Major Redbrick*	*Minor Redbrick*	*London*	*Total*
Almost certainly will not	62	35	38	32	31	48	39
Probably will not	27	34	34	34	33	27	32
Probably will	6	20	19	22	19	18	18
Almost certainly will	5	11	9	12	16	7	10
TOTALS	(154)	(116)	(245)	(462)	(159)	(237)	(1,373)

Source: 1964 Survey.

fifty-four would-be movers from Scottish universities wanted to go to Oxford or Cambridge).

The pattern was confirmed by another question. Our respondents were asked 'which of the following university posts would be most attractive to you personally: university lecturer and college fellow at Cambridge; professor at Sussex; professorial head of department at Leeds; reader in the University of London?' The results are shown in Table 10.18. The Cambridge fellowship had the most first votes,

TABLE 10.18

The attraction of various university posts for university teachers: by university group (per cent)

Which of the following university posts would be most attractive to you personally?	*Oxford and Cambridge*	*Wales*	*Scotland*	*Major Redbrick*	*Minor Redbrick*	*London*	*Total*
University lectureship and college fellowship, Cambridge	68	38	30	28	40	19	33
Professorship, Sussex	20	23	34	30	35	33	30
Professorial head of department, Leeds	8	21	23	30	13	11	21
Readership, London	3	18	13	11	12	37	16
TOTALS	(142)	(109)	(227)	(427)	(144)	(223)	(1,272)

Source: 1964 Survey.

followed by the professorship at Sussex, with the professorial headship of department at Leeds third and a readership in London fourth. However, staff of the University of London were least attracted to the Cambridge job, which was most popular among men already in Oxford and Cambridge and those in minor provincial universities in England and the University of Wales. The professorial headship of a department at Leeds and the Sussex professorship were equally attractive to those with jobs in the major Redbrick universities, and this group was the one most attracted by the most senior post in their own group.

We asked specifically about attitudes to the new universities (Table 10.19). Over 60 per cent of the respondents were not interested

TABLE 10.19

The attractions of the new universities for university teachers: by university group (per cent)

How would you view the opportunity to join the staff of one of the new universities in your present rank?	*Oxford and Cambridge*	*Wales*	*Scotland*	*Major Redbrick*	*Minor Redbrick*	*London*	*Total*
Would not consider going to any of them	78	49	63	60	48	67	61
Might go to some but not to others	22	49	33	37	48	32	36
Would accept an offer at almost any of them	1	3	3	3	4	2	3
TOTALS	(158)	(115)	(235)	(455)	(157)	(230)	(1,350)

Source: 1964 Survey.

in them at all but the remainder were distributed institutionally according to the pattern which runs through all of these questions on preferred movement.

All the evidence confirms that universities are graded according to their popularity and that Oxford and Cambridge are at the top. But what is perhaps most remarkable about this is that it calls in question the importance of money in determining mobility. The Cambridge post carries lower income than either the Sussex or the

Leeds chairs. Salary levels do not necessarily outweigh considerations of status and of social and intellectual milieu, and the relative attractiveness of the Cambridge lectureship illustrates the continued orientation of many British academics to the traditional norms. These originated in, and are still strongly associated with, Oxford and Cambridge which serve as status and intellectual models and thereby both reflect and reinforce a traditional view of the academic life.

These patterns of mobility preference may be examined finally in relation to mobility experience using the six categories of experience of service in the various university groups which we listed above (pp. 218 and 219). Our survey respondents were asked if there were any other British universities in which they would prefer to work (Table 10.20). The relative satisfaction of the Oxford and Cambridge

TABLE 10.20

Preference for another university by various groups of university teachers (per cent)

	Oxford and Cambridge teachers		*Non-Oxford and Cambridge teachers*			
	Studied at Oxford or Cambridge	Did not study at Oxford or Cambridge	Have studied and taught at Oxford or Cambridge	Have studied, never taught at Oxford or Cambridge	Have taught, never studied at Oxford or Cambridge	No contact with Oxford or Cambridge
	I	II	III	IV	V	VI
Would prefer to be elsewhere	8	9	44	52	44	33
TOTALS	(118)	(43)	(70)	(226)	(75)	(891)

Source: 1964 Survey.

dons with their own positions is remarkable. Less than a tenth would prefer another place compared with upwards of a third in the other groups and over half of those who began as students but never had teaching posts in the two ancient universities. Moreover, as we saw in Table 10.16, of would-be movers, most named Oxford or Cambridge as the university to which they wanted to move. Again the Oxford and Cambridge dons are much more likely to think of themselves as permanently settled–three-quarters compared with half in the other groups (Table 10.21). And this is not, apparently, affected by expec-

TABLE 10.21

Expectation of permanence in present post by various groups of university teachers (per cent)

	Oxford and Cambridge teachers		*Non-Oxford and Cambridge teachers*			
	Studied at Oxford or Cambridge I	Did not study at Oxford or Cambridge II	Have studied and taught at Oxford or Cambridge III	Have studied, never taught at Oxford or Cambridge IV	Have taught, never studied at Oxford or Cambridge V	No contact with Oxford or Cambridge VI
Expect to remain in present post until retirement	76	74	46	54	46	54
TOTALS	(118)	(43)	(70)	(226)	(45)	(891)

Source: 1964 Survey.

tations of promotion to a chair (Table 10.22).[1] Expectations of a professorship are highest among the mobile group III. They are low among those who are Oxford and Cambridge 'natives' who also show least inclination to move. They are at the same time low among those who studied but have never taught at these two universities, a group which also has the highest proportion of would-be movers.

Thus those whose experience has been confined to Oxford and Cambridge seem to be least affected in their conceptions of academic success by the idea of a hierarchy of professional expertise with the professorship at its apex. They are the clearest representatives of the older conception of an academic career–the working tutor who is a full member of his self-governing college. Those who began in Oxford or Cambridge but have never held a teaching post there are

[1] Given that Oxford and Cambridge dons are, on average, older we have examined the distribution shown in Tables 10.20, 21 and 22 keeping age constant. The patterns are unchanged age for age.

TABLE 10.22

Promotion expectations of various groups of university teachers (per cent)

	Oxford and Cambridge teachers		*Non-Oxford and Cambridge teachers*			
	Studied at Oxford or Cambridge I	Did not study at Oxford or Cambridge II	Have studied and taught at Oxford or Cambridge III	Have studied, never taught at Oxford or Cambridge IV	Have taught, never studied at Oxford or Cambridge V	No contact with Oxford or Cambridge VI
Believe they are more likely than others of similar age and rank to be offered a chair	18	25	30	18	22	17
TOTALS	(118)	(43)	(70)	(226)	(45)	(891)

Source: 1964 Survey.

the most discontented with their position and are not hopeful of a chair. They appear to be 'expatriate' in their outlook. The mobile groups on the other hand seem to be more integrated into the modern professional hierarchy and to be more optimistic about their own careers within it the more experience of Oxford and Cambridge they have had. Those with no Oxford and Cambridge contact are least inclined to move of all the groups other than the Oxford and Cambridge 'natives' and least likely also to think in terms of those two universities if they do want to move. They are also the most pessimistic about personal chances of a chair and thus appear to be the soldiers of the modern academic army.

CONCLUSION

We have argued and described the view that the academic career in Britain is in a transitional stage of adaptation. In Parts I and II we looked at the evolution of the institutional setting of university teaching and research. In Part III we have looked directly at the academic role. In Part IV we shall use our survey data to analyse the collective self-conception of the British academics–their attitudes and perceptions, that is, of the function of the university and society and their own roles in the universities as they see them. In preparation for this discussion, and to conclude our analysis of the development of the academic career, we may glance back and ask what is to be expected.

The opinions of men are not wholly determined by their social origins or by their professional interests or by the customary definitions which they inherit through socialisation. Men, in other words, are not cultural automata: and, even if they were, the elaborate interplay of complex social influences would still make prediction difficult. In any case highly educated men see themselves as trying to transcend the forces of class, religion, nationality, ethnicity and generation which press upon them; and indeed the institution of free enquiry, which is at the very centre of the idea of a university, is one which encourages and rewards the modification or overthrow of previously accepted views. Independent individual variation is accordingly to be expected beyond that which might be attributable to social and organisational differences in the university system. None the less the strength of traditional institutions may also be expected to influence the patterns of orientation, and the more strongly in the case of the British academics if our thesis about the distinctive English idea of a university and the assumptions implicit in a guild organisation of resident teachers is valid.

These two sets of values are rooted historically in relations between the universities and society and in the particular conditions of the social organisation of scholarship. We have emphasised the mediaeval establishment of Oxford and Cambridge in England which, together with early industrialisation, set the stage for nineteenth-century university developments and contained them within traditions opposed to the characteristics which have been postulated by Ben-David as essential to an expanded and differentiated structure of academic roles. There was, in the nineteenth century, the presence rather than the absence of metropolitan dominance and the absence rather than the presence of effective competition between independent institutions. True, there was a separate educational tradition in Scotland as well as new social pressures to incorporate science and apply it to industrial problems in London and in the provincial cities. True, too, that these influences made an impact on the character of the universities, both new and old. Nevertheless the pre-eminence of Oxford and Cambridge survived, with consequences for academic careers and attitudes that remain fundamental and are worth recapitulating.

The academic professions were accustomed to small-scale organisation over a long period. Numbers grew imperceptibly in the nineteenth century and even in the twentieth century at a rate which in no way disturbed the organisational presuppositions of the residential college. A vice-chancellor or a college principal, a head of department or even a junior teacher could carry his organisation 'in his head'. Administration was domestic and domesticated. The scale of colleges and universities did not raise problems of bureaucracy and permitted, if it did not promote, self-government. The ideals of residence and of a nationally and internationally recruited body of undergraduates were slowly and imperfectly realised during the twentieth century in the provincial foundations, but none the less remained and remain firmly held educational and social aims. The conception of teaching as requiring close contact between university teachers and students has gained rather than lost ground in the twentieth century, at least as expressed by staff/student ratios.

The academic professions were also remarkably isolated for a long time from the main pre-occupations of a changing society. Smallness contributed to isolation: but there was also the long period in which Oxford and Cambridge colleges were linked closely to the organisation of the Anglican Church and, at the same time, to a narrow segment of the class structure, providing a suitable environment for the sons of the aristocracy and gentry and so largely cut off until well into the nineteenth century from industrialism and the industrial middle classes. The alumni of Oxford and Cambridge found their way into the Church, the law and the older liberal professions, not into business. The donnish concept of professionalism was pre-industrial–an orientation to humanism, to social service and to the morals and manners of the gentleman rather than to specialised knowledge, to science and to entrepreneurship. And the dons made themselves in the same image. The ideal was an academic version of the idealised gentleman, widely cultivated and interested in the spiritual and physical as well as the intellectual welfare of the young men temporarily under their care. Again it is true that Scottish tradition was different and that the London and provincial university developments in the second half of the nineteenth century were in part responses to the need for scientific and industrial research and training. But, until the second war at least, the academic professions were a small isolate of professional life, respected for their intellectual achievements and enjoying a social prestige which reflected the 'magic' of Oxford and Cambridge. Only in the last twenty years has the development of professional work and especially research outside the universities begun to result in an assimilation of academic styles of life to the mainstream of the professional classes, or what in America has come to be called 'the Ph.D community'.

From the point of view of the structure of the academic professions, Victorian reform in Oxford and Cambridge raised the prestige and power of the working tutor and resuscitated and modernised an older conception of the academic career. There thus developed a model of the university teacher which contrasts with the emphasis on research and specialisation implicit in the departmentally organised hierarchies of academic rank under the leadership of a single professor.

The idea of the academic profession as a guild of resident teachers, united by their widely defined relation to students more than divided by their specialised research interests or professional identifications, has had a continuing influence. It has resisted the elaboration of salary differentials which might have been 'imported' from the differing market conditions for professional services outside the university. It has maintained the strongly felt principle of academic self-government and it has enabled the Association of University Teachers to exercise trade-union functions on behalf of all the academic ranks, professorial and non-professorial.

The evolution of the British universities up to the middle of the twentieth century resulted in a system heavily dominated by Oxford and Cambridge, tightly knit into the interests and educational outlook of the metropolitan higher professional classes who have controlled the size and shape of educational development through a network of 'establishment' contacts eased by shared class background in public schools and in the Oxford and Cambridge colleges themselves. Competition has accordingly been muted. An academic market place on the American model might have emerged from the nineteenth-century movements in the industrial provinces, but in fact non-conformity and regional pride which might have sustained truly independent institutions were too weak and the assimilative readiness of the national élites based on London too strong. Industrial money flowed more easily to Oxford and Cambridge than to Sheffield and Leeds. Neither cultural nor financial competition ever became serious. Instead there was absorption and modification. Science and technology found a limited place *within* the assumptions of a liberal education. Specialisation developed but within the tradition of teaching a small and highly selected body of students. Rationalisation took place but *within* the framework of a managed élitist system where the managers were men of similar background and outlook and closely connected to the metropolitan political and administrative élite.

The academic career in Britain, with Scotland as only a partial exception, has evolved concurrently with these institutional developments. The desire for personal promotion is real enough but is conditioned in ways which contrast markedly with the, perhaps caricatured, picture painted of the American market place by Caplow and McGee. The attraction of the Oxford or Cambridge fellowship remains greater than that of the professorship elsewhere for a significant minority of university teachers and especially those who have had experience of the two universities as undergraduates, graduates or dons. Mobility between the universities has not been great and has been shaped more by the Oxford and Cambridge connection than by desire for more money. Of course, on average, Oxford and Cambridge hold out material inducements and also the less tangible rewards of a style of academic life which carries great prestige. But at the same time they have strong intellectual attractions in their library and scientific resources, their teaching organisation and the quality of colleagues. Thus they reinforce and reflect a set of attitudes which may be distinguished from professional careerism through specialised research and which encourage a way of academic life emphasising teaching and, in the best sense, amateurism.

Nevertheless this weight of tradition in the institutional setting and career structure of the British academics is now being challenged. Unprecedented pressure has developed far larger numbers, greater scale and more specialisation, efficient operation, visible productivity and responsiveness to external demand. We must therefore examine the collective state of mind of university teachers in order to judge the influence they are having and will have on the course of university development.

PART IV

ACADEMIC ORIENTATIONS

Chapter 11

ATTITUDES TOWARDS EXPANSION

Our survey, and that of the Robbins Committee, came in the middle of a long and slowly accelerating period of university expansion which can be dated from the end of the second war.[1] The causes and character of this expansion are discussed elsewhere in this volume. In the present chapter we want to raise the question of how the people most directly involved in and affected by university expansion, the university teachers, perceived it and felt about it. For while the decisions about the nature and extent of British higher education are made ultimately by the highest political authorities, nevertheless the influence of the academic community on those decisions is very great. It is likely that the Robbins recommendations themselves reflected as well as stimulated a shift in sentiments in the British academic community towards an increasing acceptance of the inevitability and even the desirability of the expansion of the university system. But the question of how widely those sentiments were and are held by British academics is not answered in the public debates or in letters to the press. And the answer–essentially to the question of how university teachers see their own institutions and their development or growth–may shed light both on the nature of the academic professions and on the future of the British university system.

The Robbins Report recommended that the number of students in the university system increase from 130,000 in 1962–63 to 219,000 in 1973–74, an increase of a little less than 70 per cent in rather over a decade. When our questionnaire was distributed a year later, the recommendations (at least regarding size, though of little else) had been accepted by both the Conservative Government and the Labour Opposition which was soon to achieve power. We included a question[2]

[1] See Graphs 11.A and 11.B.

[2] The question reads as follows: Q.5 'Which of the following opinions concerning the number of students in the university system as a whole lies closest to your own opinion? In each case please assume that staff and resources are made available.'

about expansion of the system with response categories which bracketed the Robbins recommendations. The distribution of responses in our sample was as follows:

TABLE 11.1

Opinions on expanding the university system (per cent)

		% *answering*
a.	We should double the numbers or more in the next decade	27
b.	We should increase the numbers about 50% in the next decade	40
c.	We should increase the numbers about 25% in the next decade	28
d.	I think that the number of students admitted to the universities should remain about where it is now	4
	TOTAL	(1,408*)

* This includes forty-five respondents, about 3 per cent of the total, who did not answer the question for one reason or another. These cases will be omitted from the subsequent analysis. In general 'Non-responses' will be omitted from tables, except where their numbers are large enough to raise a special question or affect the character of the findings.

Response (b), favouring an increase of 50 per cent in a decade, was closest to the Robbins recommendations of about 70 per cent in 11 years; those making this response, together with the little over a quarter wanting a doubling of numbers or more, will be seen as supporting a 'significant' growth in the system as a whole. A growth of 25 per cent over a decade would be distinctly smaller than the growth of the age group and of the numbers of qualified candidates, and would make for an even more highly selective system than existed at the time of Robbins.[1] Thus, about two-thirds of the teachers in our sample supported an expansion of numbers of 50 per cent or more, while even after the powerful Robbins arguments for modest recommendations (based on projections that very quickly were exceeded by reality), roughly a third opposed any significant growth in the size of the university system. The teachers were also asked about growth in the number of places in their own subjects. We may imagine that while academics might be cautious about growth of the system as a whole, they would be more likely to see the virtues of a growth of their own subjects. But British academics are wary of growth and its presumed consequences: where only 32 per cent preferred a growth of 25 per cent or less in the university system as a whole, 40 per cent wanted to see such a low rate of growth over the next decade in their

[1] See *Higher Education*, Chap. VI, esp. paras. 147–81, esp. Table 30; also *ibid.*, Appendix One, *passim*, for detailed statistical projections.

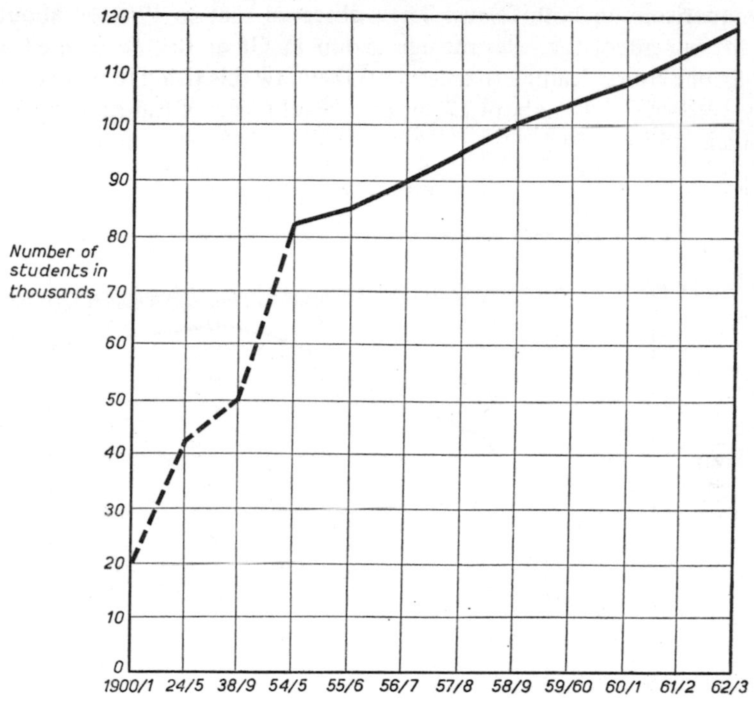

GRAPH 11.A

Students in universities (Great Britain): 1900–63*

* Source: *Higher Education*, Table 3, p. 15, and Appendix One, Table 46, p. 163.

own subjects. And where 28 per cent favoured at least *doubling* the numbers of university students overall, only 18 per cent favoured increasing the numbers in their own fields by 75 per cent or more in the next decade.[1]

The size of a university system can be discussed by reference to the numbers of students–i.e. in terms of the *institution*–or by reference to the proportion of the age group gaining a university education–i.e. in terms of the population at large, and implicitly, the needs of society. National comparisons of higher education more commonly take the latter form. The Robbins Committee provided data and

[1] See Appendix D, Table 11.32.

comparisons in both forms. They observed that in 1958–59 about 4·5 per cent of the relevant age group in Great Britain entered a full-time course leading to a degree;[1] they saw this rising to 6 per cent by 1968–69[2] and to about 17 per cent in all forms of full-time higher education by 1980.[3]

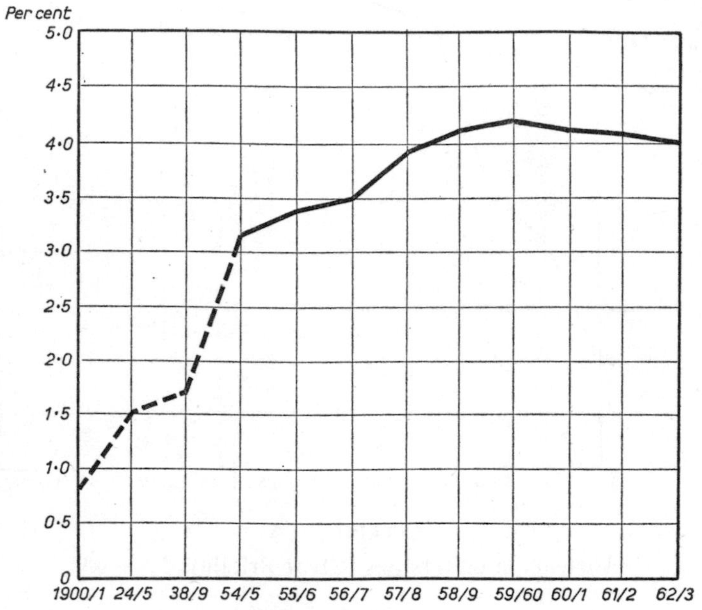

GRAPH 11.B

Percentage of age group entering universities (Great Britain): 1900–63*

* Source: *Higher Education*, Table 4, p. 16.

Our sample of British academics were asked what proportion of the age group they would like to see entering full-time higher education in Great Britain.[4] The question was asked without reference

[1] *Higher Education*, p. 42.
[2] *Ibid.*, p. 46.
[3] *Ibid.*, p. 66.
[4] **Q 10**: 'Here are some proportions of the relevant age group entering universities and other full-time institutions in different countries. Which of these proportions would you like to see in Britain? (The Robbins Report recommends raising the present proportion of 8·5 per cent to 17 per cent by 1980.)'

to a date, but in the context of a reminder of the Robbins recommendation of 17 per cent by 1980. The responses were as follows:

TABLE 11.2

Opinions on proportion of the age grade to receive higher education

	% answering
40% or more	6
30% or more	7
20% or more	39
10% or more	46
5% or less*	1
TOTAL	(1,335)

* The reader will note that the categories are not completely exhaustive, and that no provision has been made for those preferring a figure between 5 per cent and 10 per cent. This error in the construction of categories probably affects the last two figures; however, the bulk of the analysis contrasts those supporting a proportion of more than 20 per cent with those wanting to see less than 20 per cent of the age grade gaining higher education. Roughly half the sample falls into the two lower categories; the gap between 5 per cent and 10 per cent should not affect that proportion.

Thus, about half our sample would like to see a higher proportion in British higher education than Robbins envisaged by 1980; but very few (about one in eight) envisaged the kind of mass higher education, with a third or more of the age group in some form of higher education, already existing in the U.S.A. and the U.S.S.R. Here, even more clearly than in the figures on their preferences for the size of the university system, we see that the dominant view of British academics, a year after the Robbins Report, was much like that of the Report itself–supporting a moderate expansion of the present highly selective system of higher education, but opposing the transformation of that system in the direction of mass higher education.

Sources of attitudes towards expansion

The British university system has been growing rapidly since the end of World War II. In 1938–39, the last peace-time year before the war, university enrolments were about 50,000. By 1954–55, after the post-war bulge, the enrolments were 82,000, and by 1962–63 they were up to 118,000.[1] Thus, in the eight years preceding Robbins university places had increased by nearly 50 per cent, while in the twenty-four years separating 1938–39 and 1962–63 they had grown by nearly 140 per cent, not far off the increase projected by Robbins (166 per cent) for the eighteen years between 1962–63 and 1980–81. So British academics have been experiencing growth, both in their own institutions, which grew, on average, from almost 2,000 to about 4,000 students between 1938–39 and 1962–63, and in the system as a whole.[2] We might assume, therefore, that their judgements of the effects of the growth in the recent past on the quality of their students will have some bearing on their sentiments towards future expansion.

At this point we might introduce two caveats: first, the attitudes of university teachers towards future growth may be independent of their judgement of the effect of past growth on student quality, since other considerations, such as the reduction of social inequalities or the national interest, may lead them to support university expansion even if they believed it would lower student standards.[3] Secondly, judgements of the effect of past expansion on the quality of students may not *shape* attitudes towards future expansion, but rather, both past perceptions *and* attitudes towards expansion may reflect more basic attitudes about the selectivity and size of the university system, and even more basic political dispositions. We explore both of these possibilities below, but they should be borne in mind throughout the following discussion.

First, how do university teachers as a whole feel about the effects of recent expansion? Our question (6) asked: 'Do you feel that the expansion that has already taken place over the past decade has affected the quality of students admitted to your university in your subject?' The distribution of responses for the whole sample was as follows:

[1] *Higher Education*, Appendix One, Part IV, Table 46.

[2] See Appendix D, Table 11.34.

[3] For example we might quote a social psychologist who was interviewed in the early stages of the study (before the appearance of the Robbins Report): 'I favour university expansion with an emphasis that can scarcely be exaggerated . . . I think we would still get the very best people somewhere, and if there aren't any more of them I'm still in favour of getting . . . to larger numbers, even larger stupid numbers.'

TABLE 11.3

Opinions on the effect of past expansion

		% answering
a.	It has lowered the average level of ability of my students very considerably in recent years	1
b.	It has lowered the average level of ability of my students to some extent in recent years	20
c.	It has not changed the quality of my students appreciably	66
d.	The overall level of ability of my students has risen in recent years	13
	TOTAL	(1,313)

Thus, two-thirds of the teachers do not see recent expansion as having any appreciable effects on the quality of their students, and the remainder are nearly evenly divided between those who feel that quality has gone down to some extent and those who feel that average ability has risen with expansion.

It may be relevant to note the Robbins findings on the effect of the expansion (both of the universities and the sixth form) of the previous decade on the quality of university entrants.

> In 1938 only about 3 per cent of those aged nineteen were receiving full-time education; in 1962 the proportion was 7 per cent, nearly all of them in higher education.
>
> This expansion has not been accompanied by any lowering of standards, but rather the reverse. For example, . . . the percentage of the age group achieving minimum university entrance qualifications has risen by over a half since 1954, whereas the percentage entering universities has risen only by a quarter, and has actually fallen since 1959. In the last few years, in other words, university expansion has not even quite kept pace with the increase in the age group, let alone the increase in the number of those with the minimum qualifications for entrance.[1]

The rise in the number of qualified candidates has inevitably driven qualifications for entry higher, so that while 'two passes at the Advanced Level of the General Certificate of Education are the minimum qualification for entry to universities in England and Wales,' at the time of the Robbins Report 'over 80 per cent of the students have at least three.' This reflected a rise in standards of entry

[1] *Higher Education*, Chap. III, p. 12.

over the preceding decade. In 1954, 72 per cent of those gaining the minimum school entrance qualifications in England and Wales (that is, two A Level passes) gained entry to a university. By 1961 that figure was down to 59 per cent.[1] Looked at another way, it was estimated that 57 per cent of university applicants were admitted in the same year; by 1961 that figure was down to 42 per cent.[2]

There can be little question that the overall quality of university students rose during the decade preceding Robbins. Of course, there is no assurance that the overall improvement in the quality of students in the system as a whole was reflected in the experience of any particular teacher. And yet, when the overwhelming majority of teachers refuse to recognise any improvement in their students during these years, while a fifth claimed that the quality of their students was *deteriorating*, it seems likely that these judgements are strongly influenced by the widespread fear of expansion among university teachers, and by convictions that even if necessary or desirable on other grounds, expansion must necessarily be associated with a lowering of standards. This widespread fear of growth (or indeed of any kind of change) is a pervasive characteristic of the British academic, as of his institutions.

Apprehension of the effects of expansion is seen even more clearly in the teachers' anticipations of the effects of future growth on quality. Judgements of its past effects are at least constrained by personal experience (as well as by the statistical evidence reported by Robbins and then widely in the press). But the future provides an empty canvas on which the teachers could project their own hopes and fears, mostly the latter, of increasing numbers.

Our question (Q11) took the form: 'If the numbers of students doubled in the next decade with the same staff–student ratio, what would you expect to be the effect on the quality of graduates in your subject from your university?' Of the total sample, 16 per cent anticipated a 'marked deterioration' in their graduates, 50 per cent said they expected 'some deterioration,' 27 per cent thought that degree of expansion would have no effect on their graduates' quality, and only 6 per cent thought that rate of expansion would be accompanied by an 'improvement' in their graduates.

Doubling the number of university students in a decade is a somewhat higher rate of growth than the 68 per cent Robbins

[1] *Ibid.*, Appendix One, Table 14, p. 119.
[2] *Ibid.*, Table 15, p. 120. These figures exclude Oxford and Cambridge.

recommended for 1973–74, though two years after the report was published the man who produced its five volumes of statistics suggested a revision upwards of 25,000 places over the Robbins projections for 1973–74, which would mean very nearly a doubling in numbers by 1973–74 over 1962–63 enrolments.[1] Robbins gave the firmest assurances[2] in connection with his recommendations for expansion, that the quality of students would not suffer. And his Report reiterates that its projections of the numbers of qualified candidates by present standards were very conservative ones, and did not take into account a series of factors (such as the raising of the school-leaving age) which would certainly increase the numbers, and thus allow an even greater expansion without lowering standards.[3] Despite that, and in the face of the evidence of rising standards over a decade when enrolments were increasing by 50 per cent, and a question which asks the respondent to assume that growth does not affect present staff–student ratios, it is surprising to find two-thirds of the sample anticipating some deterioration in the quality of their own graduates if numbers were doubled in a decade.

Here is a clear expression of the fear of expansion noted earlier in connection with judgements of the effect of past expansion. As we shall see, these suspicions have sources in broader social and political perspectives, and also operate as an important determinant of attitudes towards expansion.

Attitudes towards expansion and apprehension regarding its effects on the quality of students

Before we explore some of the sources of this apprehension, let us consider its relation to the attitudes teachers hold towards expansion. A number of possibilities present themselves. We might expect that judgements of the effects of past expansion on student quality would affect anticipations of future effects as well as attitudes towards expansion themselves. Another possibility is that attitudes towards expansion are in some measure independent of apprehension about its effects; people may oppose expansion for other reasons despite their

[1] Professor Claus Moser, as reported in *The Observer*, 31 October 1965.

[2] See *Higher Education*, Chap. VI, paras. 137–46, for summary, and Appendix One for details, esp. Parts II–IV.

[3] *Ibid.*, p. 53; also Martin A. Trow, 'Second Thoughts on Robbins: A Question of Size and Shape', *Universities Quarterly*, March 1964, pp. 136–52.

belief in its deleterious consequences. Or third, despite the apparent relation implied in the correlation, it may be that apprehensions of the effects of expansion may not shape attitudes towards expansion, but rather that both apprehensions and attitudes may reflect more basic sentiments about the selectivity and size of the system and even more basic political dispositions.

First let us look at the relation of judgements of the effects of past expansion to attitudes towards future growth (Table 11.4).

TABLE 11.4

Recommended expansion of system, by experience of the effects of expansion on student quality (per cent)

Recommended expansion of system	*Effect of past expansion* Lowered*	No change	*Improved*
Double	12	29	46
50%	38	41	41
25%	39	28	10
None	12	2	3
TOTALS	(269)	(839)	(172)

* 'Lowered' combines those who believe expansion 'lowered very considerably' and 'lowered to some extent' the quality of their students.

Nearly half of those who believed that past expansion has been accompanied by an improvement in the quality of their students (as Robbins data suggests was true for the whole student population), favour doubling the number in the next decade, compared with only about one in ten of those who believed expansion had lowered quality. Only half of the latter group favoured expanding by even as much as 50 per cent, over the next 10 years, an increase well below Robbins' recommendations.

Similarly, those who anticipate a decline in quality attendant on growth are also less likely to support expansion (Table 11.5).

Thirdly, and not surprisingly, we find (Table 11.6) that those who have found past expansion to be associated with a decline in the quality of their students are also likely to expect a further deterioration in quality with the even higher rate of expansion posited by our

TABLE 11.5

Recommended expansion of system, by anticipation of the effects of expansion on student quality (per cent)

Recommended expansion of system	*Effect on future expansion* Marked deterioration	Some deterioration	No change	Improve
Double	15	17	46	56
50%	27	45	39	33
25%	44	33	15	11
None	14	4	1	0
TOTALS	(212)	(667)	(369)	(84)

TABLE 11.6

The relation of the experience of effects of expansion on student quality to anticipation of effects of further expansion (per cent)

Anticipation of effects	*Experience of effects of expansion on student quality* Much lower	Somewhat lower	No change	Improve
Marked deterioration	50	30	13	11
Some deterioration	33	60	50	34
No change	17	6	33	38
Improvement	0	3	5	18
TOTALS	(12)	(262)	(847)	(171)

question (a rate higher than Robbins recommended, but close to what the actual size of expansion will probably be). No appreciable proportion of any group, even of those who experienced an improvement in the quality of their students over the previous decade, anticipate an improvement in students with doubling numbers over the next ten years. And it is only this last group that has a bare majority who believe that doubling will not bring about a deterioration in student quality. It is very likely that it was the idea of doubling student numbers that generated the considerable amount of apprehension reflected in Table 11.6; though at the time of writing (1970) the growth in the numbers of qualified candidates makes it highly probable that a doubling of numbers will be achieved without any decline in standards and perhaps with an overall improvement.

On both of these questions, the judgement of past effects and the anticipation of future consequences, we are dealing with the teachers' apprehensions that growth will impair quality. We may say that those who see expansion, either retrospectively or in anticipation, as having no effects, or positive ones, on student quality, are 'not apprehensive' about expansion. Those who see negative effects *both* in the past and in the future are 'highly apprehensive'; those who see them *either* in the past or the future are 'somewhat apprehensive' (almost all of these have doubts about the future rather than the past).[1]

We see in Table 11.7 the strong relation between these apprehensions of the effect of expansion and the teachers' attitudes to growing numbers. Nearly half of those who are not apprehensive (less than a third of the total sample) favour doubling the system in a decade; 86 per cent support 'significant expansion' (50 per cent or larger increase in places). By contrast, only one in ten of the most apprehensive teachers favour doubling numbers, and less than half support 'significant expansion'.[2]

TABLE 11.7

The relation of apprehension of effects of expansion to attitudes towards expansion (per cent)

Attitudes towards expansion	*Apprehension of effects of expansion*		
	Highly apprehensive	*Somewhat apprehensive*	*Not apprehensive*
Double	10	20	49
50%	37	43	37
25%	41	33	14
None	12	4	—
TOTALS	(242)	(615)	(405)

[1] For this 'index of apprehension' see Appendix D, Table 11.35.

[2] Though it is worth noting that nearly half of these 'highly apprehensive' academics support significant expansion despite their anticipation of a decline in student quality with growth.

Expansion of the teacher's own subject

Logically, experience of expansion and attitudes towards it in one's own discipline might be largely independent of views about expanding the university system as a whole. We can imagine men (and know some) who strongly support the expansion of the system but who believe their own subjects to be as large as is necessary or desirable. But while such people exist, they are fairly uncommon, for a number of reasons.

First, academic men tend to be especially conscious of the values and virtues of their own subjects, and to want to see them strongly represented in universities. Indeed, the advancement of the subject, to which the teacher is honourably dedicated, may in part depend on its gaining a 'fair' share of the extra resources of men and money associated with university expansion. Thus, if a man is in favour of enlarging the system, he is also likely to want his own subject to grow.

Moreover, we would expect academic men to generalise their experiences of (and attitudes towards) the expansion of their own subjects both to other subjects and to the future. If men believe the quality of their students has suffered from expansion in the past, they are likely to believe this has been and will be true of other subjects and other universities.

The consistency of attitudes to expansion (of system and subject) may arise, as in the above ways, through some kind of logical processes. In addition, as we suggested earlier, all these sentiments and perceptions may be to some extent expressions of more generalised ideologies and preferences regarding university expansion.

In any event, however successfully we distinguish among these different social and psychological processes, they all tend to produce similar attitudes to both subject and system expansion. Let us see to what extent this is true empirically.

We see in Table 11.8 a strong tendency towards consistency; those who favour expansion of the system are also likely to favour a growth of numbers in their own subjects. Over half of those who favour at least doubling the total number of students, favour a growth of at least 75 per cent in their own subjects. At the other extreme, those who favour little or no growth of the system are overwhelmingly against any significant expansion of numbers in their own subjects. (A growth of 25 per cent over a decade is not in our definition

TABLE 11.8

Relationship between support for expansion of the system and of the teacher's own subject (per cent)

Recommended new places in own subject	*Recommended expansion of number of students overall*			
	Double or more	50%	25%	*Remain same*
75%	52	7	3	0
25%–75%	31	66	25	9
Under 25%	11	22	62	40
No expansion	5	5	9	52
TOTALS	(369)	(540)	(381)	(58)

'significant expansion', since it is well below Robbins' modest projections of growth of qualified candidates.) It is clear, however, that there is more support for an increase in the total number of students than there is for expansion of the teachers' own subjects. And this means that there is a considerable minority–roughly 16 per cent of our sample–who do not support a significant expansion of their own subjects (25 per cent or more) but who do support an increase of 50 per cent or more in all university places. (The group that supports a growth of their subjects but a growth of less than 50 per cent overall is less than 8 per cent of the sample.)[1]

We shall consider more closely the differences between those academic men who are consistently for or against expansion and those who favour it for the system but not for their own subjects. First, however, we shall look at some of the determinants and correlates of teachers' attitudes towards the growth of their own subjects. The connection of expansionist sentiments with apprehension regarding its past and future effects on quality can be seen at the level of the subject as well as the university system: support for expansion of the teacher's own subject is strongly associated with the teacher's estimate of its future effect on the quality of his students (Table 11.9), and only a little less strongly related to his judgement of the effects of expansion over the preceding decade (Table 11.10).

[1] See Appendix D, Table 11.33.

TABLES 11.9 AND 11.10

The relationship between support for expansion of the teacher's own subject and opinions on effects of past and future expansion (per cent)

		Recommended new places in own subject			
		None	*Less than* 25%	25–75%	75%+
11.9	Believes doubling in decade will lead to some or marked deterioration in quality of graduates in own subject	79	82	64	36
11.10	Believes the expansion over past decade has lowered quality of students admitted to own department to some extent or very considerably	35	26	19	11
TOTALS (vary slightly in the two tables)		(112)	(424)	(568)	(250)

We might imagine that support for expansion of his own subject would be related to the teacher's sense of the quality and reputation of his own department. Rapid expansion can provide the resources and opportunities to improve a weak department, and strengthen its reputation. Conversely, if increased numbers are thought to threaten standards, teachers in weak departments might oppose expansion for fear of further weakening their academic position.

There is a slight tendency for teachers in a department whose comparative *reputation* is, they believe, less than it deserves, to favour expansion of their subject more than teachers who believe their departments have the reputations they deserve or better. But there is no clear relation at all between academics' attitudes towards expansion and their own estimates of the *quality* of their departments. British academic men, from our sample, by and large, do not see expansion as a means to strengthen the quality of their departments. In this respect British university teachers differ from their counterparts in America, where expansion has long been seen as one of the major strategies for improving both the quality and the reputation of an academic subject as well as of specific departments.

Support for expansion in different subject areas

If we ask where support for given subjects is most concentrated the answer is clear: teachers in the social sciences are distinctly more likely to favour expansion of their subjects, almost four times as likely as teachers in the arts subjects, and twice as likely as teachers of science to favour an expansion of 75 per cent or more in their subjects over the next decade (Table 11.11). But it is not clear from

TABLES 11.11 AND 11.12

Attitudes towards expansion of subject and system by subject area (per cent)

	Social studies	*Technology*	*Science*	*Arts*	*Medicine*
11.11 *Expand subject* 75%+	41	25	17	11	8
11.12 *Expand system* Double or more	42	29	25	20	24
TOTALS (vary slightly in the two tables)	(214)	(178)	(404)	(349)	(136)

these figures how much this is a judgement of the special needs or opportunities of social science subjects, or how much an expression of the generally expansionist dispositions of social science teachers. For when we look at their attitudes towards expansion of the whole university system, social scientists also emerge as more likely to favour doubling total student numbers (Table 11.12).

A comparison of Tables 11.11 and 11.12 suggests that social studies teachers are more generally expansionist than teachers in other fields, and also more likely to support expansion of their own subjects. Later consideration of the social characteristics of teachers in the several subject areas will shed more light on these differences in attitudes towards expansion.

Differences between ranks on these issues are not very large; only the readers are noticeably less likely than other ranks to support significant expansion of their subjects. A little less than half the readers favour expansion of 25 per cent or more as compared with about three in five of all other ranks. Possibly research-oriented teachers (specially represented among readers) may be less interested in the growth in the numbers of students (and that of teaching duties).

This is a hypothesis we can explore when we look at attitudes towards teaching and research in Chapters 12 and 13.

Attitudes towards university expansion as an aspect of political dispositions

The strong relationships we reported between attitudes towards university and disciplinary expansion and the teacher's experience and anticipation of its effects on student quality suggest a causal connection: that these apprehensions shape expansionist or restrictionist attitudes. This argument is supported by the relationship we find between these apprehensions and teachers' feelings about the size of their departments and universities, and is at least not contradicted by our finding of an absence of relationship with judgements of the quality of the teacher's own department. It is not his judgement of the present quality of the department (university, subject, system) which influences a teacher's attitude towards expansion, but rather his concern (or lack of concern) about the effect of expansion on quality. So at least the data seem to suggest.

But these findings can be interpreted differently. It may be that attitudes towards expansion are not only, or even primarily, shaped by apprehensions regarding the effects of expansion on quality, but to a very large extent by the teacher's general political values and attitudes. Sentiments about expansion may be rooted in more fundamental ideas about the nature of the 'good society', and the role of higher education in it. These beliefs affect both the interpretation of past experience and judgements of future consequences of growth, as well as the general attitudes teachers hold towards expansion.

Evidence to support this view is provided by the university teachers' attitudes to giving university status to the CATs.[1] Clearly this policy, recommended by Robbins and adopted by the Government in the spring of 1964, was the kind of 'expansion' that would least influence the quality of students admitted to the existing universities. Reluctance to grant CATs university status, we suspect, arose largely out of concern for the 'meaning of a university degree', and reluctance to 'dilute' its standing or distinction. About two-thirds of our sample, following Robbins, favoured university status for the CATs and a

[1] The ten Colleges of Advanced Technology, recommended by Robbins for upgrading to full degree-giving universities, with expansion of student numbers and of the range of subjects offered.

little over a quarter opposed it. And there is a strong relation between these attitudes and those expressed towards expansion (Table 11.13).

TABLE 11.13

Support for granting CATs university status by attitudes towards expansion of the university system (per cent)

Grant CATs university status?	*Recommended expansion of number of students overall*			
	Double	50%	25%	*None*
Yes	85	69	50	32
No	11	25	43	61
No answer	5	6	7	7
TOTALS	(372)	(546)	(386)	(59)

Whereas 85 per cent of those who favoured doubling the numbers of university places in a decade also favoured giving CATs university status, the proportion dropped to only a third of those who opposed any university expansion, and half of those who supported expansion of less than 25 per cent. Again, granting CATs university status did not affect the quality of entrants to any existing university or subject; it did, however, affect the shape and inclusiveness of the university system. And it was the teachers' basic conceptions of the nature and functions of the university system that determined their attitudes to the CATs.

The most direct evidence of the political sources of these sentiments comes from the strong relationships between them and political dispositions.[1] The respondents were asked to place themselves on the political spectrum ranging from 'Far Left' through 'Moderate Left' and 'Centre' to 'Moderate Right' and 'Far Right'. The distribution of responses on this spectrum was as follows:

TABLE 11.14

Location on 'political spectrum' (per cent)

	% *answering*
Far Left	4
Moderate Left	47
Centre	27
Moderate Right	18
Far Right	1
No answer	3
TOTAL	(1,408)

[1] The influence of political attitudes and loyalties is explored more fully in Chapter 15.

Nearly half the sample located themselves on the Moderate Left; over a quarter in the Centre, nearly a fifth on the Moderate Right and small proportions at both extremes. This positioning on a political spectrum is closely related to party identification[1] (Table 11.15).

TABLE 11.15

Party support related to political position (per cent)

	Political position				
Party	*Far Left*	*Moderate Left*	*Centre*	*Moderate Right*	*Far Right*
Labour	87	71	10	2	8
Conservative	0	6	55	91	83
Liberal	3	16	21	4	0
Other	6	1	1	0	0
None	3	7	13	3	8
TOTALS	(62)	(624)	(337)	(345)	(12)

About seven out of ten on the Left have 'generally supported' Labour; an even higher proportion, nearly nine out of ten, of those on the Right have generally supported the Conservatives. Half of those in the Centre are also Conservative supporters, with the remainder chiefly Liberals or having no party preference.

There is little doubt, from what we know of political attitudes and their genesis, that these are formed prior to and independently of the teachers' experience in the university. They are associated with much more basic experiences and more general social and political values. It is highly unlikely that many teachers have changed their political dispositions because of their views on university expansion. Therefore, the strong relationship between left-wing politics and expansionist attitudes suggests that these attitudes are part of much more comprehensive sets of social and political views (Tables 11.16 and 11.17).

Support for doubling student numbers in a decade declines from 60 per cent of those who place themselves on the Far Left to 12 per cent of those who place themselves on the Right (Table 11.16).[2] The

[1] Given in Q.53: 'What party have you generally supported?'

[2] Only twelve respondents, less than 1 per cent of the total, identified themselves on the Far Right. They appeared on these questions as highly restrictionist –for example, none of them favoured doubling student numbers–but because of their small numbers they were combined in these and succeeding tables with the much larger group who place themselves on the Moderate Right, in most cases without great effect on the distribution of responses of that category. The reader must keep in mind that the great bulk of those on the Right are men who identify themselves with the Moderate Right.

TABLES 11.16 AND 11.17

Various attitudes on university system expansion by political position (per cent)

Table 11.16	Political position					
Expand university system	*Far Left*	*Moderate Left*	*Centre*	*Moderate Right – Far Right*		
Double	60	34	21	12	12	0
50%	30	42	44	35	34	9
25% or less	10	24	35	53	54	91
Table 11.17						
Proportion of the age grade						
40%+	31	8	3	2	2	9
30%+	19	9	4	5	5	0
20%+	28	44	37	34	33	9
Less than 20%	22	40	56	60	6I	82
TOTALS (vary slightly)	(58)	(625)	(364)	(238)	(249)	(11)

proportion supporting 'appreciable growth' (that is, 50 per cent or more in a decade) fell from nine in ten of teachers on the Far Left to three-quarters of those on the Moderate Left, to two-thirds in the Centre, to well under half of men on the Right. Similarly, general political dispositions are very strongly related to teachers' conception of the proportion of the age group which should at some indefinite future time gain higher education (Table 11.17). The figures here are very striking. The proportions supporting expansion to more than 20 per cent of the age group declines from 78 per cent on the Far Left to 40 per cent on the Right.

These findings are surprising only to those who may believe that views on higher education are insulated from broader political and social attitudes. The Left, in Britain as elsewhere, has generally supported the extension of citizenship rights and public services, but with respect to education has, to a large extent, accepted the meritocratic principle of equality of access, and has supported reforms designed to increase the proportions of working and lower-middle-class students in grammar schools and universities. Admission by selective examination and the grants available for university students, for example, both aim to reduce the disadvantages faced by able students from poor homes in the competition for scarce places: but both are compatible with a small intake to meritocratic institutions. As Robbins documented, and as events since Robbins have dramatically shown, the numbers of 'qualified' students have been growing rapidly–and a considerable expansion of higher education is required even by meritocratic principles. Labour supporters are more likely than Conservatives to want to keep pace with the growth of qualified students, since an even more 'meritocratic' intake is likely to be less 'democratic' as well.

What is perhaps more surprising is how little support there was at the time of Robbins even on the Left for the extension of university places to larger proportions of the whole population. The meritocratic principle defines the democratic impulse among British academics of almost all persuasions. Support for anything like mass higher education–30 per cent or more of the age group–comes from only half of the Far Left, and from very small proportions of any other political group. Expressed differently, only 13 per cent of the whole sample want such a system of higher education. Nearly half of the whole sample wants to see less than 20 per cent of the age group in higher education. 22 per cent of the Far Left and 61 per cent of the Right (combining Far Right and Moderate Right) preferred to restrict higher education to under 20 per cent of the age group. These views are realistic in that the Robbins recommendations saw only 17 per cent of the age group in full-time higher education of all kinds by 1981.[1] The prospects for mass higher education are very remote if these attitudes determine the structure and growth of the British system. It seems that Robbins was not more but perhaps less conservative than the mass of British academics. When even the large body of Moderate Leftists would not 'like to see' a system of mass higher education in Britain, pressure for expansion beyond the Robbins recommendations is not likely to come from within the universities.[2]

Nevertheless, while the relation of political position to expansionist sentiments is clear, it is not a perfect one. Of special interest are the nearly two out of five men on the Left who want a system of higher education which is attainable by less than a fifth of the population, as well as the smaller number of men on the Right and Centre who would like to see a much larger proportion of the age group in higher

[1] *Higher Education*, p. 66.

[2] Pressure for university expansion everywhere comes more from the 'consumers'–potential students and their parents, and from employers in industry and government–than from the 'producers'.

education. These could be an important minority, if economic and attitudinal pressures for a breakthrough develop in Great Britain.

Political dispositions and attitudes towards expansion of own subject

A position on the political spectrum implies certain attitudes to a broad range of social and cultural questions. While many men (and perhaps especially academics) pride themselves on the independence of their judgement and their abhorrence of 'ideology', nevertheless, a political position implies also a measure of consistency on a range of public issues, and over time. (This consistency need not be incompatible with independence of mind: as an American voter once observed to a pollster, 'Just because I've voted Republican in every election for forty years doesn't mean I haven't made up my own mind.') Higher education in Britain in the 1960's was certainly a public and a political issue, despite the fact that it had not figured prominently in the party debates or in the post-war general elections. But, reflected only imperfectly in the party documents and perhaps cutting more deeply in the party rank and file than between the party leaders, are profound differences between the British 'Left' and 'Right' over the nature and functions of higher education. And we have seen evidence of those differences in Tables 11.16 and 11.17 which show the strong relation of political position to attitudes on university expansion.

But political dispositions colour a wider range of attitudes, sentiments and perceptions regarding university expansion than merely the policy question of whether and how much the system as a whole should expand, or how large a proportion of the age group should gain a higher education. For example, no political party or position is clearly identified with the expansion of any given subject. Yet Table 11.18 shows a clear relation between teachers' general political dispositions and their feelings about the expansion of their own subjects.

The pervasive influence of political sentiments is more strikingly seen in their influence on men's perceptions of what is an objective fact: that is, whether recent expansion has affected student quality.[1] As we see in Table 11.19, nearly a third of the men on the Far Left

[1] The fact is, as we noted earlier, that the quality of entrants to British universities, at least as measured by their G.C.E. qualifications, rose sharply over the decade prior to our survey. See *Higher Education*, Appendix One, pp. 118–19.

TABLE 11.18

Attitudes towards expansion of own subject by political position (per cent)

Expand own subject	*Political position* Far Left	Moderate Left	Centre	Right
75% or more	46	22	15	7
25%–75%	26	44	42	41
Less than 25%	28	34	42	52
TOTALS	(61)	(642)	(370)	(256)

believed recent expansion had been accompanied by a rise in student quality, as compared with only 7 per cent of the men on the Right. On the other hand, nearly twice as many men on the Right as on the Left thought that the quality of their students had declined in the previous decade.

TABLE 11.19

Judgements of the effects of past expansion on the quality of students in own university and subject, by political position (per cent)

Effect of expansion on student quality	*Political position* Far Left	Moderate Left	Centre	Right
Lowered (very greatly or to some extent)	17	15	24	30
No change	52	68	66	64
Improvement	31	17	10	7
TOTALS	(54)	(610)	(356)	(250)

TABLE 11.20

Anticipation of the effects of future expansion on the quality of students graduated from own university and subject, by political position (per cent)

Anticipation of effects of expansion on student quality	*Political position* Far Left	Moderate Left	Centre	Right
Deterioration (some or marked)	38	62	67	80
No change	38	31	27	17
Improvement	23	7	6	3
TOTALS	(60)	(636)	(375)	(256)

The relation of political position to these judgements of the effects of expansion on quality is even greater with respect to future growth than it is for past expansion, as we can see by comparing Table 11.20 with Table 11.19. In every category of political position our university teachers are more pessimistic about the effects of a doubling in a decade than about the effects of the (70 per cent) expansion in numbers over the previous decade. But in addition, the differences between the Far Left and the Right are greater. Apart from the relatively small group on the Far Left (the only category to show a majority who are relatively optimistic about future growth), between 40 and 50 per cent of all the other teachers are more apprehensive about future growth than about the effects of recent expansion. Certainly the figure suggested in our question, of doubling numbers in a decade, was frightening to a great majority of university teachers, though it is not so much higher than Robbins' estimate (with his firm assurances of no decline in quality) and very likely close to the degree of expansion that will actually be achieved (also without a decline in quality).

There are two distinct points to be made about Table 11.20; first, the high degree of apprehension with which most teachers contemplated the growth of higher education even after Robbins; and second, the differences between teachers of different political persuasions. It is unlikely that the academic standards of conservative teachers are higher than those of men of the Left; differing judgements about the past and likely future effects of increasing numbers partly reflect different and preconceived views about the desirability of expansion, rooted in basic political dispositions. (We can see the relation of political disposition to apprehension very clearly by using the index of apprehension introduced on page 254.)[1]

We have been speaking of the bearing of political position and 'dispositions', rather than party support or identification. Yet much political research has shown the independent influence of party identification on positions people take with respect to specific issues; on many matters, people bring their positions on issues into line with party identification rather than select their party to be consistent with their position on some given issue.[2] And, indeed, party identification is often a more powerful determinant of issue position that is political predisposition.

This seems to be the case with respect to university teachers'

[1] See Appendix D, Table 11.36.

[2] See, for example, Angus Campbell and others, *The American Voter*, John Wiley, 1960, esp. Chap. VI, pp. 168–87.

attitudes towards university expansion. There is a very marked difference on these questions among teachers who 'generally support' different parties, as we see below (Tables 11.21 and 11.22).

TABLES 11.21 AND 11.22

Attitudes towards expansion of university system by party support

11.21 *Expand university system*	*Party support* Labour	Conservative	Liberal	None
Double	38	18	24	28
50%	41	35	47	40
25% or less	21	47	29	33
TOTALS	(520)	(448)	(184)	(101)

11.22 *Recommended proportion of the age grade*	*Party support* Labour	Conservative	Liberal	None
40%	10	3	4	9
30%	9	5	7	6
20%	44	37	39	32
Less than 20%	37	55	49	54
TOTALS	(509)	(444)	(180)	(104)

Moreover, as we would expect, there is a close, though far from perfect, relation between party support and political position (Table 11.23).

TABLE 11.23

Political position by party support (per cent)*

Political position	*Party support* Labour	Conservative	Liberal	None
Far Left	10	0	1	2
Moderate Left	83	8	53	43
Centre	6	41	40	46
Moderate Right	1	49	6	8
Far Right	—	2	0	1
TOTALS	(534)	(454)	(182)	(96)

* Cf. Table 11.15.

Labour supporters are heavily concentrated on the Left, Conservatives divided between the Centre and Right, and Liberals between the Centre and the Moderate Left.

However, when we look at the distribution of attitudes towards expansion by party support, controlling for political position, we find that while differences still obtain between the party supporters, they are somewhat reduced within any given category of political position. We show this in Tables 11.24 and 11.25 only for the Moderate Left and Centre, where we have a sufficient number of cases in the several categories of party support.

TABLE 11.24

Attitudes towards expansion of the university system by party support within categories of political position (per cent)

*Expand university system**	*Labour*	*Moderate Left* *Conservative*	*Liberal*
Double	36	33	28
25% or less	21	42	29
TOTALS	(429)	(36)	(97)
		Centre	
Double	28	23	19
25% or less	31	37	28
TOTALS	(32)	(180)	(72)

* Columns do not add up to 100% since middle categories (50%) are omitted.

TABLE 11.25

Recommended proportion of age grade to gain higher education by party support within categories of political position (per cent)

Recommended proportion of age grade	*Labour*	*Moderate Left* *Conservative*	*Liberal*
Less than 20%	36	35	51
TOTALS	(419)	(37)	(95)
		Centre	
Less than 20%	59	51	51
TOTALS	(32)	(179)	(71)

On the whole, as we can see in these tables, political position rather than party allegiance is the more important influence on attitudes to expansion. Moreover, political dispositions are related to attitudes towards every kind of expansion. We have already seen this in relation to increasing the total of student places, and to growth of the teacher's own subject. We also find Left–Right dispositions strongly related to the teacher's feelings about the size of his university and department.

TABLES 11.26 AND 11.27

Feelings regarding the size of own department and university, by political position (per cent)

	Political position			
11.26 *Size of own university*	*Far Left*	*Moderate Left*	*Centre*	*Right*
Too big	20	22	26	25
About right	31	41	43	54
Too small	49	37	31	21
TOTALS	(59)	(638)	(368)	(257)
11.27 *Size of own department*				
Too big	5	5	4	8
About right	37	47	50	57
Too small	58	48	46	35
TOTALS	(59)	(627)	(360)	(250)

Where almost half of the men of the Far Left believe their universities are too small, only about one in five of men on the Right think likewise. Differences in feelings about the size of their departments vary similarly. Academics of all political persuasions are more inclined to think of their departments as too small compared with their universities. Men of the Left are not disproportionately concentrated in small universities or departments. Rather, their political dispositions lead them to favour larger educational units, as well as a larger educational system, and against those sentiments their present institutions are more likely to seem too small.

Political position and granting university status to CATs

Earlier we observed that granting university status to CATs was a special test of expansionist sentiments, since it was the kind of expansion that had little or no effect on the quality of students admitted to or graduated from the other universities, and therefore could not be linked to a deterioration of student quality. Nevertheless, as we showed (Table 11.13) there was a very strong relation between support for upgrading the CATs and support for increasing the number of university places. The relation of these views regarding the CATs to political dispositions can be seen clearly in Table 11.28.

TABLE 11.28

Support for granting CATs university status by political position (per cent)

Should CATs be given university status?	*Political position* Far Left	*Moderate Left*	*Centre*	*Right*
Yes	85	81	67	50
No	15	19	33	50
TOTALS	(60)	(613)	(357)	(244)

Where granting university status to the CATs was supported by over 80 per cent of the Left (and there was very little difference between the Far Left and the Moderate Left on this issue), the Right divided almost exactly in half on the question. (Among the tiny group on the Far Right, only a quarter supported giving CATs university status.) Here is clear evidence of the connection between restrictionist sentiments and conservative political views, with the element of the effect of expansion on student quality largely absent. The objection to the CATs, as we noted earlier, was largely on traditional grounds, having to do with the supposed 'non-vocational' character of 'liberal studies', and the dilution and adulteration of the meaning of the university degree if it were granted to technologists.[1]

If there is an ideological component in attitudes towards university expansion, as the strong relationships of these attitudes with political disposition suggest, then we should find these relationships strongest among those most interested in politics (Table 11.29).

[1] As examples we might quote from the pilot interviews: An economist at a small Redbrick university: '. . . I belong to the, shall we call it, depth school–that a university is a place where one has an unique opportunity . . . to think, to really probe deeply–and, therefore, I am against technologies being taught vocationally. I'm not sympathetic to the vocational idea of a university.' ('Would you want to see expansion take place?') 'Not if it meant that the idea of a university was going to change, no. I would prefer to see separate institutions.' Or, an economist at London: 'I have . . . thought sometimes that there are already people at a university for whom a university education is rather a waste. I think . . . some . . . come just in order to get a degree to get promotion and a higher salary . . . they aren't living a kind of university life . . . under the universities [there should be] a very strong sort of technical institute level of things where they could get all the technical skills that a country like this wants.' Or, a lawyer at London: 'To have pressures built up to hand out degrees of a very much lower standard to a lot of people who couldn't possibly get them now would be a rather unsatisfactory state of affairs.' (But this man was prepared to see degrees given to graduates from CATs.)

As we see in Table 11.29, the relationship between support for a significant expansion of university places and political position is strongest among those 'extremely interested' in politics. If we look at the figures closely, we can note that among those on the Left and Centre, interest in politics 'activates' their general political dispositions and makes them more relevant to the issue of university expansion;[1] while, by contrast, among the men of the Right (whose attitudes towards university expansion we might suggest are more 'traditional' than 'political') there are no appreciable or consistent differences in attitudes towards expansion between those interested in politics and those who are less so.

The combined effect of political position and apprehension of the effect of expansion on quality on attitudes towards expansion

We have shown that those who have experienced, or anticipate, a decline in the quality of their students, which they associate with university expansion, are much less likely to support significant expansion than those who see it either as having no appreciable effect on student quality or as serving to raise it. We have also seen the marked relation of attitudes towards expansion with political dispositions. And further, we have seen that these apprehensions of the effects of expansion on quality are also closely related to political positions. We now want to consider the joint influence of these perceptions and orientations on attitudes towards expansion.

Table 11.30 shows the independent and cumulative relation of political position and apprehensions of effect of expansion on talent, to attitudes towards expansion of student places overall. Among the teachers on the Left who tend to believe expansion will on balance lead to an improvement of student quality, 79 per cent support doubling numbers in a decade and 96 per cent support expansion by 50 per cent or more. By contrast, of the men on the Right who are apprehensive of the effects of expansion, only 7 per cent support doubling and 37 per cent an expansion of 50 per cent or more. Nearly two-thirds (63 per cent) of this group want to expand by less than 50 per cent over the decade.[2]

Another way of looking at this data is to ask what categories of

[1] The proportion who want the system to double in a decade only exceeds 40 per cent among those on the Left and Centre who are 'extremely interested' in politics.

[2] For other attitudes related to politics and apprehension simultaneously, see Appendix D, Tables 11.37–39.

TABLE 11.29

Attitudes towards university expansion by political position, within categories of political interest (per cent)

	Political interest											
	Extremely interested			*Moderately interested*			*Only slightly interested*			*Not interested*		
Expand system	*Left*	*Centre*	*Right*	*Left*	*Centre*	*Right*	*Left*	*Centre*	*Right*	*Left*	*Centre*	*Right*
Double	50	41	25	33	21	7	30	17	21	21	12	5
50%	37	35	19	43	48	40	36	42	22	50	38	45
25% or less	13	24	56	24	31	53	34	42	58	29	50	50
TOTALS	(187)	(34)	(16)	(381)	(189)	(145)	(111)	(113)	(73)	(14)	(34)	(20)

TABLE 11.30

Attitudes towards university expansion by degree of apprehension,* within categories of political position (per cent)

	Political position											
	Far Left			*Moderate Left*			*Centre*			*Right*		
Expand the university system	*Not apprehensive*	*Somewhat apprehensive*	*Highly apprehensive*	*Not apprehensive*	*Somewhat apprehensive*	*Highly apprehensive*	*Not apprehensive*	*Somewhat apprehensive*	*Highly apprehensive*	*Not apprehensive*	*Somewhat apprehensive*	*Highly apprehensive*
Double	79 } 97	44 } 94	17 } 50†	55 } 90	25 } 71	15 } 56	38 } 79	17 } 67	5 } 44	28 } 78	10 } 40	7 } 37
50%	18 }	50 }	33 }	35 }	46 }	41 }	41 }	50 }	38 }	50 }	30 }	30 }
25%	0	0	17	10	27	33	21	30	45	22	53	51
None	3	6	33	0	2	11	0	3	12	—	7	12
TOTALS	(28)	(18)	(6)	(218)	(285)	(80)	(110)	(160)	(78)	(40)	(131)	(67)

* The 'index of apprehension' used here is described in Appendix D, Table 11.37 and note. See also above, Tables 11.6 and 11.7 and text.

† The percentages in this column are reported only to fill out the table and allow independent manipulation of the numbers. No significance is attached to percentages based on six cases.

TABLE 11.31

Ratio of proportion of expansionists to proportions of whole sample in categories of apprehension and political position*

	Political position											
	Far Left			*Moderate Left*			*Centre*			*Right*		
	Not apprehensive	*Somewhat apprehensive*	*Highly apprehensive*	*Not apprehensive*	*Somewhat apprehensive*	*Highly apprehensive*	*Not apprehensive*	*Somewhat apprehensive*	*Highly apprehensive*	*Not apprehensive*	*Somewhat apprehensive*	*Highly apprehensive*
R	1·8	1·1	0·42	1·4	0·62	0·35	0·92	0·42	0·12	0·67	0·22	0·17

* Xd = No. of doublers in category
ΣXd = No. of doublers in sample
N = No. of cases in category
ΣN = No. of cases in sample

$$R = \frac{\frac{Xd}{\Sigma Xd}}{\frac{N}{\Sigma N}}$$

political position and apprehension supply the bulk of the teachers who favour doubling the system. These are, after all, the supporters of expansion of the university beyond the recommendations of Robbins; it is from them, presumably, that pressure from within the universities for further expansion will come. We want to know not only the size of this potential 'ginger group', but its character and social composition as well.

One way to do this is to compare the proportions a category supplies to the whole sample with the proportion it supplies to this group of expansionists. Dividing the latter proportion by the former gives us an index number which measures the relative contribution of that category to the body of 'expansionists' (or 'doublers'). An index number of one means that the category supplies expansionists in the same proportion as its size within the whole sample; and an index number below one means that the category is under-represented among the doublers, and contrariwise for the categories with index numbers of more than one. In Table 11.31 we see that the men on the Far Left who are not apprehensive about the effects of expansion on quality are almost twice as likely as average to support doubling. They, together with the Moderate Left who are not apprehensive, supply about half of the 'expansionists' though only comprising about a quarter of the whole sample.

But while the men of the extremes of politics and apprehension are pretty largely in the expansionist or restrictionist camps, there remain large groups in the middle of both variables whose attitudes cannot be explained by reference to their positions on those variables. For example (in Table 11.30), of men in the Centre who are 'somewhat apprehensive', about two-thirds support expansion of 50 per cent or more, another third oppose that much growth. Of men in the same political position but who are 'not apprehensive' of the effects of expansion on student quality, about three-quarters support significant expansion. But how do these men differ from those in the same political and apprehension categories who do not support expansion? Clearly, we must look further to explain more.

The apprehension of British academics regarding expansion–of the system, their own subjects, their departments and universities–is, we suggest, a fear of the future. And what is feared is not 'a deterioration in the quality of my students' so much as the unknown problems that significant expansion may bring with it. To many British academic men, expansion is the source of threat, of unanticipated and undesired consequences, of dangers, rather than of challenge and opportunity.

The fear of the future, if we are right, is one reflection of a central quality of British society, which shows itself more generally as a fear of modernisation, automation, immigration, Americanisation, of all sorts of processes which have unknown outcomes. The British, including the academic community, will accept 'reforms' if they believe they know or can foresee the controlled extent and consequences of change. This is the mark of a conservative society; and the wariness and resistance to large-scale expansion of the system of higher education on the part of the British academics, across nearly the whole of the political spectrum, is one aspect of this mood and outlook.

Chapter 12

TEACHING AND RESEARCH ORIENTATIONS I: INSTITUTIONAL DETERMINANTS

The tension between teaching and research is a central problem in modern universities. It arises out of differences among academics over the relative importance of the two main functions of universities – the transmission and the creation of knowledge. The arguments, which start with strongly held beliefs about the primacy of university functions, also raise issues regarding the right allocation of resources, the needs of the student and of the state, the relative importance of graduate versus undergraduate education, the proper size of institutions, and the balance of subjects in the university and the curriculum. Behind these arguments are the academic men and the differing ways they define the academic role for themselves. The bulk of academic men believe, in principle, that the academic role should involve both teaching *and* research. Indeed, the most common response to the question 'which' is the answer 'both'. But this evades the problem rather than answers it. Choices frequently must be made, and the question arises, for individuals as for departments, universities, and systems of higher education, what relative emphasis should be placed on these activities which compete for time, energy and money.

In this and the following chapter, we shall see how British academic men answer this question. First, we shall simply report the responses of our sample of university teachers to questions about their own preferences as between teaching and research; and the quantitative production of books and scholarly articles will give some indication of the different emphases. Then we shall report the teachers' views on the importance of research in academic work. We shall then examine the relation, if any, among these attitudes to research.

But our main interest is not in a descriptive account of the extent of research activity, but in distinguishing (i) the characteristics of men who are more interested in research than teaching (and the other way around); (ii) their location within the university system; and (iii) the relation of preferences for research or teaching to other values and attitudes–views about expansion, the power and status of professors and other issues of university life. The tension between teaching and research is a major cleavage in university life. But because universities (unlike research institutes or American liberal arts colleges) exist to serve both functions, the conflicts must be contained and compromise must be reached. We want to know how the conflicting demands of research and teaching are 'resolved'–by the academics themselves and within the university system. Finally, the evidence may suggest trends in the research activities of university teachers, as the system grows and changes its functions and the balance of studies within it.

In this chapter, then, we describe the teaching and research leanings of British academic men, as revealed both by their expressed attitudes and by their research work. We then look more closely at the distribution of these preferences within the university system and the academic profession. In Chapter 13 we pursue our inquiries into the sources of attitudes to research and teaching by examining the social and educational biographies of university teachers, and the rewards and difficulties they experience in the two branches of their work. We also try to relate attitudes to research and teaching to other attitudes which academics display towards British education and their own academic environment.

Reported research activity

Early in the questionnaire our respondents were simply asked (Q17) 'Do your own interests lie primarily in teaching or research?' The question was of course framed in terms of their *interest* or preference, and so need not necessarily reflect either what they in fact do, or what they believe that they should be doing; how far these are related is a question for exploration.

We find (Table 12.1) that roughly one-third are primarily interested in teaching; but of the remaining two-thirds only 10 per cent describe themselves as interested in research almost to the exclusion of teaching, and more than half describe themselves as interested in both but leaning towards research; again, this perhaps evades the question, as a 'leaning' may perhaps be slight enough to be no more than a bow in the

TABLE 12.1

Interest in teaching or research

	% *answering*
Very heavily in research	10
In both, leaning towards research	54
In both, leaning towards teaching*	36
TOTAL	(1,368)

* Owing to a printing error, the fourth possibility 'Very heavily in teaching' was omitted from the main university questionnaire.

direction of creative scholarship. Without further analysis it is not easy to learn much from this question.

A more certain indicator of research activity is actual publication of research work. We asked two questions on this topic, first, on the number of articles published and, secondly, on the number of books. There are very few topics that do not allow of at least preliminary publication of journal articles, and this therefore we take as the most important measure of research work done during a teacher's lifetime.

TABLE 12.2

Number of academic articles published (per cent)

None	7
1 to 4	22
5 to 10*	23
10* to 20	20
More than 20	27
TOTAL	(1,404)

* These two categories overlap: but they were offered to respondents as approximate groups, and not coded from precise numbers given by respondents.

Nearly half our sample have published more than 10 articles, and the median would be around 9 (Table 12.2). Only 7 per cent have never published any. Of those who had published articles, 79 per cent had done so in 1963 or 1964, the years immediately prior to the survey, and only 6 per cent had not published since 1960 or earlier. It is clear that the number of university teachers whose lack of interest in research has led them not to publish at all is very small.[1]

[1] For a discussion of productivity among American academic men, see L. W. Hargens and Warren O. Hagstrom, 'Sponsored and Contest Mobility of American Academic Scientists', *Sociology of Education* (40), 1967, and the literature cited there.

The question of book publication is rather more problematic. Many scientists, for example, never find it necessary to publish books at all, since their research may be reported in a series of articles, which are produced more quickly and reach their fairly small audience efficiently and cheaply. Indeed the relationship between book and article publication is quite different in different faculties.[1] Moreover, many books that are published in scientific fields are textbooks for teaching purposes, which grow out of lecture notes compiled for teaching as much as from original research. It is with these qualifications that we present the next table.

TABLE 12.3
Number of books published (per cent)

None	65
1	18
2	7
3	3
4	2
5	1
6 or more	3
TOTAL	(1,405)

Almost two-thirds of our sample have never published a book; of the remainder roughly half have published one book only and the other half more than one. It is noteworthy, however, that exactly half the sample said that they were presently preparing a book for publication: and exactly half of these had not yet published a book.

We referred earlier to the three questions with which we have to deal in this context: the preferences of academics, their actual behaviour, and their feelings as to what they should be doing, their conception of what defines the role of an academic man. Among a series of statements with which they were asked to agree or disagree was the following (Q.49(i)): 'An academic man's first loyalty should be to research in his discipline. The teaching of students and the running of his university should be second to this first duty of an academic career.' We saw above (Table 12.1) that the majority of university men expressed a preference for research as against teaching. We might expect therefore that a majority would similarly agree with this statement. In fact (Table 12.4) only 4 per cent agree without reservations, and only just over one-third agree at all

[1] See Appendix D, Table 12.34.

(compared with two-thirds who expressed a personal preference for research (Table 12.1)), while 22 per cent reject the statement altogether. This suggests that there may be a conflict between men's personal preferences and their sense of what their duty as academic men requires. This is a question to be explored further.

TABLE 12.4

Research as first duty (per cent)

Strongly agree	4
Agree with reservations	31
Disagree with reservations	43
Strongly disagree	22
TOTAL	(1,372)

Before we go on, it will be useful to examine the relationship among our various indicators of research orientations. How far does an expressed preference for teaching materialise in low research output? Do those with very large numbers of articles published show far greater interest in research? The relationship is very strong (Table 12.5). Of those who describe their interests as heavily in

TABLE 12.5

Number of articles published, by preference for teaching or research (per cent)

Number of articles	*Heavily in research*		*Both, leaning to research*		*Both, leaning to teaching*	
None	1	16	4	22	13	42
1–4	15		18		29	
5–10	18		22		26	
10–20	24	68	22	57	17	32
More than 20	44		35		15	
TOTALS	(131)		(720)		(491)	

research, 68 per cent, or over two-thirds, have published more than ten articles, and nearly half over twenty. Of those who lean towards teaching, on the other hand, just under one-third have published more than ten articles, and only 15 per cent more than twenty. Evidently the way our sample describe themselves reflects quite substantially their actual behaviour measured by publication of their research.

There is one obvious disadvantage in using the production of articles as an indicator of research activity: clearly age will drastically affect its usefulness. It is difficult for a 23-year-old assistant lecturer, however research-minded, to have published more than one or two articles, whereas even a highly teaching-oriented 50-year-old senior lecturer has probably published one or two.

TABLE 12.6

Number of articles published, by age (per cent)

Number of articles	*Under* 30		30–4		*Age* 35–9		40–4		45 *and over*	
0	12	57	8	35	7	26	4	18	5	17
1–4	45		27		19		14		12	
5–10	29		27		24		18		19	
10–20	12	14	21	36	25	50	27	65	17	65
Over 20	2		15		25		38		48	

In Table 12.6 we see how age affects publication. Of those under 30, almost three-fifths have published less than five articles; but after age 45 less than one-fifth have published so few. At the other end of the table, the proportion who have published more than ten increases from 14 to 65 per cent by the time they have reached the early forties. At this point, however, the proportion who have published more than ten stops increasing; but there is still a shift up to the group who have published more than twenty. This suggests that by this age academic men have settled whether they are to be researchers or not; the researchers go on publishing while the rest write no more articles. This is a matter that can be examined more directly by looking at the increase in publication with age, using the preferences which our sample expressed for teaching and research.

Table 12.7 is striking in its demonstration of how the potential for research, as expressed in the preferences of the youngest members of our sample, is apparent even below 30; there is a sharp difference between teachers and researchers even in the first age group. But as these men grow older the difference between researchers and teachers becomes increasingly sharp for every succeeding age category.[1]

[1] This can be seen most clearly if we examine the *maximum* percentage difference for each age group. This is found at *5 or more* articles for the under-30 and 30–34 group, at *10 or more* articles for the 35–39 and 40–44 groups, and *more than 20* articles for the 45 and over group. The percentage differences between 'heavy researchers' and 'teachers' then read 33 per cent, 37 per cent, 47 per cent, 60 per cent and 69 per cent. The categories of researchers and teachers become steadily more distinguishable by their research output.

TABLE 12.7

Number of articles published, by preference for teaching or research, within age categories (per cent)

Number of articles	*Under 30* High research	Lean research	Lean teaching	*30–4* High research	Lean research	Lean teaching	*35–9* High research	Lean research	Lean teaching	*40–4* High research	Lean research	Lean teaching	*45 and over* High research	Lean research	Lean teaching
0	3	10	26	0	3	18	0	3	17	0	1	9	0	2	8
1–4	40 } 43	40 } 50	50 } 76	12 } 12	30 } 33	31 } 49	12 } 12	10 } 13	35 } 52	0 } 0	7 } 8	29 } 38	0 } 0	4 } 6	19 } 27
5–10	27	35	19	31	26	31	16	26	23	9	12	31	0	13	27
10–20	23	13	6	35	22	15	31	28	17	17	35	16	5	14	20
20+	7 } 30	1 } 14	0 } 6	23 } 58	19 } 41	5 } 20	41 } 72	34 } 62	8 } 25	74 } 91	46 } 81	15 } 31	95 } 100	68 } 82	26 } 46
TOTALS	(30)	(136)	(54)	(26)	(149)	(80)	(32)	(155)	(96)	(23)	(103)	(68)	(19)	(176)	(192)

Lastly, we should examine the relation between the teachers' own preferences and their conception of the essential academic role (Table 12.8).

TABLE 12.8

Research as firms duty, by interests in research/teaching (per cent)

*Academic man's first duty is to research**	*Interest* Very heavily in research		*Both, but lean towards research*		*Both, but lean towards teaching*	
Strongly agree	15	63	5	47	1	12
Agree with reservations	48		42		11	
Disagree with reservations	29	37	38	53	53	88
Strongly disagree	8		15		35	
TOTALS	(132)		(710)		(492)	

* Q.49(i). See Appendix B.

This relationship is also very strong; almost two-thirds of the 'heavy researchers' agree, with or without reservations, that research should be the first duty of academics, as against 12 per cent of those who lean towards teaching. Perhaps it is not surprising that men's preferences and their conceptions of the role are so strongly related. And we have used that relationship to define and construct an index of 'orientations towards researching and teaching', in which a man's conception of the role and his own preferences for one or other activity weigh equally. This index, described in detail in Appendix C, consists of five possible positions. Those appearing at one extreme, 'very high research' orientation, gave their own preference as 'very heavily in research' and agreed that 'an academic man's first duty is to research'. Those at the other extreme, 'very high teaching' orientation, gave as their preference 'leaning towards teaching', and strongly disagreed with the conception of the basic academic duty as research. In between fall those who gave a consistent middle position, and those whose personal preference did not altogether accord with their conception of the academic role.[1]

[1] While for many purposes it will be useful to assign the 'deviant' cases–men who prefer research but do not see it as the academic man's 'first duty' and men who lean towards teaching but agree that research is the prime duty–to an intermediate position on the index, we will at later points be interested in these men who hold what appear to be conflicting perspectives and attitudes, and where they are found in the university system.

The institutional location of teachers and researchers

Having described the overall attitudes of British university men to research and teaching, we shall now try to show how these sentiments are distributed within the university system. Throughout the study we have located academics within the structure of British universities in three ways. First, there is the kind of university in which they work. Despite the apparent similarity of all British universities compared with a pluralistic higher education system like that of the United States–a similarity that arises out of common modes of funding, of degree standards, of recruitment of staff and students, etc.–there are important differences among the universities in England, Scotland and Wales. These derive partly from the historical circumstances which led to their establishment, partly from their somewhat different social and educational recruitment (within the relatively narrow population catered for by British universities), and also from sometimes explicit differences in educational aims and methods. Obviously it is not possible to characterise some forty-five different institutions individually, and for the purpose of this analysis we shall use the groupings described in Chapter 1. This is not to deny, of course, the possibility of large variations within these groups; at present we only suggest that differences between groups are more revealing.

Oxford and Cambridge still have a prestige that is based as much on intensive undergraduate teaching and excellent facilities for research as on ancient connections with wealth and power. London and the large Redbrick universities also, by virtue of their size alone, have better than average facilities for research. Scotland's universities represent a very old tradition that stressed something nearer equal opportunities for higher education than has been accepted in England and Wales until recently, though their teaching methods have traditionally resembled Continental rather than English universities. Wales and the 'minor Redbrick' group are small and either new or slow-growing institutions which evidently cannot and perhaps have not wished to support a large research effort. The one 'new' university in our sample, Sussex, took the improvement of undergraduate teaching as its primary mission in its early stages; the Colleges of Advanced Technology, despite their chief subjects, which seem to demand research, had very recently been technical teaching institutions with little opportunity for research. They are now moving up to university status, which would at least allow, if not demand, more research-oriented men on the staff and more time allotted to research. Our survey, shortly after the decision to elevate the CATs, may reflect changes in the climate of those institutions, but not yet major changes of substance.

Table 12.9 shows the distribution of teaching and research preferences among academic men in different university groups.[1] Preference for research is (looking at the top line of the table) roughly in line with our expectations. Oxford and Cambridge contain notably more men with a strong preference for research; the former CATs and the minor redbricks show distinctly higher proportions of men oriented towards teaching, while the differences among the other university groups are small or negligible. It is interesting that Oxford and Cambridge, despite their teaching reputation, show the highest proportion of men whose preference is research. Evidently for most of the teachers at the two universities faculty teaching is not the primary attraction of their posts, despite the emphasis placed on it there. It may be that a different picture will emerge when we examine other variables, notably the subject taught: for it is in the arts and social sciences that particular stress is laid on the tutorial system, and there may be a sharp division between members of these faculties and teachers in science. We examine this question below.

More impressive than these relatively small variations is the striking *similarity* in the distributions among the university groups. The recent CATs aside, Table 12.9 is evidence that we are dealing with a common profession, whose practitioners differ among themselves, but who are rather uniformly distributed among the several institutions that make up the British university system. Differences in the research climates between specific universities there certainly are, as we shall show later, and these differences have consequences for the research activity at those institutions. But the differences do not coincide with the historical, organisational, and geographical differences distinguishing our broad categories of university groups. We can see this even more clearly when we turn from the question of preferences for research or teaching to the question of how academics in these groups of universities conceive of their role. Table 12.10 shows the distribution of agreement with

[1] It should be noted that the last response category 'very heavily in teaching' was accidentally left off the main questionnaire, but was replaced for the CATs and Sussex. These groups are therefore not strictly comparable with the rest. However, the very small number at Sussex–which emphasises teaching–who chose that category suggests that the distribution among the main sample would not have been greatly affected by its inclusion.

Table 12.9

Interests in teaching or research, by university group (per cent)

Interest	University group: Oxford and Cambridge	London	Major Redbrick	Minor Redbrick	Scotland	Wales	Sussex	CATs
Very heavily in research	17	12	11	3	9	5	11	6
Both, but lean towards research	54	51	56	51	52	57	51	42
Both, but lean towards teaching	29	37	33	46	39	37	34 4 } 38	37 15 } 52
Very heavily in teaching				—category omitted—				
TOTALS	(156)	(233)	(462)	(140)	(243)	(116)	(134)	(376)

Table 12.10

Conception of academic role, by university group (per cent)

An academic man's first duty is to research	University group: Oxford and Cambridge	London	Major Redbrick	Minor Redbrick	Scotland	Wales	Sussex	CATs
Strongly agree Agree with reservations	5 32 } 37	5 33 } 38	4 34 } 38	1 28 } 29	5 27 } 32	6 26 } 32	3 41 } 44	2 18 } 20
Disagree with reservations	42	43	42	45	43	46	42	42
Strongly disagree	20	19	20	27	24	23	13	38
TOTALS	(154)	(235)	(463)	(145)	(242)	(116)	(134)	(379)

the statement: 'An academic man's first duty is to research in his discipline.' Again, with the exception of the recent CATs, we find remarkably small differences among the university groups. These differences are somewhat magnified through the use of the index of research orientations, which combines preferences and role conceptions (Table 12.11); the differences, though still not very large, are much in accord with our expectations (the former CATs, Wales and minor Redbrick universities showing somewhat smaller proportions of research-oriented staff).

It is when we turn to research activity, rather than attitudes and orientations, that differences among the major categories of British universities become striking. Over three-fifths of the men at Oxford and Cambridge and London have published ten or more articles, as compared with only about one in ten of the men at the former CATs, a quarter at Sussex, and little more than a third of the staff of the minor Redbrick universities (Table 12.12). This may be partly a matter of the larger concentrations of older men at Oxford, Cambridge and London, and of younger men at Sussex (and this we shall examine later). But it surely also reflects differences in the research climates of these several kinds of institutions, and in the variations in the necessary time and facilities (laboratories, research libraries, and other resources) among them. These variations affect not only how much research men within them do, but also the kinds of men they recruit and retain. Research traditions and resources shape recruitment patterns, and these in turn reinforce the emphasis given to research. We can see variations reflected in the teachers' reports of the amount of research activity they feel able to carry on during the term (Table 12.13).

The results here are interestingly different from our findings above. Londoners are notably unimpeded by the other commitments of term-time: only one-fifth of them are able to do no research in term, and more of them than any other group say that they can do a 'substantial part' of it. This accords well with their high research output. At the other end of the scale, men at the minor Redbricks do noticeably less research during term; this may be partly due to their small size,[1] which does not allow for many 'research men' who can opt out of most teaching or administration (we suspect that these are

[1] Sussex and the CATs were small at the time of our survey, and the same comment would apply here.

TABLE 12.11

Research orientation (index)* by university group (per cent)

Research orientation		University group							
		Oxford and Cambridge	London	Major Redbrick	Minor Redbrick	Scotland	Wales	Sussex	CATs
(Research)	1	8	8	7	2	5	4	9	3
	2	32 } 40	28 } 36	29 } 36	27 } 29	27 } 32	23 } 27	35 } 44	15 } 18
	3	28	26	26	19	24	32	18	25
	4	20	25	29	31	29	25	25	32
(Teaching)	5	11 } 31	13 } 38	9 } 38	21 } 52	15 } 44	15 } 40	10 } 35	26 } 58
TOTALS		(148)	(228)	(451)	(140)	(236)	(114)	(119)	(373)

* The index of research orientation is here presented in five categories, as it was computed. It will, however, be shown only in three parts hereafter. The reader should note the rough proportions in the extreme categories, which will not appear later.

TABLE 12.12

Production of articles, by university group (per cent)

Number of articles	University group							
	Oxford and Cambridge	London	Major Redbrick	Minor Redbrick	Scotland	Wales	Sussex	CATs
0	8	4	6	6	11	7	15	35
1–4	16 } 24	16 } 20	22 } 28	30 } 36	22 } 33	26 } 33	33 } 48	37 } 72
5–10	14	18	26	27	26	21	26	17
10–20	23	29	19	17	16	17	16	5
20 and over	39 } 62	33 } 62	26 } 45	20 } 37	24 } 40	29 } 46	10 } 26	6 } 11
TOTALS	(159)	(231)	(465)	(145)	(247)	(116)	(134)	(381)

TABLE 12.13

Research activity during term, by university group (per cent)

Research carried on during term	*University group*							
	Oxford and Cambridge	*London*	*Major Redbrick*	*Minor Redbrick*	*Scotland*	*Wales*	*Sussex*	*CATs*
A substantial part	25	32	27	14	26	17	15	17
A little of it	46	50	44	50	45	51	48	46
Almost none	29	18	30	36	29	32	36	37
TOTALS	(159)	(225)	(464)	(145)	(246)	(114)	(134)	(361)

especially common at London): it may also be due more simply to the fact that, as evidenced by their own preferences, there are fewer men here who *want* to research. The same comments would apply to a lesser extent to Wales. But in the middle, and clearly different from the others, fall the three remaining groups, Oxford and Cambridge, Scotland and the major Redbricks. Here are men whose commitment to research, as evidenced by their expressed preferences and their production of articles, is strong, but who are unable to carry on with it (or any substantial amount of it) because of their other commitments. This may be an example of an uncomfortable tension that is felt, as we suggested earlier, not only by the university system and its institutions, but by individual members themselves. We shall return to this point.

University rank and research orientations

It would follow from what we know of the career structure of British universities that professors would have the most active research record, but that they might currently be less engaged in research than readers. We would also expect that both of these grades would surpass all the others in research activity while senior lecturers, who occupy the only explicitly teaching grade, would do less. The distribution of scores on the index of research orientations for the different academic ranks appears in Table 12.14.

TABLE 12.14

Index of research orientation, by rank (per cent)

Research orientation	*Professors*	*Readers*	*Senior lecturers*	*Lecturers*	*Others**
Research primarily	33	42	27	35	40
Both	35	28	25	23	26
Teaching primarily	32	29	48	43	34
TOTALS	(187)	(121)	(206)	(706)	(109)

* All junior grades, including assistant lecturers, demonstrators, research posts, etc.

On the whole our expectations are borne out: readers are on average the most research-oriented group, and the least teaching oriented. Where 42 per cent of the readers stress the academic's research role and only 29 per cent his teaching role, the figures are roughly reversed among senior lecturers. The surprisingly small proportion of research-oriented professors may well reflect their other responsibilities–as we shall see, it certainly does not reflect a low level of research activity in the past. The lecturers are a very mixed group: we will want to see whether the differences in age and research interests conceal two alternative career lines, one for teachers leading to the senior lecturer grade, the other for researchers leading to a readership and possibly a professorship.

A clearer sense of the relation of rank to research and teaching emerges when we look at the actual research activity of the men in our sample, first over their whole career, as shown by their production of scholarly articles, and then currently, at least during term.

TABLE 12.15

Number of academic articles, by university rank (per cent)

Number of articles	*Professors*		*Readers*		*Senior lecturers*		*Lecturers*		*Others*	
0	1	10	0	15	1	40	9	67	20	82
1–4	1		2		14		30		40	
5–10	8		13		25		28		22	
TOTALS	(190)		(125)		(216)		(730)		(114)	

Although we saw above that readers are currently more research-oriented than professors, and that there are more research-minded lecturers than senior lecturers, Table 12.15 shows that past research activity does not altogether reflect present leanings. The rank order of cumulative research productivity corresponds to the official order of academic ranks. Professors have published more than readers, and senior lecturers more than lecturers. This is doubtless partly a result of age differences between the various ranks (which we shall examine later): for example, some lecturers have certainly been more active in research for a shorter time than senior lecturers. But it is also clear that the ranks are not so sharply differentiated in function. We suggested above that there may be two alternative career lines, one for teachers, which generally ends at the senior lecturer grade, and one for researchers, which leads to readerships and often professorships. This may be the case to some extent; but even the senior lecturers as a group did not define themselves so thoroughly (or so early) as teachers as to prevent them from publishing more than lecturers. Moreover, the distinction between readers and senior lecturers that we spoke of, while valid in many circumstances, is by no means universal throughout British universities. There are many research-oriented senior lecturers who have been promoted in recognition of their research in a situation where no readership was available.

Is the formal and informal differentiation of function between readers and senior lecturers becoming more or less pronounced at the present time? The existence of these two ranks has been a way of institutionalising the division of labour between research and teaching in some departments and universities. Whether these roles are more sharply distinguished in the future or become more similar, with the senior lectureship also as a reward for research accomplishment, will make a great deal of difference to the organisation and character of British universities. It is perfectly possible for the research and teaching roles to become more sharply differentiated without their being institutionalised in different *ranks*. In the United States this has come about through the development of research institutes and centres, with which researchers on a faculty become identified. The very much greater emphasis given to research in most large American universities threatens the role of 'teacher' with the stigma of second-class citizenship and status: and this threat materialised with the creation of a teaching-oriented college at the University of Chicago manned by a faculty that was quite separate from the research-oriented members of the graduate departments and faculties. This immediately raises the problem of recruiting able men to teaching posts which carry such a stigma; a problem encountered by even the most distinguished liberal arts colleges, though the absence of a body of men primarily devoted to research on the same campus softens the invidious distinction. The much greater status (and resources) accorded teaching in British universities has allowed the emergence of senior ranks roughly identified with research or teaching which have similar prestige. But the present apparent instability of this arrangement may, paradoxically, reflect the ascendancy of research over teaching in British universities as well. We suspect that instead of retaining the formal role differentiation in the form of different senior ranks, at the risk of one becoming distinctly subordinate to the other in status and appeal, the tendency will be for researchers increasingly to capture the senior lectureships as well, since with the growing importance of research (and graduate training) the need for more posts rewarding research distinction will probably grow faster than the number of professorships and readerships.

At the moment this is highly speculative. What is more certain is that changes in the size and functions of the British university system will place strains on the existing conceptions of these ranks; conversely, their evolution should be a sensitive indicator of changes in the roles and functions of British academics. We have already seen the extent of the difference in the research record of men in the several academic ranks. Are these reflected in differences in their present research activity, or, as near as we can get to that, their current activity during term? The data, in Table 12.16, show the very marked differences between the readers (and the 'others')[1] compared with all the other ranks.

TABLE 12.16

Research during term, by academic rank (per cent)

Research done during term	*Professors*	*Readers*	*Senior lecturers*	*Lecturers*	*Others*
A substantial part	21	41	23	21	44
A little of it	44	46	44	49	38
Almost none	34	13	32	30	18
TOTALS	(192)	(127)	(210)	(727)	(109)

The professors, or most of them, have had to put their research behind them: as a group they are least able to research during term, only one in five reporting any substantial activity. This is an interesting finding: it suggests that the organisation of British universities is such that when its most productive research men receive the reward they have earned through their contributions to learning, they are then effectively diverted into other work, chiefly academic administration. The general problem is widely recognised, though our data give it substance. The story is complicated by the fact that in subjects where knowledge is growing very rapidly, the appointment to a professorship may occur just about the time that a man's ability to contribute to new knowledge is declining. A shift of role to scientific administration for such men may be an extremely fortunate way of employing their still active energies and experience. In addition, again more commonly in the sciences but increasingly, we suspect, in other areas as well, chairs will be created that do not carry

[1] Included in the category 'others' are specific full-time research posts, filled for the most part by young men, which account both for their high level of research activities and (as yet) low level of accomplishment.

departmental administrative responsibilities; such 'research professors' may well be able to carry on a full programme of research during term. This development is dependent on the increasing separation of the professorship from the leadership of departments, a tendency warmly supported by a majority of academics (as we shall see in Chapter 13). Nevertheless, the figures in Table 12.16 suggest that a considerable amount of research activity among professors is inhibited by their other responsibilities; this is a high price to pay for the reluctance of British academics to permit the growth of a separate and specialised non-academic administrative staff. But the burdens of academic administration grow exponentially with the growth of institutions. Either more professors will in the future be able to do less research *or* teaching, or else the British universities will have to accept a measure of rationalisation of their administrative machinery. But that also, as Americans know well, carries with it a variety of consequences for the character of universities, many of them very difficult to anticipate. Growth will place great strain on the forms of administration, and thus on the existing character of British universities. The inherent conservatism of British academics and especially their reluctance to initiate reforms which threaten large though incalculable changes in the basic character of their institutions, is likely to lead them to attempt to retain the essentially amateur professorial forms of administration for as long as possible. But the growth both of student numbers and of research activity (with its new research organisations, large expenditures and ancillary personnel) will place, indeed is already placing, the traditional forms of university administration under very great strain.

Research orientation and subject taught

It is obvious from experience in the academic world–and our interviews confirm this–that the research-teaching dilemma is felt in all subjects in a university; it would doubtless be agreed that a subject in which no research remained to be done has little place in a university. But despite this we might expect differences in emphasis in different subjects. The arts subjects are the traditional centre of liberal arts teaching in British universities, as elsewhere, and it is here that we might expect to find the old dispute, of transmission versus cultivation of knowledge, resolved in favour of transmission. In the natural sciences new knowledge is being gathered so fast that it is at least arguable that no one could be an adequate teacher unless he were also engaged in his own research. Moreover, even at the undergraduate level the process of learning in the sciences is both a training in how to do research and actual participation in it, while an undergraduate in an arts subject is more likely to be engaged at best in reinterpretation or re-evaluation. We might expect, then, to find more research-oriented men in the sciences than in the arts. The same would presumably hold for the social sciences, another discipline very actively engaged in research at present, and most of all in technology, where–if anywhere–research must provide the subject's chief claim to be an academic discipline rather than a vocational training. Some of these assumptions, however, turn out to be rather surprisingly contradicted by the facts (Table 12.17).

TABLE 12.17

Index of research orientation by subject taught (per cent)

Research orientation	*Arts*	*Social science*	*Natural science*	*Technology*	*Medicine*
Research primarily	36	23	38	29	46
Both	21	23	30	23	29
Teaching primarily	41	54	31	48	25
TOTALS	(337)	(211)	(381)	(177)	(139)

We find that medicine is far the most research-oriented subject. This is perhaps not surprising; a very great part of medical research is carried on in the teaching hospitals associated with university-based medical education. But, of the strictly academic subjects, natural science comes first, with 38 per cent in the research-oriented category, closely followed by arts, with 36 per cent. Technology is third, with 29 per cent, and fourth social science, with 23 per cent, just half as many as medicine. At the teaching end of the continuum the same order holds, but (after medicine) natural science is lowest, with 31 per cent scored as 'teachers'; arts shows 41 per cent, technology 48 per cent, and social science 54 per cent. Although arts and natural science men have much the same proportion of researchers among them, there are noticeably more teachers in arts than in science. The 'pull' of the subject in natural science is definitely towards research; in arts it is more ambivalent.

The findings on social science and technology are remarkable, compared with what we had anticipated. One possible explanation, which raises more questions that it answers, is that social scientists and technologists in British universities are simply not interested in research; this would, to say the least, make them rather odd members of the international academic group of scholars in their subjects. But these are (with some exceptions) fairly new subjects to British universities: one consequence may be that their departments are relatively small, and hence that social scientists have to devote a rather larger amount of time to teaching. The other possibility is that men in these subjects feel some anxiety as to their status, and find it necessary to justify their existence inside a university: there are still a number of academics in arts subjects who express doubts as to the intellectual value of subjects such as psychology and sociology, or even the longer-established economics, and in the sciences there are doubts about the acceptability of their claim to be called rigorous sciences as well. Similarly technology is at the wrong end of the value-loaded term 'pure' science, and is sometimes seen as corrupted by its concern with immediate, 'applied' problems. The men in these disciplines probably do not take these accusations very seriously, consciously at least, and they would ask only to be judged on the quality of work they produce. But reactions to such anxieties can take other less conscious forms, and one way of countering them, without compromising their conception of their subjects, would be to emphasise conformity to other norms of British academics. It is clear from our survey that most university teachers in fact 'lean towards research' (Table 12.1), although they do not on the whole agree that research is an academic man's first duty (Table 12.4). But it may still be that social scientists and technologists either do not realise this, or hope to appeal to criticism from more old-fashioned sources by an over-emphasis on the old-fashioned virtues of teaching. Moreover, disciplines that conceive of themselves in this way tend to confirm their character by recruiting men with similar conceptions of how the applied sciences (both physical and social sciences) should conduct themselves in a university.[1] Before speculating further, however, it would be as well to look at actual research activity in the various subjects. First, is the higher emphasis on teaching a matter merely

[1] The high traditional status of medicine, the technology of the biological sciences, permits university teachers of medicine to define it as a research subject.

of preferences and attitudes, or have social scientists and technologists, in fact, published less as well?

The research orientation of medicine is just as clear here: over half our sample of university teachers in that subject have published more than twenty articles, and only 9 per cent fewer than five. Natural scientists follow, with 37 per cent having over twenty, and 20 per cent fewer than five articles. Social scientists have almost exactly the same production as arts faculty members, 20 per cent over twenty articles, and 37 per cent under five. Technologists, on the other hand, do less research: only 13 per cent have written more than twenty

TABLE 12.18

Number of articles published, by subject taught (per cent)

Number of articles	*Arts*		*Social science*		*Natural science*		*Technology*		*Medicine*	
0	11	37	12	37	2	20	9	41	2	9
1–4	26		25		18		32		7	
5–10	24		21		23		30		13	
10–20	19	39	22	42	20	57	16	29	25	77
Over 20	20		20		37		13		52	
TOTALS	(353)		(215)		(404)		(178)		(141)	

articles, and 41 per cent five or less. Moreover, 71 per cent, or nearly three-quarters of technologists, have published under ten articles, and arts men are their nearest rivals, with 61 per cent. Lastly we look at current research activity during term.

TABLE 12.19

Research during term, by subject taught (per cent)

Research during term	*Arts*	*Social science*	*Natural science*	*Technology*	*Medicine*
A substantial part	13	13	32	21	59
A little of it	45	48	51	47	31
Almost none	42	38	18	33	10
TOTALS	(351)	(219)	(406)	(174)	(130)

Still another picture emerges: once again medicine leads in research activity, for the reasons that we discussed earlier, and natural science is in second place. But technology comes third: 21 per cent of technologists say they can do a substantial amount of their research during term. In the last place comes social science and arts.

To sum up, medicine has a clear lead both in actual research activity and in its preference for and emphasis on research, and natural science comes next. Both of these would largely accord with our expectations, at least as compared with arts faculty members. Social scientists and technologists are peculiar: they are significantly lower in their expressed preference for and approval of research activity; but social scientists have a comparatively high research output, while technologists, whose output is low, do not feel especially handicapped by other term-time commitments. The indications that academics in technology are relatively less interested in research raise a whole series of questions about the place and the function of technology in modern Britain not only in the universities but throughout the society and economy. Do the best engineers (or the most research-minded, not to beg a relevant question) not take university jobs? It could be that those interested in research see it as essentially a full-time job, and are very unwilling to be distracted by teaching, which they may believe can be left to less distinguished or older men. Although the number of engineers and technologists trained in universities as opposed to on-job training is not very large in Britain,[1] this could have very important consequences for technological progress. It would be interesting to discover how much of the important research in technology in Britain is, in fact, done at universities, and how much at governmental research institutes or in private firms' research wings.[2]

We have looked at the variation in research orientations in different sectors of the university system: we shall now try to narrow the field further. We have already seen that among the ranks readers are the most research-minded, and senior lecturers the least; among the subjects, medicine puts the most emphasis on research, and social science the least. We can now ask whether these differences hold at the same time: are there particular concentrations of teaching and research interests, the former in social science senior lecturers, the latter in readers in medicine? Or if not there, where are the concen-

[1] Roughly a third of new-qualified men with engineering and technological qualifications in recent years gained their qualifications through a first degree in a university. *Report on the 1965 Triennial Manpower Survey of Engineers, Technologists and Technical Supporting Staff*, Cmnd. 3103, H.M.S.O., London, October 1965, p. 6, Table 1.

[2] See the 'Note on university technologists' at the end of this chapter.

trations? Different subjects may have different views of the function of various ranks. Table 12.20 shows research orientations broken by subject and rank simultaneously. The two groups we selected above do show concentrations: 56 per cent of readers in medicine are 'research-oriented' according to our three-part index, the largest percentage of all; the smallest proportion, 7 per cent, is found among senior lecturers in social sciences. An interesting feature of the table is the range: taking research-oriented men (the top line of the table), there are two groups with over 50 per cent in this category (both in medicine), six groups with 40–50 per cent, eight with 30–40 per cent, five with 20–30 per cent, two with 10–20 per cent (one being professors of technology), and one with under 10 per cent (the senior lecturers in social science). Four-fifths of the groups, in other words, have between 20 and 50 per cent research-oriented men amongst them, or fall within a 30 per cent range. The spread of teaching orientations, on the other hand, is somewhat wider. Two groups have over 60 per cent in the teaching-oriented category (senior lecturers in social science and technology); three between 50 and 60 per cent, seven 40–50 per cent, five 30–40 per cent, five 20–30 per cent, one 10–20 per cent (readers in natural science), and one under 10 per cent (professors of medicine). Variations in commitment to teaching appear to be rather greater than those in commitment to research.

But, in so far as there are concentrations, where are they found? If we look again at research orientations, we can see, first, that in every subject the readers score highest, with the exception of technology, where lecturers are as high. In arts, social science, and natural science, senior lecturers are lowest; in medicine they are lowest except for the thirteen 'others'; in technology, curiously enough, professors are lowest. Perhaps the lack of emphasis on research in technology results in professors being appointed on other grounds than their research achievement. On the whole, however, the differences between ranks that we saw in the system as a whole (Table 12.14) seem to apply to the ranks within each subject, though the extent of the difference varies between subjects. In arts there is a 20 per cent difference in the proportion of 'researchers' between readers and senior lecturers–just over a quarter of arts senior lecturers are research-oriented, against nearly half the readers. In social science the difference is 27 per cent–7 per cent against 34 per cent. In natural science it is only 9 per cent, in medicine 15 per cent, and in technology only 7 per cent–but the difference between readers and

TABLE 12.20

Index of research orientation by subject and rank (per cent)

Research orientation	Arts					Social science					Natural science					Technology					Medicine				
	P	*R*	*SL*	*L*	*O*	*P*	*R*	*SL*	*L*	*O*	*P*	*R*	*SL*	*L*	*O*	*P*	*R*	*SL*	*L*	*O*	*P*	*R*	*SL*	*L*	*O*
Research	37	46	26	36	44	22	34	7	27	17	37	42	33	38	47	12	29	22	30	*	42	56	41	51	31
Both	33	21	26	18	14	26	33	24	19	30	33	39	25	31	29	44	24	15	23	*	50	20	31	14	46
Teaching	30	33	48	46	41	52	33	69	54	52	29	19	42	32	24	44	47	63	46	*	8	24	28	35	23
TOTALS	(60)	(24)	(27)	(195)	(29)	(31)	(15)	(29)	(113)	(23)	(45)	(36)	(72)	(193)	(34)	(16)	(17)	(27)	(112)	(5)	(26)	(25)	(32)	(43)	(13)

Key to column headings: P = professor R = reader SL = senior lecturer L = lecturer O = other

TABLE 12.21

Index of research orientation by subject and university group (per cent)

Research orientation	University group																	
	Wales				London					Major Redbrick					Minor Redbrick			
	A	*SS*	*NS*	*T*	*A*	*SS*	*NS*	*T*	*M*	*A*	*SS*	*NS*	*T*	*M*	*A*	*SS*	*NS*	*T*
Research	31	12	26	25	39	34	43	24	44	37	20	40	34	53	47	13	20	45
Both	28	29	47	17	21	28	27	32	27	20	23	35	20	35	21	10	28	9
Teaching	41	59	28	58	39	38	30	45	30	43	57	25	46	12	32	77	52	45
TOTALS	(29)	(17)	(43)	(12)	(61)	(29)	(30)	(38)	(55)	(92)	(82)	(138)	(71)	(43)	(47)	(31)	(40)	(11)

	Scotland					Oxford and Cambridge				Sussex			CATs			
	A	*SS*	*NS*	*T*	*M*	*A*	*SS*	*NS*	*T*	*A*	*SS*	*NS*	*A*	*SS*	*NS*	*T*
Research	22	28	45	19	34	39	38	44	31	30	50	56	12	28	17	15
Both	12	24	20	28	34	28	29	32	23	21	17	17	0	28	27	24
Teaching	66	48	36	53	31	33	33	24	46	49	34	27	88	44	56	61
TOTALS	(41)	(25)	(87)	(32)	(29)	(64)	(24)	(34)	(13)	(47)	(18)	(54)	(16)	(39)	(146)	(172)

Key to column headings: A = arts SS = social science NS = natural science T = technology M = medicine

professors is 17 per cent. Lastly, there are clear differences between the subjects. If we ignore the heterogeneous category of 'others' we find that the *least* research-oriented grade (senior lecturers) in medicine has about the same proportion of researchers as the *most* research-oriented grade (readers) in natural science; and again the lowest figure for researchers in natural science, among its senior lecturers, is 33 per cent; the highest in social science, for readers, is 34 per cent. Technology has a narrower spread than social science, and fits in between the extremes of social science. Arts has a broader spread than natural science, and extends both above and below it.

To sum up, in slightly less dry and statistical terms, we have found neither overwhelming concentrations of researchers, nor the absence of concentration. Rather, we find within each subject the differences of emphasis between ranks that we found in the system as a whole, though they are weaker in medicine and in science than in arts and social science. In the former two subjects, the requirements of the discipline for research seem to have acted as levellers between the ranks. The differences between the subjects are no less strong when we look at the ranks separately–indeed, they outweigh differences between ranks so that it is possible to find three subject areas with scarcely any overlap. In other words, the subject that a man teaches is a major determinant of his interest in research; his rank causes internal variation within the bounds of his subject, but (except where the subjects are close together, as are arts and natural science, or social science and technology) does not make him look like a teacher in another area.[1]

We now turn to variations among university groups once more, looking at them in combination with subject taught, as they together bear on research orientations. In Table 12.21 we find the highest proportion of research-oriented staff, 56 per cent among the scientists at Sussex, the lowest proportion, 12 per cent, among arts teachers in the former CATs and social scientists in Wales.[2] In all the groups

[1] At the teaching end of the spectrum the story is not so very different, though perhaps less clear. There is a wider range in all subjects except in arts, and it is also interesting that in arts, technology and medicine the professors are the grade least interested in teaching. The wide range adds a significant rider to our remarks above–although medicine and natural science evidently require that each grade should have a certain very similar number of researchers, it is possible for the grade to be more differentiated as regards teaching. As a result of the wider range there is more overlap between the subjects at this end of the spectrum, but the same general pattern predominates.

[2] Followed closely by social scientists in minor Redbricks and technologists in the CATs.

that contain large universities–Oxford and Cambridge, London, the major Redbricks and Scotland, and also in Sussex–natural science and medicine show the highest proportion of researchers. At Oxford and Cambridge, London and Scotland technology comes last. Taking the groups individually, Oxford and Cambridge are interestingly homogeneous: we suggested earlier that there might be large differences here between arts and social science, on the one hand, which are most adaptable to the tutorial system, and natural science on the other. In fact, the differences among all broad divisions of study at Oxford and Cambridge are fairly small, and the emphasis on research is relatively high, even in technology, which has as many researchers as does any subject at Wales or the CATs. Sussex, however, which also uses a tutorial system, shows big differences between natural science and arts (though social science, interestingly, is here very close to natural science). London is likewise fairly homogeneous, and high in researchers, with the exception of technology. In the large Redbricks the spread is once again fairly narrow, except that this time it is social science that has the fewest researchers, while technology is not far below arts. The spread in Scotland is wider, and the order is unusual: here alone medicine is not the most research-conscious subject, falling to second place behind science, followed by social science third, arts fourth, and technology last: moreover, arts has more men interested mainly in teaching even than technology. In Wales and the minor Redbrick universities research is most emphasised in arts subjects and least in social science (technology really has too few cases to be reliable). We suggested earlier that small institutions like these really cannot support large-scale scientific research with laboratory facilities, etc.; and though they also tend to have small libraries, which might discourage research in the arts, this is evidently less important in its effects on research interests. In the CATs for once social science leads in research emphasis, followed by natural science, technology and arts.

We can also examine the subjects and see how they differ in research orientation in the different groups. The actual figures are obtainable by reorganising Table 12.21 to control for subject taught: they will not be presented in this form here; but we can spell out the order of research orientations for each subject. In arts it runs from minor Redbricks first with 47 per cent, then Oxford and Cambridge and London, major Redbricks, Wales, Sussex, Scotland, and the CATs with 12 per cent. For social science it runs from Sussex

(50 per cent), Oxford and Cambridge, London, Scotland and the CATs, major Redbrick, minor Redbrick, to Wales (12 per cent). Natural science shows Sussex in the lead (56 per cent), followed by Scotland, Oxford and Cambridge, London, major Redbrick, Wales, minor Redbrick and the CATs (17 per cent). Minor Redbrick comes first in technology (45 per cent), then major Redbrick, Oxford and Cambridge, Wales, London, Scotland and the CATs (15 per cent). For medicine it is first major Redbrick (53 per cent), then London, then Scotland (34 per cent). Giving the order alone disguises the very varying intervals–the figures should be referred to–but a few conclusions can be stated. The large institutions, Oxford and Cambridge, London, the major Redbricks and Scotland, fall in the middle or higher, and are clearly places where a considerable number of their staff in all subjects favour research. Of the rest the minor Redbricks are highest in their proportions of researchers in the arts and technology. Arts is one area in which small places can best compete, while technology is an area where other university groups are not, in fact, competing strongly. It would be interesting to know whether this is the result of some form of natural selection, or if it represents a deliberate choice of function to avoid competition in areas where larger institutions would have the advantage. Wales has not followed the same pattern; for it comes fairly low in all areas. The position of Sussex and the CATs, on the other hand, is probably not so much a response to their positions *vis-à-vis* other institutions but, as we have argued earlier, a product of their own internal characters as distinct kinds of institutions within the system.

Table 12.22 presents the number of articles published by subject and university group. The overall picture is not so very different from the results by our index, with one or two exceptions. In general, first of all, we find again as we found above (Tables 12.17 and 12.18) that in research activity, as compared with orientations, technology drops even lower in comparison to all the other subjects, and social science appears stronger, equalling and sometimes surpassing arts. Most of the remarks made above still hold true, but one exception is that the minor Redbricks, which had a relatively large number of research-minded men in arts and technology, are not especially productive in these fields. In arts they come somewhere in the middle in terms of articles published; and in technology very near the bottom.[1]

[1] We discuss the university teachers in technology in a separate note at the end of this chapter.

TABLE 12.22

Number of articles published, by subject and university group (per cent)

	University group																	
	Oxford and Cambridge				London					Major Redbrick					Minor Redbrick			
Number of articles	A*	SS	NS	T	A	SS	NS	T	M	A	SS	NS	T	M	A	SS	NS	T
0	9	4	6	15	11	3	3	0	0	6	16	2	10	2	6	16	0	9
1–4	17 }26	22 }26	3 }9	31 }46	20 }31	13 }16	10 }13	34 }34	7 }7	31 }37	27 }43	14 }16	32 }42	5 }7	30 }36	32 }48	31 }31	36 }45
5–10	24	4	11	8	20	17	13	32	11	33	27	25	30	9	24	29	24	45
10–20	23	22	22	23	31	33	23	18	29	14	22	22	15	21	20	13	17	0
Over 20	27 }50	48 }70	58 }80	23 }46	18 }49	33 }66	52 }75	16 }34	54 }83	17 }31	9 }31	37 }59	14 }29	63 }84	20 }40	10 }23	29 }46	9 }9
TOTALS	(70)	(27)	(36)	(13)	(61)	(30)	(31)	(38)	(56)	(95)	(82)	(147)	(73)	(43)	(50)	(31)	(42)	(11)

	Scotland					Wales				Sussex			CATs			
Number of Articles	A	SS	NS	T	M	A	SS	NS	T	A	SS	NS	A	SS	NS	T
0	28	12	2	19	7	13	17	2	0	29	14	2	69	31	22	43
1–4	30 }58	29 }41	21 }23	31 }50	7 }14	30 }43	22 }39	25 }27	27 }27	35 }64	33 }47	31 }33	12 }81	38 }49	41 }63	35 }78
5–10	16	12	27	31	27	13	28	18	27	22	24	31	19	23	21	13
10–20	5	21	18	16	23	20	17	16	18	9	19	21	0	3	7	5
Over 20	21 }26	25 }46	32 }50	3 }19	37 }60	23 }43	17 }34	39 }55	27 }45	5 }14	10 }29	16 }37	0	5	10	4
TOTALS	(43)	(24)	(95)	(32)	(30)	(30)	(18)	(44)	(11)	(55)	(21)	(58)	(16)	(39)	(151)	(175)

* For key to columns see Table 12.21. In some university groups, small numbers do not allow reporting of all subjects.

Again, Oxford and Cambridge, London, the major Redbricks and Scotland are high in all areas, except for the major Redbricks in social science (as before) and Scotland, which is very low in technology.

The institutional 'climate' for research

A glance at Table 12.23 bearing on research done during term shows one interesting pattern: men in the natural sciences show remarkably similar proportions in all university groups. Variations among arts and social science staff in different kinds of university are much greater. For example, while only a quarter of arts teachers in London report that they can do no research during term, the comparable proportions at major Redbricks, Wales, and Sussex are nearly a half. Similarly, where only one in six social science teachers in London cannot do any research in term, the figures elsewhere range from one in two to one in three.

Arguments about the desirability of researching during term can be made either way. From one point of view, research activities are a distraction, and necessarily reduce the time and attention a man can give to his teaching; the assumption here is that research activities must be at the *expense* of teaching. On the other side, it may be argued that unless a man carries on some of his research activities during term his students are not likely to get a sense of the nature of research activity, and of its difficulties and frustrations and rewards, but are restricted to reading about its results. The assumption here is that research enriches teaching, and that to confine research to vacations is to insulate teaching from research to the detriment of both.

Whatever the relative weight of these or other arguments for or against research during term (and they surely vary in weight in different fields and subjects), they are undoubtedly among the factors which determine whether and how much research is done. And that question, quite apart from the question of whether it *should* be done, is worth further investigation. Whether men research during term is probably partly a matter of resources (e.g., research facilities, funds, postgraduate students, light teaching loads), as well as of the teacher's own preferences. In addition, there is a powerful though subtle force at work in universities that we can only call the 'climate' for research activities. This climate, the normative ambiance within which academics work, reflects the dominant values regarding the relation

TABLE 12.23

Research during term by subject and university group (per cent)

Research during term	Oxford and Cambridge				London					Major Redbrick					Minor Redbrick			
	*A**	*SS*	*NS*	*T*	*A*	*SS*	*NS*	*T*	*M*	*A*	*SS*	*NS*	*T*	*M*	*A*	*SS*	*NS*	*T*
A substantial part	17	19	36	17	17	22	39	19	63	11	7	34	27	65	10	6	26	9
A little of it	46	48	47	58	55	62	48	64	24	37	49	52	41	25	54	56	50	27
Almost none	37	33	17	25	28	16	13	17	14	53	44	14	32	10	36	38	24	64
TOTALS	(70)	(27)	(36)	(12)	(60)	(32)	(31)	(36)	(51)	(95)	(84)	(148)	(71)	(40)	(50)	(32)	(42)	(11)

Research during term	Scotland					Wales				Sussex			CATs			
	A	*SS*	*NS*	*T*	*M*	*A*	*SS*	*NS*	*T*	*A*	*SS*	*NS*	*A*	*SS*	*NS*	*T*
A substantial part	9	24	34	12	46	14	19	16	25	7	10	25	7	26	15	17
A little of it	51	28	44	41	46	31	38	62	50	42	40	58	20	41	51	45
Almost none	40	48	22	47	7	55	44	22	25	51	50	18	73	33	34	38
TOTALS	(43)	(25)	(95)	(32)	(28)	(29)	(16)	(45)	(12)	(55)	(21)	(57)	(15)	(39)	(141)	(166)

(University group)

* For key to columns see Table 12.21.

of research to teaching, and their relative importance within the university. These norms and values both reflect and affect the availability of research resources–money, libraries, laboratories, postgraduate students. Moreover, the climate may well be affected by the character and values of a particular vice-chancellor, as well as by the scholarly or scientific distinction of the staff and especially of the leading professors in the several subjects. The climate for research at a given institution is also affected by the institution's own history and traditions, which help to define the institutional values which set priorities among conflicting activities. Whether a man does any research, when he does it during the year, and how much he does, will be affected by the research climate of his university and of his department, by the resources available to him, and by his own research leanings; these factors, though analytically distinguishable, are related to one another and mutually influence one another.

Our present study does not allow us to separate the elements in this system of forces; the only element among the immediate determinants of research activity for which we have direct data is the teacher's own research orientation. If we attempt to 'control' for differences in research orientations among individuals in order to assess the importance of the institutional context, we see (Table 12.24) that men with similar research orientations are likely to do quite varying amounts of research if they teach in different universities, or even different kinds of universities. For example, among academic men with teaching orientations, nearly half at Oxford, Cambridge and London have published ten or more scholarly articles, as compared with only a quarter of the 'teachers' at Scottish and major Redbrick universities. The differences are equally striking if we compare men with research orientations who teach in different universities. The institutional context has a similar effect on the opportunities (and motivations) to do research during term. In Table 12.25 we see that among men with research orientations, the proportion who are able to do a substantial amount of research during term varies from 17 per cent (in Wales) to 42 per cent (at London colleges). The variation in this regard between individual universities is even larger: only a quarter of 'research-oriented' teachers at Edinburgh, Leeds and Oxford are able to do a 'substantial' amount of research during term, as compared with over two-thirds in Birmingham and over half at Liverpool.

Besides variations between institutions, moreover, the climate for

TABLE 12.24

Per cent publishing *more than ten* articles, by research orientation and university/university group†

	Group						*University*								
Research orienta-tion	*Oxford and Cam-bridge*	*Lon-don*	*Major Red-brick*	*Minor Red-brick*	*Scot-land*	*Wales*	*Oxford*	*Cam-bridge*	*Birming-ham*	*Leeds*	*Liver-pool*	*Man-chester*	*Notting-ham*	*Edin-burgh*	*Glas-gow*
Research	66	71	60	51	48	51	74	57	61	50	62	63	55	50	61
Both	66	72	50	34	52	50	60	72	60	43	55*	67	30*	62	53
Teaching	49	48	26	33	25	39	48	50	25	21	33	37	30	32	20

TABLE 12.25

Per cent doing *substantial* research in term, by research orientation and university/university group†

Research	29	42	39	24	33	17	26	31	69	26	55	35	28	24	39
Both	32	34	28	15	40	22	33	32	29	29	36*	40	0*	45	53
Teaching	15	18	15	8	15	7	9	21	12	0	29	24	0	21	17

* N < 16.

† Columns do not add to 100% since these are three-variable tables presented in a shortened form, omitting those publishing fewer than ten articles (Table 12.24), and those doing less than substantial research during term (Table 12.25).

research varies by subject and department as well; and indeed, for some subjects, the norms of the discipline outweigh, and relatively reduce, the influence of institutional norms, while external support for research, both material and scholarly, may count for more than does the support of the man's own university. This, we believe, is the explanation of the much narrower variation in research activity during term among natural scientists as compared with arts men or social scientists (Table 12.23). But these figures are only suggestive. What is needed is direct study of the 'climates' for research, within disciplines, departments, and universities: how they are formed and sustained, on one hand, and how they affect the character, timing, amount and quality of research on the other.

Age and research orientations

We have been looking at institutional influences on and variations in research orientation and activity–at least so far as our data, gathered chiefly from the academics, will allow. Now we turn back to the teachers themselves, and look at an important element in a man's academic career–namely, how far advanced he is in it. For this we take age as a rough indicator, since most academic men enter academic life at much the same age, during their middle twenties, directly after taking their first degree, or after a few years of graduate work. There are of course many individual exceptions, among subjects and universities, teachers and researchers, which we believe are close enough to being randomly distributed not to affect our findings.[1]

We have seen that the number of articles published increases fairly steadily with age, at least up to about 45 or 50–an obvious enough finding. This could be due simply to the passage of time: indeed we can deduce nothing from it. But there is another question, namely, whether interests in research or in teaching do in fact vary for different age groups. If this is the case there are several possibilities; one is that in the course of their lives academics change their conceptions of their job or profession, perhaps as a result of a

[1] The one major exception may be in the 35–39 and 40–44 cohorts, whose university education and entry into academic life may have been interrupted by World War II, and who thus may have started their academic careers somewhat older, on average, than the other groups. We have not attempted to compensate for this possibility, since it is likely that the effects of war experience on the academic career are more complex than a mere delay in starting, and beyond the reach of our survey data.

reassessment of the nature of a university post, or (if they change towards greater emphasis on teaching) because they feel that they have already made such contributions as they can towards advancing knowledge, and feel their later years are best spent in passing on their own discoveries and those of younger men. In addition, as we noted earlier, age brings administrative responsibilities to many; and changes in research orientations may merely be a realistic reflection of what a man can do with his time. Another possibility is that there has been a change over the last forty years in the universities' assessments of their chief function, so that younger men hold different views not because of their own youth but because of the time they live in.

The changes which the university system has experienced in recent years have had many effects which are discussed elsewhere in this study. Expansion has been accompanied, indeed largely motivated, py a desire to make university degrees available to a larger social group, and it may be that young teachers see it as their duty now to pay more attention to their pupils, especially those from relatively poor backgrounds, than was the case in the past. But the staff/student ratios have not changed for the worse in recent years, so that expansion has not placed any direct strains on most teachers' allocation of teaching time. And despite reactions like that at Sussex in favour of an improvement in undergraduate teaching, the general trend, encouraged by the greater size and better research facilities of most individual departments, and by increasing pressures within British society for technological progress even at the expense of traditional 'liberal' educational values, has been towards a greater emphasis on research. If we add to this the idea put forward above, that youth is generally seen as the time of creativity, and old age of consolidation in academic careers, we should expect to find a steadily greater emphasis on teaching in older men. In this particular case it will be useful to start not with our index but with one of its two constituents, since this may illuminate the possibilities mentioned above. For although we have seen that personal preferences and conceptions of the academic role are in general quite closely linked, it would be possible for personal preferences to change with increasing age, while conceptions of the role of some typical academic, perhaps imagined as in early middle age, would not alter so much.

First, then, Table 12.26 examines personal preferences in different age groups.

TABLE 12.26

Interests in teaching or research, by age (per cent)

	Age group								
Interest	*Under* 25	25–9	30–4	35–9	40–4	45–9	50–4	55–9	60 *and over*
Very heavily in research	12	14	10	11	12	4	5	5	10
Both, leaning to research	70	61	58	56	53	50	48	45	25
Both, leaning to teaching	18	25	32	33	35	46	47	49	65
TOTALS	(33)	(190)	(257)	(290)	(197)	(156)	(100)	(91)	(51)

It seems that increasing proportions prefer teaching with increasing age. Under 30 there is a very weak interest in teaching (18–25 per cent); then from 30 to 45 there is relative stability, with roughly one-third leaning towards teaching, but about the same number as earlier (10–12 per cent) strongly committed to research; from 45 to 60, roughly half are predisposed towards teaching, and only 5 per cent very heavily committed to research; finally, of those over 60 almost two-thirds are teachers, but 10 per cent are 'strong researchers'. The youngest group is composed, for the most part, of assistant lecturers and very junior lecturers who have not yet made their mark, and for whom it is very important that they should publish fast. Men from 30 to 45 are chiefly lecturers, who may well be at their most productive period, but who do not have the same need to publish: they have settled into a stable pattern of balance between research and teaching. Around 45 they start being promoted in significant numbers to the senior grades, and begin taking on significant amounts of administrative work, which is further reflected in a shift away from research. This shift continues among the men over 60, though in this category there is also a small increase in the number strongly committed to research.

Preferences for research and teaching clearly differ by age. Is this also true of the level of research *activity*? If preferences are related to research work itself, we should guess that as academic men get older they will do less research during term. Besides this, older men, even before they gain a senior rank, tend to be increasingly drawn into administrative duties; and the only counterbalance to this might be that very young assistant lecturers may have an extra commitment to teaching in that they have to write new lectures and often familiarise themselves with parts of their subject about which they know little. But work, as Parkinson pointed out, expands to fill the time available, and we suspect that most men tend to revise their lectures fairly conscientiously, while the pressure of tutorials is never any less for those who give them. In fact, apart from the very young (who are still substantially students), the proportion who can do a large amount of research during term fluctuates around one quarter; but the proportion who can do *no* research during term doubles, rising from one-fifth at 25 to two-fifths at 55 and over.

TABLE 12.27

Research during term, by age (per cent)

Research during term	*Age group* Under 25	25–9	30–4	35–9	40–4	45–9	50–4	55–9	60 *and over*
A substantial part	50	27	23	28	24	18	25	24	20
A little of it	34	53	53	45	43	47	43	37	40
Almost none	16	20	23	27	33	35	32	40	40
TOTALS	(32)	(193)	(261)	(290)	(196)	(156)	(97)	(93)	(50)

As we noted earlier, a relationship such as we see in Tables 12.26 and 12.27, showing differences in research orientations and behaviour between age groups, can be interpreted in a number of different ways. First, different age groups may behave differently because of *differences in their current situation*: such as the greater importance for young men to publish if they are to gain good posts; and the difficulties older men have of carrying on research in addition to their increasing administrative responsibilities. Another interpretation emphasises the *experience* older men have had: it is suggested that over time the rewards of working with students grow, while the rewards of research decline. It may be that the effect of the concentrated research experience which many academic men have immediately after their first degree becomes gradually attentuated over time, and that in the ordinary circumstances of teaching in a British university there are for most academics few experiences of pressures to renew that involvement. Yet another interpretation would suggest that the differences reflected in Table 12.27 stem from *changes in the character of the men being recruited* to academic life over these years–

that the older men who show weaker research orientations held those orientations when they were young assistant lecturers; and that the young men entering academic life during the past two decades come with stronger research interests than their elders had at the same point in their careers.

TABLE 12.28

Conception of academic role, by age (per cent)

First duty to research	*Age group* Under 25	25–9	30–4	35–9	40–4	45–9	50–5	55–9	60 *and over*
Strongly agree	3	7	5	4	3	3	3	3	8
Agree with reservations	42	35	36	25	35	26	31	29	20
Disagree with reservations	48 } 54	38 } 58	39 } 58	47 } 71	42 } 62	49 } 71	42 } 66	48 } 67	31 } 72
Strongly disagree	6	20	19	24	20	22	24	19	41
TOTALS	(31)	(193)	(262)	(293)	(193)	(151)	(102)	(93)	(51)

It is difficult without direct and comparable evidence over time to choose among these alternative interpretations. Nevertheless, there is some relevant though indirect evidence within our own survey. Table 12.28 shows variations in the conceptions of the academic role among men of different ages. While there is a tendency for older men more often to disagree that 'an academic man's first duty is to research', the difference between age groups in their conception of the role is not nearly as large or regular as are the differences in their preferences for research rather than teaching or the difference in their research activities during term. The implication is that the academic man's conception of his role is relatively stable over time; that older men probably resembled today's young men when they entered teaching, and that it is less the norms surrounding the academic role than the individual's motivations and opportunities that change and are changed over time in the circumstances of British university life. This would suggest a combination of the first two interpretations: that for many older men the motivation to do a good deal of research grows weaker, and the competitive demands of teaching and administration are greater than they are for younger men.

But is the story the same for all subjects? It is a popular legend, for example, that no mathematician produces creative work after his twenties, and it does seem to be true that many great scientific discoveries are made by very young men; while some of the greatest books in the arts have been written in old age, as a distillation of a lifetime's experience and maturation. Is this at all borne out by our sample's orientations and behaviour? Table 12.29 shows the distribution of research orientations by subject and age. It is fascinating to see that precisely these beliefs are borne out by the attitudes of our sample. The purest example of change is in technology: of those under 30, 74 per cent are in the research-oriented category; this proportion steadily declines till it reaches only 15 per cent of those over 45, while for those in the teaching-oriented category it rises from 13 per cent under 30 to 68 per cent over 45. In natural science, among the men under 35, the men of 35–44, and the men of 45 and over, the proportions who are research-oriented are 46 per cent, 37 per cent, and 27 per cent respectively. Medicine, too, shows a small decline in research orientations over the years, though not a corresponding rise in teaching. In arts, however, there is neither a decline in research-orientation nor a rise in teaching with increasing age. In contrast with the sciences and technology, there is not the tendency to exhaust research interests and turn to teaching increasingly with age.[1]

Tables 12.30 and 12.31 show these age differences by subject separately for the two questions that make up the index of research orientations. Where they occur, the differences by age are larger and clearer with regard to 'personal preferences' (Table 12.30) than with respect to conceptions of the academic role (Table 12.31); they are very large on both questions among teachers of technology,[2] while on neither question is there any pattern of variation by age among arts teachers; and in the social and natural sciences, the youngest men (under 30) are conspicuously research minded, while the men over 45 are markedly more inclined towards teaching.

[1] The pattern in social science is irregular: while the youngest men are research-minded, as in the other sciences, and the men over 45 markedly teaching oriented, the 40–44-year-old group are markedly more research oriented than the next two younger groups. The numbers are not large, so that this could be a chance result. And yet this group were the men who entered academic life just after World War II. This 'generation' of Young Turks has had a marked effect on British social science; it may be that it is still distinguishable nearly twenty years later, by its research interests.

[2] See below, 'A note on university technologists'.

TABLE 12.29

Index of research orientation by subject and age (per cent)

Research orientation	Arts 30 –	30–4	35–9	40–4	45+	Social science 30 –	30–4	35–9	40–4	45+	Natural science 30 –	30–4	35–9	40–4	45+
Research	36	50	33	46	29	45	19	17	43	9	45	48	37	38	27
Both	17	21	19	8	30	21	22	30	17	22	30	23	32	38	33
Teaching	47	29	48	46	40	33	59	52	40	69	25	29	32	25	40
TOTALS	(53)	(56)	(58)	(48)	(122)	(33)	(27)	(46)	(30)	(74)	(88)	(73)	(76)	(48)	(94)

Research orientation	Technology 30 –	30–4	35–9	40–4	45+	Medicine 30 –	30–4	35–9	40–4	45+
Research	74	35	14	19	15	83	52	47	48	35
Both	13	27	33	15	18	17	19	25	33	37
Teaching	13	38	52	67	68	0	30	28	19	28
TOTALS	(23)	(51)	(42)	(27)	(34)	(6)	(27)	(36)	(27)	(43)

TABLE 12.30

Interests in teaching or research by subject and age (per cent)

Interest	Arts 30 –	30–4	35–9	40–4	45+	Social science 30 –	30–4	35–9	40–4	45+	Natural science 30 –	30–4	35–9	40–4	45+
Strong research	4	9	12	8	2	11	0	10	7	3	15	14	13	12	11
Lean to research	55	65	50	55	57	60	48	48	63	25	68	64	63	62	51
Lean to teaching	42	26	38	37	41	29	52	42	30	72	16	23	24	26	38
TOTALS	(55)	(57)	(58)	(51)	(127)	(35)	(27)	(48)	(30)	(75)	(92)	(74)	(79)	(50)	(100)

Interest	Technology 30 –	30–4	35–9	40–4	45+	Medicine 30 –	30–4	35–9	40–4	45+
Strong research	26	6	0	4	3	67	22	19	32	12
Lean to research	61	55	60	41	29	33	56	64	43	44
Lean to teaching	13	39	40	56	68	0	22	17	25	44
TOTALS	(23)	(51)	(42)	(27)	(34)	(6)	(27)	(36)	(28)	(43)

TABLE 12.31

Conception of academic role, by subject and age (per cent)

First duty to research	*Arts* 30 –	30–4	35–9	40–4	45+	*Social science* 30 –	30–4	35–9	40–4	45+	*Natural science* 30 –	30–4	35–9	40–4	45+
Strongly agree	5 } 37	7 } 48	8 } 32	6 } 46	5 } 35	9 } 38	0 } 21	2 } 21	0 } 40	0 } 17	5 } 40	5 } 47	4 } 35	2 } 39	6 } 31
Agree with reservations	32	41	24	40	30	29	21	19	40	17	35	42	31	37	25
Disagree with reservations	35	44	44	31	46	44	46	46	43	53	42	30	47	47	45
Strongly disagree	28	8	24	23	18	18	32	33	17	30	18	22	18	14	24
TOTALS	(57)	(59)	(62)	(48)	(125)	(34)	(28)	(48)	(30)	(77)	(91)	(76)	(78)	(49)	(96)

First duty to research	*Technology* 30 –	30–4	35–9	40–4	45+	*Medicine* 30 –	30–4	35–9	40–4	45+
Strongly agree	4 } 62	6 } 43	2 } 14	0 } 21	0 } 24	17 } 50	4 } 45	3 } 46	7 } 44	2 } 47
Agree with reservations	58	37	12	21	24	33	41	43	37	45
Disagree with reservations	29	35	52	46	32	50	37	38	37	43
Strongly disagree	8	22	33	32	44	0	19	16	19	9
TOTALS	(24)	(76)	(42)	(28)	(34)	(6)	(27)	(37)	(27)	(44)

Publication, and office-holding in scholarly societies, by age and subject

Publication is the most visible evidence of research activity, and holding office in a scholarly or scientific society a rough though useful indication of academic distinction.[1]

Table 12.32 shows the distribution of quantity of publication (in article form) by age within the several broad academic areas; while Table 12.33 shows comparable distributions of holders of national office in academic societies. These tables are revealing in several ways. First, as we would expect, older men have more publications to their credit, and are more likely to have held national office. The two notable exceptions to these linear patterns are the men over 45 in both technology and social science. In both these areas, the older men have fewer publications than the men in the age grade immediately below, and in the case of technologists, fewer office-holders as well. There is a strong suggestion here (and there is further evidence in our note on university technologists) that the men recruited to teach technology and the social sciences in British universities before World War II were markedly less research-oriented than either men in other fields, or the men in their own fields recruited to the universities after the war.

There is another interesting finding in Table 12.32, which supports the popular conception of the natural sciences as subjects in which the burden of research and discovery is carried disproportionately by young men. If we look (Graph 12.A) at the proportions who have published ten or more professional articles, we see in the natural sciences a large increase–from 16 to 55 per cent–between the men under 30 and the 30–34-year-old cohort. Among arts teachers and social scientists the increase in cumulative output is much more even over time: the slope of the curve for the arts men is almost perfectly linear.[2] The recognition that takes the form of office in academic societies, however, does not reflect the quantitative output of young scientists, but, as in other fields, for most men comes much later in their careers (Table 12.33). Perhaps that is just as well for the research productivity of the young scientists.

[1] See Alan E. Bayer and John K. Folger, 'Some Correlates of a Citation Measure of Productivity in Science', *Sociology of Education*, Autumn 1966 (39, No. 4), pp. 381–91.

[2] Over age 30, scientists also cross the ten-article level at a roughly constant rate, and at roughly the same rate as arts men, though there are fewer of them left below it at any given age.

Table 12.32

Number of articles, by subject and age (per cent)

Number of articles	Arts 30 –	Arts 30–4	Arts 35–9	Arts 40–4	Arts 45+	Social science 30 –	Social science 30–4	Social science 35–9	Social science 40–4	Social science 45+	Natural science 30 –	Natural science 30–4	Natural science 35–9	Natural science 40–4	Natural science 45+	Technology 30 –	Technology 30–4	Technology 35–9	Technology 40–4	Technology 45+	Medicine 30 –	Medicine 30–4	Medicine 35–9	Medicine 40–4	Medicine 45+
0	25	18	3	4	6	17	19	15	7	8	4	0	5	2	0	0	10	17	7	6	*	0	3	0	2
	69	56	32	24	20	66	45	34	27	28	49	14	17	14	4	50	51	43	26	30	*	15	9	0	7
1–4	44	38	29	20	14	49	26	19	20	20	45	14	12	12	4	50	41	26	19	24	*	15	6	0	5
5–10	19	22	34	28	21	26	22	19	7	27	35	31	19	12	13	25	29	31	30	32	*	33	11	7	5
10–20	12	12	22	24	22	6	15	32	40	19	14	30	21	23	13	21	16	12	30	6	*	33	39	14	16
	12	22	34	48	60	9	34	47	67	46	16	55	63	75	83	25	20	26	45	38	*	52	81	93	89
20+	0	10	12	24	38	3	19	15	27	27	2	25	42	52	70	4	4	14	15	32	*	19	42	79	73
TOTALS	(59)	(60)	(59)	(50)	(125)	(35)	(27)	(47)	(30)	(75)	(94)	(77)	(80)	(52)	(99)	(24)	(51)	(42)	(27)	(34)	(6)	(27)	(36)	(28)	(44)

* Numbers too small for percentage to be meaningful.

Table 12.33

Proportions who have held office in academic societies, by subject and age

	Arts 30 –	Arts 30–4	Arts 35–9	Arts 40–4	Arts 45+	Social science 30 –	Social science 30–4	Social science 35–9	Social science 40–4	Social science 45+	Natural science 30 –	Natural science 30–4	Natural science 35–9	Natural science 40–4	Natural science 45+	Technology 30 –	Technology 30–4	Technology 35–9	Technology 40–4	Technology 45+	Medicine 30 –	Medicine 30–4	Medicine 35–9	Medicine 40–4	Medicine 45+
Office-holders	10	20	26	40	49	19	33	36	21	42	4	17	38	53	62	8	20	21	48	36	*	26	22	46	74
TOTALS	(59)	(59)	(61)	(50)	(125)	(36)	(27)	(47)	(29)	(76)	(95)	(76)	(80)	(51)	(101)	(24)	(51)	(42)	(27)	(33)	(6)	(27)	(37)	(28)	(43)

* Numbers too small for percentage to be meaningful.

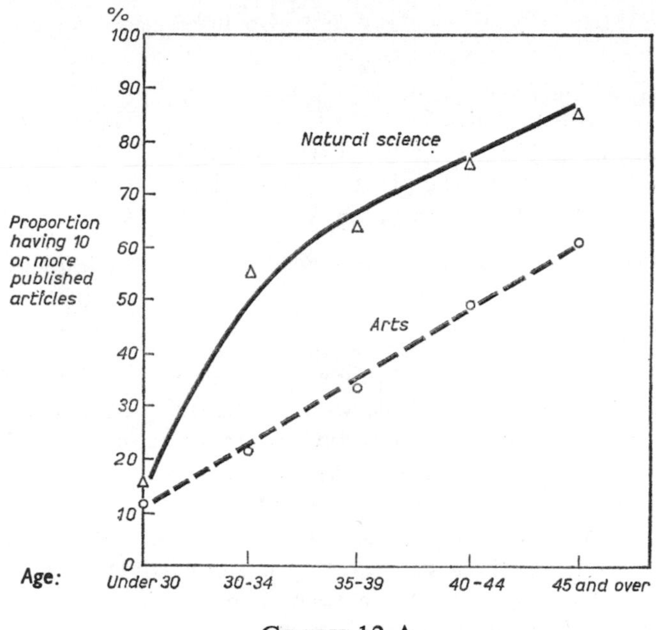

GRAPH 12.A

Rate of increase in cumulative publication of scholarly and scientific articles among university teachers in science and arts subjects. (Per cent in category having ten or more published articles.)

Differences in the proportions of office-holders in different subjects may reflect nothing more than differences in the number of academic and learned societies, and thus of offices, between fields. But within each subject we may compare the achievements of different age groups who presumably have had the same opportunities for recognition in this way. It is interesting that the difference between extremes of age is largest for natural science and medicine, then technology and arts, and finally social science. In other words, age greatly increases the chances for the honour of office-holding in science and medicine, and to some extent in arts and technology. But in social science even those under thirty have a one-in-five chance of holding office, and this has only doubled after 45. In well-established disciplines, and especially in research-oriented subjects, this kind of honorific recognition tends to come late in the career. In 'newer' subjects (newer at least to British universities), national societies are not only scholarly associations, but also instruments for defining the subject and its place in the curriculum. Young social scientists in recent decades have been seeking not merely for recognition for their own achievements, but also for status and prestige for their disciplines, and have, therefore, been conspicuously active in their national societies. Indeed, in some disciplines, genuine national societies are recent, and have been founded by the post-war generation.

Conclusion

In this chapter we have been primarily concerned with the way the British university system deals with the tension between the two major, and in some ways conflicting, components of the academic role: teaching and research. We have seen first of all that no part of the university system resolves the tension by surrendering one element of the role altogether. Everywhere it is accepted that both teaching and research (or scholarship) are legitimate activities of academic men, that both are involved in what it means to be a university teacher. It is the relative emphasis on these two functions that differs in different parts of the university system. And by a kind of academic division of labour, some parts of the institution and some sections of the profession place greater weight and invest larger resources of time, energy and money in one or the other. We have seen, always speaking relatively, and in terms of relative emphasis, that research is disproportionately concentrated in Oxford, Cambridge and London; among professors and readers, and very young lecturers and assistant lecturers; and in the arts and natural sciences (and medicine); the many refinements and qualifications of these assertions have made up the bulk of the chapter. The tension between teaching and research is in part sustained by the university system, which 'assigns' different tasks to different segments of the university, and in part by the individual university teacher, who everywhere feels the dual commitment. In the next chapter we examine differences in social origins and present attitudes and life styles which help to explain what kinds of men choose to emphasize one or the other aspect of the academic role.

When we speak of different parts of a university system being 'assigned' different roles and tasks, we are for the most part using the word in a metaphorical sense.[1] The relation of different fields of learning to the discovery and handing on of knowledge is rooted in the intellectual history of the several academic disciplines, and the circumstances surrounding their emergence from the far less differentiated organisation of the pre-modern university curriculum. Similarly, the relative emphasis on teaching and research in different universities reflects differences in institutional history, and in their functions in the scholarly and intellectual life of the nation. (On the latter score, however, an American observer may note that despite the marked differences in the history and function of, say, Manchester and Reading, their membership in a national university system makes them more alike than comparable institutions in the United States.)

While historical forces, both intellectual and institutional, have shaped the relative emphasis on teaching and research in different subjects and universities, these 'assignments' today can be seen in the different norms and expectations surrounding the academic role in different parts of the university system, and in the wide variations in the resources available for research to men differently located in it. In this chapter we have been studying not the social and historical forces underlying this functional differentiation of role among academic men, but rather the outcome of those forces as they were reflected in the variations in research orientations and activities within British universities at about the time of the Robbins Report. Present and future changes in the size and shape of British higher education will inevitably also change the distribution of research activities in the university system. One outcome may be to strengthen the research functions of technology in the universities and former CATs.

A note on university technologists

The most striking finding in Tables 12.17 and 12.18 is that the teachers of technology, even in the CATs, are so little inclined towards research. Technology without research is mere craftsmanship, just as science without research is a branch of history or philosophy. Neither subject can really justify a place for itself in the modern university

[1] However, during and since World War II, the Government, through earmarked grants and in more indirect ways, has 'assigned' certain universities specific research areas. This tendency may well increase in future.

apart from its research activities and research training, and the latter can hardly be divorced from the former. Scientists in British universities accept and reflect this in their high levels of research orientation and activity. A very large number of university technologists apparently do not. It is perhaps not inappropriate to ask–what are they doing? Or, how does one 'teach' the branches of professional engineering and applied science without engaging in research in those fields?

But there is another, and perhaps more immediately profitable question we may ask about technologists in the context of the present study. That is, who are the university teachers of technology who *do* engage in research, and in what respects do they differ from those who do little or none? It may be that there is in technology, to a higher degree than in other university subjects, a marked division of labour between the men who carry the research work of the subject and those who only teach it.

In Table 12.34 we compared research-oriented and teaching-oriented technologists in universities and in CATs, with respect to rank, age, academic careers (including class and level of degree), and also, anticipating Chapter 13, social origins. Comparable distributions are shown for research- and teaching-oriented men (within the universities only) in all other subjects combined. The most significant difference between research- and teaching-oriented university technologists (and this excludes the men in CATs) is in their age distribution (Table 12.34B). Over two-thirds of the research-oriented technologists in our sample were under 34 years of age, as compared with only a quarter of the technologist 'teachers' who were in that age group. In other fields, research men tend to be younger than teaching-oriented academics, but the differences are nowhere near so large. And it is not that technologist 'teachers' are on average so very old,[1] but rather that the technologist researchers are on average so very young. This suggests a real change in the character and orientations of the men being recruited to university posts in technology departments–and, indeed, perhaps a change in conceptions of what such departments ought to be like.[2]

Technologists differ from other academics in another way: the 'teachers' and 'researchers' among them show a larger difference in their class origins than is true for men in other fields (Table 12.34C).

[1] They are no older, on average, than 'teachers' in other fields.

[2] A similar pattern can be seen in the technologists' distribution among academic ranks (Table 12.34A): compared with other subjects, technologist 'researchers' are more likely to be lecturers or assistant lecturers.

Table 12.34

Profiles of technologists in universities and CATs, and all other subjects in universities, by research orientation, rank, age, social origin, degrees held, class of degree, and place degree gained

		University technologists			*CAT technologists*			*All others (in universities)*		
		Research	*Both*	*Teaching*	*Research*	*Both*	*Teaching*	*Research*	*Both*	*Teaching*
12.34A	*Rank*									
	Professor	4	17	8	4	0	7	15	19	12
	Reader	10	10	9	22	5	2	11	10	6
	Senior lecturer	12	10	20	7	10	12	12	16	18
	Lecturer	67	63	61	60	80	71	52	45	56
	Other	8	0	1	7	5	8	10	9	8
12.34B	*Age*									
	30 –	33 }68	7 }41	4 }26	12 }37	18 }51	9 }32	21 }42	15 }30	14 }30
	30–4	35	34	22	25	33	23	21	15	16
	35–9	12	34	26	29	23	26	19	22	22
	40–4	10	10	21	29	15	18	17	14	12
	45+	10	15	27	4	10	25	22	34	36
12.34C	*Father's occupation*									
	Professional	15	10	14	15	16	12	22	20	20
	Intermediate	46	48	35	32	42	27	45	40	40
	Skilled	35	38	43	48	37	55	29	34	32
	Semi-skilled	4 }39	5 }43	6 }51	0 }52	5 }42	4 }61	4 }34	4 }40	7 }40
	Unskilled	0	0	2	4	0	2	1	2	1
TOTALS (vary slightly)		(51)	(41)	(85)	(27)	(40)	(104)	(405)	(298)	(451)

TABLE 12.34 (*continued*)

		University technologists			*CAT technologists*			*All others (in universities)*		
		Research	*Both*	*Teaching*	*Research*	*Both*	*Teaching*	*Research*	*Both*	*Teaching*
12.34D	*Higher degrees*									
	None	34	39	39	30	52	68	35	40	48
	M.A.	18	12	21	15	20	19	11	12	15
	Ph.D.	50	51	40	55	28	14	55	48	37
12.34E	*Class of first degree*									
	1	46	41	53	26	30	18	42	45	46
	2(i)	18	7	14	19	22	8	15	14	14
	2 undivided	20	22	16	30	18	34	13	15	14
	2(ii)	2	0	2	7	10	3	2	0	1
	3/4	0	2	2	0	2	2	1	0	2
	Pass	4	7	1	4	5	17	5	3	5
	No class given	2	7	5	0	0	0	12	13	9
	No first degree	2	10	6	0	5	6	5	6	7
	Overseas	6	2	0	11	2	5	5	2	1
	Professional qualification	—	—	—	4	5	7	—	—	—
12.34F	*First degree at*									
	Oxford or Cambridge	18	20	18	0	5	3	29	33	31
	London	22	20	21	26	32	37	16	19	19
	Major Redbrick	35	29	34	48	38	31	19	16	17
	Minor Redbrick	2	0	1	0	2	4	4	3	4
	Wales	0	2	5	7	8	1	3	5	6
	Scotland	10	15	15	4	2	6	14	14	14
	Overseas	10	5	1	11	2	5	10	4	2
	None	2	10	6	0	5	6	4	6	7
	Professional qualification	—	—	—	4	5	7	—	—	—
TOTALS (vary slightly)		(51)	(41)	(85)	(27)	(40)	(104)	(405)	(298)	(451)

Over half the teaching-oriented technologists were drawn from working-class backgrounds–the highest proportion in any of these categories. The connection between working-class origins and teaching orientations holds true also, though less strongly, as we shall see in Chapter 13, for other fields. The especially strong connection among technologists is difficult to explain, except perhaps as an exaggerated identification by working-class technologists with an older conception of the academic role; and perhaps also, a somewhat stronger sense of the teacher's calling as one of *service* rather than as one of individual pursuit of personal rewards and distinction through research. But this can only be speculative.

Technologists differ from other academic men in yet another way. While in other fields 'researchers' are distinctly more likely to hold a doctor's degree than are men oriented primarily to teaching, the difference in the distribution of higher degrees as between *university* teachers and researchers in technology is relatively small (Table 12.34D). Nearly half of the technologists hold a Ph.D., second only to the natural scientists in this regard; so their relatively low levels of research activity cannot be attributed to a lack of research training. It is interesting to note here how different are the technologists in the CATs in this respect. There the relation of research orientations and the doctorate is even stronger than among non-technologists in universities.

Several other 'profile' comparisons of teachers and researchers among technologists are interesting for the surprising *absence* of difference between them. For example, it is widely believed by academic men that research is done especially energetically by men who failed to get first-class honours as undergraduates, and thus need to make their mark on academic life in other ways. Our data (see Table 12.34E) show very small differences in the distribution of classes of degrees between research- and teaching-oriented men in the universities.[1]

Perhaps equally surprising is the similarity in where men with teaching and research orientations took their first degrees (Table 12.34F). We have seen the wide differences in the level of research activity at different British universities. But these differences in the research activity of the staff are not reflected in the research orientations of their graduates who in turn become university teachers–and this is as true for technologists as for men in other fields.[2]

[1] See also below, Chapter 13.

[2] Among technologists in the former CATs, the minority of researchers were more likely to have studied at a major Redbrick, the teachers more often in London.

The sources of research and teaching orientations lie elsewhere. In part, they lie in the individual's own teaching situation: his age and rank, his subject, his present university. But they are also shaped by other personal characteristics such as class origins, and it is to these correlates in the individual's biography and social and educational perspectives that we now turn.

Chapter 13

TEACHING AND RESEARCH ORIENTATIONS II: CHARACTERISTICS AND CORRELATES

In the last chapter we tried to locate our teachers and researchers within the university system, and in doing so succeeded also in characterising the various parts of the system, its different subject areas, its ranks and the various groups of universities in terms of the encouragement and support they provide for research and teaching. We now return to the men whom we have distinguished as teachers or researchers, and try to describe them in other respects. First we ask where they come from, both socially in terms of their class origins, and then educationally. After this we explore a variety of attitudes that may be linked to interests in research or teaching, for example hopes and expectations about future careers.

First, what are their social origins? By virtue of their common occupation, university teachers would normally be thought of as members of the same social class. They have nearly all been selected in the most severe meritocratic fashion, in most cases early in their adolescence; exposed to much the same intellectual values and forms of instruction in grammar, direct-grant or public schools; attended the same universities; and have spent a good part of their late adolescence and adult years side by side in the same libraries, laboratories and common rooms. The imprint of their common calling and of their academic specialities is very strong upon them, and in many superficial ways quite obliterates differences that in other occupations reflect the early-life experience of men who grow up in different classes in modern Britain.

In Chapter 15 we show that teachers from different social backgrounds have broadly different political identifications and party loyalties, and hold different views on such directly political questions as the future character of British secondary education. But there is nothing obviously different about professional or working class backgrounds to associate the one with an interest in teaching and the other with leanings to research. It is possible, however, that men from lower-class backgrounds would be less affected by the old liberal arts tradition of British universities, and having risen by their own efforts would lay more stress on tangible achievements in the form of research, and less on the more imponderable, almost ascriptive qualities which are said to characterise a good teacher. With less of a commitment to the aristocratic and middle-class traditions of British university life, they might very well be oriented more to the production of knowledge than to the transmission of a cultural tradition. Moreover, if they still suffer from anxiety about their acceptability in a profession composed chiefly of men from middle-class backgrounds, they might find it necessary to prove their suitability for the profession by the quality of their research.

Thus, on the one hand we are suggesting that the severe selection and strong common socialisation to an academic career should override the effects of varied social origins. On the other, we are suggesting that if different social class origins do have persistent effects on the academic orientations of university teachers, they would be in the direction of stronger research leanings on the part of those from lower-class origins. Tables 13.1, 2 and 3 show the distributions

TABLE 13.1

Preference for teaching/research by father's occupation (per cent)

	Father's occupation			
Preference	*Professional*	*Intermediate*	*Skilled*	*Other manual*
Lean to teaching	34	35	39	46
TOTALS	(263)	(545)	(437)	(85)

of research or teaching preferences, conceptions of the academic role, and scores on the index of research-teaching orientations which combine those two questions. For the great majority of university teachers drawn from middle class or skilled manual backgrounds, differences in their social origins have little or no bearing on their research orientations. But the small proportion from semi- and unskilled workers' families, contrary to our expectations, shows a

TABLE 13.2

Conception of the academic role by father's occupation (per cent)

First duty is to research	Father's occupation			
	Professional	*Intermediate*	*Skilled*	*Other manual*
Agree, strongly or with reservations	37	38	34	22
TOTALS	(263)	(549)	(433)	(88)

TABLE 13.3

Index of research orientation by father's occupation (per cent)

Orientation	Father's occupation			
	Professional	*Intermediate*	*Skilled*	*Other manual*
Research primarily	36	37	31	25
TOTALS	(252)	(537)	(424)	(84)

somewhat stronger leaning not to research but to *teaching*. This may be due to the status anxiety associated with marked social mobility; in order to gain acceptance in an occupational group to which they do not altogether feel they belong, men from lower class backgrounds may take on, and indeed exaggerate, the characteristics they believe the occupation possesses–in this case, the high value traditionally placed on teaching in the university. There is another, not incompatible possibility that men from underprivileged backgrounds may feel a special obligation to teach in order to give those like themselves the encouragement they need to compete with those who started with greater advantages.

Our inquiry into differences in academic orientations of men from different social origins is, in a sense, a question of the relative power of early versus adult socialisation as they affect professional attitudes and behaviour. We can explore this question further by seeing whether differences by social origins persist among men who have been university teachers for many years. It is at least plausible that men may come to the profession with different conceptions of it arising out of their different backgrounds, but that these may disappear or become attenuated with long years of common experience in university teaching. In Tables 13.4–6 we see that the differences by social origins do not disappear among older men, but are present in every age category.

Whatever the explanation for these differences, the combination of social class origins and age makes for very marked differences in the academic orientations of university teachers. Where (Table 13.6) almost half of the young teachers of white-collar backgrounds are primarily interested in research, only one in six of the middle-aged or older teachers of working-class origins are similarly oriented. At the other extreme (not shown here) less than a third of the youngest white-collar teachers have strong leanings to teaching, as against two-thirds of the older men of manual worker backgrounds. These differences in orientation have marked consequences because of the heavy concentration of these older men of lower class origins who are mainly interested in teaching in certain academic subjects and universities. As one might expect, considering the different emphases of public and state schools in England, academic men from lower class backgrounds tend to congregate in science and technology, and there are relatively few of them in the arts.[1] We might have expected that this would make them all the more research-minded, but since this is clearly not the case we can ask whether their choice of subject makes a difference to the effect their background has on their attitudes to research. Table 13.7 gives research orientations, by subject and social origin.

In all subjects those from manual backgrounds are more teaching-oriented than the rest. But the degree to which this is the case varies. The difference is most noticeable in social science, and (allowing for the combination of the manual and skilled categories) in technology and medicine. It is still there in arts and even in natural science there is a difference in the proportion of research-oriented men from different backgrounds. The disproportionate numbers of 'teachers' among the small minority from semi- and unskilled worker origins still remains to be explained.

The university teacher's degree

Next we turn to the education of our sample. We shall look first at the degrees they hold, to find out whether these bear any relation to

[1] See Table 15.38, p. 430, and discussion there.

TABLE 13.4

Preference for teaching/research by father's occupation and teacher's age (per cent)

	Age								
	35 – Father's occupation			35–45 Father's occupation			45+ Father's occupation		
Preference	*Professional/ Intermediate*	*Skilled*	*Other manual*	*Professional/ Intermediate*	*Skilled*	*Other manual*	*Professional/ Intermediate*	*Skilled*	*Other manual*
Lean to teaching	25	31	39	31	38	44	48	55	56
TOTALS	(265)	(176)	(31)	(282)	(162)	(27)	(261)	(98)	(27)

TABLE 13.5

Conception of the academic role, by father's occupation and teacher's age (per cent)

First duty is to research									
Agree, strongly or with reservations	44	38	36	36	30	14	32	30	14
TOTALS	(265)	(178)	(33)	(282)	(159)	(28)	(263)	(95)	(27)

TABLE 13.6

Index of research orientation by father's occupation and teacher's age (per cent)

Orientation									
Research primarily	48	37	39	36	33	15	25	20	15
TOTALS	(258)	(172)	(31)	(274)	(158)	(27)	(255)	(93)	(26)

TABLE 13.7

Research orientation by subject and father's occupation (per cent)

Orientation	Arts				Social science				Natural science				Technology			Medicine		
	P	*I*	*S*	*M*	*P*	*I*	*S*	*M*	*P*	*I*	*S*	*M*	*P*	*I*	*S–M*	*P*	*I*	*S–M*
Research	32	39	37	25	27	28	17	7	43	42	35	30	32	32	24	51	41	42
Both	20	22	21	20	24	20	29	7	27	26	34	37	18	28	22	28	34	19
Teaching	48	40	42	55	49	52	54	86	30	32	31	33	50	41	54	21	24	38
TOTALS	(69)	(129)	(108)	(20)	(45)	(81)	(65)	(14)	(60)	(149)	(134)	(30)	(22)	(69)	(78)	(39)	(70)	(26)

Key to column headings: P = Professional I = Intermediate S = Skilled M = Manual

TABLE 13.8

Research orientation by class of first degree (per cent)

Orientation	Class of most recent first degree								
	I	*II(i)*	*II undivided*	*II(ii)*	*III or IV*	*Pass*	*No class*	*Gained overseas*	*No first degree*
Research	32	36	32	61	22	38	37	63	24
Both	25	24	28	6	11	23	29	23	29
Teaching	42	40	40	33	67	39	34	14	46
TOTALS	(595)	(190)	(195)	(18)	(18)	(56)	(136)	(35)	(78)

their present leanings to teaching or research. It might be, for example, that a good first degree would indicate a man's capacity to do good research work, and hence predict his interest in research, whereas a less distinguished degree would mean that he was capable of teaching adequately, but could not be expected to do very striking research. On the other hand, while the first degree is still thought of as a useful guide to a man's talents, its effects can be fairly well nullified in later life; perhaps the best way of compensating for a low-second-class or a third-class degree is to produce really good research. Table 13.8 relates research orientations to the class of first degrees gained.

In fact, there seem to be few consistent differences. The three degree classes which supply the bulk of the university teaching staff, first, II(i), and undivided second, are very little different from each other, or from the Pass and no-class degree-holders, in teaching-research orientations. Of the very few cases in each of the lower two classifications, those with II(ii)s seem to lean strongly towards research while those with thirds or fourths lean towards teaching. Apart from them, those who never gained a first degree are biased towards teaching, while those who earned their first degree overseas are definitely research-minded. But for the mass of the university staff the class of first degree does not seem to make much difference in this context.[1]

Higher degrees, however, should be a different matter. All of them, and especially the Ph.D. or other doctorate, require original research to be submitted as a thesis, and it seems likely therefore that any university teacher who has already shown his research ability by gaining a doctorate will be more interested in research than those who have not. This is examined in Table 13.9.

TABLE 13.9

Research orientation by higher degrees held (per cent)

		Higher degrees	
Orientation	*None*	*Masters only*	*Ph.D.*
Research	29	29	41
Both	25	23	27
Teaching	46	48	33
TOTALS	(540)	(179)	(609)

[1] No major differences appeared when we looked at this separately for the several subject areas. See Appendix D, Table 13.53.

In fact this is the case: only a third of the Ph.D. holders lean primarily to teaching, as compared with nearly half of those without Ph.D.s. Even so, the 'total' line (nearly as many holding no higher degrees as Ph.D. holders) suggests that there are many men with no Ph.D. and no intention of taking one whose interest in research is no less than that of 'accredited' researchers. And the breakdown by subjects taught (Table 13.10) shows, in each of them, a rather smaller difference between Ph.D. holders and the rest. (Oddly enough, the difference between Ph.D.s and others is smallest among scientists, who have the largest proportion of Ph.D.s, and whose research, one would have thought, is most closely linked to Ph.D. training. But apparently, the research tradition of science is so strong as to shape the orientation and behaviours of Ph.D.s and B.Sc.s alike.)

We have seen that the different university groups have different proportions of teachers and researchers. Since a man's first, and presumably most powerful exposure to the academic role comes when he enters a college as an undergraduate, it seems reasonable to look at where our sample first studied, to see whether any effect is still traceable in their attitudes to research and teaching later in their lives. Table 13.11 does this for the four university groups from which significant numbers of our subjects graduated. It is interesting to compare this with Table 12.20, the corresponding table for the university group in which they now teach. Curiously enough, among London graduates the arts lead the natural sciences in the proportion with research orientations, though the reverse is the case at the major Redbricks, and in Scotland. In all subjects Oxford, Cambridge and London are very similar; graduates of the Scottish universities are noticeably more interested in teaching, while graduates of the major Redbricks are also more inclined towards teaching, except in natural science where they are more research-minded than those from any other group. With the limited amount of information at our disposal it is difficult to know what to make of these findings: the differences in most cases are not very large, apart from Scottish graduates' preference for teaching, which is fairly clear. But there is a certain amount of inbreeding within the system:[1] Scottish graduates especially tend to find jobs within the Scottish universities; so that what we are seeing here may not only be the result of undergraduate education, but also a reflection of the effect of the 'climate' of a man's present university.

[1] See above, Chapter 10.

TABLE 13.10

Research orientation by higher degrees held and subject taught

Orientation	Arts			Social science			Natural science			Technology		
	None	*M.A.*	*Ph.D.*	*None*	*M.A.*	*Ph.D.*	*None*	*M.A.*	*Ph.D.*	*None*	*M.A.*	*Ph.D.*
Research	33	32	46	22	23	29	36	29	41	26	28	31
Both	24	19	19	20	20	31	31	35	30	24	16	26
Teaching	43	48	36	58	57	40	32	35	30	50	56	42
TOTALS	(171)	(62)	(101)	(125)	(35)	(48)	(80)	(31)	(271)	(66)	(32)	(80)

TABLE 13.11

Research orientation by place where first degree obtained, and subject taught (per cent)

Orientation	Oxford and Cambridge				London				Major Redbrick				Scotland			
	A	*SS*	*NS*	*T*	*A*	*SS*	*NS*	*T*	*A*	*SS*	*NS*	*T*	*A*	*SS*	*NS*	*T*
Research	36	23	35	28	38	21	27	30	36	20	47	29	28	29	42	21
Both	26	27	29	25	20	23	38	22	12	29	27	21	16	0	28	25
Teaching	37	50	35	47	42	56	35	49	52	51	25	50	56	71	31	54
TOTALS	(151)	(78)	(96)	(32)	(45)	(48)	(71)	(37)	(42)	(35)	(83)	(58)	(25)	(17)	(65)	(24)

Key to column headings: A = Arts SS = Social science NS = Natural science T = Technology

We have looked at some of the characteristics of teachers and researchers, those connected with their past history which may not only be antecedent to their present research orientations but also partly responsible for them. We next turn to another group of characteristics which are at least contemporaneous with present research orientations, and as we shall try to show, may be dependent on them. These are the use made of sabbatical leave, expectations of future career, and academic aspirations. Finally, we shall investigate whether teachers and researchers differ in their attachment to the university system.

Leave and travel

Sabbatical leave is normally allowed in British universities both to enable researchers to visit places which are particularly relevant for their work, and to allow for appointments to visiting teaching positions at other institutions. There is no general requirement that the leave be used necessarily for either purpose alone. There is therefore no *prima facie* reason to expect that either teachers or researchers would benefit specially from sabbatical leave. But perhaps researchers are more likely to take leave, since they will often have particular needs that can only be met at other institutions. Moreover, they will be known beyond their home university because of their publications. One of the chief disadvantages of being primarily a teacher is that one's reputation, however well earned, is essentially intangible, and wide recognition depends on the word-of-mouth communication of one's colleagues. The chances are therefore that a man who is primarily interested in teaching will be less widely known than his research colleagues, and so will be less likely to be invited to teach elsewhere; and if he is not interested in research he will have no excuse to invite himself. Table 13.12,[1] which tests these speculations, shows the proportions who have ever had leave, divided by subject taught and research orientations.

There are sharp differences between teachers and researchers in the natural and social sciences. In both of these faculties the chances of ever having had leave are about twice as high for researchers as teachers. In technology the tendency is in the same direction: but the chances of leave for any technologist seem to be very small (another

[1] Tables 13.12–13 (and Tables 13.54–56 in Appendix D) contain only those over 30, since leave is not easily come by in the early years, and this might cloud what clarity these tables possess.

bit of evidence on the parochialism of the university teacher in technology). In arts and medicine, it is the half-way group that is most likely to be given leave, and differences between the extreme groups are small, especially in the arts. Referring back to Table 13.19, however, we see that in these two faculties professors especially are concentrated in the middle of the research/teaching spectrum. It may well be that if we were able to introduce age or rank as an additional variable in this table we should find that the dominance of this group would disappear in these two faculties as it has in the others.[1]

The bearing of research or teaching orientations on foreign travel is shown in Table 13.13. In every faculty researchers have been abroad recently more than teachers. We have already suggested the reasons why researchers might be expected to take more sabbatical leave; these would apply even more strongly when all journeys abroad are included. Researchers might go for brief spells of field-work, or work with special equipment or facilities; and they would also go to conferences to report on their work and keep up with new discoveries in their fields. Teachers would not be affected by any of these considerations except perhaps the last, and not many of those who are predominantly teachers would be in demand for visiting lectures. So it is scarcely surprising that researchers should be greater travellers; but this is fresh evidence that research provides the passport for admission to the 'invisible college' of leaders in each field of scholarship–those who not only know of each others' work through publications, but often know each other personally through visits, conferences, and informal communications.[2]

Anticipation of academic future

We suggested previously that academics consciously define themselves as teachers or researchers early in their careers and probably do not change greatly in later life (although scientists who do their best work early in life do seem to move in the direction of teaching later on). Since there are two senior grades which are defined broadly in terms of their teaching or research functions, and since it is widely believed that professors are appointed on the basis of past research

[1] Similar tables for other aspects of leave (the date of respondents' most recent sabbatical, where and how it was spent) are given in Appendix D as Tables 13.54–56.

[2] On the 'invisible college' in science, see D. de Sola Price, *Little Science, Big Science*, Columbia University Press, 1963.

TABLE 13.12

Have you ever had leave of absence for a term or more? by subject and research orientation (per cent)

	Arts			*Social science*			*Natural science*			*Technology*			*Medicine*		
Ever had leave?	*Research*	*Both*	*Teaching*	*Research*	*Both*	*Teaching*	*Research*	*Both*	*Teaching*	*Research*	*Both*	*Teaching*	*Research*	*Both*	*Teaching*
Yes	32	43	29	52	45	24	35	31	17	12	11	9	26	38	17
TOTALS	(101)	(63)	(114)	(33)	(40)	(101)	(104)	(89)	(95)	(34)	(38)	(82)	(58)	(39)	(35)

TABLE 13.13

Have you been abroad in the past year? by research orientation and subject taught (per cent)

	Arts			*Social science*			*Natural science*			*Technology*			*Medicine*		
Have you been abroad?	*Research*	*Both*	*Teaching*	*Research*	*Both*	*Teaching*	*Research*	*Both*	*Teaching*	*Research*	*Both*	*Teaching*	*Research*	*Both*	*Teaching*
No	64	52	74	42	61	61	51	66	80	59	76	84	56	36	57
Once	20	29	16	33	20	25	27	26	16	24	14	11	24	33	29
Twice	11	13	6	15	12	7	11	6	3	12	8	4	14	26	11
Three times or more	5	7	4	9	7	7	11	3	1	6	3	1	7	5	3
TOTALS	(105)	(63)	(116)	(33)	(41)	(102)	(106)	(90)	(95)	(34)	(37)	(82)	(59)	(39)	(35)

achievements, we would expect that this self-definition would affect academic men's assessments of their future chances for promotion. Researchers can look forward to a readership and can hope for a chair. Teachers cannot realistically hope for more than a senior lectureship. So it would seem, at least. Our sample was asked three questions about their expectations of a chair, first at their present university, second at any British university, and thirdly how they thought their prospects of a chair compared with those of others of the same age and rank. The results are shown in Tables 13.14–16. In every subject area and in answer to all three questions men with primarily teaching orientations rate their chances of a chair consistently lower than researchers. There is least difference when they are asked about their prospects at their present university, where they all rate their chances as small, and teachers not greatly smaller than researchers. When they are asked about their prospects at any British university (Table 13.15) they are more sanguine, and the variations between subjects are larger. The sharpest differences between teachers and researchers are to be found among social scientists and technologists, i.e. those areas where research activity is lowest. In both areas, one half of the 'teachers' are 'almost certain' that they will not gain a chair, compared with only about one in ten of the researchers. In these subjects, presumably, the dedicated researcher is rarer and more conspicuous; and his prospects in a period of expansion are very good. Indeed, in social science, well over half the researchers think it at least 'quite probable' they will be offered a chair. But while there are differences among subjects, in general teachers and researchers accept, or at least recognise, that their preferences will affect their chances of gaining a chair.[1]

Academic aspirations

We now turn from expectations to hopes and aspirations. It was perhaps not surprising that interests in academic life affected judgements of future prospects. We can now ask, first, whether these

[1] It would be useful if we could look also at academic men's assessments of their chances for senior lectureships and readerships, to see whether, as we suppose, teachers expect to fill the former post and researchers the latter. Unfortunately, the only question asked was doubly inadequate for this purpose, in that it combined the two grades and asked about the chances of one or the other, and also introduced a limited time element. Whether as a result of this, or because men assess their prospects by different criteria than they use for the professorship (which we doubt), a tabulation showed no distinguishable pattern of relationships in any subject.

TABLE 13.14

Likely to be offered chair at present university? by subject and research orientation (per cent)

How likely?	Arts			Social science			Natural science			Technology			Medicine		
	Re-search	Both	Teach-ing	Re-search	Both	Teach-ing	Re-search	Both	Teach-ing	Re-search	Both	Teach-ing	Re-search	Both	Teach-ing
Almost certainly	0	0	1	2	5	1	1	0	0	0	0	0	0	0	0
Quite probably	6	8	3	10	8	1	6	2	4	8	9	5	14	12	6
Possibly but not probably	32	25	15	27	30	19	25	20	15	38	30	19	37	19	16
Almost certainly not	53	61	73	54	45	63	63	74	74	46	61	69	41	62	74
Not applicable	9	6	8	7	13	17	5	4	8	8	0	6	8	8	3
TOTALS	(100)	(51)	(120)	(41)	(40)	(96)	(123)	(99)	(106)	(48)	(33)	(77)	(51)	(26)	(31)

TABLES 13.15 AND 13.16

Likely to be offered chair at British university? / More or less likely than others? } by subject and research orientation (per cent)

13.15 *Likely to be offered Chair?*	*Arts*			*Social science*			*Natural science*			*Technology*			*Medicine*		
	Re-search	*Both*	*Teach-ing*	*Re-search*	*Both*	*Teach-ing*	*Re-search*	*Both*	*Teach-ing*	*Re-search*	*Both*	*Teach-ing*	*Re-search*	*Both*	*Teach-ing*
Already offered	4	10	3	13	18	3	2	4	2	2	3	4	4	4	0
Almost certainly	5	4	2	8	3	4	1	0	0	4	3	1	4	8	0
Quite probably	18	14	13	33	13	11	22	12	9	29	12	8	31	20	26
Possibly but not probably	45	45	44	35	38	27	42	42	30	52	61	32	42	32	32
Almost certainly not	26	27	28	13	35	55	34	42	59	10	21	51	19	36	42
		Δ = 2*			Δ = 42			Δ = 25			Δ = 41			Δ = 23	
TOTALS	(101)	(51)	(117)	(40)	(40)	(94)	(125)	(98)	(105)	(48)	(33)	(77)	(52)	(25)	(31)

* Δ is the percentage difference between 'researchers' and 'teachers' who believe they 'will almost certainly not' be offered a chair at a British university.

13.16 *More or less likely than others?*	*Arts*			*Social science*			*Natural science*			*Technology*			*Medicine*		
	Re-search	*Both*	*Teach-ing*	*Re-search*	*Both*	*Teach-ing*	*Re-search*	*Both*	*Teach-ing*	*Re-search*	*Both*	*Teach-ing*	*Re-search*	*Both*	*Teach-ing*
Already offered	4	10	3	13	18	3	2	4	2	2	3	4	4	4	0
More likely	23	22	11	35	10	10	22	9	8	40	15	6	25	40	23
About the same	46	45	48	30	43	43	60	64	51	40	64	51	54	36	65
Less likely	26	24	38	20	30	40	17	21	38	19	15	35	10	16	13
TOTALS	(101)	(51)	(117)	(40)	(40)	(94)	(125)	(98)	(105)	(48)	(33)	(77)	(52)	(25)	(31)

orientations in fact affect the likelihood of a man applying for jobs elsewhere; and, secondly, whether they affect the nature of the job to which he aspires. The relevant data are presented in Table 13.17. With regard to applications for posts in the previous year, differences between researchers and teachers are small. But future plans among natural scientists, technologists and teachers of medicine vary according to whether they see themselves as researchers or teachers. Adding the last two lines of the table, those who 'probably' or 'almost certainly' will apply for a post elsewhere, 39 per cent of researchers and 24 per cent of teachers in natural sciences; 44 per cent of researchers and 20 per cent of teachers in technology; 43 per cent of researchers and 28 per cent of teachers in medicine, anticipate applying elsewhere. Only in arts (22 per cent and 24 per cent) and in social science (31 per cent and 27 per cent) are there no serious differences. Why this should be so is not clear. For the others, the differences are in line with our previous findings: not only do researchers have a higher expectation of promotion to high rank, but they also act on their expectations by applying for new jobs more often. From another perspective, a primary interest in teaching turns one's energies and affections inward towards the institution–towards one's students, one's colleagues, one's syllabus. It is likely to engender 'local' as against 'cosmopolitan' attitudes[1]–an attachment to a community of fellows rather than to the international society of the discipline. All this would tend to reduce a man's inclination to move.

Table 13.18 gives a breakdown by age instead of subject, since it may be that the differences in plans and aspirations (and mobility) are more pronounced at one stage in an academic man's career, when the teacher may be settling down to a permanent post, whereas the researcher is seizing the moment to advance his career. Again adding the two bottom lines, the biggest difference between teachers and researchers is in the 30–34 age group. The under 30 group is, in fact, the most likely overall to apply for new jobs, and each group after it shows a successively smaller proportion who are inclined to move. But the difference between teachers and researchers is sharpest from 30–34, which is the period when, with the probationary grade of assistant lecturer safely behind, the teacher can forget about proving himself, and settle into the teaching duties he enjoys, while the researcher has by now published enough to make himself known, and

[1] On the distinction between 'local' and 'cosmopolitan' orientation, see our discussion in Chapter 14 and references there.

TABLE 13.17

Have applied or will apply for a post in past year/next three years, by subject and research orientation (per cent)

Applied last year/will in next three years	*Arts*			*Social science*			*Natural science*			*Technology*			*Medicine*		
	Re-search	*Both*	*Teach-ing*	*Re-search*	*Both*	*Teach-ing*	*Re-search*	*Both*	*Teach-ing*	*Re-search*	*Both*	*Teach-ing*	*Re-search*	*Both*	*Teach-ing*
Applied in past year	21	19	24	31	38	25	23	19	17	18	27	20	20	30	31
Almost certainly will not	44	47	42	31	38	41	30	33	40	22	27	44	31	53	49
Probably will not	33	26	33	35	31	31	31	37	35	30	34	33	23	15	20
Probably will	16	10	15	23	17	16	25	17	11	38	22	19	23	15	14
Almost certainly will	6	10	9	8	13	11	14	12	13	6	15	1	20	15	14
TOTALS	(124)	(72)	(140)	(48)	(48)	(114)	(145)	(115)	(119)	(50)	(41)	(85)	(64)	(40)	(35)

TABLE 13.18

Have applied or will apply for a post, by age and research orientation

Applied last year/will in next three years	*Under 30*			*30–4*			*35–9*			*40–4*			*45–9*		
	Re-search	*Both*	*Teach-ing*	*Re-search*	*Both*	*Teach-ing*	*Re-search*	*Both*	*Teach-ing*	*Re-search*	*Both*	*Teach-ing*	*Re-search*	*Both*	*Teach-ing*
Applied in past year	29	27	27	24	31	32	21	35	31	25	33	19	7	6	10
Almost certainly will not	21	29	23	15	19	25	22	25	31	37	42	33	73	66	69
Probably will not	27	29	35	35	41	41	37	29	34	34	29	48	21	24	19
Probably will	38	27	24	30	22	20	24	28	20	22	4	11	5	6	7
Almost certainly will	13	15	18	17	14	12	16	16	12	4	22	8	1	2	3
		Δ = 9*			Δ = 15			Δ = 8			Δ = 7			Δ = −4	
TOTALS	(101)	(48)	(62)	(104)	(59)	(92)	(82)	(80)	(121)	(73)	(45)	(73)	(92)	(108)	(186)

* Δ is the percentage difference between 'researchers' and 'teachers' in the proportions who 'probably' or 'almost certainly' will apply for a post in the next three years.

has reached an age where it is possible to begin applying for a post in the senior grade. Nearly half the researchers in that age group 'probably' or 'almost certainly' will apply for a post within three years, as compared to only a third of the 'teachers'.[1]

Retention in British academic life

Thus British academics have different work habits, different expectations of the future, and even different styles of life, depending on the subject they teach and their preference for teaching or research. It is therefore at least arguable that unless the university system can cater for all of them by providing them with appropriate satisfactions, some may be much more dissatisfied than others. We asked one or two questions that deal with their satisfaction with their jobs; most of these are comparative, but one possible indicator of satisfaction has a very clear meaning. They were asked whether they had ever seriously considered leaving academic life permanently. The results are shown in Table 13.19. Social science and medicine show the highest level of dissatisfaction, and the numbers who have seriously considered leaving from the arts and natural science faculties–less than one in five–are surprisingly small. But within faculties, the differences between researchers and teachers are neither large nor consistent. Academics differ among themselves in the strength of their commitment to their vocation. But apparently whether their interests lean more towards research or teaching is not a major factor in their attachment to academic life.

However, there is an alternative to leaving academic life altogether, and that is simply to leave Britain for a job in a foreign university. Our subjects were asked if they had considered taking a permanent post in a foreign country, and if so, where (Tables 13.20 and 13.21). The proportions who had considered this latter step are noticeably, indeed perhaps alarmingly, higher: in only two groups was it less than one-third. Only in the arts faculties was there no real difference between researchers and teachers: in all other subjects researchers were more likely to consider emigrating than teachers. (In the natural sciences half the researchers, as compared with only a third of the teachers, have considered emigrating.) As to where they had considered going, the only noticeable difference (Table 13.21) is that

[1] In Appendix D we discuss a series of findings (Tables 13.57–62) on the preferences of researchers and teachers for different kinds of universities.

TABLE 13.19

Have you ever seriously considered leaving academic life permanently? by subject and research orientation (per cent)

Considered leaving?	*All respondents*	*Arts*			*Social science*			*Natural science*			*Technology*			*Medicine*		
		Re-search	*Both*	*Teach-ing*	*Re-search*	*Both*	*Teach-ing*	*Re-search*	*Both*	*Teach-ing*	*Re-search*	*Both*	*Teach-ing*	*Re-search*	*Both*	*Teach-ing*
Considered seriously	23	16	16	20	36	23	28	20	21	18	20	27	27	31	35	41
Considered, not seriously	28	28	16	29	21	40	18	33	25	23	42	34	36	23	22	32
Not considered	49	56	68	51	43	36	54	46	54	59	38	39	37	44	43	26
TOTALS	(1,201)	(117)	(68)	(136)	(47)	(47)	(111)	(142)	(112)	(117)	(50)	(41)	(83)	(61)	(37)	(34)

Tables 13.20 and 13.21

Have you considered accepting a permanent post in a university abroad? by subject and research orientation

13.20 *Considered a post abroad?*	*All respondents*	*Arts*			*Social science*			*Natural science*			*Technology*			*Medicine*		
		Re-search	*Both*	*Teach-ing*	*Re-search*	*Both*	*Teach-ing*	*Re-search*	*Both*	*Teach-ing*	*Re-search*	*Both*	*Teach-ing*	*Re-search*	*Both*	*Teach-ing*
Yes	38	35	43	33	45	33	32	51	29	33	36	28	32	56	53	43
TOTALS	(1,237)	(123)	(71)	(139)	(49)	(48)	(114)	(145)	(115)	(119)	(40)	(40)	(85)	(64)	(40)	(35)

13.21 *If so, where?*	*All respondents*	*Arts*			*Social science*			*Natural science*			*Technology*			*Medicine*		
		Re-search	*Both*	*Teach-ing*	*Re-search*	*Both*	*Teach-ing*	*Re-search*	*Both*	*Teach-ing*	*Re-search*	*Both*	*Teach-ing*	*Re-search*	*Both*	*Teach-ing*
Canada	18	16	23	19	15	24	12	17	20	22	21	27	19	6	21	9
Australia or New Zealand	30	23	20	30	27	24	32	28	35	39	25	33	28	29	31	41
U.S.A.	34	37	30	33	46	28	22	42	27	19	50	27	28	52	34	36
Africa	9	11	11	10	9	8	26	5	6	10	4	0	11	4	10	9
Elsewhere	9	12	16	8	3	16	8	8	12	10	0	13	15	8	3	5
TOTALS	(534)	(56)	(44)	(73)	(33)	(25)	(50)	(104)	(49)	(59)	(28)	(15)	(47)	(48)	(29)	(22)

researchers most frequently think of going to the U.S.A., while teachers in every faculty lean towards the Antipodes. This, considering the comparative wealth of academic resources in the United States, confirms the suspicion that it is lack of research funds and facilities that leads researchers to consider leaving Britain, if not academic life altogether.

Attitudes to research: the emphasis on it, opportunities for it, and rewards in it

We began Chapter 12 by defining 'teachers' and 'researchers'. Our index combines two items so that 'researchers' are men who have a personal preference for research over teaching, and consider research as an essential part of the academic role. 'Teachers' prefer teaching in their own lives, and do not see research as necessarily a central part of their professional role. It has emerged that these expressions of preference were also reflected in behaviour in that researchers have written more articles and do more research during term. But we asked our respondents many other questions about research activities: about the emphasis placed on it by colleagues and by the universities in which they work, about the satisfactions derived from research and from other aspects of academic life, about our subjects' opinion of the quality of their own departments, and about the opportunities for research available to them. We may now discuss their answers.

Attitudes towards institutional emphasis on research

Our respondents were asked whether they thought that 'most university teachers in my subject put too much emphasis on teaching compared with research'. Very few felt strongly that most of their colleagues overemphasised teaching; only one in six believed so, even with reservations (Table 13.22). Within that broad pattern, it is scarcely surprising that in every subject researchers were more likely than teachers to see an overemphasis on teaching. But even among the researchers, no more than a third (and these were among men in arts) felt that way. It is significant that the existing high commitment to teaching among British academics is so widely accepted, even by those primarily interested in research, and even in fields like social science and technology, where a research tradition is not yet firmly established.

TABLE 13.22

'Most university teachers in my subject put too much emphasis on teaching compared with research', by subject and research orientation (per cent)

Over-emphasise teaching	*All respondents*	*Arts*			*Social science*			*Natural science*			*Technology*			*Medicine*		
		Re-search	*Both*	*Teach-ing*	*Re-search*	*Both*	*Teach-ing*	*Re-search*	*Both*	*Teach-ing*	*Re-search*	*Both*	*Teach-ing*	*Re-search*	*Both*	*Teach-ing*
Strongly agree	4	11	1	1	9	6	4	4	1	0	4	2	1	6	8	6
Agree with reservations	13	23	10	8	20	23	12	13	5	3	22	12	7	21	18	14
Disagree with reservations	49	48	56	49	53	40	50	50	58	44	43	59	43	44	46	46
Strongly disagree	35	18	33	42	18	30	35	33	36	52	31	27	49	29	28	34
TOTALS	(1,220)	(122)	(70)	(139)	(45)	(47)	(112)	(145)	(113)	(117)	(49)	(41)	(84)	(62)	(39)	(35)

TABLE 13.23

'Do you feel under pressure to do more research than you would like to do?' by subject and research orientation (per cent)

Feel under pressure		*Arts*			*Social science*			*Natural science*			*Technology*			*Medicine*		
		Re-search	*Both*	*Teach-ing*	*Re-search*	*Both*	*Teach-ing*	*Re-search*	*Both*	*Teach-ing*	*Re-search*	*Both*	*Teach-ing*	*Re-search*	*Both*	*Teach-ing*
Yes, a lot	4	4	3	7	0	2	6	3	3	4	2	7	9	3	3	3
Yes, a little	14	8	4	19	2	10	19	6	16	22	14	7	29	5	0	26
No	82	88	92	73	98	88	74	90	81	73	83	83	61	91	98	71
TOTALS	(1,231)	(124)	(72)	(140)	(49)	(48)	(114)	(146)	(115)	(119)	(48)	(41)	(85)	(64)	(40)	(35)

Similarly, Table 13.23 shows that very few academics, whatever their major subject or research interest, felt under 'a lot' of pressure to do more research than they want to do. Even if we include those who felt at least 'a little' pressure to do more research than they wish, the proportions are still, for the most part, under 30 per cent. As might be expected, in every field those who see themselves as 'teachers' feel under more pressure: in four fields, the proportions among the 'teachers' who feel under some pressure varies between 25 and 30 per cent. The highest proportion who feel these pressures (37 per cent) is found in the group which is least research-oriented–the 'teachers' in technology–where the pressure from other colleagues in their faculty should be low. (Even of the 'researchers' in technology, 16 per cent felt under pressure to do more. It would be interesting to learn where the pressure comes from.) But by and large, it would appear that the university system seems able to accommodate teachers as well as researchers without placing much pressure on them to change their direction of interest.[1]

But the tension between teachers and researchers in British universities is sharper than the question about unwanted pressure would indicate. When we turn to the delicate issue of the bases for promotion, we find very marked differences between 'teachers' and 'researchers' in every field. The question was put: 'Would you agree or disagree that promotion in academic life is too dependent on published work and too little on devotion to teaching?' In Table 13.24 we can see the marked suspicion with which research (perhaps the contemporary emphasis on research) is viewed by many academics, even by many researchers. Disregarding subject, 32 per cent of our total sample 'agree strongly' that promotion is 'too dependent' on publication; and 76 per cent agree strongly or with reservations. Differences between 'teachers' and 'researchers' on this question are, of course, quite large. Medicine apart, over 90 per cent of the 'teachers' agree with the statement, as compared with between two-thirds and two-fifths of the 'researchers'. The percentage difference

[1] It would be interesting to see comparative data for American universities which are supposed to be governed by the jungle law of 'publish or perish'. Certainly we would expect higher proportions to complain about these pressures to do more research than they wish, but the variations among fields, and between institutions of varying quality, would be most illuminating of the research climates in American colleges and universities. It would also be worth asking, both in Britain and America, where these 'pressures' emanate, and what effect they have on the quantity and quality of research done in different departments and universities.

Table 13.24

'Promotion in academic life is too dependent on published work and too little on devotion to teaching', by subject and research orientation (per cent)

Promotion too dependent on publishing	*All respondents*	*Arts* Research		Teaching	*Social science* Research		Teaching	*Natural science* Research		Teaching	*Technology* Research		Teaching	*Medicine* Research		Teaching
		Research	*Both*	*Teaching*	*Research*	*Both*	*Teaching*	*Research*	*Both*	*Teaching*	*Research*	*Both*	*Teaching*	*Research*	*Both*	*Teaching*
Strongly agree	32	13	28	44	15	19	41	16	27	54	27	44	67	14	26	34
Agree with reservations	44	31	49	47	39	60	53	48	53	39	33	41	32	44	50	49
Disagree with reservations	18	39	18	7	37	19	5	24	20	5	31	15	1	37	21	14
Strongly disagree	5	17	6	1	9	2	1	12	0	2	8	0	0	5	3	3
			Δ* = 47			Δ* = 40			Δ* = 29			Δ* = 39			Δ* = 25	
TOTALS	(1,228)	(122)	(72)	(140)	(46)	(48)	(112)	(144)	(113)	(119)	(51)	(41)	(84)	(63)	(38)	(35)

* Δ = % agree (teachers) – % agree (researchers).

Table 13.25

'Promotion in academic life is too dependent on published work and too little on devotion to teaching', by research orientation and rank (per cent)

Promotion too dependent on publishing	*All respondents*	*Research* P	R	SL	L	O	*Both* P	R	SL	L	O	*Teaching* P	R	SL	L	O
Strongly agree	32	2	10	22	18	21	15	24	40	28	32	31	47	54	54	43
Agree with reservations	44	40	50	36	41	40	48	48	36	58	57	58	50	44	38	51
Disagree with reservations	18	47	32	27	29	33	29	27	22	14	11	12	0	2	6	5
Strongly disagree	5	12	8	15	12	7	8	0	2	0	0	0	3	0	2	0
TOTALS	(1,228)	(58)	(50)	(55)	(239)	(43)	(65)	(33)	(50)	(160)	(28)	(59)	(36)	(97)	(302)	(37)

between 'teachers' and 'researchers' (in the combined 'agree' categories) varies from 25 to 47 per cent, and is largest in the arts where the research and teaching traditions are in sharpest conflict, and where a fair number of research scholars are not sure that research is yet given enough weight in academic advancement.

Nevertheless, it is still surprising that large numbers of researchers – largest of all in the natural sciences with the strongest research traditions – agree that research is given too much, and devoted teaching too little, weight in academic promotion. In part, this may be seen as one of the academic pieties: academics are always in favour of giving more 'recognition to teaching'. But these sentiments, expressed both by teachers and researchers, may be evidence of a widespread conception of the university as primarily, or at least equally, a teaching institution. In Britain, and perhaps in any modern society, this is a conservative sentiment, an expression of concern about the changes in higher education associated with the vast increases in knowledge, the rationalisation and expansion of research activity, and the resulting threatened transformation of the university into a major force for planned and unplanned social changes of all kinds.[1]

These concerns about the effects of research on the character of British universities and the academic career are largely independent of the academic man's own situation and experience. For example, in Table 13.25 we compare the sentiments regarding the role of publication in promotion among men in different ranks and with different orientations to teaching as against research. We might expect that teaching-oriented men in senior ranks would be reasonably assured of the possibilities of promotion for dedicated teachers. In fact, such men are extremely likely to fear an overemphasis on research publication, despite their own experience. The persistence of this concern, in the face of one's own experience, suggests that it is not merely a judgement of promotion practices in British universities, but rather, as we have suggested, a reflection of underlying concerns about the nature and direction of universities and their relation to society and to social change.

[1] This is Clark Kerr's view of the mission of the 'multiversity', as the central institution of 'the knowledge industry'. See *The Uses of the University*, Harvard University Press, 1963, pp. 86 ff.

The relative rewards of research and teaching

We discussed earlier the amount of research carried on by 'researchers' and 'teachers'; but one question that was not examined was how much teaching they did. We do not have data on this, but we have answers to questions about how much they enjoy research and teaching and, also, how enjoyable they find one other aspect of academic life–contact with students. These findings are given in Tables 13.26–28. It is not surprising that in every subject 'teachers' should enjoy teaching much more than researchers, though there are differences between the subjects. Natural scientists, and those in technology and medicine, do not enjoy teaching quite as much as those in arts and social science. More interesting, however, are the differences between the faculties in the proportion of researchers that enjoy teaching. In arts, nearly 60 per cent of researchers say that they enjoy teaching very much; the proportion drops to about half in social science and natural science, while of those in technology and medicine only a little over one-third enjoy teaching 'very much'. It appears that the arts, where a majority even of those whose primary interest is in research enjoy teaching very much, deserve their reputation as the core of the 'teaching' university. It is interesting that in medicine and technology, where the research tradition is, respectively, strongest and weakest, fewest researchers enjoy teaching. But these are the most clearly 'professional' subjects, where teaching is most nearly a by-product of research.[1]

Table 13.28 gives the proportions in each faculty who enjoy research. Naturally enough, researchers whatever their subject enjoy research much more than teachers. But there are interesting faculty differences among the teachers. In arts 65 per cent of the teacher group also enjoy research very much. In natural science 60 per cent do so, but in the other three faculties the proportion is 46 per cent. Once again arts faculties give the impression of being less strongly differentiated into teachers and researchers than any of the others: more of its teachers enjoy research in the humanities.

[1] Table 13.27 gives the percentages who 'enjoy their contact with students'. The results are very similar to those for teaching, with the exception that differences between extremes are smaller–those groups which very much enjoy teaching enjoy contact with students slightly less, while those who only moderately enjoy teaching enjoy contact with students slightly more. The only other difference is that social scientists in each group enjoy contact with students more even than arts men, whereas arts men enjoy teaching most of all.

TABLES 13.26–13.28

Enjoyment of university activities, by subject and research orientation (per cent)

		Arts			*Social science*			*Natural science*			*Technology*			*Medicine*		
	All respondents	*Re-search*	*Both*	*Teach-ing*	*Re-search*	*Both*	*Teach-ing*	*Re-search*	*Both*	*Teach-ing*	*Re-search*	*Both*	*Teach-ing*	*Re-search*	*Both*	*Teach-ing*
13.26 *Enjoy teaching*																
Very much	68	59	74	91	50	62	89	48	65	82	37	56	85	40	59	83
Moderately	30	38	26	9	44	38	11	49	35	18	63	44	14	55	38	17
Very little	2	3	0	0	6	0	0	3	0	1	0	0	1	5	3	0
13.27 *Enjoy contact with students*																
Very much	67	54	69	82	62	70	84	52	64	78	45	63	76	44	64	74
Moderately	31	44	29	18	36	30	15	41	34	21	55	37	24	52	33	23
Not at all	2	2	1	1	2	0	1	7	2	1	0	0	0	3	3	3
13.28 *Enjoy research*																
Very much	76	96	86	65	96	77	46	93	86	60	96	83	47	94	78	46
Moderately	21	4	12	30	4	19	43	7	13	36	4	17	48	6	18	46
Not at all	3	0	1	4	0	4	11	0	1	3	0	0	5	0	5	9
TOTALS (vary slightly)	(1,237)	(124)	(72)	(141)	(49)	(47)	(113)	(146)	(116)	(119)	(51)	(41)	(85)	(64)	(40)	(35)

We also raised the more general question not merely of whether academics enjoyed particular aspects of their work, but whether they were satisfied to be working in their present subject. Tables 13.29–30 show the answers to two questions, first, whether our respondents were pleased with having chosen their present subject, to which an overwhelming majority in every subject answered yes; and secondly, whether they ever regretted that they had not chosen another field. This question did produce some expressions of discontent–approximately 25 per cent of the total sample, fairly evenly distributed among the subjects and between those with different research orientations. (Here the researchers in medicine and technology are at opposite extremes, reflecting the research situations in their disciplines.)

Assessment of own department's teaching and research

It would be interesting to know to what extent teachers and researchers congregate in departments that are in any way singled out or respected for research or teaching. We have no way of identifying the 'better' or more widely respected departments. But we do have the assessments made by our respondents of their own department's qualities, which will enable us to see if there is any consensus among teachers that they are in good teaching departments, etc. The results are shown in Tables 13.31–35. Noticeably few men consider their department below average quality in undergraduate teaching.[1] In all the other respects in which they were asked to rate their departments there is some bias towards the 'above average' end; but the bias is much more pronounced with respect to teaching. There are several possible interpretations of this. It may be that it is almost impossible to admit that a department's undergraduate teaching is bad, since this is too fundamental to the nature of a department and would be too damaging to its members' self-respect. But we might expect that 'researchers' would not be so affected by this consideration and, in fact, they seem just as unwilling as the rest to judge their departments 'below average' in this respect. Moreover, the 'research and scholarship of its staff' is presumably even more central to a department's self-esteem, and more people seem prepared to rate this below average. An alternative interpretation is that our respondents simply do not

[1] The tendency of academic men to exaggerate the quality of their own departments is widespread. See, for example, Bernard Berelson, *Graduate Education in the United States*, McGraw-Hill, 1960.

TABLES 13.29 AND 13.30

Liking for subject, and regret for another, by subject and research orientation (per cent)

13.29 Are you *pleased* with having chosen you *present* subject:

	All	*Arts* Re-search	*Arts* Both	*Arts* Teach-ing	*Social science* Re-search	*Social science* Both	*Social science* Teach-ing	*Natural science* Re-search	*Natural science* Both	*Natural science* Teach-ing	*Technology* Re-search	*Technology* Both	*Technology* Teach-ing	*Medicine* Re-search	*Medicine* Both	*Medicine* Teach-ing
Yes	95	92	94	96	96	94	95	97	95	97	96	98	89	94	95	97

13.30 Do you sometimes *regret* that you did not choose *another field*:

	All	*Arts* Re-search	*Arts* Both	*Arts* Teach-ing	*Social science* Re-search	*Social science* Both	*Social science* Teach-ing	*Natural science* Re-search	*Natural science* Both	*Natural science* Teach-ing	*Technology* Re-search	*Technology* Both	*Technology* Teach-ing	*Medicine* Re-search	*Medicine* Both	*Medicine* Teach-ing
Yes	24	23	19	28	18	29	28	21	22	19	31	29	26	16	25	23
TOTALS (vary slightly)	(1,233)	(124)	(72)	(141)	(49)	(43)	(111)	(146)	(115)	(119)	(51)	(41)	(85)	(64)	(40)	(35)

TABLES 13.31–13.35

Assessment of department's qualities, by subject and research orientation (per cent)

	All respondents	Arts			Social science			Natural science			Technology			Medicine		
		Re-search	Both	Teach-ing	Re-search	Both	Teach-ing	Re-search	Both	Teach-ing	Re-search	Both	Teach-ing	Re-search	Both	Teach-ing
13.31 *Undergraduate teaching*																
Above average	56	61	54	72	57	56	62	50	47	53	59	55	57	39	42	58
Average	39	37	40	25	37	33	29	43	50	43	35	45	38	50	55	33
Below average	5	3	6	3	6	11	9	8	4	4	7	0	5	11	3	9
13.32 *Postgraduate training*																
Above average	30	32	26	19	34	52	38	30	27	25	50	32	41	31	46	36
Average	48	41	41	50	41	28	32	51	60	54	37	46	36	41	29	36
Below average	22	27	33	31	25	20	30	19	13	21	13	22	23	29	26	27
13.33 *Research and scholarship of staff*																
Above average	36	45	39	28	50	46	28	36	31	28	45	33	33	49	42	15
Average	50	49	50	57	45	32	44	53	54	57	47	50	46	38	44	61
Below average	14	6	11	14	5	22	29	12	15	15	9	17	21	13	14	24
13.34 *Size and breadth of coverage of field*																
Above average	45	52	42	55	58	57	51	42	32	39	48	30	41	46	28	29
Average	41	36	42	37	18	31	36	38	50	42	46	62	48	44	53	50
Below average	14	12	16	8	24	12	12	20	19	19	6	8	11	10	19	21
13.35 *Responsiveness to new ideas*																
Above average	42	38	38	40	48	56	47	45	37	30	53	35	46	55	31	29
Average	44	44	45	39	39	38	43	37	51	59	38	43	43	37	47	56
Below average	14	17	17	21	14	5	11	18	12	11	9	22	11	8	22	15
TOTALS	(1,288)	(124)	(72)	(141)	(49)	(48)	(114)	(146)	(116)	(119)	(51)	(41)	(85)	(64)	(40)	(35)

know what 'average' standards of undergraduate education are. Undergraduate teaching ability is notoriously difficult to judge among individuals and still more so between departments. There is little in the way of concrete evidence that could be used, and it is likely that academics do not have any yardstick by which to make comparisons.[1]

Be this as it may, there is little difference between teachers and researchers in their assessment of their own departments' undergraduate teaching. With respect to postgraduate training, similarly, the difference between teachers and researchers in their assessment of their own departments is small (Table 13.32), despite the fact that postgraduate training is quite different in character from undergraduate education, resembling a master–apprentice relationship rather than the teacher–pupil relations of the undergraduate years. And much of postgraduate training consists of thesis supervision. We should expect postgraduate training to be best in departments with a good research reputation, and less good where they are known for undergraduate education. But it may be that men with research orientations use more severe criteria in judging the quality of postgraduate training offered by their department, and that this obscures differences between them and other teachers in Table 13.32.

Table 13.33 deals with assessments of the 'research and scholarship of the staff' of a department. Unfortunately for our analytical purposes, though fortunately for universities and students, scholarship is not an attribute that is confined to researchers. Thus we are asking here about the overall qualities of the members of the department as academic men, though the form of the question places a certain emphasis on research. At any rate, it is clear that researchers consider their departments better in terms of research and scholarship than do teachers. The difference is relatively large in medicine, social science and arts, smaller in technology and natural science. If they are basing their replies mainly on the research abilities of the staff, this tells us simply that researchers either concentrate themselves, or at least believe that they do, in departments with better than average researchers on its staff. But if the replies also take into account the general qualities of scholarship, then the concentration is in the best departments altogether, which has a somewhat wider significance. Before we discuss this further, we should look briefly at the two tables. From Table 13.34 it appears that, medicine apart, researchers

[1] This is one reason why it is difficult to give more weight to 'teaching' in promotion, and why, also, it is easy and inexpensive to urge that this be done.

do not see themselves in larger or broader-ranging departments than teachers; in Table 13.35, again with the exception of medicine, researchers do not on average see their departments as more responsive to new ideas than do teachers.

To sum up, when asked to assess various aspects of their own departments teachers and researchers, apart from medical men, show few differences except in the assessment of the quality of research and scholarship of the staff. On that question, the researchers rank their own departments high somewhat more often than do the teachers. It may be that researchers are in fact somewhat more concentrated in stronger departments; or it may be that they simply know more about the quality of the work in their departments; or, most plausibly, that they rank their departments high on the one criterion that matters most to them. But we cannot tell much about the objective qualities of departments from these reports, in part because we cannot choose between alternative interpretations of differences we do find, in part because the absence of differences may be the product of different criteria of assessment which mask or obscure real differences between departments. This is a distinct gap in our study, and leaves unanswered a number of questions that are worthy of investigation.

Perceived opportunities and difficulties for doing research

What are the conditions under which research is done? For almost all university men it is only one of a number of demands on their time; moreover, there may well be other constraints besides lack of time which prevent them from doing as much research as they might like. Our respondents were given a list of possible handicaps to research which they might experience, and asked to indicate those which they felt were major handicaps to them. The results are shown in Table 13.36. As we might expect, teachers (in all subjects except social science) blame their teaching commitments more than do researchers; but, interestingly enough, they also blame other demands on their time more than do researchers. For all groups, however, the pressure of time is the most important handicap. The other possible handicaps are felt by researchers more than by teachers; this is natural, since they are essentially difficulties experienced *in the course of* research; whereas, lack of time is for teachers (though evidently not for researchers) a discouragement from *undertaking* research. Taking them in order, insufficient financial resources are blamed by a fairly

TABLE 13.36

Handicaps experienced in research, by subject and research orientation (per cent*)

Major handicaps	All respondents	Arts			Social science			Natural science			Technology			Medicine		
		Research	*Both*	*Teaching*	*Research*	*Both*	*Teaching*	*Research*	*Both*	*Teaching*	*Research*	*Both*	*Teaching*	*Research*	*Both*	*Teaching*
Insufficient time because of teaching commitments	52	59	61	67	60	57	58	42	41	64	36	49	68	24	21	35
Insufficient time because of other commitments	54	52	55	58	58	57	59	45	44	55	43	65	49	58	66	68
Insufficient financial resources	38	38	31	24	49	31	37	51	45	30	62	32	30	35	53	26
Slowness of machinery for obtaining equipment and/or books	21	16	22	11	16	12	8	36	29	21	43	19	16	24	18	18
Insufficient contact with other workers in your field	24	22	21	19	20	21	23	31	35	19	38	27	19	27	16	15
Insufficiencies in your library	25	37	34	28	42	29	28	21	20	18	21	19	16	27	13	3
Unresponsiveness of university administration to your needs	14	16	15	8	18	19	10	17	15	10	17	14	6	24	18	6
Unresponsiveness of department or college administration to your needs	14	17	12	9	18	17	8	15	19	9	19	5	15	18	24	18
TOTALS	(1,153)	(114)	(67)	(132)	(45)	(42)	(106)	(141)	(108)	(107)	(47)	(37)	(80)	(55)	(38)	(34)

* Percentages add up to more than 100, since multiple answers were allowed.

large proportion of all groups; but the lack of finance is particularly felt in social science, natural science and technology, which are typically the more expensive fields for research. The slowness of machinery for obtaining equipment or books does not seem very important to arts and social science; but it is a substantial handicap to researchers in science and technology. Insufficient contact with other workers is blamed by natural science, technology and medicine more than by arts and social science; and in the latter faculties it is not felt much more by researchers than by teachers. Arts and social science, on the other hand, complain more of insufficiencies in their libraries, and this is most frequently felt by researchers in those fields. Unresponsiveness to research needs, whether on the part of university or departmental administrations, is blamed roughly equally by all subjects, and more by researchers: medical researchers seem particularly to blame university administrations. It is interesting, too, that apart from the first two handicaps, affecting the time available, researchers in technology complain more about every other handicap (except library facilities) than any other group. However, when asked to say simply how adequate their resources for research were (Table 13.37), 53 per cent of researchers in arts and social science said they were adequate or better compared with 58 per cent in natural science, 67 per cent in medicine and 73 per cent in technology. Technologists may have many different causes for complaint, but it seems that fewer of them feel seriously handicapped by lack of resources than do researchers in other fields.

If we now compare researchers and teachers within fields we see, rather unexpectedly, that, except in the natural sciences, researchers are as likely as teachers to feel that resources are adequate. Common sense would suggest that those who make chief use of resources are more likely to feel their inadequacies. But this seems not to be generally the case: on the contrary, the men who do research are, if anything, more satisfied with the resources than are the teachers. It does not seem to be inadequate resources that inhibit teachers from doing more research.

Finally, our respondents were asked whether they thought the support their subject receives in the university system is more or less than it deserves (Table 13.38). In no subject was any significant number of people prepared to say that their subject was better supported than it deserved, though there were very wide differences between subjects in the level of dissatisfaction. In general, social

TABLES 13.37 AND 13.38

Apart from time, are the resources available to you adequate for your research? In the general pattern of British universities, how much support does your subject receive? } by subject and research orientation (per cent)

13.37 *Are resources adequate?*	*All respondents*	*Arts*			*Social science*			*Natural science*			*Technology*			*Medicine*		
		Research	*Both*	*Teaching*	*Research*	*Both*	*Teaching*	*Research*	*Both*	*Teaching*	*Research*	*Both*	*Teaching*	*Research*	*Both*	*Teaching*
Excellent	17	21	29	19	10	13	8	14	10	20	18	20	20	22	30	26
Adequate	44	32	28	41	43	41	45	44	53	52	55	49	50	45	35	49
Somewhat inadequate	31	32	33	32	37	43	37	36	30	24	18	29	28	28	28	20
Highly inadequate	7	14	10	8	10	4	11	6	6	3	8	2	1	5	8	6
TOTALS	(1,222)	(120)	(72)	(135)	(49)	(47)	(109)	(145)	(113)	(119)	(51)	(41)	(85)	(64)	(40)	(35)

13.38 *How much support?*																
Less than deserved	47	44	44	38	75	57	65	45	31	34	62	51	49	64	38	37
About as much as deserved	52	54	56	59	25	41	33	54	66	63	38	49	51	36	62	63
More than deserved	1	2	0	3	0	2	2	1	3	3	0	0	0	0	0	0
TOTALS	(1,225)	(123)	(71)	(141)	(48)	(46)	(111)	(144)	(115)	(116)	(50)	(41)	(80)	(64)	(40)	(35)

scientists, followed by men in technology and medicine, felt most under-privileged; and natural scientists most satisfied. Over two-thirds of the social scientists were dissatisfied, as compared with only a little more than a third of the natural scientists. But in all subjects researchers tended to be more discontented than teachers, though the differences were large only in technology and medicine. Apparently, British academics feel no contradiction in asserting both that resources for research are generally adequate, and also that they should be greater. This is perhaps a fair reflection of their needs and wishes, and a combination of realities and aspirations that is conducive to the growth of science and scholarship. A cheerful acceptance by academic men of the limitations on resources is surely the attitude least to be desired by wise vice-chancellors or ministers of state.

Membership in the 'invisible college'–modes of communication and relationship to own subject

We have referred to the concept of the 'invisible college'–that network of informal relationships and personal acquaintance which links academic men, and particularly researchers in the same discipline but different institutions. Our respondents were asked how important they thought various methods of communication were to enable them to keep in touch with current work in their subjects. The results are shown in Tables 13.39–44. The journals of academic associations are the main formal channel by which information flows about recent developments in knowledge and thought: and they are seen (Table 13.39) as 'very important', without distinction between researchers and teachers.

After journals, the next most frequently mentioned source of 'very important' communication was conversation, both with departmental colleagues and with other men in the same discipline elsewhere in Britain. The relative importance of these two kinds of conversation varies both with field and research orientations: Tables 13.42 and 13.43 should be inspected together. Over half the research scientists cite conversations with colleagues elsewhere as very important, as compared with a third of the teacher scientists and a quarter of the research men in arts subjects. Here is evidence of the 'invisible college' having its greatest importance for research men in fields with a high rate of growth of knowledge and a high level of specialisation. 'Teacher' scientists would find these contacts less necessary; and arts

Tables 13.39–13.44

How do you keep in touch with current and recent work in your subject? by subject and research orientation (per cent)

	All respondents	Arts			Social science			Natural science			Technology			Medicine		
		Research	Both	Teaching	Research	Both	Teaching	Research	Both	Teaching	Research	Both	Teaching	Research	Both	Teaching
13.39 *How important are journals and/or bulletins*																
Very important	86	76	79	79	90	83	91	88	91	87	86	93	84	92	95	91
Fairly important	14	23	21	21	10	17	9	12	9	13	12	7	16	8	5	9
Not important	0	1	0	0	0	0	0	1	1	0	2	0	0	0	0	0
13.40 *Newsletters and information bulletins*																
Very important	11	6	8	9	9	12	20	10	9	16	6	13	13	12	13	12
Fairly important	26	20	20	19	22	19	31	27	23	31	31	49	45	22	31	30
Not important	63	74	73	72	70	70	49	63	68	63	63	38	42	66	56	58
13.41 *Offprints sent by colleagues in British universities*																
Very important	15	11	13	11	11	16	9	26	19	16	14	16	15	17	16	6
Fairly important	37	36	38	34	34	21	30	34	49	42	45	42	28	47	32	32
Not important	48	53	49	55	55	53	61	40	32	42	41	42	58	36	53	61
TOTALS (vary slightly)	(1,311)	(124)	(72)	(141)	(49)	(48)	(113)	(146)	(116)	(119)	(51)	(41)	(85)	(64)	(40)	(35)

Continued on next page.

13.42 *Conversations with departmental colleagues*	*All respondents*	*Arts*			*Social science*			*Natural science*			*Technology*			*Medicine*		
		Research	*Both*	*Teaching*	*Research*	*Both*	*Teaching*	*Research*	*Both*	*Teaching*	*Research*	*Both*	*Teaching*	*Research*	*Both*	*Teaching*
Very important	42	29	33	37	51	40	43	41	39	39	54	42	44	47	70	64
Fairly important	41	37	47	40	41	38	42	43	44	37	34	42	46	45	28	27
Not important	17	33	20	22	8	23	15	16	18	25	12	15	10	8	2	9
13.43 *Conversations with colleagues in your subject elsewhere in Britain*																
Very important	40	26	31	31	33	28	35	56	41	35	65	41	37	59	58	52
Fairly important	42	50	51	45	46	46	48	30	42	43	25	46	43	34	38	30
Not important	18	24	18	25	21	26	17	14	16	22	10	13	21	6	5	18
13.44 *Correspondence*																
Very important	20	27	17	18	23	13	17	26	18	17	25	24	17	16	21	9
Fairly important	41	39	49	34	43	35	38	37	44	44	51	37	43	55	41	52
Not important	39	34	34	48	34	52	45	38	38	39	24	39	40	30	38	39
TOTALS (vary slightly)	(1,311)	(124)	(72)	(141)	(49)	(48)	(113)	(146)	(116)	(119)	(51)	(41)	(85)	(64)	(40)	(35)

men do not, for the most part, live at the edge of a rapidly moving frontier, but in the heart of a long-cultivated and slowly expanding realm. The research technologists are even more dependent on oral communication with research colleagues elsewhere, given the relatively low levels of activity in departments of technology, and thus the relatively high dilution of the minority of research-minded university technologists.

Here again the data raise numerous questions about the actual processes of scientific and scholarly communications in different fields, and the relevance of these processes to the amount and quality of research in universities. These are questions that we can raise but not answer. For example, why is it that proportionately so many more research social scientists (51 per cent) find conversation with departmental colleagues 'very important' as compared with research men in arts subjects (29 per cent)? And, why do these same research social scientists tend to value conversations *within* their departments more often than conversations with colleagues elsewhere, unlike research men in every other field (in the arts the difference is negligible)? Here again, our survey findings call for further research of a different kind: detailed studies of the intellectual life of individual academic departments.

After journals and conversation, correspondence is another form of communication, in many ways performing the same functions as conversation with colleagues elsewhere, and for the same reasons it is also mentioned more often by research men than by teachers. Newsletters and offprints serve to supplement the journals, and, with some variations by field, are about as important to teachers as to researchers.

Correlative attitudes towards other aspects of university life

Researchers and teachers are substantially different in many aspects of their lives. They differ in background, in current interests, in future prospects; they are to be found in different concentrations at different places within the university system; and they vary considerably in their behaviour and attitudes in most aspects of their work. If they are so different, we might well expect that this would be evident in other ways that are not so obviously connected with teaching or research. One way in which they might differ is in their general assessment of the nature of British university education. Table 13.45 gives the responses to a statement that 'university education in Britain puts too little emphasis on the training of experts and too much on the education of widely cultivated men'. On the whole, British academics do not agree that there is too little emphasis on training experts, perhaps because the British honours degree is specialised, though taught in a liberal way. However, there are differences between teachers and researchers on this issue.[1]

Since researchers in British universities are more likely to be experts, we would imagine that they would more often want to encourage others to travel in the same direction: while 'teachers' who, by avoiding research have also in many cases avoided specialisation and expertise, would be less likely to favour that concept of education. It turns out that this is the case: teachers in most fields are markedly more opposed to the 'training of experts' concept of education than are researchers. We should not be surprised that the great majority of academics are unwilling to come down without qualification either for the 'training' of 'experts' or the 'education' of 'widely cultivated men'. Most would reject the notion that these ends are incompatible, and many would argue that they are in fact complementary. Nevertheless, the issue persists, if only because the organisation of a curriculum forces choices which men can avoid only in rhetoric. And here it is significant that the majority view, even of the 'researchers', leans towards the position most strongly held and represented by the teachers.[2]

Whatever Ministers or industrialists may think, substantial majorities of British academics believe that British universities put quite enough emphasis on the training of experts: and consistent with this critical view of expertise and specialisation, are the majorities in every field who agree, strongly or with reservations, that a 'valid

[1] And it is an issue. The specialised honours degree has in recent years come under sharp criticism from some English academics, and these have led to less narrowly specialised courses at Sussex and other of the new universities.

[2] Table 13.45 contains one ambiguity in that it asks about 'university education in Britain' without specifying whether undergraduate or postgraduate education is meant. And indeed, the nearly half of social science 'researchers' who agreed with the statement may have been complaining about the relative paucity of provision for postgraduate training in the social sciences, while the smaller agreement given to the statement by natural scientists may reflect the better provision for postgraduate training in the scientific disciplines.

Some support for this supposition can be found in Table 13.46. The proposition was put forward there that 'valid criticism of the English universities is that they over-emphasise the single-subject honours degree'. To this question the social scientists give relatively high assent, suggesting that they are critical of specialised *undergraduate* training, while also wanting more emphasis on the training of experts at some point in the system.

Tables 13.45 and 13.46

'University education in Britain puts too little emphasis on the training of experts . . .' by subject and research orientation (per cent)

'Valid criticism of the English universities is that they over-emphasise the single-subject honours degree', by subject and research orientation (per cent)

13.45 *Under-emphasise experts*	*All respondents*	*Arts*			*Social science*			*Natural science*			*Technology*			*Medicine*		
		Research	*Both*	*Teaching*	*Research*	*Both*	*Teaching*	*Research*	*Both*	*Teaching*	*Research*	*Both*	*Teaching*	*Research*	*Both*	*Teaching*
Strongly agree	4	4	1	3	4	6	3	7	0	3	0	5	6	0	10	9
Agree with reservations	25	32	15	20	42	15	24	26	21	13	40	27	29	39	33	17
Disagree with reservations	47	49	53	41	46	65	38	54	59	45	44	54	35	45	38	51
Strongly disagree	24	15	31	36	8	15	35	13	19	40	16	15	31	16	18	23
TOTALS	(1,224)	(119)	(72)	(138)	(48)	(48)	(113)	(143)	(113)	(119)	(50)	(41)	(84)	(62)	(39)	(35)

13.46 *Over-emphasise one-subject degree*	*All respondents*	*Arts*			*Social science*			*Natural science*			*Technology*			*Medicine*		
		Research	*Both*	*Teaching*	*Research*	*Both*	*Teaching*	*Research*	*Both*	*Teaching*	*Research*	*Both*	*Teaching*	*Research*	*Both*	*Teaching*
Strongly agree	15	16	18	14	20	19	21	11	8	24	6	8	14	22	16	9
Agree with reservations	43	32	36	48	43	45	52	40	46	42	43	45	46	36	39	59
Disagree with reservations	30	30	19	27	30	34	22	38	30	22	41	35	31	39	34	22
Strongly disagree	12	22	26	11	7	2	5	12	16	12	10	13	9	3	11	9
TOTALS	(1,212)	(122)	(72)	(140)	(46)	(47)	(112)	(144)	(113)	(116)	(51)	(40)	(80)	(59)	(38)	(32)

criticism of the English universities is that they over-emphasise the single-subject honours degree' (Table 13.46). At a time when the growth of knowledge is sharply accelerating, and universities everywhere are emphasising their contributions to the production of knowledge, British academics are looking askance at their own highly specialised and research-oriented undergraduate degrees. The meaning of these sentiments is clear in the light of our finding that it is the teachers who are most likely to be critical of the single-subject degree. While about half the research men in the arts, natural sciences and technology agree with the criticism, the proportions among the scientist teachers rise to two-thirds, and among the social scientist teachers to nearly three-quarters. These criticisms have been reflected in university developments in recent years. For example, the new universities have linked their emphasis on improving undergraduate teaching to an attempt to broaden the scope of the first degree, and similar experiments are under way in the former CATs. But from another perspective, if we see an emphasis on the teaching function of the universities as a more traditional, conservative conception of the universities, then here again we find this position supported by the majority of British academic men, and by a substantial number even among the dedicated researchers.

It may well be possible to reconcile these preferences for a teaching oriented and less specialised undergraduate degree with the increasing specialisation and expansion of knowledge. But that will require far more attention to the organisation of graduate training than has been given to it by most British universities and disciplines, with the possible exception of the natural sciences. The debate over resources and expansion has dominated British university planning since World War II; but we suspect that in the coming decades the need to expand graduate education will become equally pressing. And American experience suggests that the growth of graduate training will have effects on undergraduate education as great as the growth of numbers.

Attitudes towards the British school system

If researchers and teachers have differing views about the nature of university education, this could well extend also to the secondary schools. The comprehensive school movement in England has been mainly a political concern about the social consequences of the tripartite system. But there could also be educational reasons for advocating comprehensives, such as the avoidance of too much early specialisation. Two questions were asked about the school system: the first simply proposed that the present grammar, modern and technical schools be replaced by a comprehensive system: the second specifically criticised the present secondary education system for 'premature specialisation'. Results are shown in Tables 13.47 and 13.48.

In the case of comprehensive education the differences between researchers and teachers are small. (Attitudes on this question are very strongly related to general political orientations, as we shall see in Chapter 15, but political views are unrelated to preferences for research or teaching.) By contrast in Table 13.48 we see that in all five faculty groups teachers are more concerned than researchers about the problems of premature specialisation. This fits well with their similar preference for wider degrees at universities, and their opposition to the 'training of experts' concept of higher education.[1]

University expansion

The expansion of the British universities that is taking place at present is bound to influence and be influenced by academic opinion. We have explored attitudes towards expansion in Chapter 11. Researchers may favour growth if it brings them larger departments and more facilities, but if it increases their teaching load they will probably be hostile. Teachers are most likely to disapprove if they think it will change the character of the pupils they teach for the worse. Table 13.49 shows their views on whether the university system as a whole should be expanded. In arts subjects the teachers are slightly more likely to favour expansion than the researchers, but in all other faculties it is researchers who are more in favour of it. In arts, researchers have little to gain from an expansion of the system, since their work does not depend on expensive equipment; they may lose if they are distracted from their interests by having to teach more (and, they may fear, less stimulating) pupils. In the other subjects, however, expansion may bring with it not only larger departments and more investment, but also a greater recognition of the contributions researchers can make in their subjects.

[1] But it is perhaps more important that substantial majorities of all categories of university teachers are critical of the present emphasis in the secondary schools, though almost evenly split regarding their present form of organisation.

TABLES 13.47 AND 13.48

'The tripartite system . . . should be supplanted by a system of comprehensive schools', by subject and research orientation (per cent)

'A serious shortcoming of the present system of secondary education is premature specialisation', by subject and research orientation (per cent)

13.47 *Supplanted by comprehensives*	*All respondents*	*Arts*			*Social science*			*Natural science*			*Technology*			*Medicine*		
		Research	*Both*	*Teaching*	*Research*	*Both*	*Teaching*	*Research*	*Both*	*Teaching*	*Research*	*Both*	*Teaching*	*Research*	*Both*	*Teaching*
Strongly agree	22	16	24	24	33	22	33	21	14	19	22	24	23	24	28	15
Agree with reservations	34	31	30	32	39	59	38	31	40	32	24	34	37	27	19	39
Disagree with reservations	25	27	27	26	15	13	24	30	23	28	26	21	20	31	28	33
Strongly disagree	18	26	19	18	13	7	4	18	23	21	28	21	20	18	25	12
TOTALS	(1,194)	(121)	(67)	(137)	(46)	(46)	(112)	(140)	(113)	(114)	(50)	(38)	(79)	(62)	(36)	(33)

13.48 *Premature specialisation*	*All respondents*	*Arts Research*	*Arts Both*	*Arts Teaching*	*Social science Research*	*Social science Both*	*Social science Teaching*	*Natural science Research*	*Natural science Both*	*Natural science Teaching*	*Technology Research*	*Technology Both*	*Technology Teaching*	*Medicine Research*	*Medicine Both*	*Medicine Teaching*
Strongly agree	38	34	38	42	39	49	49	33	29	42	34	37	35	40	41	43
Agree with reservations	38	33	35	40	46	40	40	30	43	35	32	44	46	33	36	43
Disagree with reservations	20	30	21	16	11	11	7	32	21	17	28	17	15	27	18	9
Strongly disagree	4	2	6	1	4	0	4	6	7	7	6	2	4	0	5	6
TOTALS	(1,217)	(122)	(68)	(139)	(46)	(47)	(112)	(144)	(114)	(118)	(50)	(41)	(79)	(63)	(39)	(35)

TABLES 13.49 AND 13.50

Should we expand the university system? / Should your subject be expanded? } by subject and research orientation (per cent)

13.49 *Expand system?*	*Arts* Re-search	*Arts* Both	*Arts* Teach-ing	*Social science* Re-search	*Social science* Both	*Social science* Teach-ing	*Natural science* Re-search	*Natural science* Both	*Natural science* Teach-ing	*Technology* Re-search	*Technology* Both	*Technology* Teach-ing	*Medicine* Re-search	*Medicine* Both	*Medicine* Teach-ing
Double	15	23	23	55	45	35	33	27	16	31	30	26	30	17	18
50%	42	37	44	23	48	40	38	44	48	29	43	44	40	39	33
25%	37	35	29	21	7	21	26	23	30	41	25	24	27	36	48
Remain as it is	7	6	5	0	0	4	3	6	6	0	3	6	3	8	0
TOTALS	(117)	(71)	(133)	(47)	(44)	(113)	(144)	(113)	(117)	(49)	(40)	(84)	(63)	(36)	(33)

13.50 *Expand subject?*	*Arts* Re-search	*Arts* Both	*Arts* Teach-ing	*Social science* Re-search	*Social science* Both	*Social science* Teach-ing	*Natural science* Re-search	*Natural science* Both	*Natural science* Teach-ing	*Technology* Re-search	*Technology* Both	*Technology* Teach-ing	*Medicine* Re-search	*Medicine* Both	*Medicine* Teach-ing
No	9	10	9	4	2	5	7	8	5	4	10	11	11	8	3
Under 25%	45	35	37	11	9	14	32	26	36	24	20	19	41	50	41
25–75%	35	46	43	46	40	43	40	50	45	42	49	48	38	37	50
Over 75%	11	8	11	39	49	39	21	16	14	30	22	22	10	5	6
TOTALS	(119)	(71)	(135)	(46)	(47)	(110)	(145)	(114)	(118)	(50)	(41)	(85)	(63)	(38)	(32)

Table 13.50 examines the attitudes of academics to expansion within their own subject. Differences on this issue are much larger between subject areas than between teachers and researchers in the same subject.[1] Nearly all the social scientists support the growth of their subject, followed by technologists, scientists, and men in the arts and medicine. (Curiously, this is close to the priorities for growth accepted by the government and the U.G.C.)

Status and power of the professoriate

Two indices of attitudes to the power and to the status of the professoriate will be discussed in Chapter 14.[2] (We show there that attitudes to research and teaching, when combined with other items into an index of cosmopolitanism and localism, have a definite bearing on views of both the power and the status of professors.) It seems useful, however, to look at these two indices here, and see what relation research orientations by themselves, within subject categories, bear to attitudes towards the professoriate. We should expect, as we suggest in Chapter 14, that researchers would be less tolerant of the *status quo*, particularly as regards the power of professors, which might impede them in their work, but also as regards their status and the limited availability of professorships.

Table 13.51 shows the distribution of attitudes to the status of professors. There is a relationship in arts, social science and natural science. In all these cases researchers are more likely to be critical of the present arrangements for allotting professorships than teachers, who are relatively content. Table 13.52 shows attitudes to the power of the professorship. Here the relationship is present in every subject, and is stronger than before in social science. It seems clear that our hypothesis is correct: researchers are less likely to approve the large powers at present held by professors. We discuss the possible reasons for this in Chapter 14.

Conclusion

In this chapter we have explored further the differences–in background, behaviour, aspirations and attitudes–of men oriented

[1] Differences between subjects in support for expansion were discussed in Chapter 11.

[2] These indices are described in Appendix D, pp. 524–26.

TABLES 13.51 AND 13.52

Attitudes to professorial status / Attitudes to professorial power — by subject and research orientation (per cent)

13.51 *Status of professoriate*	*Arts* Re-search	*Arts* Both	*Arts* Teach-ing	*Social science* Re-search	*Social science* Both	*Social science* Teach-ing	*Natural science* Re-search	*Natural science* Both	*Natural science* Teach-ing	*Technology* Re-search	*Technology* Both	*Technology* Teach-ing	*Medicine* Re-search	*Medicine* Both	*Medicine* Teach-ing
Levellers	30	20	18	34	33	25	32	24	21	27	22	25	34	32	34
Moderates	26	30	30	32	33	30	28	22	26	25	29	32	34	42	34
Elitists	44	49	53	34	35	45	41	54	52	47	49	43	31	26	31
TOTALS	(120)	(69)	(135)	(47)	(43)	(110)	(145)	(114)	(117)	(51)	(41)	(84)	(64)	(38)	(35)

13.52 *Power of professoriate*	*Arts* Re-search	*Arts* Both	*Arts* Teach-ing	*Social science* Re-search	*Social science* Both	*Social science* Teach-ing	*Natural science* Re-search	*Natural science* Both	*Natural science* Teach-ing	*Technology* Re-search	*Technology* Both	*Technology* Teach-ing	*Medicine* Re-search	*Medicine* Both	*Medicine* Teach-ing
Democrats	56	48	49	83	64	60	62	43	50	52	42	34	46	36	37
Neutrals	29	32	32	12	32	28	24	38	35	24	35	44	37	33	53
Non-democrats	15	20	19	5	5	12	14	19	14	24	22	22	17	30	10
TOTALS	(108)	(65)	(127)	(42)	(44)	(101)	(133)	(107)	(105)	(46)	(40)	(79)	(59)	(33)	(30)

principally to the teaching or research aspects of their academic roles. We have seen differences in their social origins, their secondary and higher education, their mobility and aspiration for mobility, and their perceptions and attitudes on a variety of aspects of institutional support and constraint. We looked also at their valued forms of communication, and finally at their differences on other aspects of university and educational policy and practice. All this is difficult to summarise briefly. It may be more useful to attempt a more general review of what we have found, and try to describe British academic men in a way that links their characteristics with broad tendencies in British higher education. In the next chapter, 14, we examine in detail the attitudes towards the professoriate referred to in the preceding pages. In Chapter 15 we widen our perspectives to explore the politics of academic men, especially as these are relevant to their academic roles. Finally an attempt at a general typology of British academics is presented in the concluding Chapter 16.

Chapter 14

THE ACADEMIC MAN AND HIS DEPARTMENT: ATTITUDES TOWARDS PROFESSORIAL STATUS AND POWER

As we saw in Chapter 7, the structure of teaching appointments in most British universities, as on the continent, has traditionally resembled a pyramid. All departments have a number of lecturers, usually one or two assistant lecturers, and the possibility of three senior posts, those of professor, reader, and senior lecturer. In the expansion of recent years departments have tended to increase in size; while new departments have not been created at the same rate. Thus the natural bottleneck caused by the pyramid has tended to narrow. This was brought out by figures given by Robbins: in 1927–28 the percentage of professors in the teaching population was 22 per cent, or almost one in four, while by 1961–62 it had dropped to 12 per cent, i.e., one in eight.[1] Since wastage from the profession is not very large it would not be surprising if some tension were created in the system.

Moreover, the nature of the senior posts, and particularly of the professorship, may create problems. For the role of professor involves several functions. On one hand it is very clearly understood that chairs are filled on the basis of academic distinction; the professor must be the leading member, academically, of his department and in this capacity he is expected to carry on productive research of his own. But besides his private concerns he is generally also 'head of the department'. In 1961–62, 80 per cent of professors were department heads, while 74 per cent of the heads of department were professors, 7 per cent readers, 12 per cent senior lecturers and 6 per cent others;[2]

[1] *Higher Education*, Appendix Three, Part 1, Table 7. See also Chapter 7, pp. 146–55.
[2] *Ibid.*, Appendix Three, Part I, Table 13.

presumably many of the 26 per cent of departments without a professor for head in fact had no professor. The professor as department head has heavy administrative duties; he is essentially responsible for the whole work and life of his department: for its budget, its syllabus, its staff and students. Moreover he will often substantially direct all the research that is carried on by junior members of the department. The advantages of this system are evident–a central and unified control that will give unity and consistency to the department, and a single voice that can represent it to the outer university world; as are the disadvantages–for the professor heavy administrative responsibilities, and many time-consuming concerns that may distract him from his central interests: and for junior members a possible lack of independence, allied with limited opportunities for promotion.

It may be useful to contrast this with the American system. Here the highest academic rank in a department, that of full professor, is held by up to a third of the staff members, all of whom have considerable independence in teaching and research, and parity of pay and status. Although a department has a chairman, whose administrative functions correspond to those of a professorial head in England, he is more often seen rather as first among equals than as senior *vis-à-vis* juniors. Thus while real power may not be much less concentrated (though it usually is, at least among the larger number of senior men), high status at least is more broadly distributed, and this is bound to have some effect on the wielding of power.

We are not able with our data to study directly the ways in which the patterns of departmental organisation in British universities affect the character or quality of teaching and research within them, though we have detailed the traditions of the English idea of a university in Chapter 3. We are, however, able to explore the attitudes and sentiments of academic men towards the central issues, the power and the status of the professor. We shall first see how certain attitudes on these issues are distributed among the whole academic profession, and then try to see how these views differ in different parts and levels of the university system. Finally, we shall investigate some of the sources of these attitudes. And here we will be raising questions about forces in the university and in the larger society that work to support or to modify the existing structure of academic power and status, and the extent to which the academic profession itself is, on balance, a force for conservation or change in British higher education.

Attitudes to departmental structure among university teachers

Our sample were offered four statements bearing on the professoriate, with which they were asked to agree or disagree. Tables 14.1–4 present the distribution of their answers.

TABLE 14.1

'Most British university departments would be better run by the method of circulating chairmanship than by a permanent head of department'

		Per cent who—		
Strongly agree	*Agree with reservations*	*Disagree with reservations*	*Strongly disagree*	*Total*
24	33	25	17	1,365

It is clear that more than half our sample favour a radical departure from the present method of administering departments, with or without reservations: a fairly startling finding in itself. The following question, which offers no alternative prescription, but simply gives an opportunity for criticism, is even more striking.

TABLE 14.2

'A serious disadvantage of Redbrick universities is that all too often they are run by a professorial oligarchy'

		Per cent who—		
Strongly agree	*Agree with reservations*	*Disagree with reservations*	*Strongly disagree*	*Total*
41	36	18	5	1,266*

* The unusually large number of non-respondents may be attributed to some respondents being unwilling to answer because they were unfamiliar with any Redbrick university. For those at present at Redbrick universities, the proportion of non-respondents was not unusually large.

Over three-quarters of our population are dissatisfied with the power structure of Redbrick universities.[1] These two questions are

[1] We have taken Redbrick as the paradigm for our description of British university structure; and if we include the four Welsh colleges (which are structurally very similar) under the description 'Redbrick', then some 50 per cent of university teachers are employed in this type of university; and only Oxford and Cambridge are very notably different.

primarily directed to the distribution of administrative *power* in the system. The two other questions deal with the somewhat different problem of the *number* of professorships which should be available; they are related most directly therefore to the distribution of high *status*, and do not refer to the power structure except by implication.[1]

Respondents were asked to comment on the statement that 'A university department with more than eight members of staff should have more than one member of professorial rank',[2] in an effort to discover if the steady decline in the relative number of professors had caused discontent, or rather if any further decline would be accepted by teachers as a whole. The answer to the latter question seems to be a fairly clear negative (Table 14.3).

TABLE 14.3

'A university department with more than eight members of staff should have more than one member of professorial rank'

		Per cent who—		
Strongly agree	*Agree with reservations*	*Disagree with reservations*	*Strongly disagree*	*Total*
40	37	17	5	1,370

Over three-quarters of our sample agreed, with or without reservations, that a second professor should be appointed where a department was larger than the 1961–62 average size of eight members.

Finally, we suggested what would amount to a much more radical change: that a professorship should be the normal expectation of all university teachers–a suggestion which would involve moving at least as far as any American university has towards widening opportunities for professorships (Table 14.4). Even here, 40 per cent of our sample agree with or without reservations, while only one-quarter disagree without reservations.

On first examination, therefore, there is evidence of considerable discontent with the present system, and of support even for very sweeping changes among a surprisingly high number of university teachers. How are these views distributed among universities and faculties?

[1] Our distinction corresponds to the two aspects or dimensions of democracy discussed by Max Weber: the minimisation of power and the levelling of statuses. See H. H. Gerth and C. Wright Mills (eds.), *op. cit.*

[2] The figure of one in eight was the current average in 1961–62.

TABLE 14.4

'A professorship ought to be part of the normal expectation of an academic career and not a special attainment of a minority of university teachers'

Per cent who—				
Strongly agree	*Agree with reservations*	*Disagree with reservations*	*Strongly disagree*	*Total*
13	27	35	24	1,385

Attitudes to departmental structure in different university groups

Since the internal structure of British universities varies quite substantially, it is at least possible that members of different university groups might have different views, whether as a result of varying experience, or of a process of self-selection whereby they would end up in the kind of system they prefer. Tables 14.5–8 explore this

TABLES 14.5–14.8

Percentage who agree (with or without reservations) to each statement, by university group (per cent)

	Oxford and Cambridge	*Major Red-brick*	*Minor Red-brick*	*Wales*	*Scot-land*	*Lon-don*
14.5 Departments should be run by circulating chairman	64	56	64	48	53	53
14.6 Redbricks are dominated by professorial oligarchy	82	76	79	76	75	77
14.7 Should be second professor for more than eight members	60	80	83	80	73	83
14.8 Professorship should be normal expectation	25	42	39	43	38	48
TOTALS (vary slightly)	(158)	(468)	(145)	(117)	(242)	(237)

possibility. First, we see that, Oxford and Cambridge apart, differences among men in different university groups on most of these questions are not very large. It is fairly simple to explain the higher percentages of agreement in Oxford and Cambridge on the first two questions related to administrative power. With their traditions of college autonomy, Oxford and Cambridge have their own peculiar difficulties in departmental administration which are probably responsible for the higher percentage who favour a circulating chairman; and the same tradition combined with a certain self-satisfaction would account for the large number of critics of Redbrick universities. When we turn to the question of status we find that teachers from Oxford and Cambridge are now at the other extreme: they favour change noticeably less than their colleagues from other universities; and nearest to them are those from Scotland, i.e., members of the other 'ancient' universities. This undoubtedly reflects the democratic élitism of the ancient universities, and their long tradition of colleaguial rather than hierarchical authority. But apart from Oxford and Cambridge, it is remarkable how much alike are the distributions of views on these questions among the several groups of universities.

Attitudes to departmental structure in different ranks

Since the questions of power and status that we are discussing relate to the distribution of the various ranks and the roles played by their occupants, it might be expected that attitudes would vary according to the rank held by the respondent. Tables 14.9–12 show these distributions. Again the variation is not large, with the notable, if unsurprising exception that professors disagree most often with all four statements. The difference is particularly large in the case of the most critical statement; only slightly more than half as many professors as men in other ranks agree that Redbrick universities are run by a professorial oligarchy. But even so, nearly half of the professors accept the highly pejorative overtones of 'professorial oligarchy'. It seems that the professors as a body are by no means united in defence of their present prerogatives: it is only when faced with perhaps the most radical suggestion for modifying the academic structure–of making a professorship a 'normal' expectation of the academic careers–that a large majority of professors draw back.

Attitudes to departmental structure among teachers of different subjects

There are no very striking differences in attitude between teachers in different subjects (Appendix A, Tables 14.27–30). It is noticeable

TABLES 14.9–14.12

Percentage who agree (with or without reservations) to each statement, by university rank (per cent)

	Professors	*Readers*	*Senior lecturers*	*Lecturers*	*Others*
14.9 Departments should be run by circulating chairman	51	62	58	58	58
14.10 Redbricks are dominated by professorial oligarchy	46	84	83	81	80
14.11 Should be second professor for more than eight members	75	80	83	87	75
14.12 Professorship should be normal expectation	29	43	51	40	41
TOTALS (vary slightly)	(190)	(128)	(218)	(734)	(116)

however that social scientists are consistently more in favour of change than any other group: a point which may become more intelligible when we explore some of the other sources of attitudes towards departmental structure.

Power and status: the relation between attitudes to departmental structure

We have already suggested that we are dealing here with two distinguishable (though related) problems: first, how departments should be governed, or who should have the real administrative *power* in formal terms; and second, how the *prestige* of full professorship should be allocated and how widely spread. The replies to our four questions show the association between the two issues: for there is a much closer relation between questions bearing on power and those bearing on status than for any other combinations. Table 14.13 presents the relation of the question on professorial oligarchy in the Redbrick universities and the assertion that departments should be run by circulating chairmen.

Of those who strongly agree that circulating chairmanship should replace the present system, 75 per cent also strongly agree that Redbrick universities are dominated by a professorial oligarchy,

TABLE 14.13

'Redbricks are dominated by professorial oligarchy' by 'Departments should be run by circulating chairmen' (per cent)

	Circulating chairman			
Oligarchy	*Strongly agree*	*Agree with reservations*	*Disagree with reservations*	*Strongly disagree*
Strongly agree	75	45	21	15
Agree with reservations	19	42	50	31
Disagree with reservations	6	11	27	37
Strongly disagree	1	2	3	17
TOTALS	(305)	(412)	(308)	(228)

compared with only 15 per cent of those who strongly oppose circulating chairmanship. So that while there are obviously differences between attitudes revealed by these two questions there is a large common element. It is possible, then, to construct an index to use as a summary of *attitudes to professorial power*. Those who agree with both these statements we shall call '*democrats*'; those who agree with only one of the two '*part-democrats*'; and those who disagree with both '*non-democrats*'.[1] This characterisation gives us 640 respondents who were 'democrats' (or 51 per cent of those who could be classified), 401 'part-democrats' (32 per cent) and 212 'non-democrats' (17 per cent). There were 155 respondents who could not be classified since they had not answered one or other of the questions.[2]

When we turn to attitudes towards increasing the number of professorships we find an equally strong relationship (Table 14.14). Of those who strongly agree that a professorship should be the normal expectation of a university teacher, 85 per cent also strongly agree that there should be a second professor where a department is larger than eight. This compares with 21 per cent of those who strongly disagree that a professorship should be normal. Or, adding the first two lines, as above, there is a variation from 98 to 50 per cent. Here again an index can be used to distinguish different attitudes to professorial power. Those who agree, with or without reservations, with both statements, that there should be a second professor for

[1] These terms should, of course, be taken as applying only within the particular context of departmental administration.

[2] For details see Appendix D.

TABLE 14.14

'There should be more than one professor for more than eight staff members' by 'Professorship should be normal' (per cent)

	Professorship should be normal			
Second professor	*Strongly agree*	*Agree with reservations*	*Disagree with reservations*	*Strongly disagree*
Strongly agree	85	53	26	21
Agree with reservations	13	41	50	29
Disagree with reservations	2	5	21	34
Strongly disagree	0	1	3	16
TOTALS	(181)	(374)	(475)	(330)

departments larger than eight, and that professorship should be a normal expectation, we call '*levellers*', those who agree with only one[1] we call '*moderates*' and those who agree with neither '*élitists*'. This gives us 235 'élitists' (18 per cent of those classified), 500 'moderates' (41 per cent) and 495 'levellers' (40 per cent).[2] As before, it should be noted that these characterisations are defined by their context; we do not mean to imply that those called 'élitists' are so in all respects (though we shall show later that their views on professorial status are not independent of other views).[3]

We have already suggested that these two indices relate to the rather different issues of the power and status of British university professors. The interrelations between their respective components are substantially higher than any other possible combinations. And our later analysis will make this assertion even clearer. But the two indices are themselves moderately related. Table 14.15 shows the relation between attitudes to professorial power and status, as measured by our two indices.

[1] Of these, almost all agreed that large departments should have an extra professor, but not that professorship should be normal, as can be seen in Table 14.14.

[2] For details see Appendix D.

[3] The two indices are somewhat artificial combinations, developed for the purpose of our analysis to show the relation of attitudes to power and status to other opinions and experiences of academic men. But by developing them we have to some extent muffled the effect of the original questions; we do not wish to suggest that 40 per cent of our sample are 'levellers', only that this proportion may be called 'levellers' *vis-à-vis* the other members of the sample: absolute figures are better determined by returning to the original questions.

TABLE 14.15

Attitudes to professorial status by attitudes towards professorial power (per cent)

Attitudes to professorial status	*Attitudes to professorial power* Democrats	*Part-democrats*	*Non-democrats*
Levellers	36	23	9
Moderates	30	29	28
Elitists	33	49	63
TOTALS	(627)	(395)	(208)

There is a difference of 27 percentage points between Democrats and Non-democrats in the proportion of Levellers, and 30 per cent in the proportion of Elitists. Attitudes to the status of the professor clearly are related to attitudes to his administrative power; they are, however, by no means identical.

Sources and correlates of attitudes towards professorial power and status

We now move on from a bare description of these attitudes and where they are to be found in the universities to try and explore some of their sources and correlates. We should expect that while experience plays its part in determining these attitudes (for example, a successful lecturer who sees a good chance of a professorship for himself within a few years, and who has never suffered from undue interference with his work, will probably not feel very strongly about the need for change), most teachers will approach the problems of power and status, and all other aspects of their profession, with certain preconceptions about the character of a university education, about the job they are doing, and, at a higher level, with views about the desirability of concentration or diffusion of power and status. We emphasised that the labels 'democrat', 'élitist', etc. were to be taken as applying only within their particular context; but it would be surprising if they were entirely unconnected with attitudes to wider issues. Whether for logical or emotional reasons, it is not easy to be a fervent democrat in one context, and an anti-democrat in another. We shall therefore try to relate these views on the structure of university departments to views on other topics. First, however, a brief note is necessary on the effect of experience within the immediate context.

Attitudes towards, and experience with, departmental administration

Our sample was asked 'What are the major handicaps that you experience in carrying on research?' and given a list of eight possibilities (with no restriction on the number they might check) including such items as insufficient time because of teaching commitments, insufficient financial resources, insufficient library facilities, etc., and 'unresponsiveness of your departmental administration to your research needs'. Thirteen per cent of our respondents checked this latter possibility. One would expect these people to be exceptionally dissatisfied with the present method of administration, and so it proved. Almost three-quarters of those who felt their research was

TABLE 14.16

Attitudes to professorial power by experience of 'administrative unresponsiveness' as a major handicap in carrying on research (per cent)

Attitudes to professorial power	*Mentions administrative unresponsiveness*	*Does not mention administrative unresponsiveness*
Democrats	72	48
Part-democrats	21	34
Non-democrats	6	19
TOTALS	(170)	(1,083)

suffering from the effects of the present form of departmental administration favoured change in the way departments are governed, as against half of those who did not complain of this handicap (Table 14.16). We cannot be sure that the experience of departmental unresponsiveness to research requirements *leads to* critical attitudes towards the power of the professoriate. There may be some underlying element of discontent with a man's department that leads to both criticism of its head and a feeling that it is unhelpful to one's research. Such feelings of generalised discontent (or resentment) might also be expected to be expressed in attitudes critical of the *status* of the professor.

In Table 14.17 however we see a relatively weak relation between the experience of departmental administration and the index of attitudes towards professorial status. We still cannot be sure of the causal direction. But it appears that attitudes towards professorial power are related to the experience of its exercise in the department in a way that attitudes to professorial status are not.

TABLE 14.17

Attitudes to professorial status by experience of 'administrative unresponsiveness' as a major handicap in carrying on research (per cent)

Attitudes to professorial status	*Mentions administrative unresponsiveness*	*Does not mention administrative unresponsiveness*
Levellers	49	37
Moderates	39	41
Elitists	11	22
TOTALS	(178)	(1,182)

Attitudes to departmental structure and political views

The importance of political views has already been discussed and demonstrated in Chapter 11, and will be much more fully explored in Chapter 15. As a simple indicator of a man's broad social orientations, political preference is unrivalled. Moreover, political views will reflect and affect not only a man's attitudes towards society in general and towards its major institutions (including the educational system), but also the way he assesses the operation of particular organisations and the ways they distribute power and status. We expect therefore to find a relation between political preference and our two indices and this does in fact appear (Tables 14.18 and 14.19).

TABLE 14.18

Attitudes to professorial power by political position (per cent)

Attitudes to professorial power	*Political position*			
	Far Left	*Moderate Left*	*Centre*	*Right*
Democrats	74	58	46	35
Part-democrats	21	28	36	39
Non-democrats	5	14	18	25
TOTALS	(58)	(597)	(343)	(220)

General political dispositions are closely linked to democratic preferences in the field of university administration. Proportionately twice as many of the Far Left as of the Right are democrats in their university department;[1] and while a quarter of the Right are 'non-democrats', only 5 per cent of the Far Left are. In their attitudes towards the distribution of power in the department and university, at least, the political preferences of academic men are of great importance. We must now look at their attitudes to professorial status (Table 14.19).

TABLE 14.19

Attitudes to professorial status by political position (per cent)

Attitudes to professorial status	*Political position* *Far Left*	*Moderate Left*	*Centre*	*Right*
Levellers	43	41	40	34
Moderates	42	42	39	38
Elitists	15	17	21	28
TOTALS	(60)	(636)	(368)	(256)

Here the relation is considerably weaker: it appears most clearly in the bottom line of Table 14.19 (the élitists), where there is a difference of 13 percentage points between the two political extremes (as compared with a difference of 39 per cent between political extremes on the top line of the previous table). It seems that political views affect a man's attitude to the distribution of power much more strongly than his attitude to the distribution of high status: and this, considering that politics (even in Britain) is essentially concerned more with problems of power than of status, is perhaps what we should expect.

Nevertheless, the weakness of the relationship in Table 14.19 is striking and significant. If we set the small minority on the Far Left aside, the difference between the Moderate Left (who supply the great bulk of Labour supporters among academic men) and the men of the Right is very small: they do not see the distribution of academic status in fundamentally different ways. And even on the Far Left well over half are 'élitists' or 'moderates'–making élitist responses to either or both of our questions regarding the size or accessibility of

[1] 'Democrats', of course, in the limited and relative sense determined by the nature of the index.

the professoriate; their presumed egalitarianism in the larger society is sharply insulated from their feelings about rank in the university. This is significant for the larger question of the role of the academic profession in the expansion and democratisation of British higher education. Here, in our discussion of university expansion, there is further evidence of the general conservatism of the academic profession. It is a conservatism, however, that can accommodate a measure of reform and change: some degree of expansion, though not so much as will threaten the existing character and standard of British universities; some growth in the number of professors, to handle increased administrative burdens, but not so many as to change the élite status of the rank.

The chief incentives to change in British higher education (and this may well be true in every society) do not lie within the universities themselves, but in their social environment. Expansion of British higher education is inevitable, and at a greater rate than academic men at any given moment would cheerfully accept, because of quite inexorable forces in the economy and in the rising educational aspirations of the population. There are no such powerful external forces lying behind a reform of the organisational structures of British universities, or of their constituent departments, schools or colleges. Changes will come, but rather more slowly and in response to other forced changes in size and function. Our study suggests that there is considerable support among academics for moderate changes in the power and numbers of the professoriate; it does not tell us anything about the likelihood of such changes actually occurring, the internal political processes through which they would be accomplished (or resisted), or the relevance of the state of 'public opinion' among academic men to these political processes.[1]

[1] We suspect that it matters whether 'public opinion' among academic men on some university issues (such as expansion, or departmental organisation, or the accessibility of the professoriate) is linked to their more general political attitudes and dispositions. Our guess is that where there are strong links between attitudes on academic matters and national political differences there is greater likelihood that those academics supporting specific changes can make their wishes felt in the universities, than if those attitudes towards change were distributed more randomly through the body of academic men. But this is, for the moment, pure conjecture: our present study allows us to do no more than voice these questions regarding the ways the attitudes and sentiments of academic men on academic issues enter the political process and affect their outcomes.

'Elitism' as opposition to university expansion and the expansion of the professoriate

In Britain, whose system of higher education cannot possibly at present be called 'mass education', the possession of a university degree is at least as important for the high status it confers as for what it indicates in the way of intellectual attainment. And it was clear from our interviews, and from analysis of the survey findings,[1] that resistance to expanding the number of university places often stemmed from a fear for 'the meaning of a university degree', and a reluctance to 'dilute' its standing or distinction. It seemed possible that the same or similar sentiments would be marshalled in opposition to an increase in the number of professorships available. And there is some evidence of such a connection (Table 14.20).

TABLE 14.20

Attitudes to the status of the professorship by attitudes towards expanding the university system (per cent)

	Recommended expansion			
Attitudes to professorial status	*Double*	*50%*	*25%*	*Remain as it is*
Levellers	47	39	31	32
Moderates	39	43	39	39
Elitists	14	18	30	30
TOTALS	(363)	(530)	(373)	(57)

Of those who recommend doubling the size of the university system, only 14 per cent are 'élitists' with regard to the numbers and status of the professoriate, as compared with 30 per cent, or twice as many, of those advocating little or no growth of the system as a whole. But again, one is struck as much by the moderate size of the relationship as by its existence, and especially by the very large numbers who are able to support substantial growth in student numbers without wishing to modify the distribution of status among academic ranks. This at least suggests (as did other data in Chapter 11) that a substantial part of the support for university expansion among university teachers in no way reflects a wish to *democratize* the system, but merely to strengthen and expand a continuing élitist institution. And that wish, of course, is wholly compatible with not modifying its internal

[1] See Chapter 11 and especially Table 11.15.

arrangements, except perhaps marginally in the interests of administrative efficiency.[1]

The combined effect of political position and attitudes to expanding the university system on attitudes to departmental structure

We have seen how general political dispositions and attitudes towards university expansion are related to attitudes towards the status of professors (and quite differently related to attitudes towards professorial power). We know, however, from Chapter 11, that political preference is related to support for expanding the universities. It is possible, therefore, that Table 14.20 does not represent a genuine causal link. The fact that views about expansion seem to be related to views about professors may simply reflect the fact that political preference is related to both. To explore this possibility we have to present a table which contains all three variables. This is done in Table 14.21 for attitudes to professorial power, and Table 14.22 for attitudes to professorial status.[2] When we examine Table 14.21 it is clear that within each political group, attitudes to expansion are not very clearly related to men's views of the power of professors. If, however, one looks at that table comparing the effect of different political views within categories of attitudes towards expansion, it is clear that even among those who have similar views on expanding the universities, their political position makes a substantial difference to their attitudes towards the departmental power of the professor.

For Table 14.22, however, precisely the reverse applies. When we control for politics, attitudes to expansion are still significantly related to attitudes towards professorial status; whereas political position is not consistently related to attitudes to the status of the professorship when attitudes to expansion are controlled.

Local–cosmopolitan orientations and their relation to attitudes towards academic power and status

We have been exploring the ways in which attitudes of university teachers towards academic power and status are related to broader

[1] In Appendix A, Table 14.33, we show the relation of attitudes towards expanding the university system to attitudes to professorial power. In this case there was no clear relationship at all.

[2] In these tables 'Far Left' and 'Moderate Left' are combined to provide sufficient cases for analysis; and 'expansion of 25 per cent' and 'remain as it is' are combined in a category of 'insignificant expansion', as in Chapter 11.

TABLE 14.21

Attitudes to professorial power by attitudes to expansion within categories of political position (per cent)

Attitudes to professorial power	*Left*			*Centre*			*Right*		
	Double	*50%*	*Insig-nificant*	*Double*	*50%*	*Insig-nificant*	*Double*	*50%*	*Insig-nificant*
Democrats	65	54	56	57	42	45	38	33	38
Part-democrats	22	34	27	27	40	36	35	40	38
Non-democrats	13	12	17	16	18	19	27	27	24
TOTALS	(238)	(259)	(139)	(70)	(149)	(115)	(26)	(77)	(112)

TABLE 14.22

Attitudes to professorial status by attitudes to expansion within categories of political position (per cent)

Attitudes to Professorial status	*Left*			*Centre*			*Right*		
	Double	*50%*	*Insig-nificant*	*Double*	*50%*	*Insig-nificant*	*Double*	*50%*	*Insig-nificant*
Levellers	49	39	30	46	44	31	37	33	33
Moderates	36	44	46	39	39	37	47	42	33
Elitists	13	17	23	14	17	31	17	25	33
TOTALS	(248)	(277)	(151)	(76)	(157)	(128)	(30)	(84)	(135)

values reflected in their political positions and feelings about university expansion. But these attitudes may also be linked with the tendency of academics to identify themselves primarily either with their academic disciplines, or with their immediate academic communities. We shall refer to men having these kinds of orientations – to the broader disciplines or the local academic community – as 'cosmopolitans' and 'locals'. We expect that cosmopolitans are more likely to be both 'democratic' with respect to the departmental power of the professor and also more egalitarian with regard to access to the senior academic rank. On one hand, the man oriented to the discipline, and to the movement of ideas and growth of knowledge in his subject, wherever it may be going on, is likely to see a strong head of department as at least a potential constraint on his freedom to develop his own research and scholarly interests. Power concentrated in a permanent head of department, and in a small band of senior professors – whatever their personal qualities – is not likely to be exercised primarily in the interests of the research work of junior men. Heads of departments have other, *internal* concerns; their position and administrative responsibilities tend inevitably to lead them to place emphasis on the local academic community – the university or department – within which they hold their posts and for whose welfare they bear a major responsibility. Ironically, as we have seen, the professor typically gains his position by his contribution to scholarship and science; but his appointment as head of department, or to a senior university-wide academic committee, forces him to assume local orientations.

Of course, not all professorial heads of departments surrender their own scholarly interests to the demands of their departments. Many continue their own research, and also administer their departments and universities in ways that are aimed at least in part towards facilitating the work of the cosmopolitans and researchers among their subordinates. But their roles inevitably involve a measure of conflict between their commitment on one hand to their subjects and to research, and on the other to their institutionalised responsibilities for their departments, and especially for their students who, in British universities, are the chief concern of the community.

However different professors resolve these conflicts in their own personal styles, cosmopolitan and research-oriented men are likely to identify their own interests in their own departments not so much with the benevolence of academic power as with its weakness and dispersion. Freedom for research flourishes in the cracks between the flag-stones of institutional authority: and the more flag-stones, the more cracks; the more professors, and the more diluted their power, the greater the autonomy of their subordinates. Where nominal departmental authority is held by an (inevitably) weak rotating chairman, and actually exercised by the colleaguial body of teachers of all ranks, the pull of local responsibilities (especially to teaching) is weakened, and freedom to act and pursue research outside the institution is correspondingly strengthened.

These are some of the reasons why we expect to find academic men with cosmopolitan orientations more likely to support more 'democratic' forms of university and departmental government. For somewhat different reasons we also expect that they will, on average, be more egalitarian in their views about the scarcity and status of the professorial role. For one thing, professorial power and status are related, both in reality and in the attitudes of academics towards the professoriate. On balance, the more professors, the less powerful any one of them; the more normal the expectation of becoming a professor, the more substantive equality in the department and university between men who are professors and men who are merely on their way to becoming a professor. The 'normality of expectation' of attaining the senior academic rank, as we can see very clearly in American universities, very much blurs the distinction among ranks. It makes the professorship a function much less of achievement than of age and seniority, attributes which in academic life are not legitimate bases for very wide disparities in power and status.

Men with cosmopolitan and research orientations are very much concerned with academic status and prestige: but status rooted not in academic rank in the university, but in scholarly and scientific achievement. For such men, professorial appointment is not the source of their status, but merely an acknowledgement of it by their university. Rank is the chief source of academic status only within the university, where it carries power. It counts for much less outside the university, where men are judged on their scholarly accomplishment. And if accomplishment and reputation are the real bases of a man's academic status, and not his rank, then it cannot be harmed by increasing the numbers of professors and thus diluting the honorific status attaching to the rank itself.

Thus men whose academic prestige is rooted in achievement rather than rank, and whose reference groups lie outside the university

–that is, research-oriented cosmopolitans–are less likely to be concerned with maintaining the scarcity value of rank. Moreover, when rank is more closely linked to seniority than to accomplishment, as is true especially in the natural sciences and mathematics, then the disparities between rank and scientific distinction are merely an embarrassment or inconvenience–the more easily removed the larger the number of professorships available. To explore these ideas empirically we developed an index of cosmopolitanism–localism based on teachers' interests in research versus teaching, their having held office in professional or learned societies, their publications, their use of professional journals, their attachment to their present university and their anticipation about applying for posts elsewhere.[1] At one extreme are men who are primarily oriented to research and their disciplines but not strongly attached to their present universities; at the other, men who are attached to their universities and much less so to their professional or disciplinary communities.

Let us look first at the relation between these orientations and attitudes towards professorial power (Table 14.23).

TABLE 14.23

Attitudes to professorial power by cosmopolitanism–localism (per cent)

Attitudes to professorial power	*Cosmopolitans* 1	2	3	4	5	6	*Locals* 7
Democrats	70	66	54	50	49	42	41
Part-democrats	26	28	30	30	31	36	41
Non-democrats	4	6	16	20	21	23	18
TOTALS	(54)	(93)	(244)	(305)	(229)	(137)	(73)

We see clear support for our speculative discussion above: men with cosmopolitan orientations are distinctly more likely to support statements that criticise, or proposals to weaken, the power of the professor in the department. And the relationship is continuous–there is a steady increase in these 'democratic' sentiments, the stronger the orientations to research and the discipline, and the weaker the attachments to the present university.

We find a similar relationship, as we anticipated, between cosmopolitanism and egalitarian views regarding the number and status of

[1] The construction of this index and its rationale are discussed in Appendix D pp. 526 ff.

professors, and conversely, between local orientations and élitist views about the rank (Table 14.24).

TABLE 14.24

Attitudes to professorial status, by cosmopolitanism–localism (per cent)

Attitudes to professorial status	*Cosmopolitans* *1*	*2*	*3*	*4*	*5*	*6*	*Locals* *7*
Levellers	55	55	43	41	34	27	24
Moderates	39	34	41	41	40	45	40
Elitists	5	11	16	18	27	26	35
TOTALS	(56)	(100)	(257)	(331)	(252)	(155)	(82)

Where over half of the 'cosmopolitans' are 'levellers' on our measure of these attitudes, the comparable proportion among men at the 'local' end is only a quarter to a third.

Attitudes towards professorial power, cosmopolitanism–localism and political position

We have seen earlier that attitudes towards professorial power are strikingly related to the *political position* academic men assign themselves on a national political spectrum; while attitudes towards the status of the professoriate are strongly related to *expansionist* or élitist views of the university system. We want now to see how these general orientations towards politics and higher education act in conjunction with local or cosmopolitan orientations as they jointly bear on how men feel about the power and status of high academic rank.[1] Table 14.25[2] shows the first of these joint relationships, linking political position and cosmopolitanism as they bear on attitudes toward professorial power.

Here we see very clearly the independent and cumulative influence of political position and cosmopolitanism on attitudes towards professorial power. Within categories of political position, cosmopolitan orientations continue to show a strong relation to 'democratic'

[1] In part this is explored out of concern with the possibility that the relationships in Tables 14.23 and 14.24 lead to spurious interpretations due to the relationship of cosmopolitanism with political or expansionist positions. The tables below dispel this anxiety, but the relatively weak relationships between the cosmopolitanism–localism index, and political position and support for university expansion are shown separately in Appendix D, Tables 14.38–39.

[2] In Tables 14.25–26 we have combined the two extreme positions at each end of the cosmopolitanism–localism index to give a sufficient number of cases.

TABLE 14.25

Attitudes to professorial power by cosmopolitanism–localism, and political position (per cent)

Attitudes to professorial power	Left					Centre					Right				
	Cosmopolitan	. . . .			*Local*	*Cosmopolitan*	. . . .			*Local*	*Cosmopolitan*	. . . .			*Local*
	1–2	*3*	*4*	*5*	*6–7*	*1–2*	*3*	*4*	*5*	*6–7*	*1–2*	*3*	*4*	*5*	*6–7*
Democrats	75	62	57	53	50	63	42	46	57	39	50	50	37	29	27
Part-democrats	20	30	28	28	30	34	33	30	30	44	36	33	37	38	45
Non-democrats	5	8	15	19	19	3	24	24	13	18	14	17	27	33	29
TOTALS	(84)	(121)	(169)	(117)	(99)	(38)	(78)	(79)	(61)	(57)	(22)	(36)	(49)	(45)	(49)

TABLE 14.26

Attitudes to professorial status by cosmopolitanism–localism, and attitudes to expansion (per cent)

Attitudes to professorial status	Double					50%					Insignificant expansion				
	Cosmopolitan	. . . .			*Local*	*Cosmopolitan*	. . . .			*Local*	*Cosmopolitan*	. . . .			*Local*
	1–2	*3*	*4*	*5*	*6–7*	*1–2*	*3*	*4*	*5*	*6–7*	*1–2*	*3*	*4*	*5*	*6–7*
Levellers	58	58	46	42	32	52	40	42	31	35	52	32	34	30	20
Moderates	35	34	41	38	42	37	47	43	46	41	39	39	37	33	44
Elitists	8	8	13	20	26	11	13	14	23	23	9	28	29	37	35
TOTALS	(52)	(79)	(85)	(66)	(38)	(54)	(98)	(139)	(98)	(99)	(46)	(74)	(97)	(84)	(93)

attitudes towards the professorship. Similarly, within each category of cosmopolitanism–localism, men of the Left are distinctly more 'democratic' than men of the Right. Together, their joint effect is very large: three times as many Left-wing cosmopolitans as Right-wing locals are 'democrats'. These two factors taken together have a substantial degree of predictive power and show that views on the structure of power in universities, far from being held in a vacuum, are strongly influenced by the attitudes and orientations that academic men hold towards more general issues than the specific matters about which respondents were being asked.[1]

Attitudes to professorial status, cosmopolitanism–localism, and support for expanding the university system

Finally we must look at attitudes to professorial status once again, and try to assess the weights of our two independent variables. In this case, however, there is a relationship (though weak) between the independent variables: cosmopolitans are more likely to favour expansion than locals (Appendix A, Table 14.39), presumably because expansion is likely to improve the prospects of any discipline for carrying on research, while locals would be more concerned to preserve the existing character of the institution to which they are attached.

Table 14.26, however, presents a three-variable distribution in the same format, and once again we find that both variables retain much of their impact even when the other is controlled. This is especially clear if we focus on the proportion of 'élitists' in the several categories: in every category of support for expansion, cosmopolitans are less likely to be élitist than locals; and in almost every degree of cosmopolitanism, 'expansionists' are also less likely to be élitist about the professorship. And, taken together at the extremes, 35 per cent of the localists who oppose expansion are also likely to be élitists about academic rank, as compared with only 8 per cent of the cosmopolitan expansionists.[2]

[1] In Appendix D, Table 14.40, we show the absence of a strengthened relationship when we examined the joint effect of cosmopolitanism–localism and *attitudes to expansion* on attitudes to professorial power.

[2] In Appendix D, Table 14.41, we show the joint effect of *political position* and cosmopolitanism–localism on attitudes to professorial status: again we found no strengthened relationship.

Conclusion

In this chapter we have uncovered systems of attitudes, orientations and beliefs held by academics about a variety of social, political and academic matters which show both logical and empirical relationships among their parts. In a sense, we are specifying, through this analysis of responses to survey questions, a number of distinct social-academic philosophies, held, with varying degrees of strength and consistency, by men with different characteristics and differently placed within the university system. These social-educational philosophies are linked to the larger society, to its class structure and political divisions; to the organisation of the university system, and of science and scholarship; and to the partly conflicting functions of higher education for the passing on and the creation of knowledge, through teaching and research. But these social and educational philosophies of academics are not only better understood by reference to the character of British society and its higher learning: they will also influence the rate and forms of social and educational change in Britain, and will affect as well as reflect the impact of inevitable growth on Britain's élite university system.

A recurrent if largely unanticipated theme in the preceding chapters has been the extraordinarily large bearing that university teachers' political positions and loyalties have on their more narrowly academic attitudes and behaviour. In our next chapter we explore this matter in great detail.

Chapter 15

POLITICS

We have described the academic professions in Britain as having a distinctive class (Chapter 9) and status (Chapter 10) position which has evolved out of changes in the social and institutional circumstances of intellectual work in the course of modernisation. In Chapter 11 we showed that the attitudes of university teachers to the expansion of higher education were linked to their political views and in Chapter 14 we also saw that attitudes to departmental government and administration were, in part, reflections of more general variations in political outlook.

These two relationships in themselves justify further exploration of political influences on academic life. But over and above this, politics have an interest of their own, to a sociologist as well as to a political scientist, and in a slightly different way. It is not necessary for our purposes to assert the primacy of specifically political views. Rather, we take political views as accessible and fairly clear indicators of different styles of thinking about a range of problems which is much wider than the issues which separate the national political parties in Britain today. And we can ask what are the forces, both outside and inside the universities, which create, or support, or are at variance with these views.

The plan of the chapter is dictated by these interests. First we show how political views are distributed within our sample of university men, and compare this with other groups in Britain. Second, we examine some of the possible sources of the political views of academics, concentrating on their social origins and education. Third, we look at the distribution of political dispositions in different segments of the academic community, primarily to discover whether different subjects and different types of university vary in their 'political climate'. Finally, we look at the correlates of different political views in attitudes to problems both within and outside the universities.

I. THE POLITICS OF ACADEMIC MEN

We asked our respondents two questions that bore directly on their political views. The first referred specifically to political parties, and simply asked (Q53): 'What party have you generally supported?' Among the 1,306 respondents who answered the question[1] the proportions were as follows:

TABLE 15.1

Party support

Conservative	*Labour*	*Liberal*	*Other*	*None*	*Total*
35%	41%	14%	1%	8%	(1,306)

We do not have precisely comparable figures from other studies Most studies of political behaviour are concerned with actual voting behaviour, or attitudes at one particular time. But it is interesting to compare these proportions (in reply to a questionnaire given in early 1964) with the general election figures of late 1964. If we revise Table 15.1 to exclude those who answered 'none' we find that, on the basis of their 'general support' for a particular party, we might expect 38 per cent to vote Conservative, 45 per cent Labour, 15 per cent Liberal, and 1 per cent for other parties. In the 1964 election, voting figures for the whole population were 43 per cent Conservative, 44 per cent Labour, 11 per cent Liberal and 1 per cent for all others. In other words, there seems to be slightly more support in the academic community than in the general population for the Liberal party and slightly less support for the Conservatives. This is interesting enough in itself; but, in fact, the academic profession is more unlike its counterparts in the general voting population than these figures show.

Many investigators of British political behaviour have noted that Britain shows a high degree of 'class voting'. The two major parties are widely recognised as representing the middle and working classes respectively. (Indeed, there are close formal links between the Labour party and the trades unions.) Although this may be said of most Western two-party democracies, the link seems to be particu-

[1] 102, or 7 per cent of the sample, did not answer the question.

larly strong in England.[1] University teachers are clearly members of the professional, upper middle class; and the voting behaviour of this class, at about the same time as this survey, is shown by an eve-of-election poll taken by Gallup in October 1964 (Table 15.2).

TABLE 15.2

Eve-of-election voting intentions (October 1964) by social class* (per cent)

	Social class			
	Upper middle class ('*Average plus*')	*Middle class* ('*Average*')	*Working class* ('*Average minus*')	*Very poor* ('*Very poor*')
Conservative	77	65	33	32
Labour	9	22	53	59
Liberal	14	13	14	9
(Totals not given)				

* *Source:* Henry Durant–The Gallup Poll: 'Voting Behaviour 1945–64', in R. Rose (ed.), *Studies in British Politics, 1966*. The two descriptions of the categories ('upper middle' against 'average plus', etc.) are both used by the Gallup Poll and its analysts, apparently indifferently.

Clearly, university teachers look very much more like the working class in their political affiliations than like the upper middle class to which they belong in respect to their incomes, status, education, styles of life and other objective indicators of social class.[2]

This phenomenon–the 'Leftism' of academic men compared with other professionals–has been noted before.[3] It may be explained partly by reference to the process of political socialisation, which takes place in three stages. The first is in the home and family. We shall see later in this chapter that there is quite a strong relationship between family background (especially the occupation of our respondents' fathers) and their political views in adult life. But this of itself is not enough to explain the difference between academics and

[1] A recent study by R. Alford, *Party and Society* (Rand McNally, 1963), compared four countries, Britain, U.S.A., Canada and Australia, and showed that 'class voting' was highest in Britain.

[2] A narrower segment of the population, 'higher professionals', including 'doctors, lawyers, architects, clergy, accountants, etc.', was analysed by Mark Bonham, 'The Middle Class Elector', *British Journal of Sociology*, 1952, 3. Their vote in 1951 was found to be 84 per cent Conservative, 6 per cent Labour, 10 per cent others.

[3] See, for example, S. M. Lipset, *Political Man*, Anchor Books, 1963, pp. 335–8.

other professionals, unless university teachers have much more varied social origins than other professional men. While this may be partly true, we do not believe that the difference is great enough to explain the wide divergence that we have found. The same comments apply to the next stage of socialisation, the educational experience in school and university. As to university education, Richard Rose observes that

> . . . for the small group that attends universities, this experience appears to have an important effect in breaking them loose from attitudes inculcated by their secondary school and their families, regardless of their nature.[1]

In other words, for university graduates, the experience of university life loosens the loyalties of their origins, and exposes them to the political values of the academic community. This is in part true, and as some Gallup data show,[2] differences between university students from working and middle class backgrounds are much narrower than comparable differences in the general population. This is undoubtedly a product of selective recruitment from these classes of origin, as well as of the 'homogenising' effect of undergraduate life.

The predominantly 'left-liberal' climate of most academic communities, in Britain as elsewhere, has its roots in the historical links of modern scholarship with the empirical, secular, sceptical traditions of the Enlightenment, and its political expressions in liberalism and democratic socialism. But, while these traditions help to explain the predominantly 'Left' orientations of academic men, as compared with their professional counterparts in law, medicine, accountancy, etc.,[3] we are still left with the considerable variation of political sentiments *within* the academic profession. We see this not only in the distribution of the party preferences but also in their political 'self-identifications'.

The university teachers were asked not only to say what party they supported, but also to place themselves in the political spectrum ranging from Far Left to Far Right (Table 15.3). Over half place themselves somewhere to the left of centre.

Lastly, our sample was asked how interested they were in politics. The findings are given in Table 15.4; it seems that (if we may take the categories of answers as roughly equivalent) university teachers are

[1] Richard Rose, *Politics in England*, Faber, 1965, p. 69.
[2] See note 1, p. 407.
[3] See note 2, p. 401.

very similar in this respect to the middle-class population, and almost identical to the group that left school after sixteen (Table 15.5).

We can now examine the relations between our subjects' party preferences and their self-location on a political spectrum (Table 15.6),

TABLE 15.3

Political position*

Far Left	*Moderate Left*	*Centre*	*Moderate Right*	*Far Right*	*Total*
5%	48%	28%	18%	1%	(1,362)

* Proportions recomputed omitting the 3 per cent who did not answer this question.

TABLE 15.4

Interest in politics (university teachers)

		Interested		
Extremely	*Moderately*	*Slightly*	*Not at all*	*Total*
18%	54%	22%	6%	(1,397)

TABLE 15.5

Interest in politics (national sample) (per cent)

			Interested		
Samples	*Very*	*Fairly*	*Not really*	*Not at all*	*Total*
All voters	15	37	33	15	not given
Middle class	17	52	22	9	,, ,,
Working class	14	30	38	18	,, ,,
Left school after 16	19	53	22	6	,, ,,

TABLE 15.6

Political position of supporters of different parties (per cent)

	Party support				
Political position	*Con-servative*	*Labour*	*Liberal*	*Other*	*None*
Far Left	0	10	1	29	2
Moderate Left	8	83	53	57	43
Centre	41	6	40	14	46
Moderate Right	49	1	6	0	8
Far Right	2	0	0	0	1
TOTALS	(454)	(534)	(182)	(14)	(96)

and then look at the degree of political interest expressed by those with different party loyalties (Table 15.7).

Among Conservative party supporters, a surprisingly large number of academic men place themselves in the Centre or even Moderate Left categories. It would be interesting to know what is their point of reference. It is probably that those who call themselves 'Centre' think of themselves as on the left wing of the British Conservative party. But it could also be that they are comparing themselves with a more international view of the political spectrum, or with a more historical and not immediately contemporary view. In this case it might be possible to call the present Conservative party a party of the Centre. Labour supporters are very highly concentrated in the Moderate Left category.[1]

Both Liberal supporters, and those who have not generally supported any one party, are to be found roughly in the middle between the Conservative and the Labour supporters.

TABLE 15.7

Interest in politics of supporters of different parties (per cent)

	Party support				
Interested	*Conservative*	*Labour*	*Liberal*	*Other*	*None*
Extremely	7	32	8	40	11
Moderately	57	53	56	53	36
Slightly	28 } 36	13 } 15	30 } 37	0 } 7	33 } 53
Not at all	8	2	7	7	20

TABLE 15.8

Party preference by age (per cent)

	Age				
Party	*Under 30*	*30–4*	*35–9*	*40–4*	*45+*
Conservatives	28	31	35	41	40
Labour	50	46	41	35	37
Liberal	13	12	14	16	15
Other	0	1	1	2	1
None	10	10	9	6	7
TOTALS	(214)	(249)	(278)	(185)	(377)

There is also a steady decline (at least up to age 40) in support for the Left with increasing age.

[1] We may perhaps assume that most of the very small number who support 'other' parties are supporters of either the Communist party or the small Welsh, Scottish and Irish nationalist parties, many of whose policies are to the Left of the Labour party.

TABLE 15.9

Political position by age (per cent)

	Age				
Political position	*Under 30*	*30–4*	*35–9*	*40–4*	*45+*
Far Left	7 } 62	5 } 56	4 } 55	3 } 46	4 } 48
Moderate Left	55	51	51	43	44
Centre	26	23	30	32	29
Right	13	20	16	22	23
TOTALS	(227)	(257)	(287)	(189)	(399)

Table 15.7 shows that the supporters of no party have a rather higher proportion who feel slight or no interest in politics. These latter are presumably non-voters, or reluctant voters; whereas those who do express an interest must be genuine 'floating voters'. More striking, however, are the differences between those who report consistent support of a single party. One-third of the Labour supporters describe themselves as 'extremely interested' in politics, and only 15 per cent are slightly or not interested, as compared with over a third of the Conservatives and Liberals who are relatively uninterested in politics.[1] But the difference between Conservatives and Liberals on one hand, and Labour on the other is intriguing. It may be that Labour supporters tend to be younger and so more enthusiastic; but this is the 'image' of itself that the Liberal party especially has been cultivating in recent years. The results here do not confirm that image; Liberal university men are evidently not more enthusiastic than are their Conservative colleagues.[2] The explanation of the high political interest of Labour supporters probably lies more in the nature of Left-wing ideology and ideas: it seems reasonable that, on average, those whose predilection in politics is for change would be more interested than those who simply want to preserve the status quo:[3] and that, as we suggested earlier, is one of the most noticeable characteristics of Conservative philosophy at present.[4]

[1] The proportions among the fifteen supporters of small parties are even higher, which is perhaps not surprising, since a considerable degree of interest is really a prerequisite even for noticing the existence of these parties.

[2] The youthful image projected by the Liberals in recent years is not confirmed by their support among university teachers: they gain roughly the same degree of support in all age categories. But Labour supporters are somewhat younger, on average, as Conservatives are somewhat older.

[3] The connection between political interest and preference is discussed in S. M. Lipset *et al.*, 'The Psychology of Voting', in G. Lindzey, *Handbook of Social Psychology*, Addison, Wesley Publishing Co., Reading, Mass., 1954, Vol. II, pp. 1126 ff.

[4] The relation between political orientations and interest is explored further in Appendix D, pp. 532–4 (Tables 15.49–50).

Political activity

There is another measure of political interest in the questionnaire; respondents were asked if there were any extra-academic activities that took up much of their time; and one of the options was political activity. This gives a measure of *active* interest, which can be compared with our subjects' assertions of their interest in politics in its relation to political sentiments. Tables 15.10 and 15.11 relate political activity to party support and position in the spectrum.

TABLE 15.10

Political activity 'taking up an appreciable amount of time' by party support

	Party support		
	Conservative	*Labour*	*Liberal*
Political activity as % of total mentioning any activity	2% (158)	8% (179)	6% (65)
Political activity as % of total of party supporters	1% (461)	3% (537)	2% (184)

TABLE 15.11

Political activity by political position

	Political position			
	Far Left	*Moderate Left*	*Centre*	*Right*
Political activity as % of total mentioning any activity	33% (24)	5% (214)	3% (119)	2% (104)
Political activity as % of total of category	13% (62)	2% (657)	1% (381)	1% (262)

The numbers who mentioned spending 'an appreciable amount of time' on political activities are very small. Indeed, it is only by showing them as a percentage of those who mention any activities that we can really detect a meaningful pattern which is that 'activity', like 'interest', is higher on the Left, both in terms of the spectrum and of party support, but it is only those on the Far Left who show a sharply higher level of political activity.

II. THE SOURCES OF POLITICAL SUPPORT

We have seen that academic men are on average rather more Left though no more politically interested or active than other upper middle class people. Our next step is to look for the sources of their political views in the two chief agents of early political socialisation, the family and the school.

There is relatively little in the literature on this subject that is directly helpful to us; for a large proportion of that devoted to the influence of family background concentrates on the relation between parents' and children's party support. We did not ask about parents' voting, and we shall concentrate on the social class of our subjects' parents, as measured by father's occupation and education. There is a wealth of literature on the relation between social class and politics, but not much that would relate to our somewhat unusual problem of a homogeneous occupational group coming from different backgrounds. Similarly, when we turn to the educational experience of our respondents, there is not much to guide us, since most inquiries have been devoted to the effect of different *amounts* of education. All of our subjects have had nearly the same amount, but in different types of schools.

Father's occupation

It is to be expected that academic men with working-class parents would be more likely to be Labour supporters; despite Rose's remarks (quoted above, p. 402) that university education has the effect of liberating students from the effects of their earlier experience, we should expect at least some residual effect,[1] and this is borne out by Table 15.12.

There is a very large and clear difference in party preference of men from different class origins. Only one-third of those with professional fathers support the Labour party, compared with almost two-thirds from semi- or unskilled manual backgrounds. The difference by class origin in support for the Conservatives is also marked, though some

[1] In a study of London university *students*, Abrams (in Rose, 1966, p. 142) found that children of working class parents were somewhat less likely to vote Conservative, and more likely to vote Labour, than those of middle class parents; but for both groups there had been a considerable movement towards a common centre from the voting behaviour of their parents. The difference between the groups in Table 15.12 is, however, much larger than in Abrams' university student sample.

TABLE 15.12

Party preference by father's occupation (per cent)

Teacher's party preference	*Father's occupation* Professional	*Intermediate*	*Skilled*	*Semi-skilled–Unskilled*		
Conservative	42	39	27	24	24	21
Labour	33	36	50	59	61	71
Liberal	15	14	16	6	5	0
Other	1	2	1	0	1	7
None	10	9	7	11	9	0
TOTALS	(255)	(520)	(419)	(71)	(85)	(14)

of the loss of Labour support among sons of middle-class origin goes to the Liberals. Indeed, as we see in Table 15.14, it is partly to the Liberals rather than Labour that sons of professionals turn if they have Left-wing sympathies. But men's (self-assigned) position on a political spectrum is much less closely related to their social origins than is their party preference (Table 15.13). There is, however, some

TABLE 15.13

Political position by father's occupation (per cent)

Teacher's political position	*Father's occupation* Professional	*Intermediate*	*Skilled*	*Semi-skilled–Unskilled*		
Far Left	5 } 46	4 } 51	4 } 59	7 } 60	10 } 61	31 } 69
Moderate Left	41	47	55	53	51	38
Centre	31	29	26	22	23	31
Right	23	20	15	19	16	0
TOTALS	(265)	(539)	(439)	(74)	(87)	(13)

relationship: 46 per cent of the children of professional fathers see themselves as on the Left, compared with 61 per cent of those from manual-worker families. To clarify what is happening here, we must examine the bearing of class origins on distribution of party support for each position on the political spectrum (Table 15.14). It is clear that in all categories of the spectrum, even the Right, class origins affect party preference.[1]

[1] On the general issue and research evidence, see H. Hyman, *Political 'alisation*, Free Press, 1959, Chapter IV, *passim*.

TABLE 15.14

Party preference by father's occupation, within categories of political position (per cent)

Party	*Political position*											
	Left *Father's occupation*				*Centre* *Father's occupation*				*Right* *Father's occupation*			
	Professional	*Intermediate*	*Skilled*	*Manual*	*Professional*	*Intermediate*	*Skilled*	*Manual*	*Professional*	*Intermediate*	*Skilled*	*Manual*
Conservative	7	7	3	6	55	59	49	41	93	93	86	71
Labour	67	68	77	87	9	7	15	18	0	0	3	21
Liberal	18	15	13	6	20	20	27	6	3	5	6	0
Other/None	8	11	7	2	16	13	9	35	3	3	5	7
TOTALS	(113)	(261)	(249)	(52)	(75)	(137)	(102)	(17)	(61)	(109)	(63)	(14)

Whatever their broader significance for the study of social class, social mobility, and political behaviour, in the present context these findings emphasise (a) the high degree of congruence between 'political position' and party preference: and (b) the continuing influence of class origins on voting behaviour despite general political orientations. The first of these implications reminds us that members of this highly educated and sophisticated occupation tend to develop coherent, logically consistent systems of views–and helps explain the relations we find between their political orientations and their attitudes on various educational issues, such as expansion and the professoriate. The second reminds us that adult socialisation does not obliterate the influence of early life experience and identifications, and draws attention to the effects on the academic profession of changes in the patterning of social recruitment to it–and especially of the increased recruitment from the lower middle and working class which inevitably accompanies large-scale expansion of higher education.

Father's education

We should expect the effect of the father's education to be broadly similar to that of his occupation, since education is so closely linked to future occupation. Before examining that, however, we should note one finding of the effect of length of education on a man's own political views. Rose[1] shows the voting intentions of a national sample in 1964 broken down according to the age at which the voter left school (Table 15.15).

TABLE 15.15

Voting intentions (1964) by age of leaving school (national sample) (per cent)

	Age left school				
Party	*14 or earlier*	*15*	*16*	*17–18*	*19 or later*
Conservative	37	40	58	70	58
Labour	52	49	26	15	20
Liberal	10	10	16	14	20
Other	1	2	1	1	2
(Totals not given)					

[1] Rose (1965), *op. cit.*, p. 69: source is National Opinion Polls.

It appears that the proportions voting Conservative steadily increase with length of education up to eighteen years old, but that those with higher education are more likely to vote either Labour or Liberal, and certainly less likely to vote Conservative. This may be connected both with the liberating quality of higher education which we discussed earlier, and also with a difference between the graduate professional occupations and those professions or sub-professions for which education up to eighteen is sufficient.

Among the university teachers we find steadily increasing support for the Conservatives and decreasing support for Labour with increasing education for the father, up to the age of sixteen or seventeen (Table 15.16). Beyond this point, as in the national sample shown in Table 15.15, support for the Conservatives drops, and that for Labour or the Liberals increases.[1] Once again the effect of family background is clear, though not quite as strong as it was in the case of the father's occupation.

TABLE 15.16

Party support by age at which father left school (per cent)

University teacher's party support	*Father's school-leaving age*					
	13 or earlier	*14*	*15*	*16*	*17*	*18 or later*
Conservative	26	28	38	44	45	38
Labour	50	49	44	32	38	38
Liberal	13	13	11	17	13	14
Other	1	2	0	0	0	2
None	10	9	7	8	4	8
TOTALS	(220)	(349)	(88)	(115)	(106)	(240)

But the connection between education and class is so close[2] (in Britain as in most other countries), that unless we control for class origins we cannot know how to interpret Table 15.16. In Table 15.18 we look at the bearing of father's education on the party loyalties for university teachers of middle and of working class origins separately.

[1] But, for our sample at least, it does not seem to matter *what kind* of higher education the father had. When we looked at the academics whose fathers had some higher education, we found that it made little difference to the party preferences of their sons whether their fathers had been to Oxford or Cambridge, to other universities, or to other institutions of higher education.

[2] The relation of fathers' education to their economic class is predictably large.

TABLE 15.17

Length of father's education by father's class position (per cent)

Father's school-leaving age	*Father's occupation* Non-manual	Manual
13–15	42	84
16–17	25	12
18+	33	4
TOTALS	(657)	(440)

TABLE 15.18

Party support by father's class and amount of formal education (year father left school) (per cent)

Teacher's party support	*Father's occupation* Non-manual			Manual		
	Father's school-leaving age					
	13–15	*16–17*	*18+*	*13–15*	*16–17*	*18+*
Conservative	36	46	38	22	41	39
Labour	37	33	38	59	35	39
Liberal	14	15	14	12	18	17
Other/None	13	6	10	8	6	6
TOTALS	(277)	(164)	(216)	(371)	(51)	(18)

Again the sons of men who prolonged their education past eighteen are less likely to support the Conservatives than those of men who did not go on to some kind of higher education. But more important, the difference in party loyalties of men from middle and working class backgrounds decreases the more education their fathers had. Essentially, the difference in party preference among academics of working and middle class origin is supplied almost wholly by the men whose fathers did not attend school beyond fifteen: it is among the poorly educated that class rather than education determines party allegiance *even for the next generation.* Looked at another way, differences among five of the six class and education categories in Table 15.18 are small: the Conservatives get about half of the *major* party support in all five (the range is from about 49 to 59 per cent). But among the sons of the large body of manual workers who had little formal education, support for the Tories is only 27 per cent of the major party 'vote'. Among the children of the minority of manual workers whose fathers' education exceeded the standard minimum for their class, the distribution of party preferences is almost indistinguishable from that of their middle class counterparts. This minority of workers who had gained more than the minimum working class education had in many cases acquired the political preferences as well as the education of the middle class, and we see the results in their university teacher children. The continuing effects of social origins on the party loyalties[1] of academic men could hardly be more strikingly demonstrated.

Family religious background

Religion has always been seen as important in political socialisation. The various religions and sects often provide doctrines and ideologies which may dictate or at least encourage particular political dispositions. This phenomenon is seen very clearly in the United States with its proliferation of churches. In England the Anglican Church allows a variety of opinions, both political and religious, to shelter beneath its banner; but here, too, studies have found a considerable difference between religious groups. A recent example is that of Alford,[2] who examined voting preferences in 1962 in four 'Anglo-Saxon' countries, as these varied among people of different faiths and denominations. In Table 15.19 we show his findings for a sample of the whole population of England, in terms of the intended Labour vote. Beneath it is the proportion of Labour supporters in our sample.

On the whole, the correspondence is very close, especially for those brought up in Anglican, Scots Presbyterian, or agnostic families. In the case of the Roman Catholics, the difference may be explained by the presence in the national sample of a large number of working class members (largely Irish) of the Catholic Church in England, whose class background evidently outweighs their religious beliefs. There is a small difference between the children of nonconformist parents and the nonconformists in the national sample, but it does not deviate far enough from the national average in either direction.

It appears (Table 15.20) that the Church of Scotland families provided the strongest Conservative and weakest Labour support. This church is the largest representative in Great Britain of the

[1] When we examined the distribution among university teachers on the political spectrum in the same way, we found relatively smaller variations by extent of father's education. Again, we see that social origins have their continuing effect on the politics of academic men by way of party loyalties rather than directly on political sentiments.

[2] Alford, *op. cit.*, Table 6-3, p. 136.

TABLE 15.19

(a) Proportion of Labour vote-intentions (1962) by current religious preference (national sample); (b) Proportion of Labour supporters by parents' religious preference (university teachers) (per cent)

	Church of Scotland	*Church of England*	*Roman Catholic*	*Noncon-formists*	*Jewish*	*Other*	*None (atheist, agnostic)*	*All respondents*
(a) National sample*	33	40	58	36	†	40	61	41
(b) University teachers	30	40	36	44	61	33	62	41
TOTALS	(208)	(598)	(56)	(291)	(46)	(12)	(86)	(1,306)

* No totals given by Alford. † No distribution for Jews provided by Alford.

TABLE 15.20

Party preference by parents' religious denomination (per cent)

Teacher's party support	*Parents' denomination*						
	Church of Scotland	*Church of England*	*Roman Catholic*	*Noncon-formists*	*Jewish*	*None*	*All*
Conservative	46	41	21	25	20	21	35
Labour	30	40	36	44	61	62	41
Liberal	18	10	27	21	7	11	14
Other	1	0	0	3	4	2	1
None	6	9	16	8	9	5	8
TOTALS	(208)	(598)	(56)	(291)	(46)	(86)	(1,306)

Calvinist tradition; in Britain, as in America, churches in that tradition have Conservative leanings on moral and economic issues. After them, the Roman Catholics show the least support for Labour: the Catholic Church does not, in general, favour socialist parties; but children of Catholic parents in our sample are as unlikely to support the Conservative party as even the most 'Left-wing' groups, the Jews and the agnostic/atheists. Instead, a very high proportion of them either support the Liberals or no party. We shall see below (Table 15.21) that they are fairly Left-wing. The Church of England is fairly close to, but a little more Conservative than, the average of all groups. The nonconformists, most of whose churches in Britain have traditionally favoured the Liberal or Labour parties, do so in our sample also. Lastly, those whose parents were either Jewish or had no religion prove to be the strongest Labour supporters. Again, this too has been found in other studies.[1]

Looking at the relation of religion to political dispositions (Table 15.21), we again find the Church of Scotland to be the most conservative group. The Church of England is fairly near the average, and then follow the Roman Catholics and the nonconformists close together, with the children of agnostics and, finally, Jews, the most Left-wing of all. In other words, the picture is much the same as before, with two reservations: children of Catholic parents turn out on the whole to be Left-wing non-socialists; and secondly, the differences here are considerably sharpened. Indeed, the difference in proportions who are 'Left' between Jews and the Church of Scotland group (77 per cent and 44 per cent) is greater than between men of widely different class origins (Table 15.13). Religious upbringing is a powerful determinant of political ideology and disposition.

It is now obviously necessary to look at the combined effects of religious background and social origins: it may be that religious denominations have different effects depending on the social background of the family.

In both Tables 15.22 and 15.23 we find that the differences between the religious backgrounds that we saw above (Tables 15.20–21) persist even when social origins are taken into account. Among those of both manual and middle class origins, those who grew up in the Church of Scotland are consistently furthest to the Right, while the children of Jewish or agnostic parents are furthest to the Left, both

[1] See G. Lenski, *The Religious Factor*, Anchor Books, 1963; Chapter 4, 'Religion and Politics', pp. 134–211.

TABLE 15.21

Political position by parents' religious denomination (per cent)

Teacher's political position	*Parents' denomination* Church of Scotland	Church of England	Roman Catholic	Noncon-formists	Jewish	None	All
Far Left	2	4	3	4	6	12	5
Moderate Left	42	45	50	54	71	58	48
Centre	29 } 56	30 } 51	23 } 46	28 } 42	12 } 22	20 } 29	28 } 47
Right	27	21	23	14	10	9	19
TOTALS	(216)	(618)	(60)	(309)	(48)	(89)	(1,362)

Tables 15.22 and 15.23

Party preference and political position by father's occupation and parents' denomination (per cent)

	Father's occupation											
	Non-manual						*Manual*					
15.22	*Parents' denomination*						*Parents' denomination*					
Teacher's party support	*Church of Scotland*	*Church of England*	*Roman Catholic*	*Noncon-formist*	*Jewish*	*None*	*Church of Scotland*	*Church of England*	*Roman Catholic*	*Noncon-formist*	*Jewish*	*None*
Conservative	55	45	24	30	25	24	34	33	14	18	8	12
Labour	26	35	26	34	53	55	36	51	52	56	77	77
Liberal	13	11	32	22	9	10	22	8	19	20	0	12
Other	1	0	0	5	3	3	1	0	0	1	8	0
None	5	9	18	10	9	7	7	8	14	5	8	0
TOTALS	(120)	(362)	(34)	(154)	(32)	(58)	(85)	(221)	(21)	(132)	(13)	(26)

15.23

Teacher's political position	*Church of Scotland*	*Church of England*	*Roman Catholic*	*Noncon-formist*	*Jewish*	*None*	*Church of Scotland*	*Church of England*	*Roman Catholic*	*Noncon-formist*	*Jewish*	*None*
Left	40	47	44	55	71	62	50	54	70	62	92	90
Centre	29	29	28	33	18	28	30	29	13	25	0	7
Right	31	24	28	12	12	10	20	17	17	13	8	3
TOTALS	(129)	(369)	(36)	(162)	(34)	(58)	(84)	(230)	(23)	(141)	(13)	(29)

on the political spectrum and in terms of their party support. The other groups fall in between in the same order, with the exception of the Roman Catholics. In the case of party support (Table 15.22) we find that Catholics with non-manual worker fathers support Labour as little as do those brought up in the Church of Scotland, but they support the Conservative party as little as do those from Jewish and agnostic families. However, when their fathers were manual workers they seem more willing to support the Labour party, coming near the mean for those from a similar class background. The difference is even clearer in the following table. Those from non-manual Catholic families are not noticeably Left-wing, but those from manual families are distinctly more Left-wing. In both cases support for the Labour party is somewhat less than we might expect from their position in the spectrum.

Tables 15.24 and 15.25

Political difference by class origins (% non-manual minus % manual) for university teachers of varying religious background

15.24 Party Preference

	Parents' religious denominations					
Party	*Church of Scotland*	*Church of England*	*Roman Catholic*	*Noncon-formist*	*Jewish*	*None*
Conservative	21	12	10	12	17	12
Labour	−10	−16	−26	−22	−24	−22
Liberal	−9	3	13	2	9	−2

15.25 Political Position

Political position						
Left	−10	−7	−26	−7	−21	−28
Centre	−1	0	15	8	18	21
Right	11	7	11	−1	4	7

Among Jews, Catholics and agnostics/atheists of working class origins, the proportions who identify themselves as on the Left run between 21 per cent and 28 per cent higher than among their co-religionists of middle class origins. By contrast the differences by class origins among Church of Scotland, Church of England and nonconformists are under 10 per cent. This does *not* mean that for the former groups religion is a weak determinant of political disposition; indeed, both the Jews and the agnostics/atheists are conspicuously high in support for the Left. Rather, for these groups *both* class and religious origins are strong determinants of their political dispositions; for them, as for the middle class Catholics, the influence of their deviant social statuses on their political perspectives persists into adult life, against the homogenising influence of a common higher education and adult class and occupation.

More generally, we can see from these tables that both father's occupation and family religion are important in determining the future political orientations of academics. For those of both manual and non-manual origins, as we have seen, religious variations still make a difference. Equally, within each denomination the children of manual workers are further to the Left than those of non-manual workers, and are relatively more likely to support the Labour than the Conservative party. The power of these two factors in combination can be seen by looking at the extremes. Just over three-quarters of those from manual Jewish or agnostic families are Labour supporters, against just over a quarter from non-manual Church of Scotland families. In the case of the political spectrum, the range in the same groups is from 92 to 40 per cent who are 'Left'. It is clear that though their education and their present occupations may have 'liberated' university teachers to some extent from the effect of their upbringing, it still has a very powerful effect on their political views.[1]

Secondary schooling

We have now dealt with one of the two formative influences during the childhood of our respondents, their family background. The other important agent of socialisation is, of course, the school and we should expect to find political differences according to the type of school attended.

The stratification of the British school system is both directly and indirectly related to the social class position of parents. The direct relation stems from the difference between the fee-paying 'public schools' and the free state supported system of 'grammar' and 'secondary modern' schools. In between fall the 'direct-grant' schools, independent of local authority control but supported by the central government. These schools charge fees to some pupils but are required by law to provide a certain number of free places. The three types of schools differ in their social class recruitment. Selection of the roughly 20 per cent of state school pupils who are to attend grammar schools has since 1944 been made at eleven years on the basis of one or both alternatives of intelligence tests and teachers' recommendations. The latter tend to be biased in favour of middle class children, and it has been shown that measured intelligence is also related to

[1] The residual influence of class origins on political dispositions differs for men of different religious backgrounds.

class background.[1] In any case, the result has been that grammar schools generally have more than their share of middle class children, compared with the proportion in the relevant age group, and secondary modern schools more working class children. We should expect to find in our sample also that social origin has an important bearing on the type of school attended. Table 15.26 shows, first of all, the proportions having attended different types of school, and then Table 15.27 relates this to father's occupation.

TABLE 15.26

Type of school attended

Public school	*Direct-grant*	*Grammar school*	*Other*	*None*	*Total*
21%	10%	55%	13%	1%	(1,387)

Not surprisingly, our respondents were very largely educated in one of the first three types of school, those which provide channels to the universities: fewer than 13 per cent were educated at secondary modern or technical schools, where over 70 per cent of British school children now receive their education.[2] More than half went to grammar schools, and just over one-fifth to independent public schools.

TABLE 15.27

Type of school attended by father's occupation (per cent)

	Father's occupation			
School	*Professional*	*Intermediate*	*Skilled*	*Semi- and Unskilled*
Public	47	22	8	1
Direct-grant	9	11	12	7
Grammar	32	53	68	75
Other	11	14	11	15
None	0	1	1	2
TOTALS	(271)	(552)	(441)	(88)

As in the population as a whole, the social origins of university teachers have a very clear effect on the type of school they attended

[1] A. H. Halsey *et al.*, *Education, Economy and Society*, Free Press, 1961: articles in Parts III and IV.

[2] Some indeterminate but probably large proportion of this 13 per cent was educated outside of Great Britain (6 per cent took university degrees abroad).

(Table 15.27). Almost half of the children of professional parents went to public schools, and one-third to grammar schools. At the other extreme, three-quarters of our respondents with fathers in semi- or unskilled jobs come from a grammar school background, and only 1 per cent from a public school.

The effect of differential recruitment to these types of school should be obvious. The various schools cater for groups of pupils with relatively homogeneous social backgrounds, and might therefore be expected to reinforce the political views of the dominant social group. Of course the three types of school from which most of our sample come, public, direct-grant and grammar, are all dominated by the middle class: but the public schools, particularly the most academically successful ones, contain high proportions of upper and upper middle class children, while the grammar schools have a substantial representation of working class children. Moreover, many public schools in their teaching and in other ways explicitly foster fairly conservative ideologies.

TABLE 15.28

Party support, by type of school attended (per cent)

	School			
Party	*Public*	*Direct-grant*	*Grammar*	*Other*
Conservative	49	31	33	26
Labour	26	39	45	51
Liberal	18	19	13	12
Other	1	0	2	1
None	7	11	8	11
TOTALS	(274)	(128)	(721)	(161)

We see from Table 15.28 that there is the expected relation between party support and secondary schooling. Half of the ex public school boys in our sample support the Conservative party, and one-quarter Labour. At the other extreme, of former pupils of modern and technical schools, half are Labour supporters, and one-quarter Conservative. In between, the direct-grant and grammar schools can be grouped somewhat nearer to the other state schools than to the independent public schools. The difference between fee-paying and non-fee-paying schools seems to be the most crucial.

Table 15.29 shows the relation between secondary schooling and position in the political spectrum. The differences here are somewhat smaller: 41 per cent of the public school educated teachers place

TABLE 15.29

Political position by secondary schooling (per cent)

Political position	Public		Direct-grant		Grammar		Other	
Far Left	4	41	4	57	5	56	7	58
Moderate Left	37		53		51		51	
Centre	34		24		27		24	
Right	25		20		18		18	
TOTALS	(281)		(138)		(744)		(174)	

themselves on the Left, compared with 58 per cent of those who attended modern or technical schools. Moreover, there are no significant differences among the different types of state supported schools. Even more clearly here it is the difference between fee-paying and free schools that is the crucial factor.[1]

We have already seen (Table 15.14, p. 409) that social origin has a more powerful effect on party support than on political position. Thus differences in party support between free and fee-paying schools may reflect the difference in party support of those from different social origins. In other words, the school may be an important intervening variable which by its class recruitment tends to confirm the effect of social origin: but it may not have much power to alter the party allegiance, for instance, of an upper middle class boy in a grammar school.

We can test the relative importance of social origin and schooling by examining their combined effect on party support (Table 15.30).

Though the effect of social origins is not much diminished by controlling for schooling, yet even within the same broad classes of origin the child's school has an important effect on party support. In other words, both the family and the school play independent parts in influencing future party allegiances. Thus a child sent to the type of school to which others of his class tend to go has his family's political beliefs strongly reinforced, and is more likely than others to vote according to his class.[2] The difference is especially strong in the case of manual workers' children in Table 15.30 (though this may be partly accounted for by internal variation between higher and lower strata within the group of manual workers). As far as actual party support is

[1] It may be that the differences that we found in party support among the different state supported schools (Table 15.28) are not in fact the result of schooling but rather of the differential recruitment that we saw in Table 15.27.

[2] There is the further likelihood that more conservative parents in all social classes are more likely to send their children to fee-paying schools.

TABLE 15.30

Party support by secondary schooling and father's occupation (per cent)

	Father's occupation							
	Non-manual				*Manual*			
	School				*School*			
Party	*Public*	*Direct-grant*	*Grammar*	*Other*	*Public*	*Direct-grant*	*Grammar*	*Other*
Conservative	51	32	39	29	34	29	27	19
Labour	24	39	37	43	37	40	53	66
Liberal	17	18	12	14	23	19	13	8
Other	1	0	2	1	0	0	1	0
None	7	11	9	13	6	12	7	7
TOTALS	(231)	(74)	(360)	(98)	(35)	(52)	(348)	(59)

concerned, both school and family are important. When we turn to distributions of political dispositions (Table 15.31), however, the

TABLE 15.31

Political position by secondary schooling and father's occupation (per cent)

	Father's occupation							
	Non-manual				*Manual*			
	School				*School*			
Political position	*Public*	*Direct-grant*	*Grammar*	*Other*	*Public*	*Direct-grant*	*Grammar*	*Other*
Left	40	50	51	58	50	64	60	61
Centre	34	30	29	24	28	16	26	21
Right	25	20	20	19	22	20	14	18
TOTALS	(236)	(80)	(369)	(106)	(36)	(56)	(361)	(62)

effect of social origin, which was never very strong (Table 15.13, p. 408), is further diminished. There is still some tendency for the children of non-manual workers to place themselves in the Centre or on the Right, but it is a difference of the order of 9 per cent (in the grammar schools and public schools) or at most 14 per cent (direct-grant schools). Religious background is still the most important single factor that we have found in determining political position (though not party support).

Higher education

One of the themes of this study has been that even in a highly selective university system like that in Great Britain there are considerable variations in the character or climate of the different universities. Some of the differences in internal character stem from well known factors such as the academic and social prestige of the institutions, their recruitment of students, or their size and age. We have seen some of the results of the different atmospheres of different universities in our discussions of research and teaching orientations (Chapters 12 and 13) and of attitudes to departmental structure and administration (Chapter 14), and later, we shall try to see whether the groups of universities have different political climates reflecting the political views of their staff. But at this stage we want to look at the universities where our teachers were undergraduates, to see whether these seem to have affected their political views.

As with secondary schools, one possible source of variation is the social composition of the students. It has been shown, especially by the Franks Commission for Oxford, that students' application to and selection by universities may be affected by their educational background; there are good reasons to believe that the universities therefore vary quite widely in the social origins of their students.[1]

TABLE 15.32

University group of first degree, by father's occupation (per cent)

	Father's occupation					
Group	*Profes-sional*	*Inter-mediate*	*Skilled*	*Semi-skilled*		*Un-skilled*
Oxford and Cambridge	39	33	22	14	11	0
London	15	17	23	14	15	20
Major Redbrick	15	17	25	24	25	27
Minor Redbrick	3	3	3	7	6	0
Wales	3	3	6	14	11	0
Scotland	14	14	12	22	21	20
Overseas	7	7	3	1	3	13
None	5	6	6	5	8	20
TOTALS	(274)	(554)	(446)	(74)	(89)	(15)

[1] *Franks Report*: Vol. 1, paras. 144–56. See also *Higher Education*, Appendix Two (B), Part I, Table 11, p. 9: In 1961 17 per cent of undergraduates of universities in England and Wales other than Oxford and Cambridge came from independent schools, and 70 per cent from maintained schools. In the same year figures for Oxford were roughly 50 per cent from independent schools and 33 per cent from maintained schools (estimated from *Franks Report*, Table D, p. 72). Robbins also found (Appendix Two (B), Annex (C)) that in 1955 the percentage of entrants to universities whose fathers were in manual occupations was 9 per cent at Cambridge, 13 per cent at Oxford, 21 per cent at London, and 31 per cent at other English universities.

It is quite clear (Table 15.32) that the children of fathers in the upper occupational groups are much more likely to have been educated at Oxford or Cambridge. Roughly similar proportions of students from all backgrounds were educated at London, while disproportionately large numbers of working class students were educated at Redbrick and Scottish universities.[1]

On the basis of these findings we might expect that those university teachers who did their undergraduate work at Oxford and Cambridge would turn out to be the most Conservative, and that the rest would not vary very much. But since here we are not so much interested in describing the characteristics of those educated at different places, as in discovering what effect their education had, we shall look at the different university groups, controlling for social origin at the same time (Table 15.33). Otherwise, since we know that social origin is a powerful factor in affecting political views, our findings might be contaminated by the very different backgrounds of students from one group to the next.

We find, however, that for both groups, non-manual and manual, Oxford and Cambridge graduates as a group are slightly to the Left in their party support.[2] In the non-manual group, those from Oxford and Cambridge support the Conservative party least of all: and in the manual group, they support Labour most. But there are no very large differences between the university groups, with one exception: those from Scotland are much more Conservative. This is the case not only in the non-manual group, where only Scotland produces more than 50 per cent support for the Conservatives, but also for those of working class background, where they are the only group to show a plurality for the Conservatives.

This is a very interesting finding. It seems clear from other studies[3]

[1] We also percentaged this table the other way, to show the variations in class origins of academic men from different university groups. (The table is printed in Appendix D, as Table 15.55.) We found that men educated at universities abroad came from the highest social origins: four-fifths of their fathers held non-manual occupations. Those educated at Oxford and Cambridge came closest to them; here the percentage from non-manual backgrounds was 73 per cent. After these came Scotland, the minor Redbricks, London, and the major Redbricks, in that order, with percentages from non-manual families ranging between 61 per cent and 50 per cent. Of those from Wales, two-fifths (42 per cent) came from non-manual backgrounds. Thus, as is suggested by Table 15.32, there are quite sharp differences in social origins between those who took their first degrees at different universities.

[2] The variations on the political spectrum are similar, but much smaller: see Table 15.34.

[3] A large amount of American research is summarised in Kenneth A. Feldman and Theodore M. Newcomb, *The Impact of College on Students*, Jossey-Bass Inc., 1969 (2 vols.).

TABLE 15.33

Party support, by university group of first degree and father's occupation (per cent)

	Father's occupation									
	Non-manual					*Manual*				
Party	*Oxford and Cambridge*	*London*	*Major Redbrick*	*Minor Redbrick and Wales*	*Scotland*	*Oxford and Cambridge*	*London*	*Major Redbrick*	*Minor Redbrick and Wales*	*Scotland*
Conservative	36	37	41	39	52	25	27	26	16	41
Labour	37	40	36	33	23	58	55	53	57	33
Liberal	17	15	12	17	13	10	14	11	24	18
Other/None	10	8	11	11	10	7	5	9	4	8
TOTALS	(270)	(120)	(126)	(46)	(109)	(98)	(110)	(129)	(51)	(73)

TABLE 15.34

Political position, by university group of first degree and father's occupation (per cent)

	Father's occupation									
	Non-manual					Manual				
Political position	*Oxford and Cambridge*	*London*	*Major Redbrick*	*Minor Redbrick and Wales*	*Scotland*	*Oxford and Cambridge*	*London*	*Major Redbrick*	*Minor Redbrick and Wales*	*Scotland*
Far Left	5 } 51	5 } 52	5 } 52	2 } 46	2 } 41	6 } 66	4 } 64	3 } 60	7 } 58	4 } 42
Left	46	47	47	44	39	60	60	57	51	38
Centre	31	27	28	30	32	19	25	22	31	34
Right	18	21	19	24	27	15	12	18	11	23
TOTALS	(277)	(129)	(129)	(50)	(112)	(108)	(113)	(132)	(55)	(73)

that university education does have an effect on political dispositions, even if it is simply a liberating one. It was clear from our examination of the effects of secondary schooling that schools with a more working class composition tend to produce more Labour supporters, even among pupils with the same social background. The universities, however, which also vary widely in the background of their students, do not seem to develop different political climates as a result–at least not so as to affect greatly those of their graduates who become university teachers. In other words, the social hierarchy of universities does not seem to have the same politically divisive effect as does the hierarchy of secondary schools. These remarks do not apply to the Scottish universities: but they are exceptions, since they are much more local in character than any of the other British groups. Although many English students can be found in Scottish universities, and many Scots in England, there is a much more direct channel from Scottish schools to Scottish universities than is to be found in any other geographical area, even in Wales. We have noted that teachers brought up in the Church of Scotland are relatively conservative in their political views. Most of these will have been educated at universities in Scotland,[1] and the homogeneity of these universities in this respect, despite their fairly wide social recruitment, probably does much to reinforce the political attitudes learnt in family and school.[2, 3]

[1] Actually, two-thirds of the men in our sample who were from Church of Scotland backgrounds took their first degree in a Scottish university.

[2] Indeed, it is really only those Church of Scotland men *who remained in Scotland for their first degree* who are conspicuously conservative, as we see below:

TABLE 15.35

Party preference by place of first degree (per cent)

Party	*Oxford and Cambridge, London*	*Church of Scotland Origins Place of First Degree*		*Whole Sample*
		Scotland	*All Others*	
Conservative	36	51	33	35
Labour	31	26	46	41
Liberal	24	17	21	14
Other/None	10	6	0	9
TOTALS	(42)	(126)	(24)	(1,306)

[3] While we are looking at the possible effects of university education on political views, it is worth considering two other aspects of this education–namely, the class of degree gained, and whether the respondent took any higher degrees. It is possible that the quality of academic performance may have some bearing on the impact of a university education on political views. For

Subject taught

Is there a causal relation between academic subjects and political outlook? The choice of a particular subject implies the formation of views about the nature of the world and further study continues to shape them. This is particularly clear, perhaps, in the case of the social sciences. Although most social scientists would claim, justifiably, that their research after they have chosen a problem is objective and 'value-free', yet their studies compel them to confront the social and political dilemmas of their world. And in Britain, especially, the applied social sciences have roots in the reformist traditions of political radicalism.[1]

The connections between subject and political dispositions are complex, a product both of selective recruitment of men of different political sentiments to different subjects, and of the more subtle continuing intellectual force of the subject itself. Whatever the process which links them (and we shall return to that question), we look, first, at the dispositions of the men in each subject, then at how recruitment to subjects varies by social origins, and, finally, at whether the choice of subject overrides social origins in its effect on political views.

The following tables show party support and position on the political spectrum by subject taught. In Table 15.36 the differences between subjects are, in fact, quite sharp. Social scientists are well to the Left of all the others: 70 per cent of them describe themselves as Far Left or Moderate Left. At the other extreme are the technologists and teachers of medicine, of whom 44 or 45 per cent are on the Left, and roughly a quarter consider themselves Right-wing. Similarly, in Table 15.37, two-thirds of the social scientists are Labour party supporters, compared with about half the arts teachers,

---

example, those who gain better degrees may be somehow more open-minded to change in their views, and those who stay on to study for higher degrees may be more affected by longer exposure to student life. But the differences by class of degree are not large, though there is some evidence that those who did better as undergraduates tend towards the Left. When we looked at higher degrees, similarly, there was no appreciable difference between those who took a Ph.D. as compared with Master's or Bachelor's level degrees. (See Appendix D, Tables 15.51–54.)

[1] The social sciences have also strong *conservative* roots–though stronger on the Continent than in England. See H. Stuart Hughes, *Consciousness and Society: The Reorientation of European Social Thought, 1890–1930*, Knopf, 1958; and Leon Bramson, *The Political Context of Sociology*, Princeton University Press, 1961. Lipset, in *Political Man* (*op. cit.*), pp. 336–8, gives evidence for the Leftism of American social scientists.

TABLES 15.36 AND 15.37

Political position and party support by subject taught (per cent)

15.36 *Political position*	*Arts*	*Social science*	*Subject* *Natural science*	*Technology*	*Medicine*
Far Left	5 } 58	8 } 70	4 } 49	2 } 45	3 } 44
Moderate Left	53	62	45	43	41
Centre	25	21	31	30	33
Right	17	8	20	26	23
TOTALS	(350)	(218)	(397)	(172)	(136)

15.37 *Party*					
Conservative	29	18	36	42	55
Labour	47	66	36	32	26
Liberal	15	8	17	18	8
Other/None	9	7	12	8	11
TOTALS	(329)	(205)	(308)	(170)	(133)

TABLE 15.38

Subject taught by father's occupation (per cent)

Subject	*Father's occupation* *Professional*	*Intermediate*	*Skilled*	*Semi-skilled*	*Unskilled*
Arts	30	26	28	26	21
Social science	20	16	16	20	14
Natural science	26	30	35	36	50
Technology	9	13	16	13	14
Medicine	16	14	5	6	0
TOTALS	(254)	(519)	(419)	(70)	(14)

one-third of the natural and applied scientists, and one-quarter of the teachers of medicine. In Table 15.38 we show the pattern of social recruitment to the various faculties. Social origin affects the choice of subject, though except for medicine the differences are not very large. The children of professional men who enter academic life are most likely to choose arts subjects: those from all the other categories choose natural science more often than any other area, but the preponderance of natural science increases the lower the occupational group, while choices of arts and medicine decrease. The smaller proportion in the arts may be seen even more clearly in Table 15.39

TABLE 15.39

Father's occupation by subject taught (per cent)

			Subject		
Father's occupation	*Arts*	*Social sciences*	*Natural sciences*	*Tech-nology*	*Medicine*
Professional	22	23	16	13	29
Intermediate	39	39	39	41	52
Skilled	33	31	37	40	16
Semi-skilled	5	6	6	5	3
Unskilled	1	1	2	1	0
TOTALS	(350)	(217)	(400)	(171)	(138)

which shows the distribution of social origins within the several major fields of study. These differences may be partly due to different cultural values between social classes; but it should also be remembered that the traditional strength of the public schools lies in the arts subjects, and the type of school attended probably has a powerful effect on the choice of subject. In any event, we have seen that social origins are related to subject choice, so that it becomes necessary to introduce social origins into Tables 15.36 and 15.37. This is done in Tables 15.40 and 15.41.

Controlling for the effects of social origin we find that the difference in political preferences between the subjects is as great as before. Among teachers of middle class origins, in Table 15.40, 68 per cent of social scientists describe themselves as on the Left, 53 per cent of arts teachers, 44 per cent in natural science and technology, and 42 per cent in medicine. Among men from working class backgrounds, the range is from 75 per cent (social science) to 48 per cent (technology). It appears (Table 15.41) that support for Labour ranges from 75 per cent among social scientists from manual worker families to 24 per cent (medicine, non-manual). The order is much the same as in Table 15.40. We have already suggested that one possible explanation for these differences is the different view of the nature of the world required by the subject-matter and methods of study. In the case of social scientists it is certainly true that there is a powerful pull towards the Left. In addition, we may be seeing here another factor–the influence of differing reference groups. The teacher of

TABLES 15.40 AND 15.41

Party support and political position by subject and father's occupation (per cent)

	Non-manual					*Manual*				
	Subject					*Subject*				
15.40 *Political position*	*Arts*	*Social science*	*Natural science*	*Tech-nology*	*Medi-cine*	*Arts*	*Social science*	*Natural science*	*Tech-nology*	*Medi-cine*
Far Left	6 } 53	6 } 68	5 } 44	0 } 44	3 } 42	4 } 66	11 } 75	3 } 55	4 } 48	4 } 58
Left	47 }	62 }	39 }	44 }	39 }	62 }	64 }	52 }	44 }	54 }
Centre	28	23	33	27	34	19	17	30	33	29
Right	19	9	24	29	24	14	8	15	19	12
TOTALS	(205)	(129)	(215)	(89)	(108)	(135)	(83)	(174)	(79)	(24)
15.41 *Party*										
Conservative	31	22	42	47	57	23	12	26	32	43
Labour	42	60	27	25	24	56	75	47	43	35
Liberal	16	8	17	21	8	14	9	17	14	9
Other/None	11	10	15	7	10	7	4	9	10	13
TOTALS	(197)	(119)	(206)	(89)	(107)	(124)	(81)	(167)	(77)	(23)

medicine and the teacher of technology are alike in that they can see themselves as belonging not only to an academic community but also to a profession whose members outside the university are predominantly conservative. To some extent this is true of natural scientists also, though perhaps the 'purer' the science and the more 'basic' the research the more natural scientists will take academic men as their model rather than, say, researchers employed by industry. For the most part, those in the arts and social science faculties, on the other hand, have no larger profession to which they are even loosely attached. Those whom they teach, if they wish to continue practising the subject in which they took their degrees, are compelled to remain in the universities (or perhaps schoolteaching). For this reason men in these two faculties are able to be more genuinely 'free-floating' in Mannheim's sense, while scientists, natural and applied, and teachers of medicine are in constant communication with members of the corresponding professions, and tend accordingly to take on the corresponding political colour.

For the moment this must all remain largely speculative. We have seen that differences in the political sentiments of men in different subjects are not explained by differences in social recruitment to those subjects. But the possibility remains that these differences among subjects reflect other patterns of selective recruitment to the several disciplines, rather than the influences on political sentiments of the differing views of the world that arise out of differing subjects and methods of study.

University group

We have discussed the possibility of universities developing different political characters just as they vary in other respects, as for example in research and teaching. We did not touch on the question of the political climate specifically among teachers, but simply conjectured that some atmosphere might exist in universities which would affect the political preferences of students, whether it arose basically among the students themselves or was shaped by their teachers. We found that, except for those university teachers who had taken their first degree in Scotland, there was nothing to suggest that such variations did exist; or if they did, they did not seem to affect the students. It is now appropriate, however, to look directly at the distribution of positions on the political spectrum in each university group (Table 15.42). Once again, Scotland stands out as an exception: one-quarter of the teachers in Scottish universities describe themselves as on the Right of the spectrum, and 45 per cent on the Left. Among the rest, however, the variation is very small; the proportions on the Left range from 51 to 57 per cent: Oxford has 23 per cent on the Right, but the others vary from 16 to 19 per cent. As far as abstracted political views are concerned, only Scotland is significantly dissimilar from the rest.

TABLE 15.42

Political position by present university group (per cent)

	Group					
Political position	*Oxford and Cambridge*	*London*	*Major Redbrick*	*Minor Redbrick*	*Wales*	*Scotland*
Far Left	6 } 52	5 } 51	4 } 56	6 } 57	6 } 56	3 } 45
Moderate Left	46	46	52	51	50	42
Centre	25	30	28	25	28	30
Right	23	19	16	18	16	25
TOTALS	(155)	(235)	(454)	(141)	(116)	(244)

TABLE 15.43

Party support by present university group (per cent)

	Group					
Party	*Oxford and Cambridge*	*London*	*Major Redbrick*	*Minor Redbrick*	*Wales*	*Scotland*
Conservative	38	40	32	29	28	43
Labour	40	41	41	53	46	31
Liberal	15	12	15	12	16	14
Other/None	7	6	12	6	10	12
TOTALS	(143)	(225)	(444)	(132)	(111)	(233)

Table 15.43 shows the distribution of party support. Here the variation is rather greater. Oxford, Cambridge and London fall in the middle, with fairly equal support of about two-fifths for each of the main parties. The major Redbrick universities also show two-fifths for Labour, but only one-third support the Conservatives, and there is a somewhat larger proportion favouring another party or uncommitted. The smaller Redbricks and Wales favour Labour quite substantially; around half of the teachers in these groups are

Labour supporters, and under 30 per cent Conservatives. Scotland, on the other hand, shows a 12 per cent plurality in favour of the Conservative party over Labour, compared with 24 per cent for Labour over Conservatives in the smaller Redbricks. It seems fair to say that among the teachers themselves there are significant variations of political climate between the groups of universities.

This makes our earlier discovery that the first-degree university has very little effect all the more surprising. Not only are the student bodies different, at least in their social composition, but the teachers too (now, at any rate) differ in their political views as well. Moreover, except (once again) for Scotland, the two factors run parallel: the universities with a more Labour teaching staff are more favoured by lower class students, whereas London, Oxford and Cambridge, where party support is more evenly balanced, are attended by all classes equally (London) or more by the higher classes (Oxford and Cambridge). (Table 15.32.) At this point, therefore, it seems worth re-examining both these findings. In Table 15.44 we look at party

TABLE 15.44

Party support: % of labour supporters by place of first degree and present place

	Place of first degree				
Present place	*Oxford and Cambridge*	*London*	*Major Redbrick*	*Minor Redbrick and Wales*	*Scotland*
Oxford and Cambridge	42 (106)	* (9)	* (8)	* (2)	* (5)
London	44 (57)	44 (81)	50 (24)	* (7)	* (13)
Major Redbrick	38 (107)	46 (67)	42 (161)	36 (25)	33 (36)
Minor Redbrick	54 (37)	58 (31)	52 (31)	56 (16)	* (6)
Wales	44 (23)	50 (20)	* (14)	49 (41)	* (7)
Scotland	43 (44)	39 (26)	39 (18)	* (5)	24 (111)

* Cells containing too few cases to percentage usefully.

support taking both the respondent's present university and his undergraduate institution into account simultaneously. If it turns out that teachers now at particular institutions have a characteristic political posture regardless of where they took their undergraduate degrees, we must conclude that some process of self-selection to particular university groups is at work, even though this in its turn does not seem to affect the students educated at these places. In Table 15.44 we show, for the sake of clarity, only the percentage of the staff who support the Labour party.

The lowest percentage of Labour supporters, as we might expect, is provided by men both educated and now teaching in the Scottish universities. Here the percentage is just under one-quarter. The next lowest proportion comes also from those educated in Scotland but teaching elsewhere. At the other extreme, the highest proportions are found among those now teaching in the smaller Redbrick universities, wherever they did their first degree. Apart from this, however, whether we compare by row of the table (to test the effect of undergraduate education within present groups) or by column (to see if, after education in the same type of university, men of different views choose different places to teach) there are no clear patterns to be discerned. In other words, a Scottish education produces fewer Labour supporters; the smaller Redbrick universities have more Labour supporters on their staff: otherwise there are no broad statements to be made about the political climates of the various groups.

University rank

In our search for concentrations of 'Left' and 'Right' political views within the universities, we may also look to variations by academic rank. There are several reasons for suspecting that the higher ranks may on average be more conservative. For one thing, men in higher ranks tend to be older. In any political system the old will tend to be more conservative than their juniors, partly no doubt as a result of increasing wisdom and experience, which lead them to hesitate to exchange the known for the unknown: but also because in any society that is changing, one generation's innovations will be the next generation's *status quo ante*.[1]

But there is another quality of age which bears on political views: it tends to bring more authority and responsibility, and with them a larger commitment to the existing state of affairs. Increased rank in particular brings precisely this. We have already seen, in Chapter 14, that professors were far more likely than those at lower grades to approve of the existing degree of accessibility and the existing functions of professorship. But the effect probably spreads to wider issues. Men who have gained recognition and status are likely to approve of institutions and arrangements that have recognised and

[1] The variation in political dispositions with age is shown in Table 15.9 above.

rewarded their merits. Successful men make bad revolutionaries; we may also suspect that fewer of them are likely to be ardent reformers.

The distributions of different ranks on party preference and the political spectrum are shown in Tables 15.45 and 15.46. What is

TABLE 15.45

Party support by academic rank (per cent)

	Rank				
Party	*Professor*	*Reader*	*Senior lecturer*	*Lecturer*	*Others*
Conservative	38	44	46	31	32
Labour	36	36	34	45	45
Liberal	15	12	12	16	9
Other	2	1	1	1	2
None	9	8	6	8	13
TOTALS	(178)	(121)	(204)	(687)	(110)

TABLE 15.46

Political position by academic rank (per cent)

	Rank				
Political position	*Professor*	*Reader*	*Senior lecturer*	*Lecturer*	*Others*
Far Left	1 } 45	6 } 49	4 } 46	5 } 57	8 } 57
Moderate Left	44	43	42	52	49
Centre	35	30	30	25	25
Right	21	20	24	18	17
TOTALS	(190)	(128)	(211)	(718)	(110)

surprising is not the greater conservatism of professors as compared with the lower ranks, but that the differences are as small as they are.[1] Although the power, pay and prestige of professors is very much higher than that of lecturers, for example, we do not find those large differences reflected in similarly large differences in party preferences

[1] The differences in party preference by rank are somewhat sharper, with support for the two main parties ranging from a 12 per cent plurality for the Conservatives among the senior lecturers to 14 per cent for Labour among the regular lecturers. In terms of support for Labour there is a fairly abrupt divide between the three senior grades, in all of which a little over one-third support Labour, and the lecturers and junior posts, in which nearly one-half (45 per cent) are Labour supporters. In this table, however, readers as well as senior lecturers are to the right of the professors, who are almost evenly balanced between the two main parties.

or political dispositions. Differences are of the order of 10 per cent, much smaller differences than we have seen associated with class and religious origins, or academic subject.[1]

Rank carries with it the presumption of greater age, as well as authority and prestige; and age, in turn, may affect political views in different ways than the responsibility and power of rank. Let us look briefly at the relation of rank to political preference, while controlling for variations in age among the several ranks (Table 15.47). Controlling for age reduces further the political differences by rank. Among men under forty the young professors are disproportionately Left and the senior lecturers notably Conservative; among men over forty, differences among the ranks are not very large.

Age, authority and rank clearly do have a bearing on *some* kinds of politics–specifically, as we have seen, on university politics. But positions on the national political spectrum are affected by too many other, stronger forces–for example, class origins and religion–for the bearing of academic rank to have much independent effect. Moreover, as we mentioned earlier, the major parties in Britain are both hospitable to a wide spectrum of sentiment; Labour has very strong conservative tendencies, while the Conservative leadership, especially on education and university questions, is arguably as 'progressive' as the Labour party. There may well be sharper differences between senior and junior ranks on specific social and political issues than emerges from our very general questions regarding political position and party support.

Correlates of political preference

In this chapter and in parts of earlier chapters we have explored the relationship of political loyalties and sentiments of university teachers to other attitudes and behaviour. We now summarise these findings, so as to see more clearly which aspects of the academic's life and thought are related strongly and which weakly or not at all to broader political values and attachments. We present these comparisons in clusters around a central theme or topic, in roughly weakening relationship to political sentiments (Table 15.48).

We have chosen to concentrate on relationship to the political

[1] It would be interesting to know whether this degree of similarity in the distribution of political loyalties and sentiments exist at different levels of (white-collar) rank in other institutions–say, between junior and senior executives in industry, or junior and senior civil servants or army officers.

TABLE 15.47

Party preference by rank and age (per cent)

	35–9				40–4				45+			
Party	*Professor*	*Reader*	*Senior lecturer*	*Lecturer*	*Professor*	*Reader*	*Senior lecturer*	*Lecturer*	*Professor*	*Reader*	*Senior lecturer*	*Lecturer*
Conservative	21	35	53	32	44	54	43	36	40	44	43	36
Labour	54	39	35	42	31	39	29	39	34	33	36	44
Liberal	12	10	6	16	16	7	12	20	15	13	15	15
Other/None	12	16	6	10	9	0	17	5	11	10	4	5
TOTALS	(24)	(31)	(51)	(166)	(32)	(28)	(42)	(76)	(122)	(61)	(91)	(85)

TABLE 15.48

Percentage differences between 'far left' and 'right' (Labour and Conservative) on selected attitudes

	Δ (*position*)*	averages‡	∧ (*party*)†
A. The Secondary Schools: Attitudes and Behaviour			
1 Q.49(x) 'The tripartite system of grammar, modern and technical schools should be supplanted by a system of comprehensive schools' – % agree, strongly or with reservations	66	40·0	(46)
2 and 3 Q.63 (If R has children of secondary school age or older) 'What kinds of school do they or did they attend?' – % attending private school:			
2 Sons	– 50		(– 34)
3 Daughters	– 30		(– 22)

* = % among Far Left (N = approx. 65) minus % among Right (N = approx. 260).
† = % among Labour supporters (N = approx. 535) minus % among Conservative supporters (N = approx. 460).
‡ Sign ignored.

TABLE 15.48 (*continued*)

		Δ (*position*)	averages	Λ (*party*)
B.	Attitudes towards the Expansion of the University System and the Non-University Sector of Higher Education			
1	Q.5 'Which of the following opinions concerning the number of students in the university system comes closest to your own opinion?' – % answering 'We should double the numbers or more in the next decade'	48	41·7	(20)
2	Q.10 'Which of these proportions of the relevant age group would you like to see entering universities and other full-time institutions in Britain?' – % answering '30% or more'	43		(11)
3	Q.11 'If the number of students doubled in the next decade with the same staff/student ratio, what would you expect to be the effect on the quality of graduates in your subject from your university?' – % answering 'marked' or 'some' deterioration	–42		(–15)
4	Q.8 'Do you think that the number of new places in the university system in your subject should be expanded in the next decade?' – % answering 'Yes, over 75%'	39		(14)
5	Q.49(xii) 'The essential quality of British university life should be preserved by expanding the non-university forms of higher education rather than the universities' – % agree, strongly or with reservations	–43		(–19)
6	Q.47 'Do you think that CATs ought to be given university status?' – % answering 'Yes'	35		(22)
7	Q.6 'Do you feel that the expansion that has already taken place over the past decade has affected the quality of students admitted to your university in your subject?' – % answering 'The quality of my students has risen in recent years'	24	24·7	(12)
8	Q.12 'Do you think your present university as it is now organised is . . .' – % answering 'Too small'	28		(14)
9	Q.13 'Do you think your present department is . . .' – % answering 'Too small'	22		(8)
C.	Attitudes regarding the Distribution of Power and Status in University Departments			
1	Q.49(ix) 'Most British university departments would be better run by the method of circulating chairmanship than by a permanent Head of Department' – % agree, strongly or with reservations	36	33·7	(20)
2	Q.49(viii) 'A serious disadvantage of Redbrick universities is that all too often they are run by a professorial oligarchy' – % agree strongly	26		(10)
3	Index of attitudes to distribution of power (from 1 and 2 above) – % 'democrats'	39		(18)

		Item	Value	Group	
	4	Q.49(v) ‘A university department with more than eight members of staff should have more than one member of professorial rank’ – % agree strongly	21	16·3	(6)
	5	Q.49(iv) ‘A professorship ought to be part of the normal expectation of an academic career and not a special attainment of a minority of university teachers’ – % agree, strongly or with reservations	7		(4)
	6	Index of attitudes to distribution of status (from 4 and 5 above) – % ‘élitists’	– 21		(– 9)
D.		Satisfaction with Own University, and Institutional Mobility, Past and Future			
	1	Q.28 ‘Do you anticipate that you will be applying for a post at another university in the next three years?’ – % answering ‘Almost certainly will not’	– 31	16·5	(– 11)
	2	Q.24 ‘Do you expect to remain at your present university until you retire?’ – % answering ‘Probably not’ or ‘Definitely not’	23		(8)
	3	Q.25 ‘In general, how do you feel about your present university?’ – % answering ‘It is a very good place for me’	– 20		(– 14)
	4	Q.27 ‘Have you applied for a post (including your present post) within the last year?’ – % answering ‘Yes’	15		(4)
	5	(Derived from Robbins U.T. survey.) Number of different universities in which R. has taken degrees or held posts – % one only	– 14		(– 8)
	6	(Derived from Robbins U.T. survey.) Number of different universities in which R. has held posts – % one only	– 13		(– 3)
	7	Q.26 ‘Is there another British university in which you would prefer to hold a post roughly equivalent to the one you hold here?’ – % answering ‘Yes’	11		(6)
	8	Q.32(i) ‘Since taking a university post in the United Kingdom, have you ever seriously considered accepting a permanent post in a university abroad?’ – % answering ‘Yes’	11		(4)
	9	Q.31 ‘Do you like the city or town in which your university is located?’ – % answering ‘Yes’	– 11		(– 4)

Table 15.48 (*continued*)

		Δ (*position*)	averages	∧ (*party*)
E.	Views regarding the Character, Content and Curriculum of British Education			
1	Q.49(iii) 'Valid criticism of the English universities is that they over-emphasise the single-subject honours degree' – % agree, strongly or with reservations	18	16·5	(7)
2	Q.49(xi) 'A serious shortcoming of the present system of secondary education is premature specialisation' – % agree strongly	15		(7)
3	Q.49(ii) 'University education in Britain puts too little emphasis on the training of experts and too much on the education of widely cultivated men' – % agree, strongly or with reservations	3		(– 1)
(4–9)	Q.50 'The general balance of university studies in Britain is such that the following faculties are given insufficient support' – % marking:			
4	Pure science	3	3·2	(– 4)
5	Arts	– 2		(4)
6	Law	3		(– 5)
7	Medicine	–5		(– 7)
8	Technology	3		(–3)
9	Social sciences	35		(26)

F. Attitudes towards Academic Life, and to Research and Administration			
1 Q.49(vii) 'Promotion in academic life is too dependent on published work and too little on devotion to teaching' – % agree, strongly or with reservations	– 13		(0)
(2–5) Q.18 'What are the major handicaps that you experience in carrying on research?' – % marking:			
2 'Insufficient time because of teaching commitments'	14		(5)
3 'Insufficient time because of commitments other than teaching'	– 14		(0)
4 'Insufficiencies in library'	13		(8)
5 'Unresponsiveness of your departmental or college administration to your research needs'	7	11·4	(2)
6 Q.49(xiii) 'In order to do full justice to his position, an academic man has to subordinate all aspects of his life to his work' – % agree, strongly or with reservations	– 11		(– 12)
(7–8) Q.45 'How much do you enjoy each of the following of your present activities?'			
7 'Research' – % answering 'Very much'	8		(2)
8 'Administration and policy-making in the University (College) and Department' – % answering 'Very little'	17		(4)
9 Q.17 'Do your own interests lie primarily in teaching or research?' – % answering 'Very heavily in research'	6		(1)
G. Religious and Familial Patterns			
1 Q.58 'Do you consider yourself deeply religious, moderately religious, largely indifferent to religion, or basically opposed to religion?' – % answering 'largely indifferent' or 'basically opposed'	49		(23)
2 Q.57 'What is your present religious denomination?' – % answering 'Church of England'	– 40		(– 23)
3 Q.61 'Is your wife a university graduate?' – % answering 'Yes'	30		(9)
(4–5) Q.63 (If R. has children who are or have attended an institution of higher education) – % attending university			
4 Sons	13		(17)
5 Daughters	13		(4)

spectrum, not so much because we believe this general measure to be in any sense prior to party support (although being more generalised and less bound to the contemporary characteristics of British political parties it is less susceptible to idiosyncratic interpretations), but for a more practical reason: namely, that the two extremes on the political spectrum between which we shall be giving differences are further apart than are the two main political parties; thus the differences in attitudes stand out more clearly. It should be borne in mind that the large majority of our sample falls somewhere between the extremes of 'Far Left' and 'Right'. (For comparison, differences by major party support are also given.)[1]

On the left of the table we show the particular response or combination of responses to a question; in the column marked $\triangle$ (position) we show the difference between the percentage of those on the Far Left and that of those of the Right who gave this response. Where the percentage on the Far Left is higher the figure given is positive, where that on the Right is higher the sign is negative. The next row of figures gives the average percentage difference between Far Left and Right for the bracketed questions. The third column, labelled $\wedge$ (party), shows the percentage difference on these questions between Labour and Conservative party supporters.

A. The secondary schools: attitudes and behaviour

The attitude elicited by our questionnaire which was most strongly related to general political disposition concerned the replacement of the tripartite system of secondary education by comprehensive schools (Item A.1). This issue, a major plank in Labour educational policy, and opposed by most (though not all) Conservative party leaders, placed the weight of a clearly articulated party issue behind the more general differences of sentiment regarding equality and privilege that separate the Left from the Right in Britain. The result is a difference of 66 per cent between the Far Left and Right in our sample, and of 46 per cent between Labour and Conservative supporters. These sentiments are not merely reflections of party differences, but also affect how men educate their own children: those

[1] On the spectrum, 5 per cent of the sample fall in the Far Left category, and 19 per cent in the Right (Table 15.3). Thus three-quarters of the sample are between these extremes. Party support, however, covers 76 per cent (35 per cent Conservative, 41 per cent Labour) (Table 15.1): thus only one-quarter is not included.

on the Right are not only opposed to comprehensive schooling, but are much less prepared to commit their children to the state system of secondary education, regardless of how it is organised (Item A.2). The difference in the education of their sons is very large (50 per cent); of their daughters, smaller though still considerable (30 per cent). These differences are not special to academic men, but are part of the basic and continuing cleavage in British social and political life over the organisation of secondary education, as between a system of élite schools, whether public or private, which reflects and helps sustain social and economic inequalities, and comprehensive state schools designed in part to reduce the relative importance of class origins for adult life and careers. Academic men mirror this broad social cleavage in their own attitudes and behaviour, but they live with the effects of Britain's secondary educational system more closely than do most of their countrymen.[1]

B. Attitudes towards the expansion of the university system and the non-university sector of higher education

Here we need only summarise findings discussed at length in Chapter 11. Listing the items in descending order of difference by political sentiment (or party preference) we see first that there are very large differences on questions about expansion of the university system as a whole. On questions B.1–6 we find differences of between 48–35 per cent (average $\triangle$: 41·7 per cent) between the Left, strongly supporting expansion, and the Right, broadly opposing it. Items B.5 and 6, dealing with aspects of the non-university sector of higher education, are consistent with the greater readiness of conservatives to want to preserve the élite character of the university system both by excluding technical institutions, and by insulating the universities against expansion by using the non-university sector to absorb whatever expansion is necessary.

Where academic men are asked to make judgements of past events or present realities bearing on expansion, as in items B.7–9, the Left is less apprehensive of future growth, as we noted in Chapter 11, and less inclined to see their own present universities and departments as

[1] It would be useful to see whether direct experience makes their attitudes towards comprehensive schooling, or their education of their own children, any different on average from those of other professional groups, such as lawyers or civil servants, whose work is not so directly linked to the political issues of secondary education.

'too small'. But these differences, constrained by objective realities, are smaller (average $\triangle$: 24·7 per cent) than are the differences between Left and Right in their basic attitudes and anticipations of the future effects of expansion (Items B.1–6).

C. Attitudes regarding the distribution of power and status in university departments

Category C deals with a subject we discussed in detail in Chapter 14, the feelings of academic men towards the distribution of power and status within their own departments. As we saw there, political sentiments are quite strongly related to attitudes regarding the power of chairmen, rather less so to views about the status of the professorship. On the issue of professorial power, differences on items C.1–3 average 33·7 per cent between the Far Left and the Right; on the matter of professorial status, items C.4–6, differences average 16·3 per cent.

D. Satisfaction with own university, and institutional mobility, past and future

In Category D we group a number of items concerning the academic's satisfaction with his present post and the facts, preferences and anticipations surrounding individual mobility between universities. There is no obvious relation of these matters to broader political sentiments; yet we find moderate but consistent differences between men on the Left and Right: the average differences on the nine items in Category D is 16·5 per cent. Men on the Left are in general less satisfied with their present positions, and more mobile, both in fact and intention. But before we suggest that political conservatives are also more likely to be conservatives in their own careers, we would want to see whether there are marked differences in mobility between subjects and ranks, which as we know are also correlated with differences in political sentiments.

E. Views regarding the character, content and curriculum of British education

While there are very marked differences between the Left and Right regarding the *organisation* of both secondary and higher education–the Left wanting expansion and comprehensive schools, the Right defending the small élite systems–the differences between Left and Right regarding the character and curriculum of British education are much smaller. On items E.1 and 2, those on the Far Left are somewhat more likely to be critical of specialisation, both in secondary and higher education (average difference on the two items: 16·5 per cent). But there is almost no difference on what might be thought of as a conservative educational value–the education of 'widely cultivated men' as opposed to 'the training of experts' (item E.3). And when we look at views regarding the desirable level of support for various university subjects, we find, with one exception, almost no differences between Left and Right. The exception is in their views of the social sciences, which the Left is much more likely to see as inadequately supported. We have seen that social scientists are distinctly more Left, on average, than men in other subject areas; but support for the claims of the social scientists is not confined to the Left academics who happen to be social scientists. In a sense, the social sciences have a political image and a constituency among the Left both within and outside the academic world in a way that is true of no other subject. But with that exception, the pattern is of remarkably small differences by political sentiments regarding the general character and content (if not the organisation) of British education.

The relatively small differences here are as significant for British higher education as are the large differences on issues of university expansion and organisation: the latter, in the British academic tradition, are legitimately political issues; the former are not. This fact may help to account for the relatively small differences; but that they are relatively small helps to insulate these academic issues from the external forces of national politics, and thus indirectly to preserve the academic freedom and autonomy of British education. We can imagine the result if the character and curriculum of the universities was itself an issue between Left and Right; the direct introduction of national political sentiments and loyalties into academic decision-making would severely strain the freedom of universities to make these decisions on intellectual and academic rather than political grounds.[1] Nevertheless, the broad consequence of this insulation of the curriculum from national politics is to strengthen the conservative

[1] This is increasingly the case in some American colleges and universities. See Martin Trow, 'Reflections on the Transition from Mass to Universal Higher Education', *Daedalus*, Winter 1970, pp. 1–42.

tendencies of British education, since the consensus tends to develop around the traditional liberal and 'gentlemanly' conceptions of higher education–what we have called the distinctive English idea of a university.

F. Attitudes towards academic life, and to research and administration

We have explored the distribution and sources of attitudes towards research and teaching in great detail in Chapters 12 and 13. These personal sentiments towards the primary activities of the profession are not strongly correlated with political dispositions. Differences between Far Left and Right on various aspects of research, teaching, administration, and the bases for promotion are clustered in Category F; the average differences on these nine items are only 11·4 per cent. Men on the Left are a little more oriented towards research, a little less inclined to subordinate all other aspects of life to their work. But politics are certainly not a major source of differences on these basic academic issues.

G. Religious and familial patterns

In category G we see marked differences between men of the Far Left and Right in their religious identifications, which we would expect, and in the higher education of their wives and children, which we would not. Men of the Far Left are much more likely to marry university graduates, and somewhat more likely to have children attending university. We tend to underestimate the influence of personal experience, and that of members of one's family, on the attitudes of academic men towards academic questions; it is not quite seemly for such personal experience to be invoked in academic argument. But while men of the Right are more likely to come from homes in which a parent was a university product, men of the Left have more university experience in their own families. It would be interesting to explore the implications of this fact for their attitudes towards, say, university expansion.

Politics and the academic man

We have now produced a fairly thorough description of the political views of university teachers, starting by exploring their origins, in so far as they can be discovered, moving on to locate them in the system, and finally showing how they are reflected in the opinions and styles of life of our subjects. We have tried, because that is our own interest, to show that academic men do not hold their views as a result of some process of pure reasoning, but that their views are quite substantially the product of their environment and experience. Some of their attitudes to academic life can be understood in the light of their position within the university system; others correspond in consistent ways with their political views, which we believe to have been largely formed before entering the academic profession. But to say that university teachers take positions on academic and political issues in largely predictable ways is not to condemn them. There is a strain towards consistency in the views men hold, the stronger the more reflective and intellectually responsible they are. Moreover, deciding questions 'on their merits' is a laudable aim; but it is impossible without an idea of what constitutes merits, and these ideas rest on values acquired in large part prior to and outside the university. Some of these values unite British academic men: a scrupulous honesty in intellectual life, a dedication to the highest academic standards, a strong sense of responsibility to their students. Others divide them, and among these are conceptions of the size and functions of British higher education in the future, and the closely related question of the character of British education more generally. Our problem and method leads us to focus on the latter, but our consideration of British academic men and their institutions will be woefully distorted if we do not pay sufficient attention to the powerful cohesive and integrative forces in the society, the university, and the academic profession. But it is in the nature of integrative forces to be conservative in their consequences, while change entails and is achieved through conflict. The forces working for growth and change in British higher education are very strong, though stronger outside–in the politics of democratisation and the economics of modernisation–than inside the universities themselves. The question to which we must turn is how the British universities, and their staffs, will respond to these forces: to what extent they will resist, to what extent contain and divert, to what extent accept and be changed by the forces coming to bear on them. To some unknown degree the distinctive virtues of British universities–their freedom based on autonomy, their high standards, their capacity to preserve, add to and transmit the values of the society's high culture–are based on their profound conservatism in defence of their small size and élite functions. Finally, therefore, we must ask, even if we cannot answer, the question of how expansion and change will affect the existing strengths and virtues of the élite British university system; and whether there are not strengths and virtues it may gain as well as lose in the course of change. Our answers to these questions will involve our own social and political values, as they do those of the university teachers whose values and attitudes we have been studying.

Chapter 16

CONCLUSION: A TYPOLOGY OF ORIENTATIONS

Our primary object in this book has been to describe the university teaching professions in Britain. We chose to do so at a crucial moment in the history of the universities. The Robbins Committee had made its recommendations for systematic expansion of higher education, had for the first time put forward an explicit plan of development up to 1980 and had seen its essential proposals accepted by both of the major political parties. University expansion was nothing new: it had been going on throughout the twentieth century but was now redefined and widely accepted not only as socially necessary but also as part of a growing investment in education and science with a major claim on parliamentary attention and government resources.

Expansion was also familiar in the sense that hitherto it had been contained within a traditional form of organisation and a set of educational assumptions which we have described as the distinctive English idea of a university and which, in a word, can be labelled élitist. The essential basis of élitism is best defined here in terms of the typology of educational systems outlined by Max Weber.[1] Weber's principal reference was to the aims and functions of whole systems of education and not to the differentiation of function between particular organisations within them. His attention, moreover, was for our purposes relevantly confined to those forms of education which are aimed at producing members of the élite or ruling strata of societies. Most educational systems have been so restricted and from this point of view Weber distinguished three broad types of social personality; the charismatic, that of the cultivated man and the expert. These three types of personality are called for by three corresponding types of power and authority in society. The first is that of the charismatic leader whose personal gift or mission is magically or divinely inspired. The second characterises a wide range

[1] H. Gerth and C. Wright Mills, *op. cit.*, pp. 416 ff.

of élites, whose authority is sanctioned by custom and tradition, of which the gentlemanly strata of eighteenth and early nineteenth century Britain and Europe provide examples. The third corresponds to the rational and bureaucratic forms of authority typical of advanced industrial societies. These are ideal types but the transition from the second to the third defines the modern history of higher education in Europe though it has little to say about recent developments towards mass education.

In Britain this transition from traditional to rational-legal forms of authority has manifested itself in the university in a continuing struggle to replace an education appropriate to the requirements of amateur, gentlemanly administrators in an imperial power by curricula designed to satisfy the growing demand for professional competence based on the natural or social sciences. Selection for university education in a society which is transitional between the two types is typically ascriptive by class and social connection but never entirely so, for it also allows assimilation of at least a minority from the lower strata chosen for their intellectual potential. Merit so defined became increasingly important from the beginning of high Victorian expansion of the universities.

What we have seen as most distinctive of the British and especially the English universities was the strong organisational expression of careful and intensive education for scholarship and social leadership in residential institutions with high staff/student ratios, intimate teaching methods intermingled with domesticity, a total immersion in the academic milieu (albeit for a relatively short time by international standards) and an assured scholarship income for those selected intellectually rather than socially. It was, as Ralph Turner has argued, a sponsorship rather than a contest system of social ascent. It was, in other words, a minimal adaptation of ascriptive selection and therefore took place characteristically early in the school career. The later the selection, the more attenuated are ascriptive advantages. However, it must be added that sponsorship does not preclude sharp competition for academic and professional honours within the circle of selected students. The first class degree was, and remains, the passport to a highly restricted and respected stratum of the professional classes.

This element in Victorian academic life in Britain was related, of course, to the tradition of research and scholarship carried on by professors and dons. The teaching and research traditions lived together in the nineteenth century with increasing ease as the merit element in selection was strengthened and while research was mainly directed to increasing basic knowledge rather than to its potential social applications. Indeed these two developing features of the British universities go far to explain what Ben-David saw as 'rather baffling to observers accustomed to use the German "idea of the university" as a yardstick of measuring academic accomplishment. . . . They admired English universities for the quality of their graduates; criticised them for their mediocre performance in many fields and their seeming indifference towards the active promotion of research; and were mystified by the nevertheless brilliant work of some English scientists.'[1]

Expansion in the twentieth century up to and including that which followed the Robbins Report in the 1960's had been assimilated to these traditions with their high academic standards, lavish staffing and amenitics and generally élitist assumptions. But the question has to be raised whether continued growth of numbers and functions will not first strain and then transform both the normative and the organisational forms of British higher education. We are especially interested in how the values and attitudes of British university teachers will influence the rate at which these changes will occur and the forms they will take.

The government is the final arbiter of numbers and money but the university teachers themselves are the managers of expansion. Their assumptions and preoccupations are therefore crucial. According to our survey data in Chapter 11 about two-thirds of British academics support the modest growth of the university system recommended by Robbins: the opposition of the other third to any significant expansion of the system is more remarkable than the majority view, given the cautious assumptions on which the Robbins projections were based. Robbins wanted 17 per cent of the relevant age group to receive higher education by 1980. Half of the academics supported this or more but very few, about one in eight, envisaged the kind of mass system, with a third or more of the age group in some form of higher education which already exists in the U.S. or the U.S.S.R. The dominant view is one supporting a modest expansion of the present highly selective system but opposing the transformation of that system in the direction of mass higher education.

British academic men differ among themselves in their attitude

[1] See above, Chapter 1, p. 37.

towards the changes in the universities that are already under way or are likely to accompany further growth. At first glance it may seem that university teachers differ along a single dimension which we might call 'traditional-expansionist' with men at opposite ends of the continuum holding different conceptions of the academic role, of university government, and above all of the primary function of the university in society.

We have argued that these attitudes are largely the outcome of a combined effect of political predispositions and apprehension about the relation between expansion and the quality of university life. Within the British spectrum, as we saw in Chapter 15, university teachers are a 'leftist' group. Their political affiliations are more like those of manual workers than like the upper middle class to which, as we described them in Chapters 9 and 10, they belong in respect of their incomes, status, education and styles of life. At the same time they are worried about the future; two-thirds anticipated some or even marked deterioration of the quality of their own graduates if numbers were doubled in a decade. The sources of leftism are partly buried in the sceptical traditions of the Enlightenment: more proximately they are to be found in a slowly widening base of social recruitment, which contrasts for example with a narrow public school and Oxford arts avenue into the administrative class of the Civil Service,[1] and in the alienation of the new generation of educated middle class youth, some of whom are already junior university teachers, particularly in the social sciences. But the sources of apprehension are also strongly entrenched in the traditional English idea of a university which stems from the pre-industrial guilds of Oxford and Cambridge and which, despite all the pressures of industrialisation and modernisation, continues to exercise a powerful influence on opinion in senior common rooms. This idea continues in the minds of university teachers in Britain as a linked set of normative conceptions about the number and character of possible guests at the academic table, their appropriate intellectual diet and the manner of its digestion. The fear is that expansion will destroy these conditions for the perpetuation of the academic succession.

A summary of the variations in outlook among university teachers has to combine their attitude to the nature of the academic system and the role they see themselves as playing in it. The weight of

[1] A. H. Halsey and Ivor Crewe: *Social Survey of the Civil Service*. Evidence submitted to the committee under the chairmanship of Lord Fulton, Vol. 3 (I), H.M.S.O., 1969, Chapters III and XIII.

tradition defines the system in élitist terms, albeit that the character of the élite is increasingly meritocratic. The push of social demand for higher education and the lesser pull of occupational opportunity for graduates are both towards expansion. These forces divide the academics in one way. Similarly tradition is oriented towards the passing on of a valued humanistic culture while external demand and internal career chances are invitations to be concerned with discovery and innovation, to research rather than to teach. This divides the academics in a second way. Thus our analysis suggests that basic differences in academic orientations are represented not in a continuum but more accurately by a typology. One dimension of this typology refers to the conception of the university as either an élite, or as a relatively open and popular institution. The other dimension points to conceptions of the university teacher's primary role as either a creator of knowledge or as a teacher and transmitter of values and culture (Table 16.1).

These stark polarities of course do not do justice to the complex views and attitudes held by individual university teachers nor do they capture the nuances of thought and feeling by which men manage to maintain conceptions of the universities and of their academic roles which reflect *both* expansionist and élitist values, and which accept *both* teaching and research as legitimate and complementary functions of the university. Nevertheless, as we have seen in the preceding chapters, men do differ in the emphasis they place on these values, the priorities they put on their embodiment in university organisation, and in the allocation of both national and personal resources. And it is the *relative* emphasis in their values and orientations, we suggest, that is crucial during a period of expansion and change when men can oppose, or attempt to delay, or welcome, or even try to accelerate the changes which are associated with the expansion and democratisation of British higher education.

TABLE 16.1
A typology of academic orientations

Conceptions of the primary academic role	*Conceptions of the university*	
	Elitist	*Expansionist*
Research: the creation of knowledge	1	2
Teaching: the transmission of knowledge and the shaping of character	3	4

Recognising, therefore, that any such typology is more an analytical and heuristic device than an effort to characterise individual men and their views, we may find it useful to examine the types of academic orientation generated by these dimensions.[1]

Elitist researchers

An outlook combining élitism with research is one held by those concerned very much with intellectual brilliance and creativity, which they take to be largely genetically given and statistically rare. The function of an educational system, on this view, is to identify the small minority of really able and gifted people and then to create the intellectual environment in which promise can be developed and realised. The universities are first and foremost the institutions where this identification and education of the select minority should take place. It is in a university that academic men of high intellectual ability can find the first class minds among the students and, through close personal attention, encourage them to make their own scientific contributions. The purest examples of these attitudes are found among the professors, but they are not restricted to any particular rank, faculty or university group. Since this orientation is concerned more with brilliance and achievement, and less with character and ascribed status it has been the 'progressive', 'reformist' force for change from the middle of the nineteenth century to the middle of the twentieth century. The prestige and legitimacy which these views have gained in the past, associated as they have been with the high standards and great scientific achievements of the British universities, make them now the most formidable bulwarks of conservatism in British university life. The élitist research orientation is the most powerful conservative force against expansion and the most reliable defence against erosion of standards. It dedicates the university to a single-minded meritocracy.

Elitist teachers

The second outlook, combining élitism with teaching, is also concerned with identifying 'alpha' men, but is concerned somewhat more with the character and qualities of mind of the rather larger number of undergraduates who will go on to positions of leadership in

[1] An empirical profile of this typology is presented in Appendix F.

society. These attitudes are, traditionally, the natural extensions of the values and conceptions which have governed the leading public schools: they are concerned less with brilliance and creativity than with the transmission of the sensibilities and modes of thought of those who may be expected to guide the destinies of the larger society. Elitist teachers are somewhat apprehensive of what they see as an 'overemphasis' on research, precisely because of the danger that research interests may narrow rather than broaden students' perspectives, and also because a heavy emphasis on research can be subversive of those personal qualities and commitments to social leadership which are their prime concern in their work with students. They tend to see the undesirable effects of undue research emphasis in scientists and social scientists, many of whom, from their point of view, are not genuinely educated men.

These views, still probably the most widely held of our four types of academic orientation, provide the backcloth against which all reform and expansion is played out. There are, of course, great variations in the way they are expressed and defended: for some they are a defence of traditional privilege, and are associated with class feelings and snobberies. For others they are an expression of certain humanistic values, a tenacious adherence to the essentially élitist character of any education that can properly be called higher, part of a defence not merely of an élite institutional system but of a conception of civilised society. The position is hard to defend, even with a Black Paper, in an egalitarian age. Those who hold these opinions, in whatever form, are very much on the defensive not merely against the radical reformers but also against the much larger body of moderate progressives who are concerned with the consequences of élite conceptions of the university for British society and its economy.

But interestingly, in contemporary Britain, these traditionalist views are rarely argued–they come increasingly to take the form of sentiments rather than an articulated philosophical position. The Robbins Report did not bother to address itself to this position, but rather spent most of its space and statistical resources in reassuring the élitist researchers that the moderate expansion it was recommending would not be accompanied by a decline in standards. Nevertheless, these sentiments are at once most vulnerable and most resistant to the growth of numbers, and to the expansion of graduate education and organised research in British universities. They are, as we have suggested, very widespread among academic men: they shape thousands of unpublished decisions made in colleges and committees, and will continue to influence the rate and form of change in the 1970's. From one point of view this outlook reflects the definition of a university as a place in which to nurture the moral and intellectual character of a gentlemanly class. From another point of view it struggles against the fragmentation of excellence into intellectual specialisms and the disappearance from the campus of moral concerns.

Expansionist researchers

Third is the combination of expansion and research orientations which has provided the characteristic drive behind the development of the large American graduate schools. It represents the strongest challenge to the conservatism of the older restrictionist tradition of research-mindedness and there is strength in its promise of fruitful application to the technical and managerial problems of society. The essential function of the university, on this view, is that of the intellectual spearhead for economic growth. Men with these orientations are less concerned with the identification and nurture of the rare first-class minds than are the élitist researchers, and tend to identify the growth of knowledge with the growth of research resources, organisation and numbers of people. They are more likely, also, to accept a larger direct social role for the universities. They are likely to be the most influential advocates of university reform and expansion within the universities, since they oppose to the traditional élitist conception of the university the values of research and the expansion of knowledge which are institutionalised within the university. Nevertheless, in the British context, men with these attitudes are more likely to support a moderate than a radical expansion of the university system, in part because there is a certain element of élitism in all scholarship and science, a passionate concern for quality if not privilege. And it was this concern to which Robbins was speaking when he recommended an expansion keyed to the maintenance of existing academic standards.

Expansionist teachers

Finally there is the combination of expansion with a teaching orientation. The direction here is towards the university with no walls.

It can claim its antecedents in extra-mural and extension movements and in its modern guise it seeks new mass institutions for the post-adolescent. It is strongly represented in the social science faculties. Its primary concern is with the fundamental problem of transforming a socially restricted 'cultural heritage' into a 'common culture' but what this means in terms of organisation as well as content is a vast unknown. Men who hold these views characteristically stress the popular functions of education in providing opportunities for all to achieve their highest potential, and in raising the level of knowledge and skill of the whole population. This essentially extends to higher education the basic justification for mass primary and secondary education, and inevitably de-emphasises the élite university functions of training for intellectual or political leadership or of creating knowledge. It is not surprising, therefore, to find that those who hold these views towards the university are by far the strongest supporters of the comprehensive principle in secondary education, and are most likely to oppose specialisation, both in secondary school and the university. These attitudes, while represented throughout British universities, appear to have very little weight in current discussions of the future of the universities. They are, however, more substantially represented in the institutions of further education, which are likely to be the basis for much of the expansion of the later 1970's and for any movement towards mass higher education in the future.

In conclusion, however, we would emphasise the common characteristics of university opinion rather than its differences and point to the problems which are likely to become sharper in the future.

A commonplace observation points to the British capacity for both accomplishing and containing change through conservative institutions. This is nowhere clearer than in the evolution of British universities over the past century and a half. In England, for example, the two corrupt, stagnant aristocratic universities of the eighteenth century have become the forty odd meritocratic and creative universities of today growing at a rate which will bring their student numbers to 450,000 by 1982. And yet, these changes have so far been contained within what are essentially traditional universities devoted primarily to traditional functions.

What are the traditional functions of the university and what is happening to them today?

First, the universities transmit the knowledge, attitudes and values which are thought to make men civilised. Second, they discover new knowledge and new ideas. Third, they select, form and give recognition to a social élite: the learned professions, the higher civil service, the political, and (though less in Britain than on the Continent), the commercial and industrial leaders, as well as the teachers in preparatory secondary schools where children are educated for their accession to élite status. And fourth, they provide higher vocational training, particularly for the older professions of medicine, law, the clergy, and university teaching.

In the past all of these functions could be discharged more or less adequately by small élite university systems with strong traditions and customs changing relatively slowly. The transmission of a high culture, for example, is itself a powerfully conservative function. The conception of that culture to be passed on through the universities was, for hundreds of years, gradually secularised and broadened beyond its mediaeval and classical limits; but it was still easily carried and contained within the old conception of the élite university. The invention in Germany of the scientific research institute associated with the university, and the slow assimilation there and elsewhere of science, history, and more recently the social sciences into the curriculum, has also been compatible with the small size and élite character of the old university.

With respect to the third function, the size of the élites being selected and trained was also compatible with the university system as it existed. There was, until recently, a relatively small demand for graduates, and a small capacity to absorb them in the economy. The structure of primary and secondary education in European countries also ensured that the number of candidates for the university system would be small. And finally, the universities were well able to provide a limited amount of vocational training for the old learned professions.

What is happening to those traditional functions of the university? First, there is an increasing demand from larger groups in the population for a share in and possession of the high culture, a demand which is not met by the transmission of that culture through the élite university. There has been over the past half-century, in Britain as elsewhere, an erosion of the legitimacy of class cultures. In every modern society there is a growing feeling that it is right for all men to claim possession of the high culture of their own societies. In schools and through the mass media, ordinary people are encouraged to share in this national and international heritage, both for its own sake and because it is the mark of a cultivated man. And side by side with this tendency there emerges a kind of instrumental or vocational function of high culture, the possession of which becomes the sign of eligibility for certain élite positions. This tendency also lies behind the enormous growth of demand for higher liberal education.

Second, there is the dramatic advance of scientific research, perhaps best known of all the forces promoting university expansion. This growth is symbolised by Robert Oppenheimer's observation that of all scientists who ever lived, 90 per cent of them are alive today. This remark tells us something not only about the institution of science, but also about the universities and research centres in which most of it exists.

Third, there has been a growth both in the size of the older prestigious professions, and also in the numbers of new professions and semi-professions which demand or purport to require a higher education. There is also a demand on the part of growing numbers for higher education which is not linked to membership in any élite, either the old or the new. This latter development is associated with changes in the educational aspirations of the middle and working classes. Increasingly throughout the class structure, very markedly already in the middle classes but visible also among the growing technician-working class, higher education is coming to be seen as part of the decencies of life rather than one of its extraordinary privileges. Gradually moving down through the class structure, some kind of higher education comes to be seen as appropriate not just for people of a higher class or extraordinary talent, but as possible and desirable for youngsters of moderate talent and ambition. This strong trend towards higher standards of educational achievement in every social and economic class is associated with the abolition, or at least the amelioration of selection by wealth, the democratisation of the lower levels of schooling, and especially of the academic preparatory school. In many European countries, including Britain, we see a movement towards the various forms of comprehensive secondary schools that are a prerequisite for the development of mass non-élite higher education. These changes in the educational standard of living of the general population are confounding projections of university expansion in almost every European country, and most certainly those of the Robbins Committee.

Fourth, on the matter of vocational training, we see what has come to be an insatiable demand on the part of the economy and the occupational structure for more and more highly trained people for the new or emerging professions and semi-professions: technical, organizational, cultural, welfare. Behind this lie both economic and political forces: for example, the creation of the welfare state generates whole new categories of occupations for which higher education is required. Moreover, the extension of secondary education, and the expansion of higher education, makes teaching itself one of the major consumers of educated manpower.

These pressures for expansion are reflected in the growth of higher education in every industrial society. Sweden had 14,000 university students in 1947. By 1962 that number had tripled to 45,000; by the early 1970's they anticipate a further doubling to about 90,000, who will then comprise about 15 per cent of the relevant age group. France anticipated a growth in its university population between 1960 and 1970 from 200,000 to 500,000. Denmark doubled its university student population between 1960 and 1966, from 15,000 to 30,000; by 1975 it will double again to 60,000, and will then comprise about 18 per cent of the age group. In the United Kingdom, as we have seen, the Robbins Report anticipated student numbers growing from about 130,000 in 1962 to 220,000 by 1973, and to nearly 350,000 by 1980; and these figure have already been revised to 450,000 by 1982.

But these numbers conceal, or perhaps foreshadow, two fundamentally different trends, or forces which will be reflected in trends. One of these is the *expansion* of the élite universities–the growth of traditional university functions in the traditional, if somewhat modified forms. The other is the *transformation* of élite university systems into systems of mass higher education, performing a great variety of new functions (at least, new to the universities) for a much larger proportion of the university age group. Up to the present, in Britain as on the Continent, growth has mainly been a matter of expanding the élite university system. But the older institutions cannot expand indefinitely; they are limited by their traditions, organization, functions and finance. It is likely that an increase of enrolment in higher education beyond about 15 per cent of the age group requires not merely the further expansion of the élite university systems, but the development of mass higher education through the growth of popular institutions.

But while the expansion of the universities carries difficult problems in its train, the development of extensive non-élite forms of higher education in some relation to the universities creates larger and more intractable problems, having to do with the status of university graduates and teachers, the autonomy of institutions, and the relation of both non-élite and élite forms of higher education to governmental authorities. The pressures for equivalent support and a similar government for all forms of higher education is very great, and yet the privileges, freedoms, and levels of support of the universities are made possible precisely by their relatively small size and insulation from the political and economic mainstream–that is, by their élite status. The growth of non-élite forms of higher education will pose problems and create difficulties for the universities far beyond those associated with their own current expansion.

The first response of progressive university people to pressure for expansion is to absorb it into the universities. To such men, the expansion of the university system is the natural way of expanding higher education. Moreover, they see the advantages of a larger system, and in many cases, of larger institutions: greater resources, new staff appointments, opportunities for all kinds of reforms and innovations through the creative allocation of new funds rather than the much more difficult reallocation of existing resources.

The stubborn resistance of the conservatives among academic men only confirms the progressives in the rightness of their cause. All the traditional élitist slogans–'more means worse', 'the cream rises', and so forth–have been widely discredited both by research and by recent experience, and moreover are manifestly irrelevant to the needs of social institutions and the demands of relevant populations.

Most European societies need and can afford a considerable expansion of their university systems. Universities can grow from three to six, ten or even fifteen thousand, additional universities can be created and staffed, and numbers can double or triple in two decades, as we have seen between 1950 and 1970, without changing the fundamental character of the university system. Strains appear: there are difficulties in recruiting staff, and in building so much so fast; the old leisurely administrative machinery groans under its new loads; and the traditional supremacy of the single professor as head of department, and as member of the professorial oligarchy in university government, is challenged by the growth both of staff and of knowledge.

But the most difficult problems associated with growth arise not so much in connection with university expansion itself, but with the development of pressures for a system of higher education to provide places for 20, 30 or even 40 per cent of the age group. In no society, we suggest, can élite institutions such as the British universities provide for that kind of mass higher education and remain élite institutions. For one thing, their academic standards are too high; for another, their costs are too high, costs which are a function of élite university salary scales, staff/student ratios, amenities, and above all, of their expensive provisions for research and scholarship.

But as we have seen at many places in this study, British academic men, even the progressives and expansionists among them, are not prepared for an expansion which would threaten the central characteristics of élite universities. They want to strengthen the universities, not destroy them, and support moderate and controlled expansion which will allow the preservation of the characteristics of the university as they know it. It was precisely the Robbins argument that university numbers could be substantially increased *without* lowering academic standards or the staff/student ratio that won it support from a broad spectrum of academic opinion, as well as implementation of its recommended expansion by both Conservative and Labour governments.

But the continuing expansion of the university system, which fills the horizons and absorbs the energies of academic men and government committees, is not the first stage of the development of mass higher education. The institutions of mass higher education must differ in fundamental respects from the élite universities–they cannot be merely the further extension of university expansion. They must differ in cost. No society can yet afford to educate 30 per cent of its youth at the cost of education at Harvard, Oxford, or Sussex. The popular institutions are forced into a less rigid emphasis on high or traditional academic requirements for admission. They have to acquire a vocational and service emphasis. They have to recruit their staff more widely. They have to submit to a lesser degree of autonomy, in their relation to the governmental agencies which provide funds. In so far as the universities monopolise higher education, the result will be either to inhibit expansion, or to threaten the traditional forms and freedoms of university life.

It is easy, and not very useful, to suggest that university teachers in their own interest should welcome the development of non-university forms of higher education which, by absorbing the bulk of future expansion, can insulate the universities against the devastating effects of mass higher education on their standards, character and autonomy. But university men, as our study shows, are basically conservative; even those who are boldest and least conservative in their own intellectual lives want to preserve and strengthen the institutions which make their scientific and scholarly achievements possible. Expansion means change; change holds promise, but also a threat. There is little evidence that the British university professions have given much thought to either the promise or the threat which expansion holds for their institutions, much less to the role of the university in the larger and more varied system of mass higher education which lies just over the horizon.

What, then, will happen to the universities? There can be little doubt that the numbers target for 1980 will be reached and passed. Probably the universities will form a smaller sector of the higher education system than Robbins envisaged. The binary policy will, however, be seen as one step along the road at least to a threefold division including an extramural sector (external degrees, N.C.A.A. and the Open University) which already had more than 30,000 students in 1968, and possibly to a pluralism in which there is a more complex division of intellectual labour between institutions. Such developments need not and almost certainly will not result in large universities on the American model. Indeed there are no foreseeable *institutional* conditions which would make the English idea of a university impossible within a more varied system of higher education.

On the other hand there must be some fear that the average quality of academic staff will decline and, given the unequal starting points and the muted competition permitted by the bureaucratisation of salaries and conditions, high ability is likely to concentrate as it has already in Oxford and Cambridge and to a lesser extent in London, and only in particular departments elsewhere in the system. The great danger is that this informal hierarchy, combined with governmental anxiety over the cost of the 'higher education industry' as a whole, may defeat the development of pluralism. It will require imaginative forbearance from the central planners as well as parliamentary goodwill and tolerance to ensure that the different academic styles and values will find somewhere to express themselves.

In this study we have been exploring the characteristics and sentiments of British university teachers. We have been looking for the sources of change and of resistance to change among them. What we have found is a profession differing within itself on many specific issues, but largely agreed on the rightness of the British university as it now exists, and rather cautiously committed, with few exceptions, to the defence of that institution against the pressure and incalculable changes of the future. These men and their views will have considerable weight in shaping the forms of response of British universities to the growing pressures for mass higher education which are beginning to emerge in the larger society.

APPENDICES

Appendix A

THE CATs IN TRANSITION[1]

I. Introduction[2]

In 1964, at the time when the CAT survey was undertaken, these colleges were in the position of 'universities-designate'. In other words, they were still officially Colleges of Advanced Technology, without degree-giving powers and the other perquisites of university status, but they were aware of the promotion that was coming. They were already admitting freshmen undergraduates to read for degrees to be awarded three years later; and most were also changing or upgrading their faculty recruitment policies. In any event, our survey gives us a picture of these institutions at the point of transition; and one of the chief foci of our analysis will be the question of adaptation to the new university status.

II. Institutional characteristics: age, subject and rank

We turn first to the basic parameters of the two groups of teachers – their age distributions, and the proportions of men teaching in each

[1] By Oliver Fulton.

[2] In this appendix we shall be comparing the teachers in three CATs with the whole sample of university teachers derived from our and the Robbins Committee's main questionnaire. The survey covered Brunel College in London, and the colleges at Birmingham and Salford. (For further details, see Appendix C.) We shall be looking both at institutional differences (in proportions of subjects taught, age and rank distribution, and the origins and past experience of teachers, etc.) and at differences between the individual teachers at the two types of institutions (in attitudes and personal orientations). We shall compare the responses of both groups to a variety of questions which we shall treat as if they were identical. The reader should remember, however, that six months separated the administering of the follow-up survey instrument to the universities and to the CATs; while for the university teachers occasional items of background information are derived from the Robbins questionnaire of 1962: thus 'age' for the universities should be interpreted as age in 1962, while 'age' for the CATs is age in late 1964. With a few exceptions, however, the questionnaires were identical; and we believe that it is reasonable to interpret most responses in identical ways.

subject area and at each university rank. Perhaps not surprisingly, the two populations in 1964 were quite sharply different.

Table A.1 shows the age distributions of CAT and university

TABLE A.1

Age distribution, CATs and universities (per cent)

Age	*CATs (1964)*	*Universities (1962)*
Under 30	18	17
30–4	27	19
35–9	22	21
40–4	16	14
45 and over	17	29
TOTALS	(361)	(1,405)

teachers. The CAT faculty was much more narrowly clustered, particularly in the 30–9 group into which half of them fall, compared with two-fifths of the university faculty. Nearly twice as many of the latter as the former were over 45. Both groups, however, had about the same proportion of teachers under 30. This distribution presumably reflects the periods of large-scale expansion in the two types of institution, assuming that most teachers joined either the university system or the CATs between the ages of 21 and 25. For it was in the early 1950's that the CATs were so designated and given special support by the Ministry of Education; before this time they had simply been local technical colleges. Their high rate of growth in the next ten years is reflected especially in the 30–34 age group, which represents over a quarter of all their teachers, a relatively larger proportion than the same age group forms in the universities, which themselves were growing at the time. In recent years the CAT growth rate has been closer to that of the universities.[1]

Table A.2 shows in parallel the proportions of teachers in different subject groups for CATs and universities. As they stood in 1964 the CATs clearly deserved their title, for almost half of their teachers were in technology, and another two-fifths in natural science, leaving only 14 per cent to be divided between social science (10 per cent) and the arts (4 per cent). These latter two areas, however, occupy over 40 per cent of all university teachers, and less than one-third as many university teachers are technologists as is the case for the CATs.

[1] See, e.g., Sir James Mountford, *British Universities*, Oxford University Press, 1966.

TABLE A.2

Subject distributions, CATs and universities (per cent)

Subject	*CATs*	*Universities*
Arts	4	26
Social science	10	16
Natural science	40	29
Technology	46	13
Medicine, dentistry, agriculture, veterinary science	0	16
TOTALS	(383)	(1,404)

But it may be somewhat more revealing to look at the emphasis on subjects in different age groups (Table A.3). The universities do not

TABLE A.3

Subject by age, CATs and universities (per cent)

	CATs			*Universities*		
Subject	*30–*	*30–9*	*40+*	*30–*	*30–9*	*40+*
Arts	4	4	4	25	20	30
Social science	12	9	10	16	14	18
Natural science	54	38	33	41	28	25
Technology	29	49	53	10	17	10
Other	0	0	0	8	20	17
TOTALS	(66)	(177)	(118)	(233)	(562)	(608)

present any very consistent pattern, except that (again if we take age differences to reflect changing patterns of recruitment) they seem to have been recruiting more natural scientists in recent years (and perhaps fewer teachers of medicine, although the late age of qualification in medicine probably affects this proportion in those under 30). But there is a much clearer pattern in the CATs. There is no real change in the proportion of teachers in arts or social science; but technology and natural science have almost changed places in their proportions, with over half of all those under 30 in science, compared with over half of all those over 40 in technology. It is clear that as a preparation for becoming universities the CATs had at least been broadening their scientific base, although in 1964 there was no sign that they were expanding appreciably beyond science and technology.

In Table A.4 we show the spread of appointments by rank, for the CATs and universities.[1]

[1] This is another case where our figures are not strictly comparable, since our survey followed up a sample of university teachers selected two years earlier

Here there are very striking differences. Looking first at the overall distribution (on the right) we see that the universities had notably higher proportions in all the senior ranks, and most of all at the professor level. In the universities, 15 per cent of all teachers were professors (a 'true' 12 per cent, on the basis of all academic staff including temporary posts)[1] compared with only 4 per cent in the CATs. And all senior ranks combined made up 42 per cent at the universities, and just over half that figure–22 per cent–at the CATs. It is true that the CAT teachers were a much younger group of men (see above); and it could be therefore that their age affects their chances of promotion (although even if this were so, it would mean that the CATs were able to get by with a smaller proportion of professors and other senior ranks). But when we look at the age breakdowns in Table A.4 we see that for each age group the proportions of all senior ranks are lower for the CATs, and consistently so from the youngest to the oldest teachers. It is true that the CATs were still at the transition point at the time of this survey, and had not yet fully adapted to the university scale of ranks: but the picture that these figures reveal is one of distinctly poorer brothers to the full universities.

III. The background of the CAT faculty: social and educational origins and qualifications: non-academic experience

In Table A.5 we show the social origins of teachers in the CATs and universities. In general, as can be seen from the overall summary on the right of the table, teachers at CATs were notably more likely to come from lower class origins than those at universities. 53 per cent of the CAT faculty's fathers were in working class occupations, as against 39 per cent of those of the university faculty. But when we look at the age breakdowns a more interesting pattern emerges. In the universities, as we have seen elsewhere, the trend is towards increasing 'democratisation'. Of those who were over 44 in 1962 only one-third

---

by the Robbins Committee. Thus, most of those who at the time of the original survey were assistant lecturers, demonstrators, or who held other temporary posts, had either been promoted or left the university. The result is that whereas according to the U.G.C. returns for 1961–62 (*Higher Education*, Appendix III, p. 13, Table 7) 22 per cent of all university academic staff were 'Assistant Lecturers, demonstrators and others', this figure was reduced to 8 per cent by the time of our follow-up. In order to assure reasonable comparability, therefore, we present the distributions of the four established, non-probationary grades.

[1] See note 1, p. 471.

Table A.4

Rank, CATs and universities, by age (per cent) (permanent ranks only)

	Age											
	30 –		*30–4*		*35–9*		*40–4*		*45+*		*All*	
Rank	*CAT*	*University*	*CAT*	*University*	*CAT*	*University*	*CAT*	*University*	*CAT*	*University*	*CAT*	*University*
Professor	0	0	1	2	2	7	5	18	17	35	4	15
Reader	0	0	1	3	6	10	12	15	8	17	7	10
Senior lecturer	0	3	2	7	15	19	17	25	23	24	11	17
Lecturer	100	97	96	88	76	64	66	42	52	24	78	58
TOTALS	(39)	(172)	(23)	(248)	(80)	(280)	(58)	(194)	(60)	(390)	(329)*	(1,290)*

* Totals in these summary columns do not add to the totals of the other categories since a small number of non-responses to specific questions were omitted.

Table A.5

Social origins (father's occupation), CATs and universities, by age (per cent)

	Age											
	30 –		*30–4*		*35–9*		*40–4*		*45+*		*All*	
Father's occupation	*CAT*	*University*	*CAT*	*University*	*CAT*	*University*	*CAT*	*University*	*CAT*	*University*	*CAT*	*University*
Professional	14	19	13	21	9	15	12	18	9	25	11	20
Intermediate	34	35	30	37	35	43	39	45	42	43	35	41
Skilled	43 } 52	38 } 46	45 } 57	37 } 43	49 } 57	37 } 42	39 } 48	30 } 37	46 } 50	25 } 32	44 } 53	33 } 39
Semi-/Unskilled	9	8	12	6	8	5	9	7	4	7	9	6
TOTALS	(65)	(227)	(95)	(259)	(78)	(287)	(56)	(195)	(57)	(397)	(373)*	(1,368)*

* See note to Table A. 4.

came from working class families; while in the youngest group, those who were under 30 in 1962, nearly half came from such families. In the CATs, however, the position was more complex. The proportions of middle and working class children were steady in the oldest two groups, and near the overall average. Then for the next two groups there was a rise in the proportion from working-class backgrounds, coinciding, as we saw above, with the sharply increased expansion of and recruitment to the CATs. In the youngest age group, however, those under 30 in 1964, the proportion from middle class backgrounds had risen again. This suggests (although the size of the change is small) that the CATs, once they knew that they were to become universities, had begun to resemble universities more closely in their recruitment.[1] This phenomenon of 'convergence' towards common norms for universities is one that we shall be seeing again later in this Appendix.

Table A.6 gives the type of secondary school attended by the university and CAT teachers. The details of the pattern detected above in Table A.5 are much less clear; but in general we can see that as we move from the oldest to the youngest groups in the universities, the proportion who attended public schools diminishes–while there is no clear pattern in the CATs. Overall, the CATs were somewhat more dominated by grammar school pupils than were the universities, and distinctly less by the public schools.

Table A.7 shows the university group from which our respondents took their most recent first degree. Contrary to our discoveries elsewhere, there seems to have been very little change over time, except that in the case of the CATs steadily more younger teachers seem to have come from the major Redbrick universities, largely at the expense of those without degrees (see the last two lines of the table), and partly also of London. In general, it seems that, as we might expect from the two previous tables, many more university than CAT teachers studied at Oxford or Cambridge (and also rather more in Scotland); and the difference was made up by the heavy preponderance of London and the large Redbrick universities, which between them educated two-thirds of the CAT faculty.

[1] The reader should note that such statements as this are convenient shorthand descriptions of complex phenomena. In personifying an institution in this way we do not mean to imply a human process of decision; for while it is possible that the CATs deliberately changed their basis for making appointments, it is also possible and perhaps more likely that different men began to apply for posts there, once their future as universities was secure.

TABLE A.6

Secondary school attended, CATs and universities, by age (per cent)

	Age											
	30 –		*30–4*		*35–9*		*40–4*		*45+*		*All*	
School	*CAT*	*University*	*CAT*	*University*	*CAT*	*University*	*CAT*	*University*	*CAT*	*University*	*CAT*	*University*
Maintained	70	59	69	57	67	58	61	51	71	52	68	55
Direct-grant	12	14	6	10	10	11	9	10	5	8	8	10
Public	9	17	15	18	9	18	7	25	11	26	10	21
Other	9	10	10	14	13	12	23	14	12	14	13	13
None	0	0	0	1	1	1	0	1	0	1	0	1
TOTALS	(66)	(230)	(94)	(259)	(78)	(293)	(57)	(198)	(56)	(404)	(372)*	(1,387)*

* See note to Table A. 4.

TABLE A.7

Place of first degree, CATs and universities, by age (per cent)

	Age											
	30 –		*30–4*		*35–9*		*40–4*		*45+*		*All*	
Place of first degree	*CAT*	*University*	*CAT*	*University*	*CAT*	*University*	*CAT*	*University*	*CAT*	*University*	*CAT*	*University*
Oxford or Cambridge	11	31	8	26	11	26	5	30	15	34	10	30
London	23	16	28	16	29	21	43	20	35	18	30	18
Major Redbrick	44	21	36	26	36	18	28	18	17	17	34	20
Minor Redbrick	8	5	8	3	4	5	2	4	2	1	5	3
Wales	4	4	4	5	2	5	5	2	3	5	4	5
Scotland	2	14	4	13	2	16	0	13	3	13	3	14
Overseas	6	6	4	8	10	3	5	6	2	3	5	5
No first degree	0	3	1	3	2	6	3	7	12	8	3	6
Professional qualification only	3	0	6	0	2	0	9	0	12	0	6	0
TOTALS	(66)	(233)	(97)	(263)	(80)	(298)	(58)	(199)	(60)	(408)	(383)*	(1,402)*

* See note to Table A. 4.

We turn next to the question of educational qualifications. Table A.8 shows the class of first degree attained by our samples of CAT and university teachers. Overall (see right of table) it is clear that, in terms of first degree honours, CAT teachers tended to be less well qualified. Almost 60 per cent of the university faculty gained first or upper second class degrees, as against 44 per cent of the CAT faculty. And only half as many CAT teachers as university teachers gained firsts. But the age breakdown tells a rather different story of current trends. With respect to first class honours alone, the universities have been remarkably stable over time,[1] fluctuating between 44 and 48 per cent for the five age groups. And the CATs had never come higher than 26 per cent, with a low of 15 per cent gaining 'firsts' in the 35–39 age group–in which group 20 per cent gained only third, fourth or pass degrees. But if we look at the percentages holding either 'firsts' or 'upper seconds' (which is often taken as a more reliable criterion of academic merit) there is a remarkable change. For the universities show a rise from 54 per cent for the 45 and over age group to 70 per cent for those under 30, who took their degrees less than ten years ago. But the CATs had risen from 29 per cent, far below the universities, for the over-44 group, to 68 per cent for the under-thirty's; in other words the CATs had increased their standards of intake so as almost to equal the universities, at a time when the universities' own standards were rising. This is a special kind of 'convergence', since the universities were moving not towards but away from the CATs taken as a whole. But it is a remarkable example of 'anticipatory socialization', in that the CATs were already taking on some of the qualities and standards of the universities which they were later to become. The same phenomenon can be seen in Table A.9 (from which the youngest age group has been excluded, since many of them had not yet had time to complete higher degree qualifications): university teachers as a whole were more likely to have acquired postgraduate degrees than teachers at the CATs, and particularly to have Ph.D's. But the gap was narrowing for the younger teachers, and in the youngest group CAT staff were approximately as likely as were university staff to have at least one second degree.

But the most striking difference between the universities and the CATs is still to come. We have seen that teachers at CATs, though somewhat different in background from those at universities in social and educational origins and qualifications, nevertheless were

[1] See also Robbins, Appendix III, Section 5, pp. 19–23.

TABLE A.8
Class of first degree, CATs and universities, by age (per cent)

	Age											
	30 –		30–4		35–9		40–4		45+		All	
Class of first degree	*CAT*	*University*	*CAT*	*University*	*CAT*	*University*	*CAT*	*University*	*CAT*	*University*	*CAT*	*University*
1	24 } 68	44 } 70	23 } 43	44 } 58	15 } 34	46 } 58	26 } 42	48 } 62	22 } 29	45 } 54	22 } 44	45 } 59
2(i)	44	26	20	14	19	12	16	14	7	9	22	14
2 undivided	12	14	28	16	26	15	31	13	30	17	25	15
2(ii)	6	2	9	2	5	2	0	1	2	1	5	1
3, 4, pass	4	2	8	9	20	5	9	5	13	7	11	6
Unclassified	0	6	0	9	0	12	2	10	0	11	0	10
Overseas	6	3	4	3	10	2	5	3	2	3	5	5
No first degree	0	3	1	3	2	6	3	7	12	8	3	6
Professional qualification only	3	0	6	0	2	0	9	0	12	0	6	0
TOTALS	(66)	(233)	(97)	(264)	(80)	(298)	(58)	(199)	(60)	(408)	(383)*	(1,402)*

* See note to Table A. 4.

TABLE A.9
Higher degree, CATs and universities, by age (per cent)

	Age†									
	30–4		35–9		40–4		45+		All	
Higher degrees	*CAT*	*University*	*CAT*	*University*	*CAT*	*University*	*CAT*	*University*	*CAT*	*University*
Ph.D.	41	52	28	48	26	54	30	43	33	46
Master's only	19	10	20	13	19	13	7	16	17	13
None	40	38	52	39	55	33	63	41	50	41
TOTALS	(97)	(264)	(80)	(296)	(58)	(195)	(57)	(406)	(380)*	(1,395)*

* See note to Table A. 4. † "30-" category omitted since many in it were completing higher degrees.

comparable, if as poor relations, and were coming to resemble their more privileged colleagues more closely all the time. And it might seem that these two groups of teachers were really very similar in their past experience. But the history of the development of the CATs was very different from that of the universities, not only in their scientific and technological emphasis, but also in the contacts with local industry which marked their early careers, and still play a large part in their present day degree courses for undergraduates. It turns out that such contacts were very much a part of the careers of CAT faculty members, as we can see in Table A.10. In all, only 1 per cent of university teachers had ever been employed in industrial research and development; but for the CATs the comparable figure was 41 per cent. One-third of all the CAT natural scientists had worked in industrial research and development, and over half of their technologists. In this respect at least, the CAT teachers were much less solidly connected to the academic world than their university colleagues, very few of whom had ever held a non-academic job.

IV. Orientations and opinions, within and outside the institution

(*a*) *Teaching and research*

The attitudes of the faculty of the CATs towards teaching and research, in terms of personal preferences, personal achievements, and conceptions of academic norms, have already been described quite extensively in Chapter 12.[1] The CATs emerged as much less research minded, not only than the universities as a whole, but even than the most teaching-oriented university groups, in personal preference, in their conception of the central academic role, and in research productivity. It was only when we looked at their professed ability to do research in term that they resembled any other groups of institutions. This was still true when we looked at subject areas within fields, with the sole exception of social science. In all other subject areas, including technology, which appears to put very little emphasis on research throughout academic life, the CATs were less likely to favour or practise research than any other group. In Chapter 12 we suggested that a possible explanation for this finding was the CATs' only very recent change to the university standard, with its emphasis on research as a reasonable and proper occupation

[1] See especially Tables 12.9–13, 12.20–22, 12.33 and text.

TABLE A.10*

Proportions who have been employed in 'industry: research and development', CATs and universities, by subject

	Natural science	*Technology*	*All*
CATs	34% (153)	53% (175)	41% (383)
Universities	2% (410)	4% (179)	1% (1,408)

* This table shows the relation between three variables more economically than in a larger table which would include rows showing those who had not been so employed. For this reason the columns do nct add to 100%.

TABLE A.11

'Apart from time, are the resources available to you adequate for the kind of research you are doing?', CATs and universities, by subject (per cent)

	Subject							
	Social science		*Natural science*		*Technology*		*All*	
Research resources	*CAT*	*University*	*CAT*	*University*	*CAT*	*University*	*CAT*	*University*
Excellent	10 } 44	9 } 53	7 } 45	17 } 65	8 } 57	19 } 71	7 } 49	19 } 62
Adequate	33	44	38	48	49	51	42	44
Somewhat inadequate	20	38	42	30	38	26	37	31
Wholly inadequate	36	9	13	5	5	3	13	7
TOTALS	(39)	(216)	(143)	(406)	(170)	(177)	(366)*	(1,384)*

* See note to Table A. 4.

for faculty members. Until this change the CATs had been thought of as institutions, albeit advanced, for teaching only.

Table A.11 provides a small addition to our information on research and teaching in the CATs. When we looked at academic men's assessment of available resources for research in the universities we found that there was a tendency for non-researchers to rate research facilities more highly, no doubt because they were unlikely to have any personal experience of the frustrations of attempting to do research. One might expect, therefore, that the CATs would rate their resources fairly highly. In fact, however, they consistently considered them poorer than did their university colleagues in all three subject areas for which we have sufficient numbers. It may be, therefore, that the CATs contain a larger proportion of genuinely frustrated researchers than do the universities (though it may also be, in the light of their stated preferences, that those who complain of inadequate resources were simply rationalizing their own preference for teaching).

(*b*) *Attitudes to university expansion*

If one were to speculate on how the members of the CATs' teaching staff might feel with regard to university expansion, it would be possible to make two fairly convincing cases. The first, that they would be strongly in favour of expansion, would be based on the consideration that they were themselves part of the current, post-Robbins wave of university growth. Indeed, part of the projected increase in university undergraduate numbers is a technical increase supplied by the 'stroke of the pen' which turned the CATs into full degree-giving institutions. Thus the CAT teachers should favour expansion as leading to increased prestige–and pay–for themselves. On the other hand, by the time of our survey, the Robbins recommendation to upgrade the CATs had already been accepted, and therefore any further expansion beyond Robbins' figures could be seen as a 'dilution' of the CATs' newly acquired high status. A choice between these predictions would depend on guessing whether questions about expansion would be interpreted as a guarantee of parity or a threat to new prestige. But it might be that the CATs would tend to favour expansion in so far as their teachers come from somewhat lower class backgrounds, on average, than university teachers, and might therefore follow the politically left-wing line that favours expansion (Chapter 11, passim).

When we come to look at the figures, however, such speculation is seen to have been relatively unrewarding: for the teachers in the CATs turned out to be astonishingly like those in the universities. There was a very slight difference in the proportions who recommended expanding the university system–with the CATs favouring expansion, especially doubling, a little more (Table A.12). But the difference was

TABLE A.12

'Should we expand the university system?', CATs and universities (per cent)

Recommended expansion	*CATs*		*Universities*	
Double in next decade	33	71	27	67
50%	38		40	
25%	24		28	
Remain as it is	4		4	
TOTALS	(368)		(1,363)	

TABLE A.13

Recommended proportion of age-grade for full-time higher education, CATs and universities (per cent)

Recommended proportion	*CATs*	*Universities*
40%+	7	6
30%+	7	7
20%	39	39
10%	46	46
<10%	1	1
TOTALS	(365)	(1,335)

very small; and Table A.13, which shows the recommended proportions of the age grade to attend institutions of higher education full time, reveals no difference at all between the universities and CATs. This is all the more surprising in the light of Tables A.14 and A.15, for here we see that although one quarter of the CAT teachers believed that the quality of their students had declined in the past decade (Table A.14) (thus flying in the face of the Robbins report which maintained that it had become harder for qualified students

TABLE A.14

'Has expansion of past decade affected quality of students in your subject?' (per cent)

Effect of past expansion	*CATs*	*Universities*
Lowered considerably	3	1
Lowered somewhat	21	20
No change	51	66
Improvement	25	14
TOTALS	(322)	(1,313)

TABLE A.15

'If the number of students doubled in next decade, what would be the effect on quality of graduates from your institution in your subject?' (per cent)

Effect of future expansion	*CATs*		*Universities*	
Marked deterioration	9		16	
Some deterioration	40		50	
No change	35	51	27	33
Improvement	16		6	
TOTALS	(372)		(1,372)	

to get into universities, so that presumably the CATs would have been experiencing a rise in quality in the remainder), a substantially higher proportion of teachers in CATs than in the universities also believed the Robbins claim that standards had risen. Moreover, half of them, compared with only one-third of university teachers, were prepared to believe that quality would not decline with a doubling of numbers in the next decade (Table A.15). In spite of all this, they were no more in favour of expansion than are teachers at the universities. In other words, when we consider the evidence provided by their own experience, the CATs appear to have been educationally more conservative than the universities. We shall see shortly, however, that they *were* politically somewhat more conservative; and since we know (see Chapter 11) how much political dispositions affected attitudes to expansion among university teachers, it is necessary to look again at attitudes to expanding the system, taking politics into

TABLE A.16

'Should we expand the university system?', CATs and universities, by political position (per cent)

	Politics							
	Far Left		*Left*		*Centre*		*Right*	
Expand system	*CAT*	*University*	*CAT*	*University*	*CAT*	*University*	*CAT*	*University*
Double in next decade	60	60	40	34	27	21	18	12
50% increase	15	30	39	42	37	44	44	34
25% increase	15 } 25	3 } 10	19 } 20	21 } 24	33 } 36	31 } 35	27 } 38	47 } 54
Remain as it is	10	7	1	3	3	4	11	7
TOTALS	(20)	(60)	(142)	(636)	(119)	(371)	(73)	(254)

account (Table A.16). In this table it can be seen that, with the possible exception of those on the 'far left' whose numbers in the CATs are small, the CAT teachers turned out to be somewhat *more* expansionist than university men who placed themselves in the same category of the political spectrum. And in view of their experience this seems more reasonable. Nevertheless, we are struck more by the smallness of these differences than by the fact that they existed. What is clear is that the CATs, even before elevation to university status, had quite thoroughly accepted the élite conception of a relatively small university system, with only a third overall in favour of the Robbins recommendation of doubling the system in a decade. And indeed, in some respects they were even more élitist than the university teachers: when asked whether they favoured expanding the non-university forms of higher education rather than the universities (essentially the 'binary' solution) nearly two-thirds of CAT teachers approved this as compared with only half the university teachers (Table A.34).

(*c*) *Attitudes to departmental structure*

We turn now to attitudes in the CATs regarding the structure of academic departments, and in particular to their views on the role of the professor as the chief wielder of power and controller of the department, and on the status of the professoriate as it is affected by the number of professorships available. It would be difficult to know what to predict here, first because a university-type departmental structure was presumably something of an innovation at the CATs, and attitudes might not yet have hardened; and secondly, as regards the power of the professor, most complaints at universities seemed in our interviews to be the result of supposed interference with junior members' research; and it is clear that a lot less research was being done at the CATs, which might have reduced this source of friction. Moreover, as was suggested above and will be shown below (d), the CAT faculty was somewhat more conservative politically than the universities, and we know that conservative political views affect teachers' views in favour of greater professorial power. On the other hand, we saw in section II that there was a considerably smaller proportion of professors at the CATs; and a consequence of this could be both hostility to an unusual concentration of power and a tendency to favour widening the accessibility of professorial status.

TABLE A.17

Attitudes to professorial power, CATs and universities (per cent)

Attitudes to professorial power	*CATs*	*Universities*
Democrats	44	51
Part-democrats	35	32
Non-democrats	21	17
TOTALS	(310)	(1,253)

TABLE A.18

Attitudes to professorial status, CATs and universities (per cent)

Attitudes to professorial status	*CATs*	*Universities*
Levellers	30	39
Moderates	39	40
Elitists	31	21
TOTALS	(369)	(1,360)

In the event, we see (Table A.17) that the CATs were somewhat *less* likely to have 'democratic' views on the power of professors than were the universities; though the difference is not large. Similarly, but more surprisingly, in Table A.18 the CATs were more élitist than the universities. But we have to look more closely at both these findings. In Table A.19 we examine attitudes towards professorial power within categories of political dispositions; and we find that (except on the 'far left' where the same caution should be used as previously), the CATs were still somewhat less 'democratic' than the universities. In other words, their non-democracy presumably derived from some institutional difference, and not merely from the different political make-up of the CATs and universities. It is possible that the 'more royalist than the King' attitude of parvenus played a part here. Table A.20 shows attitudes to professorial status in a similar format. We found in Chapter 14 that political dispositions had only a very small relationship to this question in the universities; and the same seems to be true here for the CATs. In any event, in each category of political disposition CAT teachers still turned out to be somewhat more élitist than their university counterparts.

TABLE A.19

Attitudes to professorial power, CATs and universities, by political position (per cent)

	Political position							
	Far Left		*Left*		*Centre*		*Right*	
Attitudes to professorial power	*CATs*	*Universities*	*CATs*	*Universities*	*CATs*	*Universities*	*CATs*	*Universities*
Democrats	50	74	48	58	41	46	38	35
Part-democrats	36	21	30	28	40	36	38	39
Non-democrats	14	5	22	14	19	18	24	25
TOTALS	(14)	(58)	(119)	(597)	(105)	(343)	(63)	(220)

TABLE A.20

Attitudes to professorial status, CATs and universities, by political position (per cent)

	Political position							
	Far Left		*Left*		*Centre*		*Right*	
Attitudes to professorial status	*CATs*	*Universities*	*CATs*	*Universities*	*CATs*	*Universities*	*CATs*	*Universities*
Levellers	50	43	24	41	36	40	24	34
Moderates	17	42	42	42	38	39	41	38
Elitists	33	15	35	17	26	21	35	28
TOTALS	(18)	(60)	(144)	(636)	(118)	(368)	(74)	(256)

(*d*) *Political views*

We now look at political views directly. The distribution of self-assigned political position and party support are found in Tables

TABLE A.21

Political position CATs and universities (per cent)

Political position	*CATs*	*Universities*
Far Left	6	5
Moderate Left	40	48
Centre	34	28
Moderate Right	19	18
Far Right	1	1
TOTALS	(365)	(1,362)

TABLE A.22

Party support, CATs and universities (per cent)

Party	*CATs*	*Universities*
Labour	41	41
Conservative	27	35
Liberal	24	14
Other	1	1
None	7	8
TOTALS	(350)	(1,306)

A.21 and A.22. In neither case are the differences substantial. The universities show a slightly lower proportion describing themselves as 'centre' and slightly higher as 'moderate left', but the difference is one of only 8 percentage points. Similarly the two groups show an identical amount of support for the Labour party; while the CAT teachers were somewhat less likely to support the Conservatives, and more likely to favour the Liberals. But, as we pointed out earlier, six months separated the two surveys–the last six months of a Conservative government; and it may be that the difference represents a change of opinion in the population, and not an abiding difference between CATs and universities.

(*e*) *Other attitudes–(i) to university teaching*

There are two items in our questionnaire which directly address the educational ideology of the British B.A. degree, one attacking the 'single-subject honours degree' which is the chief emphasis of all the major English universities outside Oxford, Cambridge and the post-war foundations; and the second criticising the philosophy which is thought to lie behind the single-subject degree, that of the 'training of experts' versus the 'education of gentlemen'. On both of these issues the CATs might be expected to have had special views. They were new institutions, and so would not need to be tied to the concept of the single-subject degree to the same degree as the major Redbrick universities, which have invested their energies in it for some years. But at the same time they were very much teaching institutions, and scientific and technical institutions, and presumably would favour the 'training of experts' as an appropriate function for 'technological universities'. It turns out that there was not very much difference on the first issue (Table A.23) between them and the universities. There

TABLE A.23

'Valid criticism of the English universities is that they overemphasise the single-subject honours degree', CATs and universities (per cent)

	CATs		*Universities*	
Strongly agree	17	62	15	59
Agree with reservations	45		44	
Disagree with reservations	32		29	
Strongly disagree	6		12	
TOTALS	(373)		(1,362)	

TABLE A.24

'University education in Britain puts too little emphasis on the training of experts and too much on the education of widely cultivated men' (per cent)

	CATs		*Universities*	
Strongly agree	7	39	4	30
Agree with reservations	32		26	
Disagree with reservations	48		47	
Strongly disagree	14		23	
TOTALS	(375)		(1,370)	

was rather more disagreement on the second question (Table A.24) where, as expected, the CATs turned out to be noticeably, if not very substantially, more in favour of the training of experts than the universities.

Other attitudes–(ii) to secondary-school teaching and structure

There were also two questions relating to opinions on secondary schools in the questionnaire. The first relates to the topic of 'premature specialisation'–which has long been a favourite complaint of dons, schoolmasters and schoolchildren alike. Indeed, the deploring of premature specialisation has become one of the academic pieties, to be repeated in a ritualistic manner on frequent occasions, without (with some laudable exceptions) any very serious attempt to modify the conditions which require it. It can be seen that three-quarters of our sample of university teachers, and almost the same proportion of CAT teachers, found themselves able to agree with the statement quoted (Table A.25), with or without reservations. This was not a divisive issue.

TABLE A.25

'A serious shortcoming of the present system of secondary education is premature specialisation' (per cent)

	CATs		*Universities*	
Strongly agree	32	73	38	76
Agree with reservations	41		38	
Disagree with reservations	22		20	
Strongly disagree	6		4	
TOTALS	(377)		(1,377)	

The question of comprehensive schools was at the time of our surveys a much more real dispute; but as we saw in Chapter 15 the positions taken on this issue were very closely related to political views; and we have discovered above that politically the CATs and universities were not too different. In any event their views on this subject were almost identical (Table A.26).

V. The 'styles of life' at CAT and university

In this final section of findings we show briefly the responses of CAT teachers to various questions which, while many of them are not closely related to our central concerns, may still help to fill out the picture of academic life for a teacher at a CAT as against one at a university. The first of these (Table A.27) is not directly academic at

TABLE A.26

'The tripartite system . . . should be supplanted by . . . comprehensive schools' (per cent)

	CATs		*Universities*	
Strongly agree	21	58	23	57
Agree with reservations	37		34	
Disagree with reservations	23		26	
Strongly disagree	19		18	
TOTALS	(374)		(1,350)	

TABLE A.27

Per cent of those married to graduate wives (CATs and universities) by age

	Under 30	*30–4*	*35–9*	*40–4*	*45+*
CATs	32 (44)	35 (81)	16 (71)	21 (47)	19 (47)
Universities	47 (176)	41 (222)	45 (253)	41 (173)	41 (339)

all: it relates to the kind of wives that our respondents married, and in particular whether or not they were university graduates. It turns out that there were rather sharp differences, especially among the older teachers. For example, of those over 44, one-fifth of the CAT teachers were married to graduates, and two-fifths of the university teachers. But there was a tendency for the younger teachers at CATs to look more like the university faculty they were shortly to become, in this respect as well as others, and the proportion with graduate wives increased sharply for the two youngest groups. The differences between CAT and university teachers probably derive in part from the lower social origins of the CAT teachers, but more substantially, doubtless, from the fact which we discovered earlier that so many of the latter had held industrial or other non-university jobs, which would provide them with greater chances for exogamy than university lecturers–a large part of whose feminine company is provided by their students.

Turning to the following tables (A.28 and A.29) we see the incidence of leave and travel. In both these categories CAT teachers are

TABLE A.28

Per cent who have ever had a leave of absence (CATs and universities) by subject

	Social science	*Natural science*	*Technology*	*All*
CATs	15 (39)	7 (153)	5 (175)	6 (383)
Universities	34 (208)	22 (404)	10 (178)	26 (1,361)

TABLE A.29

Per cent who have been abroad in the past year (CATs and universities) by subject

	Social science	*Natural science*	*Technology*	*All*
CATs	28 (39)	14 (152)	16 (175)	18 (352)
Universities	41 (222)	33 (410)	24 (178)	36 (1,405)

considerably worse off than their university counterparts. But it is interesting to note that, of all subjects when compared with their opposites *in the same subject*, CAT technologists, relatively speaking, appeared best treated; though this is a rather limited advantage since technology was the least privileged of the main university subject areas.

As for leaving the British university system altogether (Tables A.30

TABLE A.30

Per cent who have considered a post abroad (CATs and universities) by subject

	Social science	*Natural science*	*Technology*	*All*
CATs	18 (38)	33 (153)	32 (175)	31 (382)
Universities	36 (223)	38 (408)	32 (177)	38 (1,398)

and A.31), university teachers seem to have thought of taking a post abroad more often than CAT teachers of the same subject–except for technologists, where the proportions are the same. But when the choice is of leaving academic life anywhere–permanently–for another kind of job, there are no very consistent differences, even though we might have expected that the CAT faculty, so many of whom have been away from the warmth of academia already, would find it easier to face going back into the cold.

Looking at the milder step of applying for a post at another institution or college (Tables A.32 and A.33), we find that, except in social science, CAT teachers are more likely to have applied for a new

TABLE A.31

'Have you ever considered leaving academic life permanently?' (CATs and universities) by subject (per cent)

	Social science		*Natural science*		*Technology*		*All*	
	CAT	*University*	*CAT*	*University*	*CAT*	*University*	*CAT*	*University*
Seriously	20	28	22	20	22	25	21	24
Not seriously	33	24	26	28	28	38	28	28
No	46	48	52	53	50	38	51	49
TOTALS	(39)	(216)	(153)	(400)	(174)	(176)	(382)	(1,354)

TABLE A.32

Per cent who applied for a post last year (CATs and universities) by subject

	Social science	*Natural science*	*Technology*	*All*
CATs	21 (38)	29 (153)	29 (174)	28 (381)
Universities	28 (222)	21 (406)	21 (178)	22 (1,399)

post in the year before they completed the questionnaire (though this could include applying for the job they now hold); while in all subject areas they were less certain they would not want to move in the next three years. Whether this was an expression of discontent with their present jobs or simply of youth and ambition is a matter for speculation.

There is one last item, which could have fitted in our discussion of attitudes towards expansion, but is perhaps equally appropriate here. Respondents were asked (in an admittedly somewhat value-loaded question, which referred to the 'preservation . . . of the essential quality of British university life') whether further provision of higher education should be supplied by expanding the non-university forms of higher education, or by expanding the universities. In view of the CATs' attitudes towards university expansion, which fairly closely resembled those of the universities themselves, one might expect agreement on this question too. And since it is clear that in several ways the CATs are (or were in 1964) the poor relations of the university system, it might well be that they would oppose any continuation of the type of experiment in expansion which turned them into universities. We find, in fact, that they were considerably more strongly opposed to any such 'binary system', as it later came to be called, than the universities (almost two-thirds opposing, compared with half). In other words, although they may, like the universities, have been somewhat élitist in terms of the students they would admit, they were not so selective with regard to institutional admission and promotion. And this in turn implies a certain degree of self-approval.

VI. The future

At this transitional moment in their history, the CATs were a peculiar phenomenon–'universities-designate' under the U.G.C., with the

TABLE A.33

'Do you expect to apply for a post at another institution in the next three years?' (CATs and universities) by subject (per cent)

Expect to apply	*Social science*		*Natural science*		*Technology*		*All*	
	CAT	*University*	*CAT*	*University*	*CAT*	*University*	*CAT*	*University*
Certainly not	22	41	24	35	26	34	25	40
Probably not	46	32	40	35	42	34	41	32
Probably yes	22 } 33	17 } 27	28 } 37	18 } 31	22 } 32	26 } 32	24 } 34	18 } 28
Certainly yes	11	10	9	13	10	6	10	10
TOTALS	(37)	(219)	(149)	(404)	(171)	(172)	(372)*	(1,376)*

* See note to Table A. 4.

understanding that they were now to be treated, and to behave, like full universities 'on the academic gold-standard', but still with a substantial legacy from their past as local technical colleges, and a lot of leeway to make up. Some problems, such as the low proportion of senior ranks, and the relative lack of research facilities and such perquisites as leave and travel opportunities, are not hard to remedy, even in a relatively stable institutional pecking-order like Britain's, granted a fair allocation of funds and determined leadership within the institutions. And some of the changes we detected in the younger age groups show that these problems are being attacked. But there are more intractable problems; and chief among these is the residue of staff from earlier years. In terms of the typology developed in Chapter

TABLE A.34

'The essential quality of British university life should be preserved by expanding the non-university forms of higher education rather than the universities' (CATs and universities) (per cent)

	CATs		*Universities*	
Strongly agree	9		17	
Agree with reservations	28		32	
Disagree with reservations	42	64	33	50
Strongly disagree	22		17	
TOTALS	(369)		(1,366)	

15, a very large proportion of the CAT faculty fall into the élitist-teacher category, perhaps the most unsuitable for what are intended to be flourishing technological universities, which might become the spearhead of the once-promised technological revolution. The best scientists and technologists are clearly those with a strong personal interest in research; and among them élitist-researchers, such as can be found very widely in Britain, can contribute to a country's well-being, far out of proportion to their personal contacts with students. Expansionist-researchers, however, would probably be the best type of faculty members to dominate the CATs, as they do in many great American universities, combining a devotion to high academic achievement (and the prestige that it brings the institution), with a strong commitment in principle to mass higher education. Alternatively, expansionist-teachers could be of great use in a type of

TABLE A.35

Typology of academic orientations: CATs and universities (per cent)

	CATs	*Universities*
Elitist-researchers	12	25
Expansionist-researchers	7	11
Elitist-teachers	56	48
Expansionist-teachers	25	16
TOTALS	(358)	(1316)

institution which was after all primarily intended to train large numbers of technologists. But considering the almost overwhelming emphasis on devotion to teaching rather than research which is at present characteristic both of the CATs and of all academic technology, this might be the greatest danger. For what is clearly needed, and what the CATs were intended to supply, is large numbers not of well-trained technicians, but of scientists and technologists taught to innovate. At the moment of transition the CATs were dominated not just by teachers, but by élitist-teachers; and this majority threatened to set the tone of the institution. As well as funds for research, it would take a major influx of young teachers interested both in large-scale expansion, and in research for its own sake, to fulfil the hopes which the Robbins Committee, and many others, saw in the CATs.

Appendix B

QUESTIONNAIRES

The following is the part of the Robbins Committee's university teacher questionnaire used in this study:

1. Name
2. University
3. Sex: Male
   Female
4. Age at the 31st December, 1961
5. Marital status: Single
   Married with children
   Married without children
6. Post held: (a) Professor
   (b) Reader
   (c) Senior Lecturer
   (d) Lecturer (or college fellow of not less than 3 years standing *not* being Research Fellow)
   (e) Assistant Lecturer (or college fellow of *less* than three years standing not being Research Fellow)
   (f) Demonstrator
   (g) Research post
   (h) Other post (write in)
8. In which Faculty do you primarily work?
9. In which department do you primarily work? (Write in where applicable)
10. What is your main subject?
18. A. First Degree(s)
    If you obtained more than one first degree please answer in respect of each.

Names of First Degree(s) Obtained	Institution at which Obtained	Class* Obtained	Date of Completing Degree Course
One ...			
Two ...			
Three ...			

* If degree taken in more than one part give the class awarded on last part.

B. Higher Degree(s)

Please list all higher degrees other than those for which further study is not required.

	Name of Qualification	Institution at which Obtained	Date of Award
One ...			
Two ...			
Three ...			

19. Please list in chronological order in the manner shown below the sectors in which you have held full-time appointments. In the University sector please give the grade of each full-time post, and the name of the University. For posts in other sectors the name of the post need not be given, and successive posts within one sector should be aggregated.

List of Sectors

A. University: full-time research posts.
B. University: other posts.
C. School teaching.
D. Other teaching.
E. Industry or commerce: research and development.
F. Industry or commerce: other posts.
G. Public Service (including nationalised industries) research and development.
H. Public Service: other posts.
J. Other posts (including military service).

Dates*	Sector (Indicate by Letter)	Length of Time	G.B./ Abroad	Grade (of any University Post)	Name of University

* Please state *month and year* when you took up duties in your present post.

The following is the follow-up questionnaire sent to all available respondents to the Robbins questionnaire:

1. University and/or College
2. University Department (if any)
3. Subject
4. Post (please give exact title of both university and college post)
5. Which of the following opinions concerning the number of students in the university system as a whole lies closest to your own opinion? In each case please assume that staff and resources are made available
   (a) We should double the numbers or more in the next decade
   (b) We should increase the numbers about 50 per cent in the next decade
   (c) We should increase the numbers about 25 per cent in the next decade
   (d) I think that the number of students admitted to universities should remain about where it is now
6. Do you feel that the expansion that has already taken place over the past decade has affected the quality of students admitted to your university in your subject?
   (a) It has lowered the average level of ability of my students very considerably in recent years
   (b) It has lowered the average level of my students to some extent in recent years

(c) It hasn't changed the quality of my students appreciably
(d) The average level of ability of my students has risen in recent years

7. Do you think that CATs ought to be given university status?
Yes No
8. Do you think that the number of new places in the university system in *your subject* should be expanded in the next decade?
   (a) No
   (b) Yes, but under 25 per cent
   (c) Yes, between 25 per cent and 75 per cent
   (d) Yes, over 75 per cent
9. Most of the new universities established since the war have been located in small town or rural areas. Are you in favour of that policy, or do you favour locating new universities in the large cities?
   (a) I favour locating new universities in small towns and/or rural areas
   (b) I favour locating new universities in the large cities
10. Here are some proportions of the relevant age group entering universities and other full-time institutions in different countries. Which of these proportions would you like to see in Britain? (The Robbins Report recommends raising the present proportion of 8·5 per cent to 17 per cent by 1980.)
    40 per cent or more 20 per cent or more 5 per cent or less
    30 per cent or more 10 per cent or more
11. If the number of students doubled in the next decade with the same staff/student ratio, what would you expect to be the effect on the quality of graduates in your subject from your university?
    (a) Marked deterioration (c) No change
    (b) Some deterioration (d) An improvement
12. Do you think your present university as it is now organised is:
    Too big About right Too small

(Questions 13 to 16 concern departments. If you do not belong to a department or equivalent teaching and research unit, please skip to Question 17.)

13. Do you think your present department is:
    Too big About right Too small
14. In its quality as a whole, how would you say your department

stands in relation to departments in the same subject at other British universities?

Much higher than average
Higher than average
About average
Lower than average
Much lower than average

15. How does the general reputation of your department in the academic world compare with your assessment of its quality as a whole?
    (a) It has a better reputation than it deserves
    (b) It has the reputation it deserves
    (c) It has a lower reputation than it deserves
16. Compared with similar departments in other British universities would you describe your department as above, below or average in the following respects? Above average, average, below average.
    Its teaching of undergraduates
    Its training of post-graduate students
    The research and scholarship carried on by its staff
    Its size and breadth of coverage of the field
    Its responsiveness to new ideas
17. Do your own interests lie primarily in teaching or in research?
    Very heavily in research
    In both, but with a leaning towards research
    In both, but with a leaning towards teaching
18. What are the major handicaps that you experience in carrying on research?
    Insufficient time because of teaching commitments
    Insufficient time because of commitments other than teaching
    Insufficient financial resources
    Slowness of machinery for obtaining equipment and/or books, etc.
    Insufficient contact with other workers in your field
    Insufficiencies in your library
    Unresponsiveness of university administration to your research needs
    Unresponsiveness of your departmental or college administration to your needs
19. Do you feel under pressure to do more research than you would actually like to do?
    Yes, a lot   Yes, a little   No

20. Apart from time, are the resources available to you (library, literary facilities, etc.) adequate for the kind of scholarly or scientific research you are doing?
    Excellent Somewhat inadequate
    Adequate Highly inadequate
21. Are you able to carry on research during term?
    A substantial part of it Only a little of it Almost none
22. Have you ever had a leave of absence for a term or more while on the staff of any British university? Yes No
    If yes: What kind of leave?
    Paid or partly paid sabbatical leave
    Unpaid leave of absence
    Paid or partly paid leave of absence
23. If you have had such a leave:
    (a) How recent was the latest?
    (b) Was it from your present university?
    (c) What was its duration?
    (d) Where did you spend it?
    (e) What did you do during your leave?
24. Do you expect to remain at your present university until you retire?
    Definitely yes Probably no Don't know
    Probably yes Definitely no
25. In general, how do you feel about your present university?
    It is a very good place for me
    It is a fairly good place for me
    It is not a good place for me
26. Is there any other British university in which you would prefer to hold a post roughly equivalent to the one you hold here?
    Yes No Don't know
    If yes, which one (if more than one, give highest preference)?
27. Have you applied for a post (including your present post) within the last year? Yes No
28. Do you anticipate that you will be applying for a post at another university in the next three years?
    Almost certainly will not Probably will
    Probably will not Almost certainly will
29. How would you view an opportunity to join the staff of one of the new universities at a higher rank?
    I would not consider going to any of them
    I might go to some but not to others

I would accept an offer at almost any of them
I already hold a chair at my present university

30. How would you view an opportunity to join the staff of one of the new universities at your present rank?
    I would not consider going to any of them
    I might go to some but not to others
    I would accept an offer at almost any of them
31. Do you like the city or town in which your university is located?
    Strong liking — Moderate dislike
    Moderate liking — Strong dislike
32. (i) Since taking a university post in the United Kingdom, have you ever seriously considered accepting a permanent post in a university abroad? Yes No
    (ii) *If yes*, where have you considered going?
    Canada
    Australia or New Zealand — Africa
    United States — Somewhere else (specify)
33. Which of the following university posts would be most attractive to you personally? (Would you mark them 1, 2, 3, 4 in order of preference?)
    University Lecturer and College Fellow at Cambridge
    Professor at Brighton
    Professorial head of a department at Leeds
    Reader in the University of London
34. (FOR THOSE BELOW THE RANK OF PROFESSOR)
    How likely do you think it is that you will eventually be appointed to a Chair at your present university?
    Almost certainly — Almost certainly not — Possibly, but not probable
    Quite probably — Not applicable
35. (FOR THOSE BELOW THE RANK OF PROFESSOR)
    How likely do you think it is that you will eventually be offered a Chair in a British university?
    Already offered — Possibly but not probably
    Almost certainly — Almost certainly not
    Quite probably
36. (FOR THOSE BELOW THE RANK OF PROFESSOR)
    Do you think of yourself as more or less likely than other university teachers of your age and rank to be offered a Chair eventually?
    Already offered — About the same
    More likely — Less likely

37. (FOR ASSISTANT LECTURERS AND LECTURERS)
    Do you expect to be offered a Senior Lectureship or Readership?
    Already offered   In 10 years or more
    Within 5 years   Never
    In 5–10 years
38. Since gaining your first academic appointment, have you ever seriously considered leaving academic life permanently?
    Yes, have given it serious consideration
    Yes, considered it, but not seriously
    No
39. Have you ever held office in a national or international academic, learned or professional society?   Yes   No
40. How many academic articles have you published?
    None   5 to 10   More than 20
    1 to 4   10 to 20   Year latest article was published
41. Have you written a book which was published?
    (a) Yes
    (b) No
    (c) If yes, how many
    (d) Year latest book was published
42. Are you preparing a book for publication?   Yes   No
43. How do you keep in touch with current and recent work in your subject? Please indicate the importance to you of the following methods–Very important, fairly important, not important
    Reading journals and/or bulletins
    Newsletter and information bulletins
    Offprints sent to you by colleagues in British universities
    Conversation with department colleagues
    Conversation with colleagues in your subject at other British universities
    Correspondence
44. Have you been abroad for primarily professional and scholarly reasons during the past 12 months?   Yes   No
    If yes, how many times?
45. How much do you enjoy each of the following of your present university activities?   Very much, moderately, very little
    Teaching   Research
    Contact with students   Discussions with colleagues
    Administration and policy making in the university (college) and department

46. Are you pleased with having chosen your present subject?
    Yes No
47. Are you sometimes regretful that you did not choose to work in another academic field? Yes No
48. Are there any public activities outside your university duties that take up an appreciable amount of your time? Yes No
    If yes, what are they?
49. Please indicate your agreement or disagreement with the following opinions: Strongly agree, agree with reservations, disagree with reservations, strongly disagree
    (i) An academic man's first loyalty should be to research in his discipline. The teaching of students and the running of his university should be second to this first duty of an academic career
    (ii) University education in Britain puts too little emphasis on the training of experts and too much on the education of widely cultivated men
    (iii) Valid criticism of the English universities is that they over-emphasise the single-subject honours degree
    (iv) A professorship ought to be part of the normal expectation of an academic career and not a special attainment of a minority of university teachers
    (v) A university department with more than eight members of staff should have more than one member of professorial rank
    (vi) Most university teachers of my subject put too much emphasis on teaching compared with research
    (vii) Promotion in academic life is too dependent on published work and too little on devotion to teaching
    (viii) A serious disadvantage of Redbrick universities is that all too often they are run by a professorial oligarchy
    (ix) Most British university departments would be better run by the method of circulating chairmanship than by a permanent Head of Department
    (x) The tripartite system of grammar, modern and technical schools should be supplanted by a system of comprehensive schools
    (xi) A serious shortcoming of the present system of secondary education is premature specialisation
    (xii) The essential quality of British university life should be

preserved by expanding the non-university forms of higher education rather than the universities

(xiii) In order to do full justice to his position, an academic man has to subordinate all aspects of his life to his work

50. 'The general balance of university studies in Britain is such that the following faculties are given insufficient support'. Mark the faculties to which, in your opinion, this statement applies:

Pure science / Medicine
Arts / Technology
Law / Social sciences

51. In the general pattern of British university education do you feel that your own subject receives:

Less support than it deserves
About as much support as it deserves
More support than it deserves

52. How interested are you in politics?

Extremely interested / Only slightly interested
Moderately interested / Not interested

53. What Party have you generally supported?

Labour / Liberal / None
Conservative / Other

54. Where would you place yourself in the following political spectrum?

Far Left / Centre / Far Right / Moderate Left / Moderate Right

55. (i) What is (was) your father's occupation? Please be as specific as possible: for example, if a teacher, at what level of education?
(ii) Is (was) he self-employed or an employee?

56. In what religious denomination were you brought up?

57. What is your present denomination?

58. Do you consider yourself:

Deeply religious / Largely indifferent to religion
Moderately religious / Basically opposed to religion

59. What was the age at which your parents left school?

	Mother	*Father*
13 or younger		
14		
15		
16		
17		

18 or older
don't know

60. Did either have any higher education?

	Mother	*Father*
University (where)		
Other higher education (kind)		

61. Is your wife a university graduate? Yes No
62. In what kind of school did you get the major part of your secondary education?

Grammar	None
Direct-grant	Other (specify)
Public school (which)	

63. Do you have any children of secondary school age or older?
Yes No *If yes,* what kinds of schools are they attending or did they attend?
Age
Sex
Type of secondary education
Type of further education. If university, which?

The questionnaire sent to teachers at the CATs and Sussex contained the items both from the Robbins study and from our own questionnaire.

Appendix C

RESEARCH OPERATIONS AND THE SAMPLE

The inquiry began in 1963 with a series of interviews, long and open-ended, among university teachers at the Universities of Birmingham, Cambridge, the London School of Economics, Reading, Leicester and Edinburgh. Altogether 114 university teachers were interviewed in 1963. These interviews, which averaged two to three hours in length, were recorded on tape and then transcribed in full. The teachers who were interviewed were chosen to provide a roughly representative sample of all academic ranks and subjects.

The next step was to base a national questionnaire on the interview material. For this purpose we negotiated with the Robbins Committee to re-survey the one-in-five sample of university teachers surveyed by them in 1962 (the results of the original Robbins Survey are in Appendix III of the Report of the Committee on Higher Education). The number of people in the original Robbins sample was 3,498 of whom 3,098 had responded. Of this 3,098 we in fact approached 2,865, the rest having had their identification erased on a random basis in order that the Robbins questionnaires could be shown to interested parties.

A questionnaire, reported in Appendix B, was developed during 1963, in part on the basis of the intensive open-ended interviews we have described. This questionnaire was informally pre-tested and revised a number of times. With the questionnaire in hand, our follow-up inquiry was launched in April 1964 with a circular letter asking the original respondents to indicate their willingness or unwillingness to be re-surveyed. Those who were willing to participate further were then sent the questionnaire in April and May of 1964. The response rate on this main follow-up inquiry was as follows: the sample 2,865, questionnaires returned 1,408; proportion of questionnaires returned 49 per cent. Proportion of questionnaires returned, subtracting from the original table those who had in the meantime died, retired or were absent abroad, 51 per cent.

A comparison of the Robbins population and sample and the Achieved Follow-up sample will give some basis for a judgment of the representativeness of the latter.

Grade of university sample* (per cent)

Grade	*Total population*	*Robbins achieved sample*	*Follow-up achieved sample*
Professors	11·5	12·7	12·1
Readers	6·5	6·2	6·5
Senior lecturers and lecturers	58·0	60·9	65·8
Assistant lecturers and demonstrators	12·3	12·3	9·8
Research staff	6·0	5·5	4·1
Other grades	5·7	2·4	1·6
All grades	100·0	100·0	100·0
Numbers	14,849	3,006	1,408

* The first two columns are from *Higher Education*, Appendix Three, Table W.7, p. 229.

Our achieved sample somewhat undersamples the lower grades, and especially the 'other grades' who are probably most mobile and difficult to reach. We do not introduce these 'other grades' anywhere into the analysis; elsewhere we do not believe the differences in these distributions distort the relationships we uncover or our interpretations of them.

We made a closer comparison of the *joint* age-grade distribution of the Robbins sample with the follow-up achieved sample.[1] The fit remains very close within most cells. Again we undersampled the youngest men in the marginal academic positions. But again we have no reason to believe that the pattern of response to our questionnaire produced findings which would not have been true for the whole population or for Robbins' achieved sample.

In 1965 a decision was made to extend the follow-up inquiry to include a new university (Sussex) and three Colleges of Advanced Technology (Salford, Birmingham and Brunel). The Sussex questionnaires went out in April 1965 to every member of the faculty who had

[1] The comparison was with *Higher Education*, Appendix Three, Table 31, p. 33.

not already filled in a questionnaire through having been a member of some other university and included in the main sample. The total number distributed to teachers at Sussex was 180, and 134 completed questionnaires were returned, a response rate of 74 per cent.

The extended survey of the CATs took place in November and December of 1964. The numbers involved were as follows:

	Total number of faculty	*Questionnaires returned*
Salford	289	168
Birmingham	267	143
Brunel	128	72

These figures give a total of 383 returned questionnaires representing a response rate of 56 per cent, i.e., 56 per cent for Brunel, 53 per cent for Birmingham and 58 per cent for Salford.

In the case of Sussex and the three CATs it should be noted that we included the essential information from the original Robbins inquiry as well as our own follow-up questions in a composite questionnaire.

These follow-up questionnaires were coded and punched at Oxford, and analysis began using punched cards in Oxford, with the data transferred to tapes the following year in California.

Appendix D

INDEX CONSTRUCTION, ADDITIONAL TABLES AND NOTES

NOTES TO CHAPTER 11

TABLE 11.32

Opinions on expanding the respondent's own subject

Q.8 'Do you think that the number of new places in the university system in your subject should be expanded in the next decade?'

	Percentage
No	8
Yes, under 25%	31
Yes, between 25% and 75%	42
Yes, over 75%	18
TOTAL	(1,371)

TABLE 11.33

Proportions of sample supporting expansion of system, subject, both or neither

	%
Support significant expansion of system (50% or more) *and* significant expansion of subject (25% or more)	52
Support significant expansion of system but *not* significant expansion of subject	15
Support significant expansion of subject but *not* significant expansion of system	8
Support significant expansion of *neither*	24
TOTAL	(1,348)

APPENDIX D

Table 11.34

Growth of institutions in the British university system, 1938–63

Full-time students: Sources (1938–9) *University Grants Committee Returns* for 1938–9, 1954–5 and 1962–3, *Commonwealth University Yearbooks*, 1957 and 1964.

	1938–9		% *to*	*1954–5*	% *to*	*1962–3*
Birmingham	1,433		119	3,135	52	4,766
Bristol	1,005		165	2,666	37	3,642
Cambridge	5,931		34	7,934	14	9,040
Durham, Durham Colleges	412		167	1,098	62	1,775
Durham, King's College/ University of Newcastle	1,297		117	2,817	47	4,145
Exeter	422		111	889	98	1,763
Hull	—*			727	167	1,942
Leeds	1,757		93	3,398	64	5,561
Leicester	—*			638	170	1,724
Liverpool	2,055		42	2,919	62	4,738
London	13,191		38	18,201	24	22,644
Manchester	2,108	} 2,462	88	4,637	62	7,515
Manchester College of Technology	354	}				
Nottingham	582		255	2,066	36	2,814
Oxford	5,023		43	7,187	22	8,803
Reading	584		90	1,110	59	1,764
Sheffield	767		162	2,010	75	3,524
Southampton	268		310	1,100	72	1,892
North Staffordshire	—			520	64	852
Sussex	—			—		434
England	37,189		70	63,052	42	89,338
Aberystwyth	663		65	1,096	63	1,787
Bangor	485		73	839	88	1,576
Cardiff	970		51	1,467	51	2,221
Swansea	488		68	821	129	1,877
Welsh National School of Medicine	173		40	242	—35	157
Wales	2,779		61	4,472†	70	7,618
England and Wales	39,968		69	67,524	44	96,956
Aberdeen	1,211		36	1,652	48	2,445
Edinburgh	3,205		44	4,608	46	6,710
Glasgow	4,175		14	4,748	23	5,860
Glasgow R.T.C.	515		155	1,315	51	1,988
St. Andrews/Dundee	928		96	1,820	67	3,044
Scotland	10,034		41	14,143	42	20,047
TOTALS	50,002		63	81,667	43	117,003‡

* Not then supported by U.G.C.

† Disparity in A.U.B.C.'s own figures.

‡ There is a disparity of approximately 1 per cent between this (A.U.B.C.) total and the Robbins Committee's total for this year of 118,400.

Index of apprehension

Items: Q. 6 'Do you feel that the expansion that has already taken place over the past decade has affected the quality of students admitted to your university in your subject?' ('Ability lowered considerably' or 'Ability lowered to some extent' coded 0, 'No appreciable change' or 'Ability has risen' coded 1.)

Q.11 'If the number of students doubled in the next decade with the same staff/student ratio, what would you expect to be the effect on the quality of graduates in your subject from your university?' ('Marked deterioration' or 'Some deterioration' coded 0, 'No change' or 'An improvement' coded 1.)

TABLE 11.35

Index of apprehension

Score	*Number*	%
0 ('highly apprehensive')	247	19
1 ('somewhat apprehensive')	632	49
2 ('not apprehensive')	413	32
TOTAL 1,292: 116 cases, or 8% of the sample, were not scored.		

TABLE 11.36

Index of apprchension by political position (per cent)

	Political position			
Index of apprehension	*Far Left*	*Moderate Left*	*Centre*	*Right*
Highly apprehensive	11	14	22	27
Somewhat apprehensive	33	49	46	56
Not apprehensive	56	37	32	16
TOTALS	(54)	(598)	(353)	(245)

TABLES 11.37–11.39

Opinions regarding university expansion by degree of apprehension, within categories of political position (per cent)

	Political position											
	Far Left			*Moderate Left*			*Centre*			*Right*		
	Not apprehensive	*Somewhat apprehensive*	*Highly apprehensive*	*Not apprehensive*	*Somewhat apprehensive*	*Highly apprehensive*	*Not apprehensive*	*Somewhat apprehensive*	*Highly apprehensive*	*Not apprehensive*	*Somewhat apprehensive*	*Highly apprehensive*
11.37 *Proportion of age group*												
30%+	59	18	34	24	14	9	10	5	5	15	7	2
20%+	33	35	17	44	44	36	45	39	25	44	32	26
Less than 20%	8	47	50	32	41	55	45	55	70	41	62	72
11.38 *CATs university status*												
Yes	97	65	83	90	77	69	84	62	53	58	50	38
11.39 *Expansion of places in own subject*												
No	7 } 21	22 } 39	33 } 50	3 } 18	6 } 39	16 } 55	6 } 27	7 } 35	13 } 55	8 } 31	12 } 54	12 } 64
Under 25%	14	17	17	15	33	39	21	38	42	23	42	52
25%–75%	25	33	17	44	46	40	47	44	37	50	43	30
75%+	52	28	33	38	16	6	26	11	8	20	4	6
TOTALS (vary slightly)	(29)	(18)	(6)	(217)	(289)	(83)	(111)	(157)	(78)	(40)	(134)	(67)

TABLE 12.35

Publication of books by publication of articles, within subject categories (per cent)

Number of books	Arts: Number of articles					Social science: Number of articles					Natural science: Number of articles				
	0	1–4	5–10	10–20	20+	0	1–4	5–10	10–20	20+	0	1–4	5–10	10–20	20+
0	76	73	51	29	14	81	76	54	40	21	100*	97	87	78	53
1	18	15	32	30	17	15	19	24	19	12	0	3	10	18	26
2	3	8	8	23	17	0	4	15	15	17	0	0	3	2	11
3+	3	4	8	18	53	4	2	7	26	50	0	0	0	2	10
TOTALS	(38)	(93)	(84)	(66)	(72)	(26)	(54)	(46)	(47)	(42)	(9)	(73)	(91)	(80)	(151)

Number of books	Technology: Number of articles					Medicine: Number of articles				
	0	1–4	5–10	10–20	20+	0	1–4	5–10	10–20	20+
0	100*	96	87	75	58	100*	100*	89	71	55
1	0	4	9	21	29	0	0	5	23	24
2	0	0	0	4	4	0	0	5	3	12
3+	0	0	4	0	8	0	0	0	3	8
TOTALS	(16)	(57)	(53)	(28)	(24)	(3)	(10)	(19)	(35)	(74)

* N's too small to be reliable: presented for completeness only.

APPENDIX D

Index of research orientation

Items: Q.17 Do your own interests lie primarily in teaching or in research? ('Very heavily in research' coded 0, 'Both, but leaning to research' coded 1, 'Both, but leaning to teaching' coded 2, 'Very heavily in teaching' (CATs and Sussex only) coded 2.)

Q.49(i) An academic man's first loyalty should be to research in his discipline. The teaching of students and the running of his university should be second to this first duty of an academic career. (Trichotomized: 'Strongly agree' or 'Agree with reservations' coded 0, 'Disagree with reservations' coded 1, 'Strongly disagree' coded 2.)

TABLE 12.36

Index of research orientation

	Score	*N*	%
Research	0	84	6
	1	372	28
	2	340	25
	3	366	27
Teaching	4	172	13
		1,334	

74 cases (5% of sample) not scored.

NOTES TO CHAPTER 13

Note on preference for particular universities

Our sample were asked about the kind of post that they would accept if offered them, or would prefer if they were given a choice. The first of these questions referred specifically to the new universities, and the second offered four different jobs at different institutions.[1] In some ways it may be more revealing to regard these questions as describing for us the character of the posts offered, rather than, as has been our

[1] These are Question 29–30 and 33 in Appendix B.

TABLE 13.53

Research orientation by class of first degree and subject taught (per cent)

	Arts				Social science				Natural science				Technology			
Orientation	*I*	*II(i)*	*Un-div. II*	*Pass/ Un-class.*	*I*	*II(i)*	*Un-div. II*	*Pass/ Un-class.*	*I*	*II(i)*	*Un-div. II*	*Pass/ Un-class.*	*I*	*II(i)*	*Un-div. II*	*Pass/ Un-class.*
Research	32	50	33	48	24	21	14	33	38	34	43	29	27	38	30	21
Both	26	16	18	12	19	24	33	20	30	36	32	29	20	12	27	43
Teaching	42	34	49	40	56	55	53	47	32	31	25	42	53	50	42	36
TOTALS	(181)	(44)	(45)	(25)	(94)	(42)	(36)	(15)	(204)	(59)	(60)	(24)	(85)	(24)	(33)	(14)

TABLE 13.54

Aspects of leave by research orientation and subject taught (per cent)

	Arts			Social science			Natural science			Medicine		
Latest leave	*Re-search*	*Both*	*Teach-ing*	*Re-search*	*Both*	*Teach-ing*	*Re-search*	*Both*	*Teach-ing*	*Re-search*	*Both*	*Teach-ing*
Before 1959–60	49	58	49	20	14	28	48	38	17	28	12	*
1960 or 1961	23	16	14	40	71	47	17	21	33	28	47	*
1962 or after	29	26	38	40	14	25	36	41	40	44	41	*
TOTALS	(35)	(31)	(37)	(20)	(21)	(32)	(42)	(28)	(15)	(18)	(17)	(6)

* N's too small to be reliable.

procedure previously, describing the implications of the question in advance, and trying to derive from the results statements about the characteristics of researchers and teachers. Regarding the new universities, at the time of the survey Sussex was the only new university with a sizeable faculty, and may then have been regarded as more typical of the new universities than it is thought now, especially since the next two new universities, Norwich and York, resembled Sussex in their emphasis on undergraduate teaching. But even then there were differences between them, and the questionnaire allowed for this with the possible answer 'I might go to some, but not to others.' Thus it is not easy to interpret the results of these tables. Table 13.57 offers the possibility of going to a new university at a higher rank, broken by subject and research orientation; Table 13.59 asks about taking a post at a new university at the same rank as at present. Tables 13.58 and 13.60 are the corresponding tables broken by age instead of subject.

Table 13.57 shows that researchers in arts would be relatively reluctant to go even at a higher rank. At Sussex, certainly, and quite largely at other new universities, the brunt of curricular reform and improved teaching has been borne by the arts and to a lesser extent the social science faculties or schools, and it is clear that arts researchers are aware of this in the comparatively high proportion who would not consider any new university. This does not altogether hold true for social science and natural science, but in both of these areas there is a higher proportion of teachers than of researchers who would accept at almost any. There is no clear pattern in technology and medicine.

Table 13.58 is obscure; in nearly every age group the two extremes of teachers and researchers resemble each other more than they do the intermediate group. But above the age of 35 a general trend seems to emerge, namely that as before researchers are relatively distrustful of the new universities, and teachers find them more attractive.

In Table 13.59 we find that very few academic men in any subject area, whether researchers or teachers, would consider going to almost any new university at the same rank. We are left to compare those who would consider some (unspecified) universities with those who would not consider any. In arts and social science especially, and also in natural science, researchers once again prove much more unwilling than teachers to contemplate going to a new university. In technology and medicine there is no real difference.

TABLES 13.55 AND 13.56

Aspects of leave by research orientation and subject taught (per cent)

13.55	Arts			Social science			Natural science			Medicine		
Leave spent where:	*Research*	*Both*	*Teaching*	*Research*	*Both*	*Teaching*	*Research*	*Both*	*Teaching*	*Research*	*Both*	*Teaching*
At home	26	30	26	12	5	10	15	12	0	11	0	*
Elsewhere in Great Britain	6	7	12	18	5	23	3	8	6	6	6	*
America	35	41	29	35	47	39	69	48	62	67	69	*
Western Europe	13	11	21	6	5	19	5	8	6	6	0	*
Africa	3	7	3	12	5	6	0	4	6	0	12	*
Asia	3	0	6	0	21	0	3	0	6	0	6	*
Eastern Europe, U.S.S.R.	3	4	3	12	5	3	0	0	0	0	0	*
Middle East	6	0	0	0	0	0	3	8	12	6	6	*
Australia, N. Zealand	3	0	0	6	5	0	3	12	0	6	0	*
TOTALS	(31)	(27)	(34)	(17)	(19)	(31)	(39)	(25)	(16)	(18)	(16)	(6)

13.56 *How was leave spent?*	Arts			Social science			Natural science			Medicine		
	Research	*Both*	*Teaching*	*Research*	*Both*	*Teaching*	*Research*	*Both*	*Teaching*	*Research*	*Both*	*Teaching*
Full-time research	47	48	59	61	37	44	68	65	44	39	38	*
Teaching, visiting professor	32	31	14	17	21	16	12	15	19	17	19	*
Touring, teaching, visiting several universities	9	3	14	0	11	12	12	8	19	22	25	*
Other	11	17	14	22	32	28	8	12	19	22	19	*
TOTALS	(34)	(29)	(37)	(18)	(19)	(32)	(40)	(26)	(16)	(18)	(16)	(6)

* N's too small to be reliable.

TABLE 13.57

Would consider going to new university at higher rank? by subject and research orientation (per cent)

New university at higher rank?	Arts Re-search	Arts Both	Arts Teach-ing	Social science Re-search	Social science Both	Social science Teach-ing	Natural science Re-search	Natural science Both	Natural science Teach-ing	Technology Re-search	Technology Both	Technology Teach-ing	Medicine Re-search	Medicine Both	Medicine Teach-ing
I would not consider any	26	21	18	15	9	15	16	11	15	16	7	14	13	14	34
Might some, not others	47	55	56	60	52	48	65	60	57	66	63	66	52	46	38
Accept at almost any	11	4	14	13	22	22	9	18	19	12	10	14	17	11	28
Already hold Chair	15	17	9	13	15	15	10	11	9	6	20	5	15	30	0
TOTALS	(123)	(71)	(138)	(47)	(46)	(110)	(146)	(114)	(117)	(50)	(41)	(85)	(60)	(37)	(32)

TABLE 13.58

Would consider going to new university at higher rank? by age and research orientation (per cent)

New university at higher rank?	Under 30 Re-search	Under 30 Both	Under 30 Teach-ing	30–4 Re-search	30–4 Both	30–4 Teach-ing	35–9 Re-search	35–9 Both	35–9 Teach-ing	40–4 Re-search	40–4 Both	40–4 Teach-ing	45+ Re-search	45+ Both	45+ Teach-ing
I would not consider any	9	4	8	15	5	13	21	7	8	21	7	14	27	27	28
Might some, not others	71	71	71	71	80	67	57	61	60	56	51	60	27	36	39
Accept at almost any	19	25	19	10	7	19	17	20	24	7	16	15	7	7	14
Already hold Chair	0	0	0	3	4	0	5	12	7	17	27	8	36	29	18
TOTALS	(101)	(48)	(59)	(100)	(56)	(89)	(81)	(75)	(120)	(72	(45)	(72)	(91)	(107)	(177)

TABLE 13.59

Would consider going to new university at same rank? by subject and research orientation (per cent)

New university at same rank?	*Arts*			*Social science*			*Natural science*			*Technology*			*Medicine*		
	Re-search	*Both*	*Teach-ing*	*Re-search*	*Both*	*Teach-ing*	*Re-search*	*Both*	*Teach-ing*	*Re-search*	*Both*	*Teach-ing*	*Re-search*	*Both*	*Teach-ing*
I would not consider any	72	66	54	70	61	47	63	49	59	64	49	65	70	78	69
Might some, not others	25	32	42	30	35	45	36	49	37	32	46	32	25	19	28
Would to almost any	3	0	3	0	2	7	1	2	3	2	5	2	3	0	3
TOTALS	(123)	(71)	(138)	(47)	(46)	(110)	(146)	(114)	(117)	(50)	(41)	(85)	(60)	(37)	(32)

TABLE 13.60

Would consider going to new university at same rank? by age and research orientation (per cent)

New university at same rank?	*Under 30*			*30–4*			*35–9*			*40–4*			*45+*		
	Re-search	*Both*	*Teach-ing*	*Re-search*	*Both*	*Teach-ing*	*Re-search*	*Both*	*Teach-ing*	*Re-search*	*Both*	*Teach-ing*	*Re-search*	*Both*	*Teach-ing*
I would not consider any	52	42	44	69	59	47	75	65	61	74	56	57	67	65	65
Might some, not others	44	58	51	30	41	49	22	29	36	24	38	39	29	33	28
Would to almost any	3	0	3	1	0	3	2	4	3	1	4	4	3	0	5
TOTALS	(101)	(48)	(59)	(100)	(56)	(89)	(81)	(75)	(120)	(72)	(45)	(72)	(91)	(107)	(177)

Table 13.60 gives the variation within age categories. In every category researchers are less willing than teachers to think of taking a post in a new university. And once again (compare Table 13.18) it is in the age category 30–34 that the biggest difference is to be found between teachers and researchers. The difference is small for those under 30 (and they are also the group most willing to go to a new university at the same rank, perhaps because they could hardly expect at that age to be promoted above the lecturer grade); it is largest for the 30–34 group; from 35–39 and 40–44 it is smaller again and has almost disappeared in those over 45, who are however consistently unenthusiastic.

These data suggest something about the general view of the new universities from within the university system. They seem to have the reputation which we described above, of being, more than other places, teaching institutions. Research-minded men at the time of the survey tended to avoid them, particularly in the years when they had their reputations to make by a large research output: and teachers were more attracted by them. The teaching emphasis is evidently seen as strongest in the arts and social sciences, but is present also in natural science. (It is perhaps not significant that the same results were not found in technology and medicine, since at the time of the questionnaire no new university had departments in either of these fields.)

Our final question in this field of academic aspirations provided a list of four positions, each of which would have very different responsibilities. Respondents were asked to choose which would be most attractive to them. They were a university lecturer and college fellow at Cambridge, a professor at Brighton, a professorial head of department at Leeds, and a reader in the University of London.

In Table 13.61, among arts men the Cambridge post is particularly favoured, and more so by researchers than by teachers. Researchers also are relatively attracted by the London readership; while the Brighton professorship appeals to all groups roughly equally, and the Leeds post, though not attractive to many, is more so to teachers than to researchers. In social science Cambridge again appeals to the largest proportion, but not differently to teachers and researchers. The former favour a Brighton professorship, and the latter are much more attracted by the London readership. In natural science it is the Leeds post that appeals most to researchers, and Brighton to teachers, while a London readership is not attractive to any groups, and

TABLE 13.61

Which university post would be most attractive to you? by subject and research orientation (per cent)

Which post preferred?	Arts			Social science			Natural science			Technology			Medicine		
	Re-search	Both	Teach-ing	Re-search	Both	Teach-ing	Re-search	Both	Teach-ing	Re-search	Both	Teach-ing	Re-search	Both	Teach-ing
University Lecturer and College Fellow at Cambridge	42	40	36	35	22	37	35	41	33	30	11	28	10	23	33
Professor at Brighton	21	18	23	20	38	37	30	33	43	20	53	31	23	36	27
Professorial Head of Department at Leeds	9	12	19	12	13	13	24	20	15	34	21	29	46	31	24
Reader in the University of London	26	25	21	31	22	10	9	5	8	12	13	14	21	15	15
TOTALS	(116)	(67)	(132)	(49)	(45)	(101)	(142)	(111)	(111)	(50)	(38)	(78)	(61)	(39)	(33)

TABLE 13.62

Which university post would be most attractive to you? by age and research orientation (per cent)

Which post preferred?	Under 30			30–4			35–9			40–4			45+		
	Re-search	Both	Teach-ing	Re-search	Both	Teach-ing	Re-search	Both	Teach-ing	Re-search	Both	Teach-ing	Re-search	Both	Teach-ing
University Lecturer and College Fellow at Cambridge	31	32	31	29	12	34	27	20	26	28	40	37	53	49	40
Professor at Brighton	27	45	29	29	32	32	23	43	46	30	33	26	17	26	29
Professorial Head of Department at Leeds	25	11	16	30	33	25	26	24	20	19	12	21	18	14	19
Reader in the University of London	18	11	24	15	23	11	26	16	11	23	16	18	12	10	13
TOTALS	(99)	(44)	(58)	(101)	(57)	(85)	(78)	(76)	(114)	(69)	(43)	(68)	(77)	(97)	(161)

Cambridge is so to all. Technology is confused by the rather odd preferences of the middle group, but the trend such as it is seems to resemble natural science in that researchers single out Leeds differentially, and teachers Brighton. In medicine researchers favour Leeds and London, teachers Cambridge.

This table provides an interesting background to Tables 12.20 and 12.21 which showed the effect of combinations of university group and subject and rank on research orientations. From the examples here we learn first that a Cambridge post is more attractive to many university men even than a professorship elsewhere, and that it attracts both researchers and teachers more or less equally (except in medicine). Evidently it is possible to use the same post at Cambridge as a place from which either to conduct research using all the facilities of a large university, or to take advantage of its tradition of intensive undergraduate teaching. A professorship at Brighton is seen as primarily a teaching post by social scientists and natural scientists; but the other subjects do not define it so clearly in this way. The post of professorial head of a department at Leeds clearly implies an emphasis on teaching to arts men, but natural scientists, technologists and those in medicine obviously feel that it is a good place for research. This may very well represent a genuine difference between different subjects at Leeds in their emphasis on and capacity for research. Lastly the London readership is seen as offering good opportunities for research by arts, medicine, and particularly social science, while natural science and technology simply do not find it attractive.[1]

NOTES TO CHAPTER 14

Index of attitudes to professorial power

Items: Q.49(ix) 'Most British university departments would be bettern run by the method of circulating chairmanship than by a permanent Head of Department' (Dichotomized: 'Strongly agree' and 'agree with reservations' coded 0, 'disagree with reservations' and 'strongly disagree' coded 1.)

[1] Table 13.62 shows the distribution of preferences among these different posts among teachers and researchers of different ages. (See p. 523.)

APPENDIX D

Q.49(viii) 'A serious disadvantage of Redbrick universities is that all too often they are run by a professorial oligarchy' (Dichotomized: 'Strongly agree' and 'agree with reservations' coded 0, 'disagree with reservations' and 'strongly disagree' coded 1.)

TABLES 14.27–14.30

Percentage who agree (with or without reservations) to each statement, by subject taught

	Social science	*Natural science*	*Technology*	*Arts*
14.27 Q.49(ix) Departments should be run by circulating chairman	70	60	45	55
14.28 Q.49(viii) Most Redbricks are run by professorial oligarchy	88	76	74	77
14.29 Q.49(v) Should be second professor for more than 8 members	79	79	76	76
14.30 Q.49(iv) Professorship should be normal expectation	42	38	39	37
TOTALS (vary slightly)	(210)	(403)	(178)	(350)

TABLE 14.31

Index of attitudes to professorial power

Score		*Number*	%
0	'Democrats'	640	51
1	'Part-democrats'	401	32
2	'Non-democrats'	212	17
	TOTAL	1,253	

155 respondents (or 11% of the sample) could not be scored.

Index of attitudes to professorial status

Items: Q.49(v) 'A university department with more than eight members of staff should have more than one member of professorial rank' (Dichotomized: 'Strongly agree' and 'agree with reservations' coded 1, 'disagree with reservations' and 'strongly disagree' coded 0.)

Q.49(iv) 'A professorship ought to be part of the normal expectation of an academic career and not a special attainment of a minority of university teachers' (Dichotomized: 'Strongly agree' and 'agree with reservations' coded 1, 'disagree with reservations' and 'strongly disagree' coded 0.)

TABLE 14.32

Index of attitudes to professorial status

Score		*Number*	%
0	'Elitists'	280	21
1	'Moderates'	549	40
2	'Levellers'	531	39
	TOTAL	1,360	

48 respondents (or 3% of the sample) could not be scored.

TABLE 14.33

Attitudes towards professorial power, by attitudes towards expansion of the university system (per cent)

Attitudes towards professorial power	*Recommended expansion* Double	50%	25%	*Remain as it is*
Democrats	61	46	46	54
Part-democrats	24	37	33	33
Non-democrats	15	17	21	13
TOTALS	(341)	(497)	(331)	(48)

The indices of cosmopolitanism and localism

The terms 'cosmopolitan' and 'local' were first used by Robert Merton in a study of patterns of influence in a small town. These two types of residents were both clearly influential within their community, but their influence took different forms, and stemmed from different characteristics. The locals were influential because their lives were lived, and all their interests lay, entirely inside the community; while the cosmopolitans were respected because they provided links with the outer world. The terms were taken over and somewhat transformed by Alvin Gouldner, who proposed their use in the analysis of organizations (in the first instance, in the study of an American college). He described cosmopolitanism and localism as 'latent social roles' (latent since they are not formally prescribed or recognized by the organization); and they represent ways of examining the common conflict in an organization between its needs for loyalty and for the expertise which requires an attachment to an outer professional world. Gouldner saw the two as polarities, which were theoretically (and in practice) mutually exclusive. Three factors served to differentiate the types: (i) loyalty to the community or organization – locals high, cosmopolitans low; (ii) commitment to professional skills and values – locals low, cosmopolitans high; (iii) reference group orientation – locals inner, cosmopolitans outer.

We attempted to construct an index which would permit us to locate British university teachers along a dimension of cosmopolitanism-localism. In our initial explorations we discovered that indicators of cosmopolitanism were not highly related to indicators of localism, and we thus began by constructing two indices of, respectively, cosmopolitanism and localism, each of which measured one of the first two of the three factors referred to above. Cosmopolitans were those who showed a high commitment to professional skills: locals those who showed a high loyalty to their own university. The items used were as follows (details of scoring, etc., may be found below):

For cosmopolitanism:

(1) those whose interests lay heavily or mostly in research, as opposed to those whose interests lay mostly in teaching
(2) those who had ever held office in a national or international academic, professional, or learned society
(3) those who had published more than 10 academic articles
(4) those who felt that reading journals or bulletins was a 'very important' way for them to keep in touch with current work in their subject.

For localism:

(1) those who felt their present university or college was 'a very good place for me.'

(2) those who did not anticipate applying for another post in the next three years.

The resulting indices showed no relationship (see below). It was found, however, that while either index separately was useful in analysis, the combination of the two was considerably more powerful: in other words the difference on a variety of dependent variables between 'cosmopolitan-non-locals' and 'non-cosmopolitan-locals' was considerably greater than that between either cosmopolitans and non-cosmopolitans or between locals and non-locals. It was therefore decided to create an index of 'cosmopolitanism-localism' which would combine the two into a less unwieldy form. We describe below the construction of the separate indices for 'cosmopolitanism' and 'localism', and then show how they were combined into the single index of 'cosmopolitanism-localism' that we use in the body of the chapter.

Index of cosmopolitanism

Items: Q.17 'Do your own interests lie primarily in teaching or research?' (Dichotomized: 'Very heavily in research' and 'in both, leaning towards research' scored 1, 'in both, leaning towards teaching' scored 0.)

Q.39 'Have you ever held office in a national or international academic learned or professional society?' ('Yes' scored 1, 'No' scored 0.)

Q.40 'How many academic articles have you published?' (Dichotomized: 'None', '1 to 4' and '5 to 10' scored 0, '10 to 20' and 'more than 20' scored 1.)

Q.43 'How do you keep in touch with current and recent work in your subject? Please indicate the importance to you of the following methods: . . . Reading journals and/or bulletins.' (Dichotomized: 'Very important' scored 1, 'Fairly important' and 'Not important' scored 0.)

Index of localism

Items: Q.25 'In general, how do you feel about your present university (or college)?' ('It is a very good place for me' scored 2, 'It is a fairly good place for me' scored 1, 'It is not a good place for me' scored 0.)

Q.28 'Do you anticipate that you will be applying for a post at another university in the next three years?' (Trichotomized: 'Almost certainly will not' scored 2, 'Probably will not' scored 1, 'Probably will' and 'Almost certainly will' scored 0.)

TABLE 14.34

Cosmopolitanism index

	Non-cosmopolitan . . . . *cosmopolitan*					
	0	*1*	*2*	*3*	*4*	*Total*
Number	35	279	454	341	211	1,320
%	3	21	34	26	16	

88 cases (or 6% of the total sample) could not be scored.

TABLE 14.35

Localism index

	Non-locals . . . . *locals*					
	0	*1*	*2*	*3*	*4*	*Total*
Number	56	265	361	328	348	1,358
%	4	20	27	24	26	

50 cases (or 4% of the total sample) could not be scored.

Table 14.36 shows the relation (or absence of relation) between the two indices.

TABLE 14.36

Index of localism by index of cosmopolitanism (per cent)

		Non-cosmopolitans . . . . *cosmopolitans*				
		0	*1*	*2*	*3*	*4*
Non-locals	0	3	4	4	6	1
	1	20	18	26	15	16
	2	17	28	30	27	18
	3	40	25	21	24	26
Locals	4	20	24	19	28	39
TOTALS		(35)	(272)	(437)	(324)	(205)

APPENDIX D

Index of cosmopolitanism–localism

The two earlier indices were combined, by the process of scoring localism as it stands, and reversing the scores on the cosmopolitanism index: i.e., 0 scored 4, 1 scored 3, etc. The resulting index had a range from 0 to 8, with localism scoring high, cosmopolitanism low. The two extreme categories, 0 and 8, were too small to be useful, and were therefore combined with the nearest category, giving a range when revised from 1 to 7.

TABLE 14.37

Index of cosmopolitanism–localism

	Cosmopolitans	. . .	. . .	. . .	. . .	. . .	*locals*	
	1	*2*	*3*	*4*	*5*	*6*	*7*	*Total*
Number	56	100	263	342	266	159	87	1,273
%	4	8	21	27	21	12	7	

135 cases (or 10% of the total sample) could not be scored.

A note on the additive index

The most common type of index used in survey analysis resembles most of those used in this chapter (attitudes to professorial power and to professorial status, and cosmopolitanism and localism) in that it is formed from items that are clearly related to each other. The rationale for this procedure is that the relationship demonstrates that there is a common element in the items concerned: construction of an index enables us to draw out this common element, and eliminate some of the differences between the items that are thought to be irrelevant to their common component.

But even if the items are not statistically related there may still be reasons for combining them in an index. To take a very clear example, there might be reasons for supposing that persons who are relatively old, or relatively young, are in some sense perceived as socially inferior by the mass of the population; and the same might be said of women versus men. It would be possible, therefore, and theoretically justifiable, to construct an index of 'perceived social inferiority' from the two items of sex and age. But in a normal population we would not find any correlation between sex and age. Similarly in this case, although we have found no relation between cosmopolitanism and localism we may still wish to construct a composite index, setting at one extreme cosmopolitans who are also not locals, and at the other locals who are not cosmopolitans. There is a problem of interpreting the middle categories: for in these will fall both those who are cosmopolitan *and* local and those who are neither. But towards the ends of the scale at least we can be fairly sure of what it is we are measuring.

The index we have constructed justifies itself by its usefulness in the analysis. Nevertheless, there is a loss of clarity regarding the meaning of scores in the middle categories. For this reason, it may be more illuminating to combine our separate indices of localism and cosmopolitanism into a typology which would allow us to distinguish–in addition to the extreme categories of cosmopolitan-non-local, and local-non-cosmopolitan–between men whose orientations are both inward and outward, local *and* cosmopolitan, and those whose orientations are not strongly in either direction, neither towards their disciplines at large nor towards their own institutions. But the results of this approach will be reserved for a later report.

The relation of cosmopolitanism to political position and attitudes to expansion

Table 14.38 gives the relationship between political preference and cosmopolitanism-localism.

TABLE 14.38

Cosmopolitanism–localism by political position (per cent)

Cosmopolitanism–localism		*Political position* Far Left		Moderate Left		Centre		Right	
Cosmopolitans	1	6	21	4	13	4	12	5	10
	2	15		9		8		5	
	3	19		20		23		17	
	4	31		28		26		24	
	5	9	30	22	39	19	38	23	49
	6	15		12		12		16	
Locals	7	6		5		7		10	
TOTALS		(54)		(595)		(345)		(239)	

Table 14.39 gives the relationship between cosmopolitanism-localism and attitudes to expanding the university system.

TABLE 14.39

Attitudes to expansion by cosmopolitanism–localism (per cent)

Recommended expansion	*Cosmopolitans* *1–2*	*3*	*4*	*5*	*. . . locals* *6–7*
Double	34	31	27	26	16
50%	36	39	43	40	43
25%	23	27	25	31	37
Remain as it is	7	3	5	3	4
TOTALS	(152)	(256)	(330)	(261)	(236)

NOTES TO CHAPTER 15

It may be useful to look at this question of interest in politics as it relates to our subjects' place in the political spectrum. Is it simply true that the further Left, the more interest? We shall look first at the direct relationship, and then compare differences in position on the spectrum within the main parties. It may turn out that, in fact, it is the Centre that is least interested, and that the Far Left of the Labour party are those who carry the rest by their interest, while the Right of the Conservatives are more interested than others in their party.

On first inspection, before we break by party simultaneously, there seems to be a direct, unilinear relationship between interest and preference between the Centre and the Far Left (Table 15.49). There is a very faint increase in interest of the Right over the Centre, but it is very small, and even the 12 respondents who described themselves as 'Far Right' are scarcely more interested than the Moderate Right. But on the Far Left the interest is very high: compared with one third of Labour party supporters we see here that over half of those on the Far Left are extremely interested in politics.

When we look at political interest by political position within the parties (Table 15.50) we find that within all three parties, and also for those who claim to support no party, those on the Left show a higher interest in politics. And this seems to apply both to party preference and to political self-placement. Owing to different combinations of the spectrum divisions it is not always possible to compare those in the same position on the spectrum as between the parties; but this can be done for those on the Centre and Right. If we compare the third column of Labour supporters, the average of the second and third

TABLE 14.40

Attitudes to professorial power by cosmopolitanism–localism and attitudes to expanding the university system (per cent)

Attitudes to professorial power	Recommended expansion														
	Double					*50%*					*Insignificant expansion*				
	Cosmopolitan . . . . . . *Local*					*Cosmopolitan* . . . . . . *Local*					*Cosmopolitan* . . . . . . *Local*				
	0–2	3	4	5	6–8	0–2	3	4	5	6–8	0–2	3	4	5	6–8
Democrats	73	70	56	56	44	56	46	48	48	42	74	47	48	43	38
Part-democrats	20	18	26	23	35	37	37	32	34	41	24	37	31	33	33
Non-democrats	6	12	18	21	21	8	17	20	18	16	2	16	22	24	29
TOTALS	(49)	(77)	(78)	(61)	(34)	(52)	(94)	(130)	(90)	(92)	(42)	(68)	(88)	(75)	(76)

TABLE 14.41

Attitudes to professorial status, by cosmopolitanism–localism and political position

Attitudes to professorial status	Political position														
	Left					*Centre*					*Right*				
	Cosmopolitan . . . . . . *Local*					*Cosmopolitan* . . . . . . *Local*					*Cosmopolitan* . . . . . . *Local*				
	0–2	3	4	5	6–8	0–2	3	4	5	6–8	0–2	3	4	5	6–8
Levellers	57	49	42	32	26	50	39	43	42	31	61	32	38	28	31
Moderates	33	43	43	47	47	45	41	38	31	39	26	37	36	37	40
Elitists	10	9	15	22	28	5	20	19	27	30	13	32	25	35	29
TOTALS	(88)	(127)	(179)	(129)	(105)	(42)	(79)	(88)	(62)	(64)	(23)	(41)	(55)	(54)	(62)

TABLE 15.49

Interest in politics, by political position (per cent)

	Political position				
Interested	*Far Left*	*Moderate Left*	*Centre*	*Moderate Right*	*Far Right*
Extremely	56	24	9	6	8
Moderately	32	57	51	56	58
Slightly	6 } 11	17 } 19	30 } 39	28 } 38	25 } 33
Not at all	5	2	9	9	8
TOTALS	(62)	(654)	(380)	(250)	(12)

TABLE 15.50

Interest in politics, by party and political position (per cent)

	Party support									
	Labour			*Conservative*			*Liberal*		*None*	
	Political position*									
Interested	*FL*	*ML*	*C/R*	*ML*	*C*	*MR/FR*	*FL/ML*	*C/R*	*FL/ML*	*C/R*
Extremely	54	31	13	11	8	6	7	8	19	6
Moderately	35	55	56	62	57	56	65	46	42	35
Slightly / Not at all	11	13	31	27	34	37	27	46	39	60
TOTALS	(54)	(439)	(39)	(37)	(185)	(232)	(98)	(83)	(43)	(52)

* Combined where necessary to produce a meaningful number of cases.

for the Conservatives, and the second column for the Liberals, we find that Labour supporters are more interested in politics than those of the other two parties, even when they assign themselves to the same place in the political spectrum.

TABLES 15.51 AND 15.52

Political position and party by class of first degree (per cent)

	Class of first degree								
15.51 *Position*	*I*	*II(i)*	*II*	*II(ii)*	*III/IV*	*Pass*	*No class given*	*No first degree*	*Overseas*
Far Left	5	3	5	6	0	2	4	5	8
Left	51	54	46	53	42	41	41	44	42
Centre	27	27	31	12	21	29	28	31	31
Right	17	16	18	29	37	29	27	20	19
TOTALS	(611)	(188)	(210)	(17)	(19)	(56)	(138)	(75)	(36)

15.52 Party	Class of first degree								
	I	*II(i)*	*II*	*II(ii)*	*III/IV*	*Pass*	*No class given*	*No first degree*	*Over-seas*
Conservative	31	29	35	28	30	64	47	37	29
Labour	44	47	39	56	55	20	33	38	47
Liberal	16	14	16	11	10	11	10	12	6
Other/None	9	9	10	6	5	5	9	12	18
TOTALS	(580)	(181)	(198)	(18)	(20)	(55)	(134)	(73)	(34)

TABLES 15.53 AND 15.54

Political position and party by higher degrees (per cent)

15.53 Position	None	Higher degrees Masters	Ph.D.
Far Left	5	3	4
Moderate Left	48	49	48
Centre	28	24	29
Right	19	24	19
TOTALS	(546)	(178)	(632)

15.54 Party	None	Higher degrees Masters	Ph.D.
Conservative	35	38	35
Labour	41	37	41
Liberal	12	16	15
Other/None	10	9	9
TOTALS	(536)	(171)	(593)

TABLE 15.55

Social origin (father's occupation) by university group of first degree (per cent)

Father's occupation	University group: Oxbridge	London	Major Redbrick	Minor Redbrick	Wales	Scotland	Overseas	No first degree
Professional Non-manual	27 } 73	16 } 53	15 } 50	18 } 57	11 } 42	20 } 61	28 } 80	18 } 58
Intermediate	46 }	37 }	35 }	39 }	31 }	41 }	52 }	40 }
Skilled	25	42	42	32	42	29	16	32
Semi-skilled	3 } 3	4 } 5	7 } 8	11 } 11	16 } 16	8 } 10	1 } 4	5 } 9
Unskilled	0 }	1 }	1 }	0 }	0 }	2 }	3 }	4 }
TOTALS	(399)	(249)	(267)	(44)	(62)	(189)	(69)	(77)

Appendix E

A NOTE ON CLASS ORIGINS, AGE, AND 'ACADEMIC FATE'

We can look at class origins and research orientations in yet another way–by asking how men of different age, class origins and research orientations are represented in the various subject areas in British universities. In a sense we are asking about the academic 'fate' of men of different class origins who entered university teaching before or after the war (and we can determine this roughly by separating men who were over or under 45 years of age in 1964 when we made our survey). First, we separate our sample of university teachers into four groups, combining age and class origins.

TABLE E.1

Class origins by age

	44 years or less	*45 years or more*	*Total*
	I	II	
Middle class	40·5%	20·2%	60·7%
	III	IV	
Working class	30·0%	9·3%	39·3%
	70·5%	29·5%	100·0%

We see in Table E.1 that the largest single group are the younger teachers of middle class origins (Group I) who comprise 40·5 per cent of the total. Next are the younger 'working class' teachers (Group III) who make up just 30 per cent of the total. Next are the older 'middle class' teachers (Group II) who are 20·2 per cent of the total, and finally, the smallest group are the older teachers of working class origins (Group IV) who make up 9·3 per cent of the total. Thus in our sample (and this was roughly true for the British academic professions at the time of the Robbins Survey), men under 45 made up over 70 per cent of the whole body of university teachers[1] – reflecting the rapid growth of the universities after the war. Similarly, we see in the right-hand column that 60 per cent of all university teachers are of broadly 'middle class' (i.e., non-manual worker) origins. The tendency (though it is far from achieved) towards equality of access to universities and the academic profession is reflected in the middle:working class ratio of 4:3 among younger academics as compared with 2:1 among men over 45.

Now, how are men in these age and class categories distributed in our several subject areas? We immediately get a sense of the selective recruitment to these subjects before and since the war.[2]

TABLE E.2

Representation of age–class categories in subject areas (per cent and index numbers)

Subject		*Age–Class categories* I	II	III	IV
All subjects	100%	40·5	20·2	30·0	9·3
	index	1·0	1·0	1·0	1·0
Arts	100%	36·2	24·5	27·9	11·3
	index	0·90	1·22	0·93	1·21
Social science	100%	38·2	23·0	27·0	11·8
	index	0·92	1·14	0·90	1·27
'Pure' science	100%	40·2	15·9	35·3	8·6
	index	0·99	0·78	1·18	0·92
Technology	100%	42·6	11·2	37·3	8·9
	index	1·06	0·55	1·24	0·96
Medicine	100%	52·6	28·1	16·3	3·0
	index	1·30	1·39	0·54	0·32

Key: Group I: younger men (44 or under) of middle-class origins.
II: older men (45 or more) of middle-class origins.
III: younger men of working-class origins.
IV: older men of working-class origins.

[1] We saw these in more detail in Chapter 7 on the age distribution of the academic profession. Our figures for the age distribution are very close to those of an A.U.T. Survey of 1962 of university staff shown (in brackets) in Table 7.6. The proportion of those who are 45 years or less add up to 74·2 per cent. Our category of 'younger' teachers stops a year earlier, at 44, and in those age brackets each year represents nearly 3 per cent of the whole. Subtracting 3 per cent from 74·2 per cent brings the A.U.T. figure to within 1 per cent of our sample, based on the Robbins survey which was also done in 1962.

[2] This, of course, necessarily neglects the effects of attrition, which we do not believe are large or systematic enough to affect our general findings.

We see on the top line, again, the distribution of the four age-class categories in the whole sample. On succeeding lines we see the distributions among these categories in each of the major subject areas. Clearly, where the proportion in a category in a given subject is higher than in the sample as a whole, that category is 'over-represented' in that subject. For example, where younger middle class men make up 40·5 per cent of the whole sample, they supply 52·6 per cent of the teachers of medicine. And similarly, where older working class men make up 9·3 per cent of the university teachers, they supply only 3·0 per cent of the teachers of medicine.

It is perhaps easier to see the patterns of over- and under-representation if we standardise those figures, developing an index of representation simply by dividing each figure by the proportions of that category in the total sample. An index figure greater than 1 means a concentration in the subject greater than among all university teachers: less than 1, a relative under-representation of the age-class category in the subject.

We see in Table E.2 that younger men of middle class origin (Category I) (who comprise the largest category of university teachers) are still somewhat under-represented in arts and social science, near to their overall proportions in science and technology, and markedly over-represented among teachers of medicine. But comparing those patterns with that of older middle class men (Category II) we see that the selective recruitment of middle class men to medicine was rather greater before the war, while in technology there has been a very great shift between the two age groups–older middle class men being very greatly under-represented among technologists. Looking further along the row of medicine, we see that men of working class origins are represented somewhat nearer to their proportions in the academic profession, but only by comparison with the extreme under-representation of older working class men in that subject.

The reader may find other comparisons of interest. Where the index numbers among both sets of younger men are lower than among older (i.e. where Category I < II; III < IV), as in arts or social science, it means that the subject has lost members relative to other subjects (science and technology).

This approach can be extended by introducing our index of research–teaching orientations. In Table E.3 we report only the index numbers for our four age-class categories, for those with primarily research or teaching orientations in each of our major subject areas.[1] We also repeat the index numbers from Table E.2 for each of the subject areas in the lines labelled 'All'.

TABLE E.3

Representation of research and teaching-oriented men of different age–class categories in subject areas (index numbers)

Subject	*Orientation*	*Age–Class categories* I	II	III	IV
Arts	Research	1·02	1·02	1·00	0·91
	Teaching	0·90	1·17	0·93	1·30
	All	0·90	1·22	0·93	1·21
Social science	Research	1·56	0·54	0·79	0·23
	Teaching	0·74	1·38	0·87	1·74
	All	0·92	1·14	0·90	1·29
'Pure' science	Research	1·25	0·51	1·09	0·67
	Teaching	0·90	0·99	1·01	1·40
	All	0·99	0·78	1·18	0·92
Technology	Research	1·30	0·41	1·25	0·22
	Teaching	0·79	0·79	1·32	1·32
	All	1·06	0·55	1·24	0·96
Medicine	Research	1·48	1·08	0·56	0·18
	Teaching	1·07	1·42	0·76	0·61
	All	1·30	1·39	0·54	0·32

Key: Group I: younger men (44 or under) of middle-class origins.
II: older men (45 or more) of middle-class origins.
III: younger men of working-class origins.
IV: older men of working-class origins.

This information adds a good deal to what we have learned from Table E.2. For example, we see that while younger middle class academics are slightly under-represented in the social sciences, they are greatly over-represented among those social scientists with strong research orientations. By contrast, the older working class academics are markedly over-represented in the social sciences, but markedly under-represented among the social science researchers, and thus very highly over-represented among social scientists with primarily teaching orientations. (This latter pattern is also found in technology.) And, perhaps contrary to popular stereotypes, younger men from working class origins are still under-represented in the social sciences

[1] To simplify the table, we do not include the intermediate category of those who have roughly equal commitments to research and teaching.

and among researchers especially, though to a less marked degree than in the older generation.[1]

To take another case, both older and younger working class academics are under-represented in medicine, as we have noted. But the older men are even less commonly found among the researcher medics, while the younger men of working class origins are as likely to be researchers in medicine as to be in medicine at all. Clearly, here the forces hindering the recruitment of working class youth to careers in academic medicine are declining, and the additional handicaps to their pursuing a research career are declining even more.

If there are any broad patterns to be seen in Table E.3 they may be summarised thus:

1. There is a greater tendency for younger men to have research interests than older men of the same class origins. This is true in every subject except in arts where the differences by age are small or zero. This means, among other things, that the under-representation of working class academics in research in the older generation has been wiped out, as in arts, science and technology, or greatly attenuated, as in social science and medicine.

2. There is a greater tendency for middle class men to have research interests than working class men in the same age bracket. This is true in every subject except among older science teachers, where working class men were a little less under-represented than middle class men, and again in the arts, where the differences are small.

3. Middle class men dominate or have dominated medical education, both as teachers and researchers. Older middle class men were distinctly less likely to go into either pure or applied science, but since the war, middle class recruits have come to both fields in numbers proportionate to their total in academic life, and have contributed disproportionate numbers of researchers in both areas.

Finally, there is yet another way to look at these same figures. We may say that of every hundred men entering academic life from a middle class background before the war, about 5 would become teachers of medicine with strong research interests. That would be true of only 1 in 100 men from working class origins entering before

[1] These findings on the social scientists antedate the great expansion of sociology over the past five years, which may also have been accompanied by a change in class recruitment to the subject.

the war, of about 3 working class men entering after the war, and of about 7 middle class men entering after the war. Where 16 of 100 of the older working class men would end up as teaching-oriented social scientists, that would be true of only about 7 out of every 100 middle class men who entered after the war. The 'academic fates' of these four age-class categories can be seen in Table E.4.

TABLE E.4

Proportions of men in age–class categories by research-teaching orientations and subject (per cent)

Subject	*Orientation*	*Total*	*Age–Class categories* I	II	III	IV
Arts	Research	9·7	9·8	9·9	9·7	8·9
	Both	5·7	3·9	9·5	4·7	8·9
	Teaching	11·6	10·4	13·6	10·8	15·2
	All	27·1	24·2	32·9	25·1	33·0
Social science	Research	3·8	5·9	2·1	3·0	0·9
	Both	3·9	3·3	4·5	4·1	4·5
	Teaching	9·2	6·8	12·8	8·0	16·1
	All	16·9	16·0	19·3	15·2	21·4
Science	Research	12·0	15·0	6·2	13·0	8·0
	Both	9·3	7·0	8·6	13·5	7·1
	Teaching	9·5	8·6	9·5	9·7	13·4
	All	30·8	30·5	24·3	36·2	28·6
Technology	Research	4·0	5·1	1·6	5·0	0·9
	Both	3·3	4·3	0·8	3·6	3·6
	Teaching	6·7	5·3	5·3	8·8	8·9
	All	14·0	14·8	7·8	17·4	13·4
Medicine	Research	5·0	7·4	5·3	2·8	0·9
	Both	3·3	4·1	6·2	1·1	0·9
	Teaching	2·9	3·1	4·1	2·2	1·8
	All	11·2	14·5	15·6	6·1	3·6
		100%	100%	100%	100%	100%
	TOTALS	(1,205)	(488)	(243)	(362)	(112)

Key: Group I: younger men (44 or under) of middle-class origins.
II: older men (45 or more) of middle-class origins.
III: younger men of working-class origins.
IV: older men of working-class origins.

Appendix F

AN EMPIRICAL PROFILE OF THE TYPOLOGY OF ACADEMIC ORIENTATIONS

The measure of the dimension of research-teaching orientations combined two questions asking for agreement or disagreement with the statements that 'an academic man's first loyalty should be to research in his discipline . . .' and 'promotion in academic life is too dependent on published work and too little on devotion to teaching'.[1] To measure élitist-expansionist sentiments, we used responses to a question which asked the teacher what level of size and growth of the university system he supported.[2] Of the four responses, we used only

[1] Q.49 (i) 'An academic man's first loyalty should be to research in his discipline. The teaching of students and the running of his university should be second to this first duty of an academic career.' ('Strongly agree' scored 3, 'agree with reservations' scored 2, 'disagree with reservations' scored 1, 'strongly disagree' scored 0.)

Q.49 (vii) 'Promotion in academic life is too dependent on published work and too little on devotion to teaching.' ('Strongly agree' scored 0, 'agree with reservations' scored 1, 'disagree with reservations' scored 2, 'strongly disagree' scored 3.)

Distribution of research–teaching orientations (index)

	Teaching	. . . .	. . . .	. . . .	. . . .	*Research*		
Score	0	1	2	3	4	5	6	*Total*
Number	150	320	391	272	149	56	15	1,353
%	11	24	29	20	11	4	1	100

55 cases, or 4% of the sample, could not be scored.

This index differed from that used in Chapters 12 and 13 to measure research-teaching orientations, since there we were interested in the individual's personal interests, while here we were more interested in his conception of the academic role.

[2] Q.5: 'Which of the following opinions regarding the number of students in the university as a whole lies closest to your own opinion? In each case please assume that staff and resources are made available.' 'We should double the numbers or more in the next decade'; 'we should increase the numbers about 50 per cent in the next decade'; 'we should increase the numbers about 25 per cent in the next decade'; 'I think that the number of students admitted to universities should remain about where it is now.'

the response, 'double the numbers in the next decade', to indicate the 'expansionist' position. This is at variance with our practice in Chapter 11, but here we were concerned with identifying those who support at least the rate of expansion in the post-Robbins decade: anything less cannot for our present purposes be called 'expansionist'.

This gave us four possible types of attitudes to expansion and to research and teaching: those who opposed expansion and favoured research (category 1), those who favoured expansion and favoured research (category 2), those who opposed expansion and favoured teaching (category 3) and those who favoured expansion and favoured teaching (category 4). We show the derivation of this typology from the index of attitudes to the academic role and Question 5 (attitudes to expanion) below.

A typology of academic orientations
(categories assigned)

		'Should we expand the university system?'			
Research-teaching orientations (index)		*Remain as it is*	*25%*	*50%*	*Double*
Research primarily	6	1	1	1	2
	5	1	1	1	2
	4	1	1	1	2
	3	1	1	1	2
	2	3	3	3	4
	1	3	3	3	4
Teaching primarily	0	3	3	3	4

The numbers and proportions of academic men in each of our categories, measured in these ways, appears in Table 16.1.

The proportions and numbers in each of these categories are of no great significance, since they are so largely a function of the specific indicators and cutting points used. They are shown here to give the reader a sense of the stringency of the criteria used for allocation to any given category. We have used rather more stringent criteria here than in other chapters (and thus admit smaller numbers) in the definition of 'researchers' and 'expansionists'; these decisions we feel justified by our interests in the characteristics and location of the minorities who will carry the burden of reform and expansion within the university system (Table 16.2).

But perhaps of greater interest is some evidence bearing on differences among these several categories. Table 16.3 gives a brief profile of those who hold these different orientations.

APPENDIX F

TABLE 16.2

The distribution of academic orientations

	Elitist	*Expansionist*
Researchers	1 25% (330)	2 11% (148)
Teachers	3 48% (628)	4 16% (210)

92 cases (7% of the sample) could not be classified.

TABLE 16.3

A profile of the types of academic orientations (per cent)

	1 *Elitist Re-searchers (100%)*	*2* *Expan-sionist Re-searchers (100%)*	*3* *Elitist Teachers (100%)*	*4* *Expan-sionist Teachers (100%)*
(1) Age:				
34 years or under	35	50	31	41
(2) Rank:				
Professors	20	14	11	11
Readers	13	9	8	6
Senior lecturers	13	13	17	16
Lecturers and assistant lecturers	51	59	58	60
(3) Subject:				
Arts	34	16	25	21
Social science	8	19	15	28
Pure science	29	36	30	21
Technology	9	12	15	16
Medicine	15	12	8	7
(4) Expect to remain at present university till retirement:				
Definitely or probably yes	57	45	59	47
(5) Since taking a U.K. post, have you ever seriously considered taking a permanent post abroad?				
Yes	38	49	33	42
(6) Party support:				
Labour	35	51	35	59
(7) Political spectrum:				
Left	47	71	45	71
(8) Interested in politics:				
Extremely	13	30	13	31

TABLE 16.3 (*cont.*)

	1 Elitist Researchers (100%)	*2* Expansionist Researchers (100%)	*3* Elitist Teachers (100%)	*4* Expansionist Teachers (100%)
(9) Father's occupation:				
Middle class	64	62	59	54
(10) Father self-employed	29	41	29	28
(11) Secondary school:				
Grammar	52	51	56	64
Public school	26	18	21	15
(12) Deeply or moderately religious	50	38	58	40
(13) An academic man must subordinate all aspects of his life to his work:				
Agree, strongly or with reservations	65	58	50	43
(14) The tripartite secondary system should be replaced by comprehensives:				
Agree, strongly or with reservations	43	72	51	81
(15) A major shortcoming of secondary education is premature specialisation:				
Agree, strongly or with reservations	66	75	79	87
(16) English universities overemphasise the single-subject honours degree:				
Agree, strongly or with reservations	46	59	61	72

Expansionist researchers are younger: half are 34 years or younger as compared with about a third of the élitist categories (1).[1]

Elitist researchers are more likely to be professors (2). They are over-represented among teachers in the arts and medicine; expansionist researchers are over-represented in science; expansionist teachers are heavily over-represented in social science (3).

The researchers are somewhat less likely to think of leaving their university, or to have thought of taking a permanent post abroad (4 and 5). (By contrast, researchers in the United States are more mobile.)

The élitists are less likely to vote or identify themselves as Left and

[1] Numbers in brackets refer to tables within Table 16.3.

are less likely to be extremely interested in politics (6, 7, 8). They are more likely to be at least moderately religious, especially the élitist teachers (12). The élitist researchers are most likely to come from middle class origins (9), but the expansionist researchers are distinctly more likely to have had fathers who were self-employed, and perhaps reflect their entrepreneurial spirit (10). The élitist researchers are most likely to have been to a public school (11), and to believe that an academic man must subordinate all aspects of his life to his work (13).

Elitist researchers are least likely, and expansionist teachers most likely, to agree that the present secondary system should be replaced by comprehensives (15); that premature specialisation is a major shortcoming of secondary education (16); and that English universities over-emphasise the single-subject honours degree (17).

Appendix G

SELECT BIBLIOGRAPHY

Abrams, M., 'Cambridge Recruits to University Teaching', *Universities Quarterly*, 17.3, June 1963.

Armytage, W. H. G., *Civic Universities*, Ernest Benn, 1955.

Ashby, Sir Eric, *Universities: British, Indian, African*, Weidenfeld & Nicolson, 1966.

—— *Technology and the Academics*, London, Macmillan, 1958.

Association of University Teachers, *The Internal Government of Universities*, 1964.

—— *The Remuneration of University Teachers*, 1961–62, 1964–65, 1967–68.

—— *University Government and Organisation*, 1965.

—— *The University Lecturer*, 1961.

Barker, Sir Ernest, *British Universities* (revised edition), Longmans, Green, 1949.

Beloff, Michael, *Plateglass Universities*, Secker & Warburg, 1968.

Ben-David, J. and Zloczower, A., 'Universities and Academic Systems in Modern Societies', *European Journal of Sociology*, vol. 3, no. 1, 1962.

Berdahl, R. O., *British Universities and the State*, Cambridge University Press, 1959.

Bridges, Lord (chairman), 'Report of the syndicate on the relationship between the University and the Colleges', *Cambridge University Reporter*, 10 March 1962.

Brittain, Vera, *The Women of Oxford*, George G. Harrap, 1960.

Caplow, T. and McGee, R. C., *The Academic Market Place*, Basic Books, 1958.

Cardwell, D. S. L., *The Organisation of Science in England*, Heinemann, 1957.

Chapman, A. D., *The Story of a Modern University: A History of the University of Sheffield*, Oxford University Press, 1955.

Charlton, H. B., *Portrait of a University 1851–1951*, Manchester University Press, 1951.

Collison, P., 'The Qualifications of Academics', *Universities Quarterly*, 10.3, June 1956.

—— 'Career Contingencies of University Teachers', *The British Journal of Sociology*, Vol. XIII. No. 3, September 1962.

Collison and Millan, 'University Chancellors, Vice Chancellors and College Principals: a Social Profile', *Sociology*, Vol. III, No. 1, January 1969.

Daiches, David (ed.), *The Idea of a New University: An Experiment in Sussex*, André Deutsch, 1964.

Evans, B. E., *The University of Wales: a Historical Sketch*, Cardiff, 1953.

Flexner, Abraham, *Universities, American, English, German*, Oxford University Press, 1930.

Franks, Lord (chairman), *Report of Commission of Inquiry*, 2 Vols., Oxford University Press, 1966.

Fulton, Sir J., *Experiment in Higher Education*, Tavistock Pamphlet No. 8, 1964.

Gillie, W. B., *A New University: A. D. Lindsay and the Keele Experiment*, Chatto & Windus, 1960.

Herklots, H. G. C., *The New Universities: An External Examination*, Benn, 1928.

Hetherington, Sir Hector, *The British University System, 1914–1954*, Aberdeen University Studies, No. 133, 1954.

Humberstone, T. L., *University Reform in London*, Allen & Unwin, 1926.

Kerr, J., *Scottish Education: School and University from Early Times to 1908*, Cambridge University Press, 1910.

Kneller, G. C., *Higher Learning in Britain*, Cambridge University Press, 1955.

Lawlor, John (ed.), *The New University*, Routledge & Kegan Paul, 1968.

Lazarsfeld, P. and Thielens, W., *The Academic Mind*, Glencoe, Ill., The Free Press, 1958.

Mansbridge, A., *The Older Universities of England*, Longmans, Green, 1923.

Marris, P., *The Experience of Higher Education*, Routledge & Kegan Paul, 1964.

Martin, H. (ed.), *The Life of a Modern University*, S.C.M. Press, 1930.

Moberly, Sir Walter, *The Crisis in the University*, London, S.C.M. Press, 1949.

Newman, Cardinal J. H., *The Idea of a University*, 1852, Doubleday, 1959.

Perkin, H. J., *Innovation in Higher Education: New Universities in the United Kingdom*, O.E.C.D., 1969.

—— *Key Profession*, Routledge & Kegan Paul, 1969.

Plessner, H. (ed.), *Untersuchungen zur lage der deutschen Hochschullehrer* (Investigations into the Position of the German University Teacher), Gottingen, Vandenhoeck and Ruprecht, 1956.

Proctor, Mortimer, *The English University Novel*, University of California Press, 1957.

Rashdall, H., *The Universities of Europe in the Middle Ages*, 3 Vols., Oxford, Clarendon Press, 1936.

Robbins, Lord, *The University and the Modern World*, Macmillan, 1966.

Robertson, Sir Charles G., *The British Universities*, Revised ed., Methuen, 1944.

Rose, Jaspar and Ziman, John, *Camford Observed*, Gollancz, 1964.

Rothblatt, Sheldon, *The Revolution of the Dons: Cambridge and Society in Victorian England*, Faber, 1968.

Shimmin, A. H., *The University of Leeds*, Cambridge University Press, 1954.

Simmons, J., *New University*, Leicester University Press, 1958.

Simon, Sir Ernest (later Lord, of Wythenshawe), *The Development of British Universities*, Longmans, Green, 1944.

Sloman, A. E., *A University in the Making*, British Broadcasting Corporation, 1964.

Sparrow, John, *Mark Pattison and the Idea of the University*, Cambridge University Press, 1967.

Summerkorn, I., *British Academic Women*, London University Ph.D. Thesis, 1966.

Truscott, B., *Red Brick University*, revised ed., Pelican Books, 1951.

Wilson, Logan, *The Academic Man*, New York, Oxford University Press, 1942.

Znaniecki, Florian, *The Social Role of the Man of Knowledge*, New York, Columbia University Press, 1940.

INDEX

As there are recurrent references to Oxford University, Cambridge University and the Robbins Report throughout the book, separate entries have not been included in the index.

INDEX

INDEX

INDEX

INDEX

INDEX

INDEX